Crime in a Free Society

Selections from the President's Commission
on Law Enforcement and Administration
of Justice

Robert W. Winslow

San Diego State College

Dickenson Publishing Company, Inc., Belmont, California

Library of Congress Catalog Card No.: 68–21053
Printed in the United States of America

Preface

The readings in this book are drawn from the ten-volume report of the President's Commission on Law Enforcement and Administration of Justice, a nineteen-man commission appointed by President Lyndon B. Johnson. The most comprehensive study of crime and criminal justice undertaken in the Nation's history, the report is based upon eighteen months' work with one hundred and seventy-five consultants and hundreds of advisers representing a broad range of opinions and professions; countless visits to courts, prisons, and police stations; three national conferences; five national surveys; hundreds of meetings; and interviews with tens of thousands of people.

In the choice of materials for this volume, selections have been drawn both from the *General Report: The Challenge of Crime in a Free Society* and from the various task force reports—*The Police, The Courts, Corrections, Organized Crime, Science and Technology, Assessment of Crime, Narcotics and Drug Abuse,* and *Drunkenness.*

This book, designed for the academic study of criminology, does not duplicate the Commission's *General Report,* which is primarily intended for the lay reader. Moreover, although the *General Report* contains lengthy discussions of plans for controlling crime, one must refer to the task force reports for the research on which these plans are based. By contrast, *Crime in a Free Society* deals extensively with both the research studies and the generalizations and conclusions. In addition, the book covers research findings from over 300 surveys, polls, and research projects, whereas the *General Report* discusses only a few field surveys. Special attention has been given to national surveys—conducted by Gallup, Harris, the National Opinion Research Center, the Bureau of Social Science Research, and the President's Commission itself—of victimization; unreported crime; and public attitudes toward causation, methods of correction, and police practices. These surveys represent a significant contribution to the study of crime in the United States, being both recent and unprecedented in scope and magnitude.

Chapter 1 discusses the widespread nature of crime in America, its costs, its victims, public attitudes, and the effectiveness of the criminal justice system. Chapter 2 assesses the incidence of major crimes, both reported and unreported, and discusses whether the rate of crime is increasing. Chapter 3 evaluates current sources of crime statistics, suggests new sources, and proposes a plan for the national collection of statistics. Chapter 4 and 5 trace the factors involved in crime and discuss current explanations for these variations.

Chapters 6–10 discuss special offenses—professional crime, white-collar crime, organized crime, narcotics and drug abuse, and drunkenness—including extent, types, characteristics of offenders, control efforts, and treatment programs.

Chapters 11–13 focus on the criminal justice system—the police, the courts, and corrections. Chapter 11 emphasizes the problem of police-community relations and includes suggested personnel changes. Chapter 12 points to problems at various phases of the adjudication process and proposes improvements. Chapter 13 contains a typology of offenders and recommends improvements in traditional correctional institutions.

The last chapter describes the Commission's master plan for the control of crime nationally, at the state and local level, and at the level of citizen organizations.

Robert W. Winslow

Contents

v

1 Introduction

There is much crime in America, more than ever is reported, far more than ever is solved, far too much for the health of the Nation. Every American knows that. Every American is, in a sense, a victim of crime. Violence and theft have not only injured, often irreparably, hundreds of thousands of citizens, but have directly affected everyone. Some people have been impelled to uproot themselves and find new homes. Some have been made afraid to use public streets and parks. Some have come to doubt the worth of a society in which so many people behave so badly. Some have become distrustful of the Government's ability, or even desire, to protect them. Some have lapsed into the attitude that criminal behavior is normal human behavior and consequently have become indifferent to it, or have adopted it as a good way to get ahead in life. Some have become suspicious of those they conceive to be responsible for crime: adolescents or Negroes or drug addicts or college students or demonstrators; policemen who fail to solve crimes; judges who pass lenient sentences or write decisions restricting the activities of the police; parole boards that release prisoners who resume their criminal activities.

The most understandable mood into which many Americans have been plunged by crime is one of frustration and bewilderment. For "crime" is not a single simple phenomenon that can be examined, analyzed and described in one piece. It occurs in every part of the country and in every stratum of society. Its practitioners and its victims are people of all ages, incomes and backgrounds. Its trends are difficult to ascertain. Its causes are legion. Its cures are speculative and controversial. An examination of any single kind of crime, let alone of "crime in America," raises a myriad of issues of the utmost complexity.

Consider the crime of robbery, which, since it involves both stealing and violence or the threat of it, is an especially hurtful and frightening one. In 1965 in America there were 118,916 robberies known to the police: 326 robberies a day; a robbery for every 1,630 Americans. Robbery takes dozens of forms, but suppose it took only four: forcible or violent purse-snatching by boys, muggings by drug addicts, store stickups by people with a sudden desperate need for money, and bank robberies by skillful professional criminals. The technical, organizational, legal, behavioral, economic and social problems that must be addressed if America is to deal with any degree of success with just those four kinds of events and those four kinds of persons are innumerable and refractory.

The underlying problems are ones that the criminal justice system can do little about. The unruliness of young people, widespread drug addiction, the existence of much poverty in a wealthy society, the pursuit of the dollar by any available means are phenomena the police, the courts, and the correctional apparatus, which must deal with crimes and criminals one by one, cannot confront directly. They are strands that can be disentangled from the fabric of American life only by the concerted action of all of society. They concern the Commission deeply, for unless society does take concerted action to change the general conditions and attitudes that are associated with crime, no improvement in law enforcement and administration of justice, the subjects this Commission was specifically asked to study, will be of much avail.

Of the everyday problems of the criminal justice system itself, certainly the most delicate and probably the most difficult concern the proper ways of dealing individually with individuals. Arrest and prosecution are likely to have quite different effects on delinquent boys and on hardened professional criminals. Sentencing occasional robbers and habitual robbers by the same standards is clearly inappropriate. Rehabilitating a drug addict is a procedure that has little in common with rehabilititing a holdup man. In short, there are no general prescriptions for dealing with "robbers." There are no general prescriptions for dealing with "robbery" either. Keeping streets and parks safe is not the same problem as keeping banks secure. Investigating a mugging and tracking down a band of prudent and well-organized bank robbers are two entirely distinct police procedures. The kind of police patrol that will deter boys from street robberies is not likely to deter men with guns from holding up storekeepers.

Robbery is only one of 28 crimes on which the Federal Bureau of Investigation reports in its annual Uniform Crime Reports. In terms of frequency of occurrence, it ranks fifth among the UCR's "Index Crimes," the seven serious crimes that the FBI considers to be indicative of the general crime trends in the Nation. (The others are willful homicide, forcible rape, aggravated assault, burglary, theft of $50 or over, and motor vehicle theft.) The Index Crimes accounted for fewer than 1 million of the almost 5 million arrests that the UCR reports for 1965. Almost half of those arrests were for crimes that have no real victims (prostitution, gambling, narcotics use, vagrancy, juvenile curfew violations, and the like) or for breaches of the public peace (drunkenness, disorderly conduct). Other crimes for which more than 50,000 people were arrested were such widely different kinds of behavior as vandalism, fraud, sex offenses other than rape or prostitution, driving while intoxicated, carrying weapons, and offences against family or children. Each of the 28 categories of crime confronts the community and the criminal justice system, to a greater or a lesser degree, with unique social, legal, correctional, and law enforcement problems. Taken together they raise a multitude of questions about how the police, the courts, and corrections should be organized; how their personnel should be selected, trained and paid; what modern technology can do to help their work; what kinds of knowledge they need; what procedures they should use; what resources they should be given; what the relations between the community and the various parts of the criminal justice system should be.

And so, when the President asked the Commission to "deepen our understanding of the causes of crime and of how society should respond to the challenge of the present levels of crime," he gave it a formidable assignment.

Crime and society's response to it resemble a gigantic disassembled jigsaw puzzle whose pieces the Commission was asked to assemble into as complete and accurate a picture as it could. It was charged with discovering whether the popular picture of crime in America is how it really looks and, if not, what the differences are; with determining how poverty, discrimination and other social ills relate to crime; with ascertaining whether America's system of criminal justice really works the way the public thinks it does and the books say it should and, if it does not, where, when, how, and why it does not.

Commission observers rode in police cars, sat in courtrooms, visited prisons, walked the streets of city slums. Commission interviewers questioned victims of crime about their experiences; professional criminals about their methods of operation; citizens about their attitudes toward the police; convicts about their daily lives; policemen, prosecutors, judges and correctional officials about the jobs they perform and the problems they meet every working day. The Commission convened a conference at which State representatives, assigned by the Governors to work with the Commission, shared knowledge and exchanged opinions; it sponsored a symposium at which scientists and technological experts analyzed ways science and technology could be used to control crime; it co-sponsored a national conference on legal manpower needs.

The Commission brought to its offices in Washington, often for weeks or months, several hundred crime specialists—police, court and correctional officials, professors of criminal law, criminologists, sociologists, social workers, statisticians, psychiatrists, technological experts—so that they could tell in detail what they knew and what they thought. Members of the Commission's full-time staff, drawn from diverse professions and backgrounds, visited and corresponded with other hundreds of such experts. The staff collected its own statistics and other data, along with data from other agencies, for comparison and analysis. It read hundreds of books and papers dealing with subjects from police administration to juvenile-gang subcultures, from criminal sentencing codes to correctional theory.

The Commission did not—it could not—find out "everything" about crime and the criminal justice system. It became increasingly aware during its work that, far from seeking to say the last word on crime, its task was rather a step in a long process of systematic inquiry that must be continued and expanded by others. But the work the Commission was able to do did deepen its understanding; and, the Commission hopes and believes, it does provide a basis for a vigorous and effective program for meeting crime's challenge to the Nation.

[*The President's Commission on Law Enforcement and Administration of Justice,* The Challenge of Crime in a Free Society (*Washington: U.S. Government Printing Office, 1967*), *pp. 1–3.*]

The Economic Impact of Crime

One way in which crime affects the lives of all Americans is that it costs all Americans money. Economic costs alone cannot determine attitudes about crime or policies toward crime, of course. The costs of lost or damaged lives, of fear and of suffering, and of the failure to control critical events cannot be measured solely in dollars and cents. Nor can the requirements of justice and law enforcement be established solely by use of economic measures. A high percentage of a police department's manpower may have to be committed to catch a single murderer or bomb-thrower. The poor, unemployed defendant in a minor criminal case is entitled to all the protections our constitutional system provides—without regard to monetary costs.

However, economic factors relating to crime are important in the formation of attitudes and policies. Crime in the United States today imposes a very heavy economic burden upon both the community as a whole and individual members of it. Risks and responses cannot be judged with maximum effectiveness until the full extent of economic loss has been ascertained. Researchers, policymakers, and operating agencies should know which crimes cause the greatest economic loss, which the least; on whom the costs of crime fall, and what the costs are to prevent or protect against it; whether a particular or general crime situation warrants further expenditures for control or prevention and, if so, what expenditures are likely to have the greatest impact.

The number of policemen, the size of a plant security staff, or the amount of insurance any individual or business carries are controlled to some degree by economics—the balance of the value to be gained against the burden of additional expenditure. If the protection of property is the objective, the economic loss from crime must be weighed directly against the cost of better prevention or control. In view of the importance and the frequency of such decisions, it is surprising that the cost information on which they are based is as fragmentary as it is. While statements about the cost of various crimes are often made, the actual extent of information is very small. Some cost data are now reported through the UCR[1] and additional data are available from individual police forces, insurance companies, industrial security firms, trade associations and others. Books, newspaper articles and scholarly journals also provide some information, but the total amount of information is not nearly enough in quantity, quality, or detail to give an accurate overall picture.

The only comprehensive study of the cost of crime ever undertaken in this country was that made by the Wickersham Commission.[2] It set forth in detail a conceptual framework for discussing the economic cost of crime and recommended that further studies be made, particularly in the areas of organized crime and commercialized fraud. However, except in the area of statistics concerning the cost of the criminal justice system, where some progress has been made, the lack of knowledge about which the Wickersham Commission complained 30 years ago is almost as great today.

This Commission did not have the resources to attempt a complete study of the costs of crime. But it was able to gather some new information concerning neighborhood businesses through its survey of eight precincts in three cities,[3] and about losses to individuals through the NORC national survey of 10,000 households.[4] The national survey indicated very sizable losses to individuals, as shown in Table 1.

From the information obtained in the surveys and other sources available,

[1] See, e.g., Federal Bureau of Investigation, *Crime in the United States, Uniform Crime Reports* (Washington: U.S. Government Printing Office, 1965), tables 14–15, p. 105 (hereinafter cited as UCR, 1965).

[2] U.S. National Commission on Law Observance and Enforcement, *Report on the Cost of Crime* (Washington: U.S. Government Printing Office, 1931), (hereinafter referred to as the *Wickersham Costs Report*). The Cambridge Institute of Criminology has begun a thorough study of the cost of crime in Great Britain. The design for this study is discussed in J. P. Martin, "The Cost of Crime: Some Research Problems," *International Review of Criminal Policy*, No. 23 (New York: United Nations, 1965), pp. 57–63; and J. P. Martin and J. Bradley, "Design of a Study of the Cost of Crime," *The British Journal of Criminology*, 4:591–603, October 1964. The Cambridge Institute reports that it has not found any similar studies in other European countries.

[3] The principal results are reported in Albert J. Reiss, Jr., *Studies in Crime and Law Enforcement in Major Metropolitan Areas* (Field Surveys III, President's Commission on Law Enforcement and Administration of Justice, Washington: U.S. Government Printing Office, 1967), vol. I, sec. 1 (hereinafter cited as the Reiss studies, Field Survey III). Two preliminary reports contain additional information: Stephen Cutler and Albert J. Reiss, Jr., *Crimes Against Public and Quasi-Public Organizations in Boston, Chicago, and Washington, D.C.* (A special survey for the President's Commission on Law Enforcement and Administration of Justice, 1966); and Albert J. Reiss, Jr., *Employee Honesty in Businesses and Organizations in Eight Police Precincts of Three Cities* (A special survey for the President's Commission on Law Enforcement and Administration of Justice, 1966).

[4] Philip H. Ennis, *Criminal Victimization in the United States; a Report of a National Survey* (Field Surveys II, President's Commission on Law Enforcement and Administration of Justice, Washington: U.S. Government Printing Office, 1967) (hereinafter referred to as the NORC study).

Table 1—Estimated Losses to Individuals from Property Crimes, by Offense.

Offense	Average loss in dollars			National loss (in millions of dollars)
	Gross loss [1]	Recovered [1]	Net loss [1]	
Robbery	274	4	271	49.4
Burglary	191	20	170	312.7
Larceny $50 and over	160	51	109	128.1
Auto theft	1,141	982	159	63.5
Larceny under $50	21	6	15	42.4
Malicious mischief	120	18	102	209.8
Forgery and counterfeiting	323[2]		323[2]	26.2[2]
Consumer fraud	99	20	78	18.3
Other fraud (bad checks, swindling, etc.)	906	150	756	368.8

[1] Detail may not add to total due to rounding.
[2] There were only 9 instances in which losses from forgery and counterfeiting were reported.

SOURCE: NORC survey, p. 16.

the Commission sought to establish the economic impact of crime. This information is most usefully presented not as an overall figure but as a series of separate private and public costs. Knowing the economic impact of each separate crime aids in identifying important areas for public concern and guides officials in making judgments about priorities for expenditure. Breakdowns of money now being spent on different parts of the criminal justice system, and within each separate part, may afford insights into past errors.[5] For example, even excluding value judgments about rehabilitative methods, the fact that an adult probationer costs 38 cents a day and an adult offender in prison costs $5.24 a day suggests the need for reexamining current budget allocations in correctional practice.

Economic Impact of Individual Crimes

The picture of crime as seen through cost information is considerably different from that shown by statistics portraying the number of offences known to the police or the number of arrests:

    ☐ Organized crime takes nearly twice as much income from gambling and other illegal goods and services as criminals derive from all other kinds of criminal activity combined.

[5] See generally the models developed by the Commission's Task Force on Science and Technology in chapter 5 of its report. Also President's Commission on Law Enforcement and Administration of Justice, *The Challenge of Crime in a Free Society* (Washington: U.S. Government Printing Office, 1967), fig. 5 at pp. 262–263; fig. 6 at pp. 264–265, and table 5 at p. 265 (hereinafter referred to as *President's Commission, General Report*); National Council on Crime and Delinquency, "Correction in the United States," in President's Commission on Law Enforcement and Administration of Justice, *Task Force Report: Corrections* (Washington: U.S. Government Printing Office, 1967), appendix A, p. 194.

☐ Unreported commercial theft losses, including shoplifting and employee theft, are more than double those of all reported private and commercial thefts.

☐ Of the reported crimes, willful homicide, though comparatively low in volume, yields the most costly estimates among those listed on the UCR crime Index.

☐ A list of the seven crimes[6] with the greatest economic impact includes only two, willful homicide and larceny of $50 and over (reported and unreported), of the offenses included in the crime Index.

☐ Only a small proportion of the money expended for criminal justice agencies is allocated to rehabilitative programs for criminals or for research.

Employee theft, embezzlement, and other forms of crime involving business, which appear in relatively small numbers in the police statistics, loom very large in dollar volume. They make up the bulk of the more than $2 billion which business annually loses in crimes for which losses can be estimated. Direct stealing of cash and merchandise, manipulation of accounts and stock records, and other forms of these crimes, along with shoplifting, appear to constitute a tax of 1 to 2 percent on the total sales of retail enterprises, and significant amounts in other parts of business and industry. In the grocery trade, for example, the theft estimates for shoplifting and employee theft almost equal the total amount of profit. Yet Commission and other studies indicate that these crimes are largely dealt with by business itself. Merchants report to the police fewer than one-quarter of the known offenses. Estimates for these crimes are particularly incomplete for nonretail industries.

Fraud is another offense whose impact is not well conveyed by police statistics. Just one conspiracy involving the collapse of a fraudulent salad oil empire in 1964 created losses of $125 to $175 million. Fraud is especially vicious when it attacks, as it so often does, the poor or those who live on the margin of poverty. Expensive nostrums for incurable diseases, home-improvement frauds, frauds involving the sale or repair of cars, and other criminal schemes create losses which are not only sizable in gross but are also significant and possibly devastating for individual victims. Although a very frequent offense, fraud is seldom reported to the police. In consumer and business fraud, as in tax evasion, the line between criminal and civil fraud is often unclear. And just as the amount of civil tax evasion is much greater than the amount of criminal tax fraud, the amount of civil fraud probably far exceeds that of criminal fraud.

Cost analysis also places the crimes that appear so frequently in police statistics—robbery, burglary, larceny, and auto theft—in somewhat dif-

---

[6] The crimes and their estimated costs are gambling, $7 billion; driving while intoxicated, $1.8 billion; fraud, $1.3 billion; willful homicide, $750 million; loan-sharking, $350 million; and narcotics, $350 million. The amounts involved in unreported larceny are not clear but are large enough to make larceny one of the 7 most costly crimes.

ferent perspective. The number of reported offenses for these crimes accounts for less than one-sixth the estimated total dollar loss for all property crimes and would constitute an even lower percentage if there were any accurate way of estimating the very large sums involved in extortion, blackmail, and other property crimes.

This is not to say, however, that the large amounts of police time and effort spent in dealing with these crimes is not important. Robbery and burglary, particularly residential burglary, have importance beyond the number of dollars involved. The effectiveness of the police in securing the return of better than 85 per cent of the $500 million worth of cars stolen annually appears to be high, and without the efforts of the police the costs of these crimes would doubtless be higher. As with all categories of crime, the cost of property crimes cannot be measured because of the large volume of unreported crimes; however, Commission surveys suggest that the crimes that are unreported involve less money per offense than those that are reported.

The economic impact of crimes causing death is surprisingly high. For 1965 there were an estimated 9,850 homicide victims. Of the estimated 49,000 people who lost their lives in highway accidents, more than half were killed in accidents involving either negligent manslaughter or driving under the influence of alcohol. An estimated 290 women died from complications resulting from illegal abortions (nearly one-fourth of all maternal deaths). Measured by the loss of future earnings at the time of death, these losses totaled more than $1½ billion.

Single events that occur sporadically such as riots or the sabotage of a commercial airliner sometimes cause sizable losses. The Watts riots, for example, caused property losses of more than $40 million.[7] Antitrust violations reduce competition and unduly raise prices; the price-fixing conspiracy in the electrical industry alone cost the public very large sums of money.[8] The economic impact of many such crimes is hard to assess, however. Building code violations, pure food and drug law violations, and other crimes affecting the consumer have important economic consequences, but they cannot be easily described without further information. Losses due to fear of crime, such as reduced sales in high crime locations, are real but beyond measure.

Economic impact must also be measured in terms of ultimate costs to society.[9] Criminal acts causing property destruction or injury to persons not only result in serious losses to the victims or their families but also in the withdrawal of wealth or productive capacity from the economy as a whole.

---

[7] Governor's Commission on the Los Angeles Riots, *Violence in the City—An End or a Beginning?* (Los Angeles: Office of the Governor, 1965), p. 1.

[8] President's Commission on Law Enforcement and Administration of Justice, *Task Force Report: Crime and Its Impact—An Assessment* (Washington: U.S. Government Printing Office, 1967), chapter 8, "White Collar Crime."

[9] See generally *Wickersham Costs Report*, pp. 68–69.

Theft on the other hand does not destroy wealth but merely transfers it involuntarily from the victim, or perhaps his insurance company, to the thief. The bettor purchasing illegal betting services from organized crime may easily absorb the loss of a 10¢, or even $10, bet. But from the point of view of society, gambling leaves much less wealth available for legitimate business. Perhaps more important, it is the proceeds of this crime tariff that organized crime collects from those who purchase its illegal wares that form the major source of income that organized crime requires to achieve and exercise economic and political power.

.   .   .   .   .

The Victims of Crime

.   .   .   .   .

Although information about victims and their relationships to offenders is recorded in the case files of the police and other criminal justice agencies, it is rarely used for systematic study of those relationships or the risks of victimization. To discover variations in victimization rates among different age, sex, race, and income groupings in the population, the Task Force analyzed information on these items obtained in the national survey by NORC.

Table 2—Victimization, by Income

[Rates per 100,000 population]

Offenses	Income			
	$0 to $2,999	$3,000 to $5,999	$6,000 to $9,999	Above $10,000
Total_____	2,369	2,331	1,820	2,237
Forcible rape_____	76	49	10	17
Robbery_____	172	121	48	34
Aggravated assault_____	229	316	144	252
Burglary_____	1,319	1,020	867	790
Larceny ($50 and over)_____	420	619	549	925
Motor vehicle theft_____	153	206	202	219
Number of respondents_____	(5,232)	(8,238)	(10,382)	(5,946)

SOURCE: Philip H. Ennis, "Criminal Victimization in the United States: A Report of a National Survey," (Field Survey II, President's Commission on Law Enforcement and Administration of Justice, (Washington: U.S. Government Printing Office, 1967), adapted from table 14, p, 31. Hereinafter referred to as the NORC study.

Rather striking variations in the risk of victimization for different types of crime appear among different income levels in the population. The results shown in Table 2 indicate that the highest rates of victimization occur in the lower income groups when all index offenses except homicide are considered together. The risks of victimization from forcible rape, robbery, and burglary, are clearly concentrated in the lowest income group and decrease steadily at higher income levels. The picture is somewhat more erratic for the offenses of aggravated assault, larceny of $50 and over, and vehicle theft. Victimization for larceny increases sharply in the highest income group.

National figures on rates of victimization also show sharp differences between whites and nonwhites (Table 3). Nonwhites are victimized disproportionately by all Index crimes except larceny $50 and over.

Table 3—Victimization, by Race

[Rates per 100,000 population]

Offenses	White	Non-White
Total	1,860	2,592
Forcible rape	22	82
Robbery	58	204
Aggravated assault	186	347
Burglary	822	1,306
Larceny ($50 and over)	608	367
Motor vehicle theft	164	286
Number of respondents	(27,484)	(4,902)

SOURCE: NORC study, adapted from table 16, p. 33.

The rates for victimization shown for Index offenses against men (Table 4) are almost three times as great as those for women, but the higher rates of burglary, larceny and auto theft against men are in large measure an artifact of the survey procedure of assigning offenses against the household to the head of the household.

The victimization rate for women is highest in the 20 to 29 age group. In

Table 4—Victimization, by Age and Sex

[Rates per 100,000 population]

Offense	Male						
	10–19	20–29	30–39	40–49	50–59	60 plus	All ages
Total	951	5,924	6,231	5,150	4,231	3,465	3,091
Robbery	61	257	112	210	181	98	112
Aggravated assault	399	824	337	263	181	146	287
Burglary	123	2,782	3,649	2,365	2,297	2,343	1,583
Larceny ($50 and over)	337	1,546	1,628	1,839	967	683	841
Motor vehicle theft	31	515	505	473	605	195	268
	Female						
	10–19	20–29	30–39	40–49	50–59	60 plus	All ages
Total	334	2,424	1,514	1,908	1,132	1,052	1,059
Forcible rape	91	238	104	48	0	0	83
Robbery	0	238	157	96	60	81	77
Aggravated assault	91	333	52	286	119	40	118
Burglary	30	665	574	524	298	445	314
Larceny ($50 and over)	122	570	470	620	536	405	337
Motor vehicle theft	0	380	157	334	119	81	130

SOURCE: NORC study, adapted from table 17, pp. 34-35.

fact the victimization rates for women for all the index offenses reported, with the exception of larceny, are greatest in this age group. The concentration of offenses against women in this age group is particularly noticeable for forcible rape and robbery and much less apparent in aggravated assault and the property crimes.

For men the highest Index total rate falls in the 30 to 39 age category, a result heavily influenced by the burglaries assigned to men as heads of households. Actually, all the Index property offenses against men show peak rates in the older age categories. This is probably due not only to their role as household heads but also to the fact that at older ages they are likely to possess more property to be stolen. Crimes against the person, such as aggravated assault and robbery, are committed relatively more often against men who are from 20 to 29 years of age.

Thus, the findings from the national survey show that the risk of victimization is highest among the lower income groups for all Index offenses except homicide, larceny, and vehicle theft; it weighs most heavily on the nonwhites for all Index offenses except larceny; it is borne by men more often than women, except, of course, for forcible rape; and the risk is greatest for the age category 20 to 29, except for larceny against women, and burglary, larceny, and vehicle theft against men.

Victim-Offender Relationships in Crimes of Violence

The relations and interactions of victims and offenders prior to and during the criminal act are important facts to know for understanding and controlling crime and assessing personal risks more accurately. The relationships most often studied have been those involving crimes of violence against the person, especially homicide and forcible rape. Typical of the findings of these inquiries are the results of an analysis of criminal homicides in Philadelphia between 1948 and 1952.[10] This study clearly demonstrated that it is not the marauding stranger who poses the greatest threat as a murderer. Only 12.2 percent of the murders were committed by strangers. In 28.2 percent of the cases studied, the murderer was a relative or a close friend. In 24.7 percent he was a member of the family. The murderer was an acquaintance of the victim in 13.5 percent of the cases.

. . . . . .

Unfortunately, no national statistics are available on relationships between victims and offenders in crimes other than criminal homicide. How-

[10] Marvin F. Wolfgang, "Patterns of Criminal Homicide" (Philadelphia: *University of Pennsylvania Press,* 1958). See also Menachem Amir, "Patterns of Rape and the Female Victim" (unpublished Ph.D. thesis, The University of Pennsylvania, 1965); Albert J. Reiss, Jr., *Studies in Crime and Law Enforcement in Major Metropolitan Areas* (Field Surveys III, President's Commission on Law Enforcement and Administration of Justice, Washington: U.S. Government Printing Office, 1967), vol. I, sec. 1, table 6, p. 35 (hereinafter referred to as the *Reiss studies*).

ever, the District of Columbia Crime Commission surveyed a number of
other crimes. Its findings on victim-offender relationships in rape and aggravated assault closely resemble those for murder:

> Almost two-thirds of the 151 [rape] victims surveyed were attacked
> by persons with whom they were at least casually acquainted. Only
> 36 percent of the 224 assailants about whom some identifying infor-
> mation was obtained were complete strangers to their victims: 16 (7
> percent) of the attackers were known to the victim by sight, although
> there had been no previous contact. Thirty-one (14 percent) of the
> 224 assailants were relatives, family friends or boyfriends of the
> victims, and 88 (39 percent) were either acquaintances or neigh-
> bors.[11]

And among 131 aggravated assault victims, only 25 (19 percent) were
not acquainted with their assailants:

> Fourteen (11 percent) of the victims were attacked by their spouses,
> 13 (10 percent) were attacked by other relatives, and 79 (60
> percent) were assaulted by persons with whom they were at least
> casually acquainted.[12]

Again, as in murder, a substantial number (20 percent) of the aggravated
assaults surveyed by the District of Columbia Crime Commission involved a
victim and offender who had had trouble with each other before.[13]

Another source of the concern about crime, in addition to its violence and
its frequency, is the extent to which it is assumed to involve interracial
attacks. Therefore a key question in any assessment of the crime problem is
to what extent men or women of one racial group victimize those of
another. For evidence on the way in which the race and sex of victims and
offenders might affect the probability of criminal assault, the Commission,
with the cooperation of the Chicago Police Department, studied 13,713
cases of assaultive crimes against the person, other than homicide.[14]

As shown in Table 5, it is Negro males and females who are most likely to
be victimized in crimes against the person. A Negro man in Chicago runs
the risk of being a victim nearly six times as often as a white man, a Negro
woman nearly eight times as often as a white woman.

The most striking fact in the data is the extent of the correlation in race
between victim and offender. Table 5 shows that Negroes are most likely to
assault Negroes, whites most likely to assault whites. Thus, while Negro
males account for two-thirds of all assaults, the offender who victimizes a
white person is most likely also to be white.

[11] *D.C. Crime Commission Report, supra* note 9, at p. 53.
[12] *Id.* at p. 76.
[13] *Id.*
[14] *Reiss studies, supra* note 10, vol. I, sec. 1, pp. 38–72.

Table 5—Victim-Offender Relationships, by Race and Sex in Assaultive Crimes Against the Person (Except Homicide)

	Offenses attributable to—				
	White offenders		Negro offenders		All types of offenders
	Male	Female	Male	Female	
Victim rate for each 100,000:[1]					
White males	201	9	129	4	342
White females	108	14	46	6	175
Negro males	58	3	1,636	256	1,953
Negro females	21	3	1,202	157	1,382
Total population [1]	130	10	350	45	535

[1] The rates are based only on persons 14 years of age or older in each race-sex category' The "total population" category in addition excludes persons from racial groups other than Negro or white.

SOURCE: Special tabulation from Chicago Police Department, Data Systems Division, for period September 1965 to March 1966, reported in Reiss studies, supra note 24, vol. 1, section 1, adapted from table 6, pp. 35-36.

The President's Commission on Crime in the District of Columbia discovered similar racial relationships in its 1966 survey of a number of serious crimes. Only 12 of 172 murders were interracial.[15] Eighty-eight percent of rapes involved persons of the same race.[16] Among 121 aggravated assaults for which identification of race was available, only 9 percent were interracial.[17] Auto theft offenders in the District are three-fourths Negroes, their victims two-thirds Negroes.[18] Robbery, the only crime of violence in which whites were victimized more often than Negroes, is also the only one that is predominantly interracial: in 56 percent of the robberies committed by Negroes in the District of Columbia, the victims are white.[19]

The high proportions of both acquaintance between victim and offender and the intraracial character of offenses are further borne out by the findings of another study developed for the Commission. Analyzing data obtained from the Seattle Police Department, this study compared the census tract where the crime occurred with the tract (or other place) in which the offender lived. It found that a relatively large percentage of crimes against persons, as contrasted with crimes against property, had been committed in the offender's home tract—an area likely to be racially homogeneous and in which he is most likely to be known at least by sight.[20]

This analysis shows that a failure to collect adequate data on victim-offender relationships may lead to a miscalculation of the source and nature of the risk of victimization. At present the Nation's view of the crime

[15] *D.C. Crime Commission Report, supra* note 9, at p. 42.
[16] *Id.,* at p. 54.
[17] *Id.* at p. 76.
[18] *Id.* at p. 101.
[19] *Id.* at p. 56.
[20] *Reiss studies, supra* note 10, at pp. 203–216.

problem is shaped largely by official statistics which in turn are based on offenses known to the police and statistics concerning arrested offenders; they include very little about victims.

Place Where Victimization Occurs

Crime is more likely to occur in some places than in others, just as some persons are more likely than others to be the victims of criminal offenders. The police often distribute their preventive patrols according to spot maps that locate the time and place of occurrence of different types of crimes. Such information, however, has not been developed well enough to inform the public of the places it should avoid.

. . . . .

The study of victimization of individuals carried out in cooperation with the Chicago Police Department recorded the types of premises for all major crimes against the person except homicide.[21] Table 6 classifies victims by sex

Table 6—Victimization, by Sex and Place of Occurrence for Major Crimes (Except Homicide) Against the Person

[In percent]

Place of occurrence	Victims of major crimes against person	
	Male	Female
School property	3.2	2.4
Residence	20.5	46.1
Transport property	1.4	.4
Taxis and delivery trucks	2.6	
Businesses	3.2	1.1
Taverns and liquor stores	5.7	2.8
Street	46.8	30.7
Parks	.8	.5
All other premises	16.0	16.0
Total percent	100.0	100.0
Total number	(8,047)	(5,666)

SOURCE: Special tabulation from Chicago Police Department, Data Systems Division, for period September 1965 to March 1966, adapted from Reiss studies, supra note 24, vol. 1, section 1, table 34, p. 149.

in relation to the place where the offense occurred. For assaultive crimes against the person, the street and the home are by far the most common places of occurrence. Men are more likely to be victimized on the street, and women are more likely to be victimized in residences.

The findings in general are closely related to the characteristic patterns of interaction among men and women in our society. Men are more likely to meet one another outside the home. A substantial portion of assaults arises

[21] *Id.* at pp. 123–169.

from drinking—the tavern is the third most common setting for men to be victims of assault and battery—and some of the conflicts among drunks later erupt into street fights. Men and women more frequently engage in conflicts with each other in domestic settings.

Compensation to Victims of Crime

Programs granting public compensation to victims for physical injuries from violent crimes have aroused increased interest in recent years. The community has evidenced concern for the plight of victims of muggings, stabbings, and other violence. In the absence of such programs victims generally suffer losses that are not compensated in any way. Their civil remedies are most likely to be unsuccessful because of the poor financial condition and prospects of most offenders. And the criminal law generally makes no effort to use its sanctions to insure restitution to the victim. Indeed it often aggravates the victim's problem by incarcerating the offender, thus preventing him from earning money to make restitution.

Two philosophies underlie the recent movements for victim compensation. The first argues that the government is responsible for preventing crime and therefore should be made responsible for compensating the victims of the crimes it fails to prevent. The second approach, an extension of welfare doctrines, rests on the belief that people in need, especially those in need because they have been victimized by events they could not avoid, are entitled to public aid.[22]

The first modern victim-compensation programs were established in New Zealand and Great Britain in 1964. California's program, which became effective in the beginning of 1966, was the first in the United States. Only victims with limited financial resources qualify for compensation under this program. New York's victim-compensation bill, enacted in 1966, also provides compensation only for those who would suffer "serious financial hardship" as a result of the crime. Various Federal victim-compensation bills, now before the Congress, have yet to receive public hearings. The Commission believes that such hearings would provide a national forum for a much-needed debate over the philosophy, assumptions, and potential advantages and disadantages of such programs generally, and the relative merits and design of a program on the Federal level in particular.

The Commission has been impressed by the consensus among legislators and law enforcement officials that some kind of State compensation for victims of violent crime is desirable. Recent public opinion polls indicate that a considerable majority of the public is in favor of victim compensa-

[22] Gilbert Geis, "State Aid to Victims of Violent Crime," published in appendix B, President's Commission on Law Enforcement and Administration of Justice, *Task Force Report: Crime and Its Impact—An Assessment* (Washington: U.S. Government Printing Office, 1967).

tion.[23] The Commission believes that the general principle of victim compensation, especially to persons who suffer injury in violent crime, is sound and that the experiments now being conducted with different types of compensation programs are valuable.

Public Attitudes Toward Crime and Law Enforcement

.   .   .   .   .

Although it is not possible to identify all the factors that affect the rise and fall in public alarm about crime, it is a constantly recurring public theme.[24] A legal scholar recently took a look over the literature of the past 50 years and noted that each and every decade produced prominent articles about the need for strong measures to meet the then-current crisis in crime.[25] Periodically throughout the century, there have been investigating committees of the Congress, of the State legislatures, and special commissions of cities to deal with the particular crime problem of the time. It may be that there has always been a crime crisis, insofar as public perception is concerned.

Crime as a National Issue

Many circumstances now conspire to call greater attention to crime as a national, rather than a purely local, problem. Concern with crime is more typically an urban than a rural phenomenon and the rural population of the country is declining. At one time, for a majority of the population, reports of crime waves related only to those remote and not quite moral people who inhabited cities.

.   .   .   .   .

HEIGHTENED CONCERN ABOUT CRIME AS A PUBLIC PROBLEM

The national public opinion polls provide evidence of the heightened concern today about the crime problem.[26] International problems have invariably been at the top whenever open-ended questions were asked by the Gallup poll about the problems facing the Nation. Crime problems were

[23] See the Gallup poll, Oct. 29, 1965, where 62 percent of the public were in favor of compensation for the victims of crime. Also, the national survey conducted by NORC for the Commission indicated that 56 percent of the sample interviewed were in favor of compensation for victims. See NORC study, *supra* source note, table 11, p. 69.

[24] E.g., Daniel Bell, "The Myth of the Crime Waves," in *The End of Ideology* (2d. rev. ed., New York: Collier Books, 1962), pp. 151–174.

[25] Yale Kamisar, "When the Cops Were Not 'Handcuffed,' " *New York Times Magazine,* Nov. 7, 1965.

[26] Surveys by George Gallup, director, American Institute of Public Opinion, Princeton, N.J., will be referred to as Gallup polls. Those by Louis Harris, public opinion analyst, will be cited as Harris surveys.

not mentioned as an important problem by enough people to appear among the list. When the National Opinion Research Center conducted a national survey for the Commission during the summer of 1966, interviewers asked citizens to pick from a list of six major domestic problems facing the country the one to which they had been paying most attention recently.[27] Crime was second most frequently picked from among the list of domestic problems; only race relations was selected by more people. (Lower income nonwhites placed more emphasis on education than crime.)

Table 7—Most Important Domestic Problem, by Race and Income

Domestic problem	Percent white		Percent nonwhite	
	Under $6,000	Over $6,000	Under $6,000	Over $6,000
Poverty	9	5	7	8
Inflation	15	17	4	4
Education	12	19	23	21
Crime	27	22	19	22
Race relations	29	34	32	38
Unemployment	8	3	15	7
Total	100	100	100	100
Number	(3,925)	(6,461)	(1,033)	(462)

Source: Philip H. Ennis, "Attitudes Toward Crime," Interim Report to the President's Commission on Law Enforcement and Administration of Justice, 1966 (mimeo).

In a consideration of local rather than national problems people rank juvenile delinquency higher on the scale than almost any other issue, including adult crime. Gallup polls reported in 1963 that when persons were asked to name the top problems in their community from a list of 39, juvenile delinquency was second in frequency of selection—exceeded only by complaints about local real estate taxes. The third most frequently mentioned problem was a not completely unrelated matter in the public's perception—the need for more recreation areas.

Whether more concerned about adult or juvenile crime, most people think the crime situation in their own community is getting worse, and, while substantial numbers think the situation is staying about the same, hardly anyone sees improvement. A Gallup survey in April 1965, showed this pessimistic perception of the problem prevailed among men and women, well educated and less well educated, and among all age, regional, income, and city groupings.

SOURCES OF PUBLIC ATTITUDES ABOUT CRIME

From analysis of the results of its surveys of the public, the Commission tried to determine to what extent this increased public concern about crime

[27] Philip H. Ennis, *Criminal Victimization in the United States:* A Report of a National Survey (Field Surveys II, President's Commission on Law Enforcement and Administration of Justice, Washington: U.S. Government Printing Office, 1967) (hereinafter referred to as the NORC study).

was a reflection of personal experience as a victim, or vicarious impressions received from acquantances, the mass media, or other sources. Although it was not possible to answer this question fully, the available data indicate that for most people attitudes about serious crimes and crime trends come largely from vicarious sources. This is especially the case with the crimes of violence which, although the focus of the public's concern, are relatively rare.

Very few incidents in which citizens have been victimized by crime were of such great significance in their lives as to be readily remembered for any length of time. This conclusion is one of the findings from the intensive methodological work undertaken for the Commission by the Bureau of Social Science Research in Washington, D.C., in preparation for surveys of the public regarding victimization.[28] This was first observed in pretest interviewing that showed extremely pronounced "recency effects"; that is, the bulk of such incidents as respondents did report were incidents that had occurred within the very recent past—in the space of just the last few months. A very steep decline occurred when the number of cases of victimization were plotted by month of occurrence from the present into the past—even for as short a period as 1 year. While the investigators were ultimately able to achieve far greater exhaustiveness of reporting through methods that facilitated recall and led their respondents to give more time and effort to the task of remembering, even these revised methods showed pronounced effects of forgetting.

This effect is even very evident in the dates victimized citizens gave for crimes mentioned in response to questions about the worst crime that had ever happened to them or to any member of their household. Taking the most remote of any incidents of victimization mentioned by each respondent, over half had occurred during the previous 18-month period and 60 percent in the past 2 years. Only 21 percent of all incidents described as "the worst ever" were said to have happened more than 5 years ago.[29]

The seriousness of most crimes reported by the citizens interviewed by BSSR also led to the inference that people generally do not readily remember minor incidents of victimization, though relatively trivial criminal acts, such as vandalism and petty larcenies from automobiles and of bicycles, are undoubtedly much more prevalent than are more serious offenses.[30]

These observations may help explain why the surveys of citizens conducted for the Commission found little statistical relationship between having been directly victimized by crime and attitudes toward most aspects of the crime problem. Undoubtedly, if there had been sufficient cases to

[28] Albert D. Biderman, Louise A. Johnson, Jessie McIntyre, and Adrienne W. Weir, *Report on a Pilot Study in the District of Columbia on Victimization and Attitudes Toward Law Enforcement* (Field Survey I, President's Commission on Law Enforcement and Administration of Justice, Washington: U.S. Government Printing Office, 1967) (hereinafter referred to as the BSSR study).

[29] *Id.* at p. 40.

[30] *Id.* at p. 33.

relate reliably the personal experiences and attitudes of persons suffering victimization from the most serious crimes of rape, aggravated assault, robbery, etc., a direct relationship would have been found in such cases. However, for all victims as a group in contrast to nonvictims, having been personally victimized did not influence perceptions of whether crime was increasing or not, or the degree of a person's concern with the crime problem in most instances. The NORC national survey did show that victims tended to have somewhat more worry about burglary or robbery. This was true for both males and females as can be seen in Table 8, though

Table 8—Concern of Victims and Nonvictims About Burglary or Robbery

[In percentages]

Worry about burglary or robbery	Victim	Nonvictim
Males:		
Worried	69	59
Not worried	31	41
	100	100
Number of males	(1,456)	(3,930)
Females:		
Worried	84	77
Not worried	16	23
	100	100
Number of females	(2,399)	(6,189)

Source: NORC survey, supra note 5, adapted from tables 48 and 50, pp. 77–79.

females, whether they had been victimized or not, were more concerned about their safety than males. However, other data from the NORC survey show that recent experience of being a victim of crime did not seem to increase behavior designed to protect the home. Almost identical proportions, 57 percent of victims and 58 percent of nonvictims, took strong household security measures.[31]

. . . . .

A further indication of the importance of vicarious impressions in forming the public's perceptions of crime is that a majority of citizens almost everywhere think that the situation right where they live is not so bad. While the predominant opinion is that the crime situation is terrible and getting worse, most people tend to think of the situation as one that characterizes places other than their own immediate neighborhood. In the nationwide NORC study for the Commission, 60 percent of those questioned compared their own neighborhood favorably to other parts of the community in which they lived with regard to the likelihood that their home would be broken into, while only 14 percent thought their area presented a greater hazard.[32] This is the case even in areas that are regarded by the police as very crime-ridden. In the BSSR survey of residents of areas

[31] Philip H. Ennis, *supra* source note, table 1.
[32] NORC study, *supra* note 27, table 47, p. 76.

in Washington, D.C., that have average-to-high crime rates, only one out of five of those interviewed thought his neighborhood was less safe than most in the city.[33] Surveys conducted for the Commission by the Survey Research Center of the University of Michigan concerning public attitudes about crime in four medium-to-high crime rate police precincts in Boston and Chicago found that 73 percent of the respondents thought their own neighborhoods were very safe or average compared to other neighborhoods in relation to the chances of getting robbed, threatened, beaten up, or anything of that sort.[34]

Almost half of the nationwide sample contacted by the NORC survey said there was no place in the city in which they lived (or suburb or county for those not living in cities) where they would feel unsafe. Two-thirds of the respondents say they feel safe walking alone when it is dark if they are in their own neighborhood. Responses to the question: "How likely is it that a person walking around here at night might be held up or attacked—very likely, somewhat likely, somewhat unlikely or very unlikely?" were very heavily weighted toward the "unlikely" direction.

PERSONAL FEAR OF CRIME

The core of public anxiety about the crime problem involves a concern for personal safety and to a somewhat lesser extent the fear that personal property will be taken. Perhaps the most intense concern about crime is the fear of being attacked by a stranger when out alone. According to the NORC survey, while two-thirds of the American public feel safe about walking alone at night in their own neighborhoods, the remaining one-third do not. In Table 8, as noted above, women worry more than men about the risk of burglary or robbery. According to an April 1965 Gallup survey, the percentage of people feeling unsafe at night on the street is higher in large cities than in smaller ones and higher in cities than in rural areas.

Recently studies have been undertaken to develop an index of delinquency based on the seriousness of different offenses.[35] They have shown that there is widespread public consensus on the relative seriousness of different types of crimes, and these rankings furnish useful indicators of the types of crime that the public is most concerned about. Offences involving physical assaults against the person are the most feared crimes and the greatest concern is expressed about those in which a weapon is used.

Fear of crime makes many people want to move their homes. In the four police precincts surveyed for the Commission in Boston and Chicago, 20

[33] BSSR study, *supra* note 28 at p. 121.

[34] Albert J. Reiss, Jr., *Studies in Crime and Law Enforcement in Major Metropolitan Areas* (Field Surveys III, President's Commission on Law Enforcement and Administration of Justice, Washington: U.S. Government Printing Office, 1967), vol. I, sec. 2, p. 30 (hereinafter referred to as the *Reiss studies*).

[35] Thorsten Sellin and Marvin E. Wolfgang, *The Measurement of Delinquency* (New York: John Wiley & Sons, Inc., 1964), table 69, p. 289.

percent of the citizens wanted to move because of the crime in their neighborhoods, and as many as 30 percent wanted to move out of the highest crime rate district in Boston.[36]

Fear of crime shows variations by race and income. In the survey in Washington, the Bureau of Social Science Research put together an index of anxiety about crime. It found that Negro women had the highest average score, followed by Negro men, white women, and white men. Anxiety scores were lower at the higher income levels for both Negroes and whites.[37]

The NORC survey asked people whether there have been times recently when they wanted to go somewhere in town but stayed at home instead, because they thought it would be unsafe to go there. Sixteen percent of the respondents said that they had stayed home under these conditions. This type of reaction showed marked variation with race; one out of every three Negro respondents had stayed home as contrasted with one in eight whites.[38]

People also take special measures at home because of the fear of unwanted intruders. The national survey showed that 82 percent of the respondents always kept their doors locked at night and 25 percent always kept their doors locked even in the daytime when the family members were at home. Twenty-eight percent kept watch-dogs and 37 percent said they kept firearms in the house for protection, among other reasons.[39]

The special city surveys disclosed that a substantial number of people take other measures to protect themselves from crime. In Boston and Chicago 28 percent had put new locks on their doors primarily, as one might expect, because they had been victimized or were worried about the high crime rate in the area. Another 10 percent had put locks or bars on their windows; this occurred primarily in the highest crime rate areas. Nine percent said they carried weapons, usually knives, when they went out, and this figure rose to 19 percent in the highest crime rate district in Boston.[40]

The close relationship between worry about crime and the taking of strong precautionary measures is further demonstrated by the results from the national survey. Respondents were asked how much they worried about being victimized by robbery or burglary and their responses were related to their tendency to take strong household security measures. Persons worried about both burglary and robbery are most likely to take such precautions, about 50 percent more likely than those who are worried about neither.[41]

Perhaps the most revealing findings on the impact of fear of crime on people's lives were the changes people reported in their regular habits of life. In the high-crime districts surveyed in Boston and Chicago, for exam-

[36] *Reiss studies, supra* note 34, p. 31.
[37] BSSR study, *supra* note 28, p. 124.
[38] NORC study, *supra* note 27, table 44, p. 74.
[39] Philip H. Ennis, *supra* source note to table 1.
[40] *Reiss studies, supra* note 34, pp. 103–106.
[41] NORC study, *supra* note 27, table 48, p. 77.

ple, five out of every eight respondents reported changes in their habits because of fear of crime, some as many as four or five major changes. Forty-three percent reported they stayed off the streets at night altogether. Another 21 percent said they always used cars or taxis at night. Thirty-five percent said they would not talk to strangers any more.[42]

.   .   .   .   .

Attitudes Toward Causes and Cures

Attitude surveys involving questions on the causes of crime and measures for remedying the situation yield results reflecting differences in fundamental beliefs regarding man and society. Some regard punitive and repressive measures as the best means for coping with problem while others prefer measures of social uplift. Some see inherent and immutable differences between the character of those who commit crimes, on the one hand, and the ordinary citizen on the other. Others see criminal tendencies as modifiable by instruction or changes in environmental circumstances. Some view many current social changes as leading toward a progressively more law-abiding citizenry; others see in them the undermining of moral beliefs and constraints which keep men law-abiding.

While there undoubtedly are some persons whose views fit neatly into this liberal versus conservative polarity, this is by no means universally so. The lack of a rigid polarity is evidenced by conflicting poll and survey results, especially between notions of causes and cures, and between ideas of appropriate actions in general or in concrete cases.

A Gallup poll in August 1965 asked people what they thought was responsible for the increase in crime in this country. The major share of the reasons people mentioned were things having directly to do with the social or moral character of the population, rather than changes in objective circumstances or in law enforcement. Gallup classified more than half of all the answers given under the category "Family, poor parental guidance." About 6 percent of the answers gave breakdown in moral standards as the reason for increased crime. A variety of other directly moral causes were given in addition, such as: people expect too much, people want something for nothing, and communism. Relatively few (12 percent) of the responses were in terms of objective conditions such as unemployment, poverty, the automobile, or the population explosion. Inadequate laws and the leniency of the courts were mentioned by 7 percent and not enough police protection by only 3 percent.

The responses to a query by Harris the same year were classified differently but a similar pattern emerges. Disturbed and restless teenagers was mentioned by more persons than any other cause and poor police departments by very few.

---

[42] *Reiss studies, supra* note 34, p. 103.

Harris later asked specifically why people become criminal rather than the reasons for an increase in crime. Most respondents attributed criminality to environmental and developmental factors rather than inborn characteristics, emphasizing such factors as poor training and companions, sometimes simply bad environment.

Table 9—Why People Become Criminals

	Total public, percent
Upbringing	38
Bad environment	30
Mentally ill	16
Wrong companions	14
No education	14
Broken homes	13
Greed, easy money	13
Too much money around	11
Not enough money in home	10
Liquor, dope	10
Laziness	9
For kicks	8
No religion	8
No job	8
No chance by society	7
Born bad	5
Feeling of hopelessness	4
Moral breakdown of society	3
Degeneracy, sex	2
Failure of police	2

NOTE: Percentages add to more than 100 because people volunteered more than 1 cause.
Source: Harris poll, conducted in 1965 and reported in 1966.

Although a majority of persons queried tended to think of inadequate moral training rather than inherent weaknesses when asked about the cause of crime, their response concerning the best way to cope with the problem tended to depend upon how the issue was phrased. For example, the BSSR survey in Washington asked citizens what they thought was the most important thing that could be done to cut down crime in the city.[43] Their responses were classified as to whether a repressive measure, a measure of social amelioration, or one of moral inculcation was being advocated. (Repressive measures included such things as more police, police dogs, stiffer sentences, cracking down on teenagers. Social amelioration included advocacy of such things as more jobs, recreation and youth programs, better housing, and improved police-community relations. Moral measures were better child training, religious training and revival, community leadership, and, most simply, teach discipline.) Sixty percent of the respondents recommended repressive measures, as compared with 40 percent who suggested social and amelioration or moral inculcation.

Further evidence of this tendency to think of repressive measures as the way to deal with some aspects of the crime problems is contained in the answers to the question, "In general, do you think the courts in this area deal too harshly or not harshly enough with criminals?" asked in a 1965 Gallup survey. The majority of responses was not harshly enough; only 2 percent said too harshly. The BSSR study in Washington avoided the use of

[43] BSSR study, *supra* note 28, p. 134.

the word criminal by asking whether the sentences given by courts in Washington were generally too lenient or too harsh. Again, most respondents, including Negroes, thought the courts too lenient.[44]

However, when survey items pose alternatives rather than general open-ended questions, they have yielded somewhat different results. The NORC national study asked people whether the main concern of the police should be with preventing crimes from happening or with catching criminals. All but 6 percent of those asked felt they could make a choice between these two emphases—61 percent chose preventing crimes and 31 percent catching criminals.[45]

Another question by the Harris poll in 1966 posed these alternatives:

> Leading authorities on crime feel there are two ways to reduce crime. One way is to head off crime by working with young people to show them that nothing can be gained through a life of crime. Another way is to strengthen our law enforcement agencies to make it hard for criminals to get away with crime. While both ways might be desirable, if you had to choose, which one would you favor: trying to stop criminals before they begin or strengthening the police force to crack down on crime?

More than three-fourths of respondents chose "work with young people," only 16 percent "strengthen police." There were 8 percent who were not sure which was preferable.

A nonpunitive approach was also evident in a third question in the same survey which asked people to choose between corrective and punitive goals for prisons. Again, over three-fourths of the respondents chose correction as the alternative, only 11 percent punishment. Apparently, when the alternatives are put sharply enough, especially in dealing with the misbehavior of young people, the general preference of the public for preventive or rehabilitative rather than repressive measures emerges.

The tendency to be nonpunitive and repressive when considering the handling of youthful offenders is strikingly illustrated by the results of a 1963 Gallup survey. A sample was drawn from 171 communities across the Nation to sit in judgment on a hypothetical case. The respondents were asked how they would deal with a 17-year-old high school student from their own community who was caught stealing an automobile. They were told he had no previous record. Fewer than 10 percent recommended confinement of any sort: the largest number said they would give him another chance (Table 10).

These survey results indicate the existence of public attitudes endorsing current trends in the criminal justice field that would increase the effectiveness of law enforcement and at the same time greatly expand preventive

[44] *Id.* at p. 135.
[45] NORC study, *supra* note 27, p. 59.

Table 10—How Public Would Deal with Youth Caught Stealing a Car (Rank Order of Answers)

1. Give him another chance, be lenient.
2. Put him on probation; give him a suspended sentence.
3. Put him under care of psychiatrist or social worker.
4. Put him in an institution: jail, reformatory, etc.
5. Release him in the custody of his parents.
6. Punish his parents; fine them.

Source: Gallup polls, 1963.

and rehabilitative efforts, particularly with young people. Though at first glance public attitudes toward the causes and cures for crime might appear contradictory, a more careful analysis suggests that the public assumes different attitudes toward different aspects of the crime problem. This provides potential support for many different types of action programs ranging all the way from increased police powers and more severe penalties for crime to the benign types of treatment and prevention programs.

CITIZEN INVOLVEMENT IN CRIME PREVENTION

Public concern about crime can be a powerful force for action. However, making it one will not be easy. The Washington survey asked people whether they had ever "gotten together with other people around here or has any group or organization you belong to met and discussed the problem of crime or taken some sort of action to combat crime?"[46] Only 12 percent answered affirmatively, although the question was quite broad and included any kind of group meeting or discussion. Neither did most persons believe that they as individuals could do anything about the crime in their own neighborhoods. Just over 17 percent thought that they could do something about the situation.

The question of what could be done to reduce crime was put to administrators and officials of public and quasi-public organizations in three cities.[47] These officials suggested ameliorative measures, such as greater equality of opportunity, rehabilitative, recreational and youth programs more frequently than did the sample of the general population. These citizens in positions of responsibility also relied to a great extent on the police; almost as many suggested improved and augmented police forces as suggested the social measures. There was, however, much greater emphasis on improvement in the moral fiber and discipline of the population than was true of the sample of the general population. Administrators of parks, libraries, utility companies, housing projects frequently stressed greater respect for property, for persons, or for the police; they believed that education could inculcate these values in the population. As these officials were responsible for organizations which suffered considerable loss through vandalism, it

[46] BSSR study, *supra* note 28, unpublished supplement.

[47] Stephen Cutler and Albert J. Reiss, Jr., *Crimes Against Public and Quasi-Public Organizations in Boston, Chicago, and Washington, D.C.* (Ann Arbor: University of Michigan, Department of Sociology, 1966). A report to the President's Commission on Law Enforcement and Administration of Justice (mimeo).

seemed reasonable to them that greater respect for property would solve much of the crime problem. School officials proposed more alternative activities for youth while park and traffic officials emphasized more police activity and better police-community relations, reflecting their own perceived need for more patrolling.

These administrators and officials who were interviewed also acknowledged a number of ways in which they might help to reduce crime. Some suggested that they might cooperate with the police in ways calculated to make law enforcement easier. Others thought that they might cooperate in neighborhood and community programs, particularly by donating money for youth activities. The largest number of suggestions, however, involved what might be termed extension of the organizations' services. Electric companies considered more and brighter street lights, park offiicials more parks and recreational programs, and school principals more youth programs and adult education. Another category of responses by officials concerned participation in activities directed toward community goals. They thought that integration of work crews and the support of community relations programs might be helpful. Interestingly, some of these suggestions were not offered until the officials were specifically asked what their organizations might do. Park officials, for example, did not suggest recreational and other alternative activities as a means of reducing crime until asked what park departments might do. Nonetheless, these administrators and officials did see the potential of their own organizations as useful in reducing crime, creating the possibility that they might do something other than rely on the police. They also take a broader view of crime prevention than does the general public. Understandably, they might as citizens and organizations feel more competent to participate effectively in these broader programs while other segments of the public are more likely to believe that control and prevention is not within their province.

AMBIVALENCE REGARDING POLICE PRACTICES AND LAW ENFORCEMENT

The public surveys show that there is a considerable willingness to permit practices the police and law enforcement agencies consider important—but not an unqualified willingness. The complexity of the feelings about the relative rights of the police and the accused person is apparent in the responses of persons questioned by the BSSR in Washington and also in the results of the national study.

As one might expect, a substantial majority of the respondents in Washington, 73 percent, agreed that the police ought to have leeway to act tough when they have to.[48] In addition, more than half—56 percent—agreed that there should be more use of police dogs, while less than one-third (31 percent) disagreed. However, the person who takes a strong position on one question may refuse to do so on another. Further, there is

[48] BSSR, *supra* note 28, p. 146.

little consistency between a general respect and sympathy for police and willingness to enlarge police powers. Table 11 shows that there is some tendency for those with high police support scores to be willing to give the police greater power, but that there are also many who regard the police favorably who would restrict their power. The public's attitudes seem to be more responsive to particular issues than to anything which might be called a generalized high or low attitude toward supporting the police.

A similar ambivalence was observed in the results of the national survey conducted for the Commission.[49] There were four questions concerned with the power of the police. Forty-five percent favored civilian review boards (35 percent opposed them, 20 percent had no opinion or were indifferent); 52 percent believed that the police should have more power; 42 percent that

Table 11—Attitudes Toward Supporting Police and Approval of Certain Police Practices

[Figures in parentheses=percentages]

"The police should have leeway to act tough when they have to."

	Agree		Disagree	
Low Police Support Score[1]	136	(36.5)	59	(53.6)
High Police Support Score	237	(63.5)	51	(46.4)
Total	373	(100.0)	110	(100.0)

"There should be more use of police dogs."

	Agree		Disagree	
Low Police Support Score	100	(35.1)	86	(53.4)
High Police Support Score	185	(64.9)	75	(46.6)
Total	285	(100.0)	161	(100.0)

[1] A police support score was assigned each respondent depending on whether he gave a positive or negative response to six statements about the police.

Source: BSSR study, *supra* note 6, p. 148.

police should risk arresting an innocent person rather than risk missing a criminal; and 65 percent favored the ruling that police may not question a suspect without his lawyer being present or the suspect's consent to be questioned without counsel. These percentages indicate that individuals vary considerably from one issue to the next as to the desirability of enlarging or restricting police powers.

To test this motion, the answers of each respondent were combined to form a scale of restrictiveness or permissiveness regarding law enforcement policy (Table 12). Those consistently in favor of expanding police powers would score 0 and those most restrictive of police power would score 8. The distribution of scores in Table 13 illustrates the variations in attitudes about different law enforcement policies or issues. Only 11 percent of the respond-

[49] NORC study, *supra* note 27, pp. 64–72.

Table 12—Attitudes Toward Law Enforcement Policies

Recently some cities have added civilian review boards to their police departments. Some people say such boards offer the public needed protection against the police, and others say these boards are unnecessary and would interfere with good police work and morale. In general, would you be in favor of civilian review boards or opposed to them?

Score value		Percent
2	In favor	45
0	Opposed	35
1	Don't know	20
	N	(14,366)

Do you favor giving the police more power to question people, do you think they have enough power already, or would you like to see some of their power to question people curtailed?

Score value		Percent
0	Police should have more power	52
1	Have enough power already	43
2	Should curtail power	5
	N	(13,190)

The police sometimes have a hard time deciding if there is enough evidence to arrest a suspect. In general, do you think it is better for them to risk arresting an innocent person rather than letting the criminal get away, or is it better for them to be really sure they are getting the right person before they make an arrest?

Score value		Percent
0	Risk arresting innocent	42
2	Be really sure	58
	N	(13,488)

The Supreme Court has recently ruled that in criminal cases the police may not question a suspect without his lawyer being present, unless the suspect agrees to be questioned without a lawyer. Are you in favor of this Supreme Court decision or opposed to it?

Score value		Percent
2	In favor	65
0	Opposed	35
	N	(12,994)

Source: Adapted from NORC study, supra note 27, pp. 64–65.

ents show extreme scores advocating expansion of police power and 15 percent show extreme restrictive scores. Many give restrictive answers to some questions and permissive answers to others.

The public surveys also show that most people believe that the police do not discriminate in the way they treat members of different groups. About half of the Negro and 20 percent of the white citizens interviewed in Washington thought that Negroes get no worse treatment than other people. Among the comments of those respondents who do believe the police discriminate were that the police pick on Negroes more, they are rude to Negroes, use brutality and physical force, or else ignore Negroes more than other people. Half of the Washington respondents believed that people who have money for lawyers don't have to worry about police.[50] Somewhat fewer

Table 13—Percent Distribution, Police Policy Index

Most in favor of increasing police powers (index value):

0	7.5
1	3.6
2	16.4
3	10.7
4	16.9
5	17.1
6	12.5
7	13.1
8	2.2

Most in favor of restricting police power:

Total	100.0
N	(11,742)

[50] BSSR study, *supra* note 28, p. 144.

but nonetheless almost half of the respondents in Boston and Chicago said that the way police treat you depends on who you are.[51] In these cities, 35 percent saw rich and respectable persons as being favored by the police while 38 percent said that being a Negro makes a difference.[52] In the predominantly Negro districts in each of these cities, more persons thought that Negroes receive less than equitable treatment while in the predominately white areas more persons spoke of favorable treatment of rich persons.[53]

The single most outstanding finding of the survey in Washington, however, was not the differences between groups but rather the generally high regard for the police among all groups, including Negro men. Although the BSSR survey found that more than half of the Negro men believed that many policemen enjoy giving people a hard time, 79 percent said that the police deserve more thanks than they get. And 74 percent thought that there are just a few policemen who are responsible for the bad publicity that the police force sometimes gets.[54] It is not so surprising to find this potential for good will toward the police when it is remembered that Negroes expressed the most worry about being the victims of crime and a general reliance on the police to prevent and control crime. This was the case even among Negro men who are not well educated and who live in the poorer areas of the city with relatively high rates of crime.

In general, the surveys found public concern for safeguarding individual rights. Only 38 percent of the respondents agreed that too much attention is paid to the rights of persons who get in trouble with the police, when that question was asked in Washington, Boston, and Chicago.[55] The questions which comprised the law enforcement policy scale in the national survey also were concerned with various aspects of the relative rights of the accused and the police.[56] When asked several questions in which various extensions of police powers were posited against protections of individual rights, in only one case did a majority favor the enlargement of police power.[57] Barely more than half, 52 percent, thought that police should have more power to question people. A pronounced concern with the rights of citizens is particularly apparent when the rights issue is very explicit. It also is apparent that most persons do not perceive this concern with rights of citizens as being derogatory toward the police. Of those persons questioned in Washington who took a prorights position, more then half indicated strong respect and sympathy for the police.[58]

[51] *Reiss studies, supra* note 34, p. 42.
[52] *Id.* at pp. 43–47.
[53] *Id.* at pp. 42–47.
[54] BSSR study, supra note 28, p. 137.
[55] BSSR study, *supra* note 28, p. 149, and *Reiss studies, supra* note 14, p. 82.
[56] For a description of the police policy index, see NORC study, *supra* note 27, pp. 64–65.
[57] NORC study, *supra* note 27, p. 64.
[58] BSSR study, *supra* note 28, p. 150.

Negroes were somewhat more likely to take the rights position than white respondents but the differences were not great. The survey in Washington found that 49 percent of the Negroes and 46 percent of the white respondents did not think that too much attention was being paid to the rights of people who get into trouble with the police.[59] The same question was asked in Boston and Chicago; in both cities there were more prorights replies in the districts which were predominantly Negro than in those which were predominantly white. In Boston the proportions of prorights replies were 46 percent in the predominantly Negro district and 20 percent in the predominantly white area.[60] In Chicago it was 40 and 33 percent in predominantly Negro and white areas respectively.[61] The differences between the mean scores on the police policy index also reflected more concern with the rights of citizens on the part of nonwhite than white persons in the national sample.[62]

Another form of concern with the rights of citizens in recent years has been the question of allowing political and civil rights demonstrations. People who were questioned in the national study were asked whether such demonstrations should be allowed no matter what, should be allowed only if the demonstrators remain peaceful, or should not be allowed at all.[63] A majority of both whites and nonwhites would allow the demonstrations, most with the proviso that they remain peaceful. Among white persons there was a relationship between income and tolerance toward demonstrations. Those persons with higher incomes would more frequently allow demonstrations if they were peaceful and less frequently prohibit all demonstrations. Nonwhites tended to be more permissive regarding demonstrations regardless of income level. The upper income nonwhites, however, more often qualified their tolerance by requiring that demonstrations be peaceful. The tolerance of demonstrations as an indication of concern for rights was far from synonymous with a desire to restrict police powers as they related to the rights of citizens, however. More than 50 percent of the white respondents who would allow demonstrations would also enlarge police powers. (More of the nonwhites would restrict police powers.)

The national survey also found a strong preponderance of favorable opinion toward the Supreme Court's decision regarding right of counsel.[64] Almost three-quarters of the persons questioned approved the decision that the State must provide a lawyer to suspects who want one but cannot afford to pay the lawyer's fee. Not only does a strong majority approve the decision but no income, sex, or racial group opposes it.

---

[59] *Id.* at p. 149.
[60] *Reiss studies, supra* note 34, p. 82.
[61] *Ibid.*
[62] NORC study, *supra* note 27, p. 68.
[63] *Id.* at table 36, p. 63.
[64] *Id.* at table 40, p. 70.

Nonreporting of Crimes to the Police

Americans believe that the crime problem is a matter for police rather than citizen action. They nevertheless frequently fail to take the one essential action that they as citizens must take if the police are to intervene in any particular criminal instance. Fewer than half of the incidents of victimization uncovered by NORC in the national survey conducted for the Commission had been reported while the residents of Washington had notified the police of only 65 percent of the incidents they disclosed to BSSR interviewers.[65] NORC found considerable variation by type of crime.[66] Generally the more serious the crime the more likely the police were called. A higher percentage of grand than petty larcenies and of aggravated than simple assaults were reported, for example. Except for the more serious crimes against the person, however, crimes which were completed were reported no more frequently than the attempted crimes. It is apparent that the simple desire to recover losses or damages is not the only factor in a victim's decision for or against police notification. This study did not find that any racial or income group was any more likely than another to report to decline to report crimes.[67]

The victim's or witness' reluctance to get involved was one of the most frequently cited reasons for nonreporting.[68] Sometimes he did not want to take the time to call the police and present evidence, perhaps spending time in court and away from his work. Some persons who said they had witnessed incidents which might have been crimes did not feel it was their responsibility to intervene, that it was not their business to call the police or take any other action. A few persons expressed this sentiment by stating to the interviewers, "I am not my brother's keeper."

Others said they did not think the victim would want the police to be notified or they indicated a concern for the offender. Victims, too, were sometimes reluctant to cause trouble for the offender. In half the cases of family crimes or sex offenses (other than forcible rape) reported to NORC interviewers the police were not notified and the reason most frequently given was that it was a private rather than a police matter.[69] Similarly for all classes of offenses except serious crimes against the person, the police were less likely to be called if the offender were personally known to the victim than if he were a stranger.

The fear of reprisal or other unfortunate consequences sometimes deterred victims or witnesses from notifying the police of an incident. Some feared personal harm might come from the offender or his friends. Some

[65] NORC study, *supra* note 27, p. 42, and BSSR study, *supra* note 28, p. 40.
[66] See *supra* note 8, table 5 in chapter 2.
[67] NORC study, *supra* note 27, table 27, p. 46.
[68] *Id.* at table 24, p. 44.
[69] *Id.* at table 26, p. 46.

feared that they themselves would become the subject of police inquiry or action. In the case of property offenses the fear of increased insurance rates or even of cancellation of insurance was more likely to be the reason. Businessmen often refrained from reporting burglaries, believing that it was less expensive to absorb some of these losses than to pay more for their insurance.[70]

The most frequently cited reason for not reporting an incident to the police is the belief in police ineffectiveness; 55 percent of the reasons given for nonreporting by respondent in the national study fell in this category. This does not necessarily constitute evidence of a pervasive cynicism regarding police. The victim may instead have simply accepted that the damage had been done, there were no clues, and the police could not be expected to apprehend the offender or undo the damage. For example, in malicious mischief where it is unlikely the offender will be caught, police ineffectiveness is the preponderant reason for nonreporting.

For similar reasons, businessmen interviewed by the University of Michigan survey team said that they rarely called the police to handle cases of employee dishonesty.[71] In 46 percent of the cases where the police were not called, the reason given questions the capability of the police to do anything in the situation.[72] They do not question that the police will respond to their call but doubt whether the police would or could accept the kind of evidence they have, or they do not feel that the courts would accept the evidence even if the police formally made an arrest. These businessmen also frequently responded in terms of not wanting to get involved and preferring to handle the matter themselves. Dismissal of the employee apparently requires less time and effort than referral of the matter to the police. Their feeling that it was not worthwhile to call the police then did not always indicate a negative evaluation of the police. Ironically, many of these same businessmen who do not report instances of employee dishonesty use police records as a screening device for selecting potential employees.[73]

Another factor which may be operating here is the relationship between the employer and employee. The employer has in a sense taken some responsibility for the relationship by engaging the employee; what happens then is seen as a matter between himself and the person he has hired. Similarly, when a businessman agrees to cash a customer's check he infrequently calls the police when the check is returned for insufficient funds or other reasons. Only 19 percent of the owners and managers said they called the police when they are given a bad check, and another 8 percent said they

---

[70] Donald J. Black and Albert J. Reiss, Jr., *Problems and Practices for Protection Against Crime Among Businesses and Organizations* (Ann Arbor: University of Michigan, Department of Sociology, 1966). A report to the President's Commission on Law Enforcement and Administration of Justice (mimeo).

[71] *Ibid.*

[72] *Ibid.*

[73] *Ibid.*

would do so if they could not collect.[74] By far the most frequent response is to request that the offender make good. This is also the most frequent response in the case of shoplifting, but here there is a greater willingness to call the police. Nonetheless, only 37 percent say they call the police, and another 5 percent will call them if they cannot make the offender pay for the goods. Half of them try to make the offender pay for the goods.[75] There is, of course, greater reliance on law enforcement agencies than is apparent in these figures on nonreporting. Some businessmen suggested that they could threaten to call the police if the offender did not make restitution; in other instances the threat would be implicit.

[*The President's Commission on Law Enforcement and Administration of Justice*, Task Force Report: Crime and Its Impact —An Assessment (*Washington: U.S. Government Printing Office, 1967*), *pp. 42–45, 80–83, 85–94.*]

[74] *Ibid.*
[75] *Ibid.*

2   *The amount and trends of crime*

There are more than 2800 Federal crimes and a much larger number of State and local ones. Some involve serious bodily harm, some stealing, some public morals or public order, some governmental revenues, some the creation of hazardous conditions, some the regulation of the economy. Some are perpetrated ruthlessly and systematically; others are spontaneous derelictions. Gambling and prostitution are willingly undertaken by both buyer and seller; murder and rape are violently imposed upon their victims. Vandalism is predominantly a crime of the young, driving while intoxicated a crime of the adult. Many crime rates vary significantly from place to place.

The crimes that concern Americans the most are those that affect their personal safety—at home, at work, or in the streets. The most frequent and serious of these crimes of violence against the person are willful homicide, forcible rape, aggravated assault, and robbery. National statistics regarding the number of these offenses known to the police either from citizen complaints or through independent police discovery are collected from local police officials by the Federal Bureau of Investigation and published annually as a part of its report, "Crime in the United States, Uniform Crime Reports."[1] The FBI also collects "offenses known" statistics for three property crimes: burglary, larceny of $50 and over and motor vehicle theft. These seven crimes are grouped together in the UCR to form an Index of serious crimes.[2] . . .

The Risk of Harm

Including robbery, the crimes of violence make up approximately 13 percent of the Index. The Index reports the number of incidents known to the police, not the number of criminals who committed them or the number of injuries they caused.

The risk of sudden attack by a stranger is perhaps best measured by the frequency of robberies since, according to UCR and

[1] Cited hereinafter as UCR.
[2] UCR, 1965, p. 51.

other studies, about 70 percent of all willful killings,[3] nearly two-thirds of all aggravated assaults,[4] and a high percentage of forcible rapes[5] are committed by family members, friends, or other persons previously known to their victims. Robbery usually does not involve this prior victim-offender relationship.[6]

Robbery, for UCR purposes, is the taking of property from a person by use or threat of force with or without a weapon. Nationally, about one-half of all robberies are street robberies,[7] and slightly more than one-half involve weapons.[8] Attempted robberies are an unknown percentage of the robberies reported to the UCR. The likelihood of injury is also unknown, but a survey by the Dictrict of Columbia Crime Commission of 297 robberies in Washington showed that some injury was inflicted in 25 percent of them. The likelihood of injury was found higher for "yokings" or "muggings" (unarmed robberies from the rear) than for armed robberies. Injuries occurred in 10 of 91 armed robberies as compared with 30 of 67 yokings.[9]

Aggravated assault is assault with intent to kill or for the purpose of inflicting severe bodily injury, whether or not a dangerous weapon is used. It includes all cases of attempted homicide, but cases in which bodily injury is

[3] *Id.* at p. 6 (70 percent); *Report of the President's Commission on Crime in the District of Columbia* (Washington: U.S. Government Printing Office, 1966), p. 42 (79 percent) (hereinafter referred to as *D.C. Crime Commission Report*). See also Marvin E. Wolfgang, *Patterns in Criminal Homicide* (Philadelphia: University of Pennsylvania Press, 1958), p. 207. (Of the victims, 85.6 percent were at least casually acquainted with their attackers.)

[4] A special survey made by the UCR in 1960 of 564 cities covering about 38 percent of the U.S. population showed that more than 65 percent of all aggravated assaults occurred either within the family (22 percent) or among neighbors or acquaintances (43.4 percent). (UCR, 1960, p. 11). Of the 131 aggravated assaults studied by the D. C. Crime Commission, 81 percent involved offenders previously known to their victims; 20.7 percent of the offenders were relatives. Only 19 percent of the offenders were strangers. (*D.C. Crime Commission Report,* p. 76).

[5] See *D.C. Crime Commission Report,* p. 53, indicating that only 36 percent of all rapes surveyed were committed by complete strangers. A study in Philadelphia indicated that only 42.3 percent of the offenders were complete strangers. Of the others, 9.6 percent were strangers but the victim had general knowledge about them, 14.4 percent were acquaintances, 19.3 percent neighbors, 6.0 percent close friends, 5.3 percent family friends, and 2.5 percent relatives. See Menachem Amir, "Patterns of Forcible Rape" (Ph.D. dissertation, University of Pennsylvania, 1965), p. 496.

[6] In Great Britain, where robbery has been studied more intensively than in the United States, approximately 20 percent of the robberies involved some prior relationship. See F. H. McClintock and Evelyn Gibson, *Robbery in London* (New York: St. Martin's Press, 1961), p. 16.

[7] UCR, 1965, table 14, p. 105 based on 646 cities with a total population of 75,400,000 shows the following percentages for types of robberies:

```
Highway (street) ...........................51.4
Commercial house .........................20.2
Gas or service station ...................... 5.9
Chain store ............................... 2.7
Residence ................................. 9.1
Bank ....................................... .9
Miscellaneous ............................. 9.9
```

[8] Armed robberies accounted for 57.6 percent of the total and strong-arm robberies for 42.4 percent (UCR, 1965, p. 11).

[9] *D.C. Crime Commission Report,* p. 64.

inflicted in the course of a robbery or a rape are included with those crimes rather than with aggravated assault. There are no national figures showing the percentage of aggravated assaults that involve injury, but a survey of 131 cases by the District of Columbia Crime Commission found injury in 84 percent of the cases; 35 percent of the victims required hospitalization.[10] A 1960 UCR study showed that juvenile gangs committed less than 4 percent of all aggravated assaults.[11]

Forcible rape includes only those rapes or attempted rapes in which force or threat of force is used. About one-third of the UCR total is attempted rape.[12] In a District of Columbia Crime Commission survey of 151 cases, about 25 percent of all rape victims were attacked with dangerous weapons;[13] the survey did not show what percentage received bodily harm in addition to the rape.

About 15 percent of all criminal homicides, both nationally and the District of Columbia Crime Commission surveys, occurred in the course of committing other offenses.[14] These offenses appear in the homicide total rather than in the total for the other offense. In the District of Columbia Crime Commission surveys, less than one-half of 1 percent of the robberies and about 3 percent of the forcible rapes ended in homicide.[15]

Some personal danger is also involved in the property crimes. Burglary is the unlawful entering of a building to commit a felony or a theft, whether force is used or not. About half of all burglaries involve residences, but the statistics do not distinguish inhabited parts of houses from garages and similar outlying parts. About half of all residential burglaries are committed in daylight and about half at night.[16] A UCR survey indicates that 32 percent of the entries into residences are made through unlocked doors or

---

[10] *Id.* at p. 79. In a study of juvenile offenders in Philadelphia, Thorsten Sellin and Marvin E. Wolfgang, *The measurement of Delinquency* (New York: John Wiley & Sons, 1964), pp. 190–208, found that nearly three-fourths of all aggravated assault victims required medical treatment of some sort and 23 percent required hospitalization. See also David J. Pittman and William Handy, "Patterns in Criminal Aggravated Assault," *Journal of Criminal Law, Criminology and Police Science,* 55:462–470, December 1964. In a random sample of 241 aggravated assault cases occurring in St. Louis in 1961, 53.4 percent of the victims suffered injuries that required hospitalization. Lesser injuries were noted for the victims in the remaining cases studied (p. 465).

[11] UCR, 1960, p. 11.

[12] UCR, 1965, p. 9.

[13] *D.C. Crime Commission Report,* p. 54.

[14] UCR, 1965, p. 7; *D.C. Crime Commission Report,* p. 45.

[15] In the D.C. Crime Commission study of 172 murders, about 10 percent were incidental to robbery, and about 4 percent incidental to rape (*D.C. Crime Commission Report,* pp. 45–46, 56). The latter figure is considerably higher than that for the Nation as a whole.

[16] UCR, 1965, table 14, p. 105, based on 646 cities with a total population of 75,400,000, gives the following picture of types of burglaries:

	Percent
Residence:	
Night	25.4
Day	24.1
Nonresidence:	
Night	45.9
Day	4.6

windows.[17] When an unlawful entry results in a violent confrontation with the occupant, the offense is counted as a robbery rather than a burglary.[18] Of course, even when no confrontation takes place there is often a risk of confrontation. Nationally such confrontations occur in only one-fortieth of all residential burglaries. They account for nearly one-tenth of all robberies.[19]

In summary, these figures suggest that, on the average, the likelihood of a serious personal attack on any American in a given year is about 1 in 550;[20] together with the studies available they also suggest that the risk of serious attack from spouses, family members, friends, or acquaintances is almost twice as great as it is from strangers on the street.[21] Commission and other studies, moreover, indicate that the risks of personal harm are spread very unevenly. The actual risk for slum dwellers is considerably more; for most Americans it is considerably less.[22]

Except in the case of willful homicide, where the figures describe the extent of injury as well as the number of incidents, there is no national data on the likelihood of injury from attack. More limited studies indicate that while some injury may occur in two-thirds of all attacks, the risk in a given year of injury serious enough to require any degree of hospitalization of any individual is about 1 in 3000 on the average, and much less for most Americans.[23] These studies also suggest that the injury inflicted by family members or acquaintances is likely to be more severe than that from strangers. As shown by Table 1, the risk of death from willful homicide is about 1 in 20,000.

Criminal behavior accounts for a high percentage of motor vehicle deaths and injuries. In 1965 there were an estimated 49,000 motor vehicle deaths.[24]

---

[17] UCR, 1961, pp. 8, 10.

[18] Federal Bureau of Investigation, *Uniform Crime Reporting Handbook* (Washington: Federal Bureau of Investigation, February 1965), pp. 39–40 (hereinafter referred to as *UCR Handbook*).

[19] UCR, 1965, table 14, p. 105.

[20] UCR, 1965, p. 51. These figures based on reported index crimes. The danger of serious personal attack for crimes against the person is 184.7 per 100,000 or 1 in 556. (By offense, the rates per 100,000 are 5.1 for murder; 11.6 forcible rape; 61.4 robbery; and 106.6 aggravated assault.)

[21] See notes 3–6 *supra*, for percentages of risk, particularly the D.C. Crime Commission surveys. See note 20 *supra* and table 4 below for rates of offense. Assuming that the distribution is the same, the picture is clearer when unreported crime is considered.

[22] See President's Commission on Law Enforcement and Administration of Justice, *Task Force Report: Crime and Its Impact—An Assessment* (Washington: U.S. Government Printing Office, 1967), chapter 4, notes 4–22 and chapter 5, table 11. See also *Opportunity for Urban Excellence: Report of the Atlanta Commission on Crime and Juvenile Delinquency*, 1966, pp. 57–60.

[23] This figure includes all homicides and the Sellin and Wolfgang estimates for aggravated assault, *supra* note 10. It includes one-third of all forcible rapes (one-third are attempts; some others do not require hospitalization; see Amir, *supra* note 5). The only estimate available for robbery was that for injury, *supra* note 9. Based on percentages for other crimes, it was assumed that one-third of the total injuries might require hospitalization.

[24] National Safety Council, *Accident Facts* (Chicago: National Safety Council, 1966), p. 40.

Table 1—Deaths from Other than Natural Causes in 1965

[Per 100,000 inhabitants]

Motor vehicle accidents	25
Other accidents	12
Suicide	12
Falls	10
Willful homicide	5
Drowning	4
Fires	4

SOURCE: National Safety Council, "Accident Facts," 1965; Population Reference Bureau.

Negligent manslaughter, which is largely a motor vehicle offense, accounted for more than 7,000 of these.[25] Studies in several States indicate that an even higher percentage involve criminal behavior. They show that driving while intoxicated is probably involved in more than one-half of all motor vehicle deaths. These same studies show that driving while intoxicated is involved in more than 13 percent of the 1,800,000 nonfatal motor vehicle accidents each year.[26]

For various statistical and other reasons, a number of serious crimes against or involving risk to the person, such as arson, kidnapping, child molestation, and simple assault, are not included in the UCR Index.[27] In a study of 1,300 cases of delinquency in Philadelphia, offenses other than the seven Index crimes constituted 62 percent of all cases in which there was physical injury. Simple assault accounted for the largest percentage of these injuries. But its victims required medical attention in only one-fifth of the cases as opposed to three-fourths of the aggravated assaults, and hospitalization in 7 percent as opposed to 23 percent. Injury was more prevalent in conflicts between persons of the same age than in those in which the victim was older or younger than the attacker.[28]

Property Crimes

The three property crimes of burglary, automobile theft, and larceny of $50 and over make up 87 percent of Index crimes.[29] The Index is a reasonably reliable indicator of the total number of property crimes reported to the police, but not a particularly good indicator of the seriousness of monetary loss from all property crimes. Commission studies tend to indicate

[25] Reports to the UCR for 1965 covering 88 percent of the population indicated a total of 7,013 manslaughter cases (p. 94). According to earlier studies, 99 percent of all negligent manslaughter is due to automobile accidents (UCR, 1958, Special Issue, p. 25). The remainder is attributable largely to hunting accidents.

[26] National Safety Council, *supra* note 24, at p. 52.

[27] International Association of Chiefs of Police, Committee on Uniform Crime Records, *Uniform Crime Reporting* (New York: J. J. Little and Ives, 1929), pp. 180–182.

[28] Marvin E. Wolfgang, "Uniform Crime Reports: A Critical Appraisal," *University of Pennsylvania Law Review,* 111: 709–738, April 1963.

[29] UCR, 1965, p. 51.

that such non-Index crimes as fraud and embezzlement are more significant in terms of dollar volume.[30] Fraud can be a particularly pernicious offense. It is not only expensive in total but all too often preys on the weak.

Many larcenies included in the Index total are misdemeanors rather than felonies under the laws of their own States. Auto thefts that involve only unauthorized use also are misdemeanors in many States. Many stolen automobiles are abandoned after a few hours, and more than 85 percent are ultimately recovered according to UCR studies.[31] Studies in California indicate that about 20 percent of recovered cars are significantly damaged.[32]

Other Criminal Offenses

The seven crimes for which all offenses known are reported were selected in 1927 and modified in 1958 by a special advisory committee of the International Association of Chiefs of Police on the basis of their serious nature, their frequency, and the reliability of reporting from citizens to police.[33] In 1965 reporting for these offenses included information supplied voluntarily by some 8,000 police agencies covering nearly 92 percent of the total population.[34] The FBI tries vigorously to increase the number of jurisdictions that report each year and to promote uniform reporting and classification of the reported offenses.

The UCR Index does not and is not intended to assist in assessing all serious national crime problems. For example, offense statistics are not sufficient to assess the incidence of crime connected with corporate activity, commonly known as white-collar crime, or the total criminal acts committed by organized crime groups. Likewise, offense and arrest figures alone do not aid very much in analyzing the scope of professional crime—that is, the number and types of offenses committed by those whose principal employment and source of income are based upon the commission of criminal acts.

Except for larceny under $50 and negligent manslaughter, for which there are some national offenses-known-to-the-police data,[35] knowledge of the volume and trends of non-Index crimes depends upon arrest statistics. Since the police are not able to make arrests in many cases, these are necessarily less complete than the "offenses known" statistics. Moreover, the ratio between arrests and the number of offenses differs significantly from

[30] See *supra* note 22, chapter 3, notes 30–40, 73–92.

[31] UCR, 1965, p. 17.

[32] California Highway Patrol, Auto Status Program, unpublished data, 1966.

[33] International Association of Chiefs of Police, *supra* note 27, pp. 24–26. See also UCR, 1958, Special Issue, pp. 15–17, 20–25.

[34] UCR, 1965, pp. 43–44.

[35] UCR, 1965, tables 5–9, 12, and 14, pp. 92–105. This information is included each year in crime trends and offenses cleared data.

offense to offense—as is shown, for example, by the high percentage of reported cases in which arrests are made for murder (91 percent) and the relatively low percentage for larceny (20 percent).[36] Reporting to the FBI for arrests covers less than 70 percent of the population.[37] However, because arrest statistics are collected for a broader range of offenses—28 categories including the Index crimes—they show more of the diversity and magnitude of the many different crime problems.[38] Property crimes do not loom so large in this picture.

Nearly 45 percent of all arrests are for such crimes without victims or against the public order as drunkenness, gambling, liquor law violations, vagrancy, and prostitution. As Table 2 shows, drunkenness alone accounts

Table 2—Number and Rate of Arrests for the 10 Most Frequent Offenses, 1965

[4,062 agencies reporting; total population 134,095,000]

Rank	Offense	Number	Rate (per 100,000 population)	Percent of total arrests
1	Drunkenness	1,535,040	1,144.7	31.0
2	Disorderly conduct	570,122	425.2	11.5
3	Larceny (over and under $50)	385,726	286.2	7.7
4	Driving under the influence	241,511	180.1	4.9
5	Simple assault	207,615	154.8	4.2
6	Burglary	197,627	147.4	4.0
7	Liquor laws	179,219	133.7	3.6
8	Vagrancy	120,416	89.8	2.4
9	Gambling	114,294	85.2	2.3
10	Motor vehicle theft	101,763	75.9	2.1
	Total, 10 most frequent offenses	3,651,333	2,722.9	73.7
	Arrests for all offenses [1]	4,955,047	3,695.2	100.0

[1] Does not include arrests for traffic offenses.

SOURCE: "Uniform Crime Reports," 1965, pp. 108–109.

for almost one-third of all arrests. This is not necessarily a good indication of the number of persons arrested for drunkenness, however, as some individuals may be arrested many times during the year. Arrest statistics measure the number of arrests, not the number of criminals.

Federal Crimes

More than 50 percent of all Federal criminal offenses relate to general law enforcement in territorial or maritime jurisdictions directly subject to

[36] UCR, 1965, p. 97.
[37] UCR, 1965, p. 107.
[38] The UCR arrest tables show 29 categories; one of these, "suspicion," is not tallied in total arrest figures, however. Two of the categories, "curfew and loitering laws" and "runaway," are limited to juveniles and were added in 1964. These categories often do not involve criminal offenses. See UCR, 1965, pp. 47–49 for definition of the categories.

Federal control, or are also State offenses (bank robberies, for example).[39] Police statistics for these offenses are normally reported in the UCR, particularly when local law enforcement is involved. Such other Federal crimes as antitrust violations, food and drug violations and tax evasion are not included in the UCR. Although Federal crimes constitute only a small percentage of all offenses, crimes such as those shown in Table 3 are an important part of the national crime picture.

Table 3—Selected Federal Crimes

[Cases filed in court—1966]

Antitrust	7
Food and drug	350
Income tax evasion	863
Liquor revenue violations	2,729
Narcotics	2,293
Immigration	3,188

SOURCE: Department of Justice.

The Extent of Unreported Crime

Although the police statistics indicate a lot of crime today, they do not begin to indicate the full amount. Crimes reported directly to prosecutors usually do not show up in the police statistics.[40] Citizens often do not report crimes to the police. Some crimes reported to the police never get into the statistical system. Since better crime prevention and control programs depend upon a full and accurate knowledge about the amount and kinds of crime, the Commission initiated the first national survey ever made of crime victimization. The National Opinion Research Center of the University of Chicago surveyed 10,000 households, asking whether the person questioned, or any member of his or her household, had been a victim of crime during the past year, whether the crime had been reported, and, if not, the reasons for not reporting.[41]

More detailed surveys were undertaken in a number of high and medium crime rate precincts of Washington, Chicago, and Boston by the Bureau of

[39] There is no report of "offenses known to the police" for Federal crimes. The most complete report of Federal crimes is found in the *Annual Report of the Attorney General of the United States,* which lists the number of cases filed in court each year. More than 50 percent of the cases filed in both 1965 and 1966 related to general law enforcement in jurisdictions subject to Federal control, or were also State offenses. *The Annual Report of the Director of the Administrative Office of the United States Courts* also contains some information regarding Federal criminal offenses.

[40] Even when reported directly to a prosecutor, crimes are supposed to be included in the "offenses-known-to-the-police" reports. In practice, this often does not happen. Fraud, in particular, is often reported directly to the prosecuting officer and omitted from the police statistics.

[41] Philip H. Ennis, *Criminal Victimization in the United States: A Report of a National Survey* (Field Surveys II, President's Commission on Law Enforcement and Administration of Justice, Washington: U.S. Government Printing Office, 1967) (hereinafter referred to as the NORC survey).

Social Science Research of Washington, D.C.,[42] and the Survey Research Center of the University of Michigan.[43] All of the surveys dealt primarily with households or individuals, although some data were obtained for certain kinds of businesses and other organizations.

These surveys show that the actual amount of crime in the United States today is several times that reported in the UCR. As Table 4 shows, the

Table 4—Comparison of Survey and UCR Rates

[Per 100,000 population]

Index Crimes	NORC survey 1965–66	UCR rate for individuals 1965 [1]	UCR rate for individuals and organizations 1965 [1]
Willful homicide	3.0	5.1	5.1
Forcible rape	42.5	11.6	11.6
Robbery	94.0	61.4	61.4
Aggravated assault	218.3	106.6	106.6
Burglary	949.1	299.6	605.3
Larceny ($50 and over)	606.5	267.4	393.3
Motor vehicle theft	206.2	226.0	251.0
Total violence	357.8	184.7	184.7
Total property	1,761.8	793.0	1,249.6

[1] "Uniform Crime Reports," 1965, p. 51. The UCR national totals do not distinguish crimes committed against individuals or households from those committed against businesses or other organizations. The UCR rate for individuals is the published national rate adjusted to eliminate burglaries, larcenies, and vehicle thefts not committed against individuals or households. No adjustment was made for robbery

amount of personal injury crime reported to NORC is almost twice the UCR rate and the amount of property crime more than twice as much as the UCR rate for individuals. Forcible rapes were more than 3½ times the reported rate, burglaries three times, aggravated assaults and larcenies of $50 and over more than double, and robbery 50 percent greater than the reported rate. Only vehicle theft was lower and then by a small amount. (The single homicide reported is too small a number to be statistically useful.)

Even these rates probably understate the actual amounts of crime. The national survey was a survey of the victim experience of every member of a household based on interviews of one member. If the results are tabulated only for the family member who was interviewed, the amount of unreported victimization for some offenses is considerably higher. Apparently, the

[42] Albert D. Biderman, Louise A. Johnson, Jessie McIntyre, and Adrienne W. Weir, *Report on a Pilot Study in the District of Columbia on Victimization and Attitudes Toward Law Enforcement* (Field Surveys I, President's Commission on Law Enforcement and Administration of Justice, Washington: U.S. Government Printing Office, 1967) (hereinafter referred to as the BSSR survey).

[43] Albert J. Reiss, Jr., *Studies in Crime and Law Enforcement in Major Metropolitan Areas* (Field Surveys III, vol. I, sec. 1, President's Commission on Law Enforcement and Administration of Justice, Washington: U.S. Government Printing Office, 1967) (hereinafter referred to as the *Reiss studies*).

person interviewed remembered more of his own victimization than that of other members of his family.[44]

The Washington, Boston, and Chicago surveys, based solely on victimization of the person interviewed, show even more clearly the disparity between reported and unreported amounts of crime. The clearest case is that of the survey in three Washington precincts, where, for the purpose of comparing survey results with crimes reported to the police, previous special studies made it possible to eliminate from police statistics crimes involving business and transient victims. . . . [F]or certain specific offenses against individuals the number of offenses reported to the survey per thousand residents 18 years or over ranged, depending on the offense, from 3 to 10 times more than the number contained in police statistics.

The survey in Boston and in one of the Chicago precincts indicated about three times as many Index crimes as the police statistics, in the other Chicago precinct about 1½ times as many. These survey rates are not fully comparable with the Washington results because adequate information did not exist for eliminating business and transient victims from the police statistics. If this computation could have been made, the Boston and Chicago figures would undoubtedly have shown a closer similarity to the Washington findings.[45]

In the national survey of households those victims saying that they had not notified the police of their victimization were asked why. The reason most frequently given for all offenses was that the police could not do anything. As Table 5 shows, this reason was given by 68 percent of those not reporting malicious mischief, and by 60 or more percent of those not reporting burglaries, larcenies of $50 and over, and auto thefts. It is not clear whether these responses are accurate assessments of the victims' inability to help the police or merely rationalizations of their failure to report. The next most frequent reason was that the offense was a private matter or that the victim did not want to harm the offender. It was given by 50 percent or more of those who did not notify the police for aggravated and simple assaults, family crimes, and consumer frauds. Fear of reprisal, though least often cited, was strongest in the case of assaults and family crimes. The extent of failure to report to the police was highest for consumer fraud (90 percent) and lowest for auto theft (11 percent).

The survey technique, as applied to criminal victimization, is still new and beset with a number of methodological problems. However, the Com-

---

[44] For a discussion of this methodological problem, see BSSR survey, *supra* note 42 at pp. 31–32, 44–46. In addition to this problem, a number of other methodological issues have been given detailed consideration in the national survey report. See NORC survey, *supra* note 41, pp. 80–109.

[45] The Washington figures were adjusted on the basis of an FBI mobility survey conducted in the Washington, D.C., Standard Metropolitan Statistical Area in the fall of 1964.

Table 5—Victims' Most Important Reason for Not Notifying Police[1]

[In percentages]

Crimes	Percent of cases in which police not notified	Reasons for not notifying police				
		Felt it was private matter or did not want to harm offender	Police could not be effective or would not want to be bothered	Did not want to take time	Too confused or did not know how to report	Fear of reprisal
Robbery	35	27	45	9	18	0
Aggravated assault	35	50	25	4	8	13
Simple assault	54	50	35	4	4	7
Burglary	42	30	63	4	2	2
Larceny ($50 and over)	40	23	62	7	7	0
Larceny (under $50)	63	31	58	7	3	(*)
Auto theft	11	[2] 20	[2] 60	[2] 0	[2] 0	[2] 20
Malicious mischief	62	23	68	5	2	2
Consumer fraud	90	50	40	0	10	0
Other fraud (bad checks, swindling, etc.)	74	41	35	16	8	0
Sex offenses (other than forcible rape)	49	40	50	0	5	5
Family crimes (desertion, nonsupport, etc.)	50	65	17	10	0	7

*Less than 0.5%.
[1] Willful homicide, forcible rape, and a few other crimes had too few cases to be statistically useful, and they are therefore excluded.
[2] There were only 5 instances in which auto theft was not reported.

SOURCE: NORC survey.

mission has found the information provided by the surveys of considerable value, and believes that the survey technique has a great untapped potential as a method for providing additional information about the nature and extent of our crime problem and the relative effectiveness of different programs to control crime.

Trends in Crime

There has always been too much crime. Virtually every generation since the founding of the Nation and before has felt itself threatened by the spectre of rising crime and violence.

A hundred years ago contemporary accounts of San Francisco told of extensive areas where "no decent man was in safety to walk the street after dark; while at all hours, both night and day, his property was jeopardized by incendiarism and burglary."[46] Teenage gangs gave rise to the word "hoodlum";[47] while in one central New York City area, near Broadway, the police entered "only in pairs, and never unarmed."[48] A noted chronicler of the period declared that "municipal law is a failure * * * we must soon fall

[46] Daniel Bell, *The End of Ideology* (2d rev. ed., New York: Collier Books, 1962), p. 172.
[47] Robert V. Bruce, *1877: Year of Violence* (New York: Bobbs-Merrill, 1959), p. 13.
[48] Daniel Bell, *supra* note 46, at p. 171.

back on the law of self preservation."[49] "Alarming" increases in robbery and violent crimes were reported throughout the country prior to the Revolution.[50] And in 1910 one author declared that "crime, especially its more violent forms, and among the young is increasing steadily and is threatening to bankrupt the Nation."[51]

Crime and violence in the past took many forms. During the great railway strike of 1877 hundreds were killed across the country and almost 2 miles of railroad cars and buildings were burned in Pittsburgh in clashes between strikers and company police and the militia.[52] It was nearly a half century later, after pitched battles in the steel industry in the late thirties, that the Nation's long history of labor violence subsided.[53] The looting and takeover of New York for 3 days by mobs in the 1863 draft riots rivaled the violence of Watts,[54] while racial disturbances in Atlanta in 1907, in Chicago, Washington, and East St. Louis in 1919, Detroit in 1943, and New York in 1900, 1935, and 1943 marred big city life in the first half of the 20th century.[55] Lynchings took the lives of more than 4,500 persons throughout the country between 1882 and 1930.[56] And the violence of Al Capone and Jesse James was so striking that they have left their marks permanently on our understanding of the eras in which they lived.

However, the fact that there has always been a lot of crime does not mean that the amount of crime never changes. It changes constantly, day and night, month to month, place to place. It is essential that society be able to tell when changes occur and what they are, that it be able to distinguish normal ups and downs from long-term trends. Whether the amount of crime is increasing or decreasing, and by how much, is an important question—for law enforcement, for the individual citizen who must run the risk of crime, and for the official who must plan and establish prevention and control programs. If it is true, as the Commission surveys tend to indicate, that society has not yet found fully reliable methods for measuring the volume of crime, it is even more true that it has failed to find such methods for measuring the trend of crime.

Unlike some European countries, which have maintained national statis-

[49] *Id.* at p. 172.

[50] Carl Bridenbaugh, *Cities in Revolt: Urban Life in America, 1743–1776* (New York: A. A. Knopf, 1955), p. 110.

[51] Al Wasserman, "NBC White Paper: Terror in the Streets," unpublished script for NBC television broadcast, April 6, 1965, p. 24.

[52] See Robert V. Bruce, *supra* note 47 at pp. 131–158.

[53] See Joseph G. Rayback, *A History of American Labor* (New York: Macmillan, 1959); and Philip Taft, "Violence in American Labor Disputes," *Annals of the American Academy of Political and Social Science*, 364:127–140, March 1966.

[54] See Irving Werstein, *July 1863* (New York: Julian Messner, 1957); and Herbert Asbury, *Gangs of New York* (New York: A. A. Knopf, 1928), pp. 118–173.

[55] Robert M. Fogelson, *The 1960's Riots: Interpretation and Recommendations.* A report to the President's Commission on Law Enforcement and Administration of Justice, 1966 (mimeo).

[56] U.S. Commission on Civil Rights, *Justice* (Washington: U.S. Government Printing Office, 1961), pp. 267–268.

tics for more than a century and a quarter, the United States has maintained national crime statistics only since 1930.[57] Because the rural areas were slow in coming into the system and reported poorly when they did, it was not until 1958, when other major changes were made in the UCR, that reporting of rural crimes was sufficient to allow a total national estimate without special adjustments.[58] Changes in overall estimating procedures and two offense categories—rape and larceny—were also made in 1958.[59] Because of these problems figures prior to 1958, and particularly those prior to 1940, must be viewed as neither fully comparable with nor nearly so reliable as later figures.

For crimes of violence the 1933–65 period, based on newly adjusted unpublished figures from the UCR, has been. . . . [O]ne of sharply divergent trends for the different offenses. Total numbers for all reported offenses have increased markedly; the Nation's population has increased also—by more than 47 percent since 1940.[60] The number of offenses per 100,000 population has tripled for forcible rape and has doubled for aggravated assault during the period, both increasing at a fairly constant pace. The willful homicide rate has decreased somewhat to about 70 percent of its high in 1933, while robbery has fluctuated from a high in 1933 and a low during World War II to a point where it is now about 20 percent above the beginning of the postwar era. The overall rate for violent crimes, primarily due to the increased rate for aggravated assault, now stands at its highest point, well above what it has been throughout most of the period.

Property crime rates . . . are up much more sharply than the crimes of violence. The rate for larceny of $50 and over has shown the greatest increase of all Index offenses. It is up more than 550 percent over 1933. The burglary rate has nearly doubled. The rate for auto theft has followed an uneven course to a point about the same as the rate of the early thirties.

The upward trend for 1960–65, as shown in Table 6, has been faster than the long-term trend, up 25 percent for the violent crimes and 36 percent for the property crimes. The greatest increases in the period came in 1964, in forcible rape among crimes of violence and in vehicle theft among property crimes. Preliminary reports indicate that all Index offenses rose in 1966.[61]

---

[57] France was the first country to collect crime statistics, beginning a series for judicial officers in 1827. Interest in criminal statistics began in continental Europe in 1829; a collection plan for statistics was presented in England in 1856 and has been a regular part of an annual report since 1857. See Leon Radrinowicz, *Ideology and Crime* (New York: Columbia University Press, 1966), p. 31; Thorsten Sellin and Marvin E. Wolfgang, *supra* note 10, pp. 7–44; National Commission on Law Observance and Enforcement, *Report on Criminal Statistics* (Washington: U.S. Government Printing Office, 1931), pp. 8, 53 (hereinafter referred to as Wickersham Statistics Report and UCR, 1958, Special Issue, p. 9.

[58] UCR, 1958, Special Issue, pp. 33–37.

[59] *Id.* at pp. 20–28.

[60] The 1940 population was 131,669,275, and the 1965 estimated population was 193,818,000. The percentage increase, then, was 47.2 percent.

[61] UCR, Preliminary Report for 1966, March 15, 1967.

Table 6—Offenses Known to the Police, 1960–65

[Rates per 100,000 population]

Offense	1960	1961	1962	1963	1964	1965
Willful homicide	5.0	4.7	4.5	4.5	4.8	5.1
Forcible rape	9.2	9.0	9.1	9.0	10.7	11.6
Robbery	51.6	50.0	51.1	53.0	58.4	61.4
Aggravated assault	82.5	82.2	84.9	88.6	101.8	106.6
Burglary	465.5	474.9	489.7	527.4	580.4	605.3
Larceny $50 and over	271.4	277.9	296.6	330.9	368.2	393.3
Motor vehicle theft	179.2	179.9	193.4	212.1	242.0	251.0
Total crimes against person	148.3	145.9	149.6	155.1	175.7	184.7
Total property crimes	916.1	932.7	979.7	1,070.4	1,190.6	1,249.6

SOURCE: FBI, Uniform Crime Reports Section, unpublished data.

Arrest rates are in general much less complete and are available for many fewer years than are rates for offenses known to the police.[62] However, they do provide another measure of the trend of crime. For crimes of violence, arrest rates rose 16 percent during 1960–65, considerably less than the 25 percent increase indicated by offenses known to the police. For property crimes, arrest rates have increased about 25 percent, as opposed to a 36 percent increase in offenses known to the police during 1960–65.

Prior to the year 1933, . . . there is no estimated national rate for any offenses. UCR figures for a sizable number of individual cities, however, indicate that the 1930–32 rates, at least for those cities, were higher than the 1933 rates.[63] Studies of such individual cities as Boston, Chicago, New York, and others indicate that in the twenties and the World War I years reported rates for many offenses were even higher.[64] A recent study of crime in Buffalo, N.Y., from 1854 to 1946 showed arrest rates in that city for willful homicide, rape, and assault reaching their highest peak in the early 1870's, declining, rising again until 1918, and declining into the forties.[65]

[62] See UCR, 1958, Special Issue, pp. 39–40. Prior to 1952 UCR arrest data were based on estimates from fingerprints submitted to the FBI rather than on actual figures. See UCR, 1952, pp. 110–112.

[63] See also *Recent Social Trends in the United States* (New York: McGraw Hill, 1934), vol. II, pp. 1123–1135.

[64] See Sam B. Warner, *Crime and Criminal Statistics in Boston* Cambridge: Harvard University Press, 1934); Arthur E. Wood, "A Study of Arrests in Detroit, 1913–19," *Journal of Criminal Law and Criminology*, 21:168–200, August 1930; Edith Abbott, "Recent Statistics Relating to Crime in Chicago," *Journal of Criminal Law and Criminology*, 13:329–358, November 1922; William D. Miller, *Memphis During the Progressive Era, 1900–17* (Memphis: Memphis State University Press, 1957); Harry Willbach, "Trend of Crime in New York City," *Journal of Criminal Law and Criminology*, 29:62–75, May–June 1938; and Harry Willbach, "Trend of Crime in Chicago," *Journal of Criminal Law and Criminology*, 31:720–727, March–April, 1941; and Theodore N. Ferdinand, "The Criminal Patterns of Boston since 1849" (paper presented at American Association of the Advancement of Science meetings, Washington, revised version, September 1966).

[65] Elwin H. Powell, "Crime as a Function of Anomie," *Journal of Criminal Law, Criminology and Police Science*, 57:161–171, 164, June 1966.

Trends for crimes against trust, vice crimes, and crimes against public order, based on arrest rates for 1960–65, follow a much more checkered pattern than do trends for Index offenses. For some offenses this is in part due to the fact that arrest patterns change significantly from time to time, as when New York recently decided not to make further arrests for public drunkenness.[66] Based on comparable places covering about half the total population, arrest rates during 1960–65 rose 13 percent for simple assault, 13 percent for embezzlement and fraud, and 36 percent for narcotics violations, while for the same period, the rates declined 24 percent for gambling and 11 percent for drunkenness.[67]

The picture portrayed by the official statistics in recent years, both in the total number of crimes and in the number of crimes per 100,000 Americans, is one of increasing crime. Crime always seems to be increasing, never going down. Up 5 percent this year, 10 the next, and the Commission's surveys have shown there is a great deal more crime than the official statistics show. The public can fairly wonder whether there is ever to be an end.

This official picture is also alarming because it seems so pervasive. Crimes of violence are up in both the biggest and smallest cities, in the suburbs as well as in the rural areas. The same is true for property crimes. Young people are being arrested in ever increasing numbers. Offense rates for most crimes are rising every year and in every section of the country. That there are some bright spots does not change this dismal outlook. Rates for some offenses are still below those of the early thirties and perhaps of earlier periods. Willful homicide rates have been below the 1960 level through most of the last few years. Robbery rates continue to decline in the rural areas and small towns,[68] and arrest rates for many non-Index offenses have remained relatively stable.

Because the general picture is so disturbing and the questions it raises go to the very heart of concern about crime in the United States today, the Commission has made a special effort to evaluate as fully as possible the information available. It has tried to determine just how far this picture is accurate, to see whether our cities and our countryside are more dangerous than they were before, to find out whether our youth and our citizens are

[66] In the past, New York generally arrested drunks under a disorderly conduct statute. Currently, the Vera Institute of Justice has undertaken a project to experiment with summonses instead of arrests. See President's Commission on Law Enforcement and Administration of Justice, *The Challenge of Crime in a Free Society* (Washington: U.S. Government Printing Office, 1967, p. 236, and the Commission's *Task Force Report: Drunkenness*, appendix D.

[67] These trends may not be the same as those for the total population, however. No national estimates of rates for Part II offenses were available so no 1960–1965 comparison could be made using total national estimates. Using 1961 unpublished figures, however, the percentage changes were simple assault, 11; embezzlement and fraud, 14; narcotics, 35; gambling, −11; and drunkenness, −12.

[68] See President's Commission on Law Enforcement and Administration of Justice *Task Force Report: Crime and Its Impact—An Assessment* (Washington: U.S. Government Printing Office, 1967), p. 36, fig. 8.

becoming more crime prone than those who were in their same circumstances in earlier years, to see what lies behind any increases that may have occurred, and to determine what if anything this information tells us can be done to bring the crime rate down.

What is known about the trend of crime—in the total number of offenses; in the ratio of offenses to population, which measures roughly the risk of victimization; and in the relationship of crime trends to changes in the composition of the population, which measures roughly the crime proneness of various kinds of people—is almost wholly a product of statistics. Therefore the Commission has taken a particularly hard look at the current sources of statistical knowledge.

Factors Affecting the Reporting of Crime

From the time that police statistics first began to be maintained in France in the 1820's, it has been recognized that the validity of calculations of changes in crime rates was dependent upon a constant relationship between reported and unreported crime.[69] Until the Commission surveys of unreported crime, however, no systematic effort of wide scale had ever been made to determine what the relationship between reported and unreported crime was.[70] As shown earlier, these surveys have now indicated that the actual amount of crime is several times that reported to the police, even in some of the precincts with the highest reported crime rates. This margin of unreported crime raises the possibility that even small changes in the way that crime is reported by the public to the police, or classified and recorded by the police, could have significant effects on the trend of reported crime.[71] There is strong reason to believe that a number of such changes have taken place within recent years.

Changing Expectations

One change of importance in the amount of crime that is reported in our society is the change in the expectations of the poor and members of minority groups about civil rights and social protection.[72] Not long ago

[69] *Supra* note 57.

[70] See *supra* note 68, chapter 5, notes 1–2.

[71] For example, if all other things remain equal, including the recording of crime by police, a 10 percent increase in the rate of reporting would produce a 10 percent increase in reported crime. See also BSSR survey, *supra* note 42 at pp. 110–111.

[72] While the pace of change in expectations may be somewhat faster today, the fact of change is not. See, e.g., Roscoe Pound, *Criminal Justice in America* (New York: Henry Holt and Co., 1930), pp. 13–14: "In our nineteenth-century polity such things as one of the household haling another into court were tolerated only in extreme cases, and were repugnant to the settled polity of the law . . . Religious training was all but universal, and the pressure of the church group and its opinion of things which were done and things which were not done was exerted upon every one . . . [Today] we must rely on the law and the policeman for which was once the province of neighborhood opinion."

there was a tendency to dismiss reports of all but the most serious offenses in slum areas and segregated minority group districts.[73] The poor and the segregated minority groups were left to take care of their own problems. Commission studies indicate that whatever the past pattern was, these areas now have a strong feeling of need for adequate police protection.[74] Crimes that were once unknown to the police, or ignored when complaints were received, are now much more likely to be reported and recorded as part of the regular statistical procedure.

The situation seems similar to that found in England. The University of Cambridge's Institute of Criminology, which in 1963 conducted an exhaustive study of the sharp rise in crimes of violence, concluded in its report that:

> One of the main causes for an increase in the *recording* of violent crime appears to be a decrease in the toleration of aggressive and violent behaviour, even in those slum and poor tenement areas where violence has always been regarded as a normal and acceptable way of settling quarrels, jealousies or even quite trivial arguments.[75]

Police Practice

Perhaps the most important change for reporting purposes that has taken place in the last 25 years is the change in the police. Notable progress has been made during this period in the professionalization of police forces. With this change, Commission studies indicate, there is a strong trend toward more formal actions, more formal records, and less informal disposition of individual cases.[76] This trend is particularly apparent in the way the police handle juveniles, where the greatest increases are reported, but seems to apply to other cases as well. It seems likely that professionalization also results in greater police efficiency in looking for crime. Increases in the number of clerks and statistical personnel,[77] better methods for recording information, and the use of more intensive patrolling practices also tend to

[73] See, e.g., "The Negro and the Problem of Law Observance and Administration in the Light of Social Research," in C. S. Johnson, *The Negro in American Civilization* (New York: Henry Holt and Co., 1930), pp. 443–452. A number of studies indicating the lack of concern both in the community and the courts with intraracial crimes among minority groups are discussed in Leonard Savitz, "Crime and the American Negro" (unpublished manuscript, 1966), chapter 5, "The Differential Administration of Justice."

[74] See President's Commission on Law Enforcement and Administration of Justice, *Task Force Report: The Police*, p. 148.

[75] F. H. McClintock, *Crimes of Violence* (New York: St. Martin's Press, 1963), p. 74.

[76] See James Q. Wilson, "The Police and the Delinquent in Two Cities," in Stanton Wheeler, ed., *Controlling Delinquency* (New York: John Wiley & Sons, in press); and Ronald Beattie, "Criminal Statistics in the United States—1960," *Journal of Criminal Law, Criminology and Police Science*, 51:49–65, 53, May–June 1960.

[77] Civilian employees of police departments have increased from 8.6 percent of all employees in 1958 to 10.7 percent in 1965 (UCR, 1958, p. 99; and UCR, 1965, p. 152).

increase the amount of recorded crime.[78] Because this process of professionalization has taken place over a period of time and because it is most often a
gradual rather than an abrupt change, it is difficult to estimate what its
cumulative effect has been.

Wholly different kinds of changes have occurred in a number of cities. In
1953 Philadelphia reported 28,560 Index crimes plus negligent manslaughter and larceny under $50, an increase of more than 70 percent over 1951.
This sudden jump in crime, however, was not due to an invasion by
criminals but to the discovery by a new administration that crime records
had for years minimized the amount of crime in the city. One district had
actually handled 5,000 complaints more than it had recorded.[79]

*Table 7—Reporting System Changes—UCR Index Figures Not Comparable
with Prior Years*

Name of city	Years of increase	Amount of increase (Index offenses):		
		From	To	Percent increase
Baltimore	1964–65	18,637	26,193	40.5
Buffalo	1961–63	4,779	9,305	94.7
Chicago	1959–60	56,570	97,253	71.9
Cleveland	1963–64	10,584	17,254	63.0
Indianapolis	1961–62	7,416	10,926	47.3
Kansas City, Mo	1959–61 [1]	4,344	13,121	202.0
Memphis	1963–64	8,781	11,533	31.3
Miami	1963–64	10,750	13,610	26.6
Nashville	1962–63	6,595	9,343	41.7
Shreveport	1962–63	1,898	2,784	46.7
Syracuse	1963–64	3,365	4,527	34.5

[1] No report was published for Kansas City, Mo., for 1960.
SOURCE: "UCR," 1959–1965.

The Commission could not attempt an exhaustive study of such changes
in reporting procedures. It has noted in Table 7 a number of instances in
which the UCR indicated changes in reporting procedures for major cities
during 1959–65. All of these changes have resulted in an increase in the
level of reporting for all subsequent years. It has also noted that changes of
this sort are still taking place, being indicated in 1966 for Detroit,
Chattanooga, Worcester, Mass., and New York City, among others.[80]

· · · · ·

Insurance

Another factor that probably increases the amount of reporting for some
crimes is the sizable increase in insurance coverage against theft. It is

[78] The use of intensive patrolling practices in New York, for example, in one precinct
in 1957 resulted in a "sharp increase in certain types of crimes and offenses." See John I.
Griffin, *Statistics Essential for Police Efficiency* (Springfield, Ill.: Charles C. Thomas,
1958), p. 64.
[79] UCR, 1951, p. 97; UCR, 1953, p. 100; and Daniel Bell, *supra* note 46, at p. 152.
[80] UCR, *Preliminary Report for 1966*, March 15, 1967.

difficult to evaluate this factor. However, because many persons believe that they must report a criminal event to the police in order to collect insurance, more reporting seems likely.[81] Although not the only factor involved, one indication that this may be the case is the high rate of reporting for auto theft noted by the NORC survey. Insurance is usually involved in auto theft.[82]

Classification

One problem in comparing crime from place to place and time to time is in insuring that a given criminal act is always counted by the same name. Some classification problems are simple errors. At common law burglary applied only to homes. In most States this has now been expanded to include business establishments. In some other States it also includes other enclosures such as ships, airplanes and, in a few States locked cars. UCR reporting rules clearly exclude such things as locked cars and phone booths as subjects for burglary.[83] One of the Nation's largest police jurisdictions with one of the most capable police statistical sections has nevertheless regularly reported phone booth thefts in all recent years as burglaries, including more than 900 in 1965. If these thefts involved less than $50 they would otherwise have been reported as petty larceny and would not have been included in the overall Index rate of crimes against property for that city.

.   .   .   .   .

The overall effect of the classification problem is difficult to assess. For most offenses it is probably not great and to some extent merely involves increasing the incidence of one offense and decreasing that of another. Almost all charges. involve offenses of different degrees of seriousness, however, and consequently to some degree cause the crime problem to look better or worse than it really is.

In the case of a few offenses, classification changes over the history of the UCR have probably tended to increase the rates of reported crime somewhat, although it is difficult to tell how much. Aggravated assault is probably one of these crimes.

Factors Indicating an Increase in Crime

Many factors affect crime trends but they are not always easy to isolate. Murder is a seasonal offense. Rates are generally higher in the summer,

---

[81] See, e.g., Bureau of Criminal Statistics, *Crime and Delinquency in California, 1965* (Sacramento: Bureau of Criminal Statistics), p. 15 (hereinafter referred to as *Crime in California.*
[82] Information supplied by industry sources.
[83] UCR Handbook, pp. 26–29.

except for December, which is often the highest month and almost always 5 to 20 percent above the yearly average.[84] In December 1963, following the assassination of President Kennedy, murders were below the yearly average by 4 percent, one of the few years in the history of the UCR that this occurred.[85] Since 1950 the pace of auto thefts has increased faster than but in the same direction as car registrations.[86] During World War II, however, when there was rationing and a shortage of cars, rates for auto theft rose sharply. And in 1946 when cars came back in production and most other crimes were increasing, auto thefts fell off rapidly.[87]

The introduction to the UCR provides a checklist of some of the many factors that must be taken into account in interpreting changes in crime rates and in the amount and type of crime that occurs from place to place:

> Density and size of the community population and the metropolitan area of which it is a part.
> Composition of the population with reference particularly to age, sex, and race.
> Economic status and mores of the population.
> Relative stability of population, including commuters, seasonal, and other transient types.
> Climate, including seasonal weather conditions.
> Educational, recreational, and religious characteristics.
> Effective strength of the police force.
> Standards governing appointments to the police force.
> Policies of the prosecuting officials and the courts.
> Attitude of the public toward law enforcement problems.
> The administrative and investigative efficiency of the local law enforcement agency.[88]

A number of these factors have been changing in ways that would lead one to expect increases in the amounts of certain kinds of crime.

Changing Age Composition

One of the most significant factors affecting crime rates is the age composition of the population. In 1965 more than 44 percent of all persons arrested for forcible rape, more than 39 percent for robbery, and more than

---

[84] The UCR regularly publishes charts indicating the national monthly arrest deviations from the annual average by each of eight types of crime, e.g., UCR, 1965, p. 12.

[85] UCR, 1963, p. 6.

[86] Figures supplied by the American Automobile Association, January 1967. See also UCR for the relevant years.

[87] UCR, January 1947, p. 83.

[88] UCR, 1965, p. vii.

26 percent for willful homicide and aggravated assault were in the 18- to 24-year-old age group. For property crimes the highest percentages are found in the under 18 group—nearly 50 percent of all those arrested for burglary and larceny and more than 60 percent for auto theft.[89]

For most of these offenses the rate of offense per individual in these age groups is many times that in older groups. Of course the differences are based on arrest figures, and the national figures on offenses cleared by arrest show that 75 to 80 percent of burglaries, larcenies, and auto thefts are unsolved.[90] It is possible that older persons committing offenses against property are more successful at evading arrest, so that the age figures for arrests give a somewhat biased picture.[91]

Because of the unusual birth rate in the postwar years, the youthful high-risk group—those in their teens and early twenties—has been increasing much faster than other groups in the population. Beginning in 1961 nearly 1 million more youths have reached the ages of maximum risk each year than did so in the prior year.[92] Thus the volume of crime and the overall crime rate could be expected to grow whether the rate for any given age increased or not.

Commission studies based on 1960 arrest rates indicate that between 1960 and 1965 about 40 to 50 percent of the total increase in the arrests reported by UCR could have been expected as the result of increases in population and changes in the age composition of the population.[93]

Urbanization

Rates for most crimes are highest in the big cities. Twenty-six core cities of more than 500,000 people, with less than 18 percent of the total population, account for more than half of all reported Index crimes against the person and more than 30 percent of all reported Index property crimes. One of every three robberies and nearly one of every five rapes occurs in cities of more than 1 million. The average rate for every Index crime except bur-

[89] Estimates for total national population, based on unpublished data, Federal Bureau of Investigation, Uniform Crime Reports Section.

[90] UCR, 1965, p. 97.

[91] Based on clearances in 1964, for example, persons under 18 years of age were estimated to have committed 37 percent of the Index crimes; yet the same age group represented 48 percent of the arrests for the seven major crime categories (UCR, 1964, pp. 22–23).

[92] For example, in 1961 there were 2,754,000 15-year-olds and in 1962 the number rose to 3,723,000. See U.S. Bureau of the Census, *Current Population Reports: Estimates of Population of the United States, by Age, Color, and Sex: July 1, 1960–1965* (Series P. 25, No. 321, Washington: U.S. Bureau of the Census).

[93] See *supra* note 68, appendix D, "The Prediction of Crime from Demographic Variables: A Methodological Note." Other calculations were also made by the Task Force.

glary, as Table 8 shows, is at least twice as great—and often more—in the cities as in the suburbs or rural areas. With a few exceptions, average rates increase progressively as the size of the city becomes larger.

Suburban rates are closest to those of the smaller cities except for forcible rape where suburban rates are higher. Suburban rates appear to be going up as business and industry increase—shopping centers are most frequently blamed by local police officials for rises in suburban crime.

Although rural rates are lower generally than those for cities, the differences have always been much greater for property crimes than for crimes against the person. Until the last few years rural rates for murder were close to those of the big cities, and rural rates for murder and rape still exceed those for small towns.[94]

The country has for many years seen a steady increase in its urban population and a decline in the proportion of the population living in rural areas and smaller towns. Since 1930 the rural population has increased by less than 2 percent while the city population has increased by more than 50

Table 8—Offenses Known by City Size, 1965

[Rates per 100,000 population]

Group	Willful homicide	Forcible rape	Robbery	Aggravated assault	Burglary	Larceny $50 and over	Motor vehicle theft
Cities over 1 million	10	26	221	246	930	734	586
500,000 to 1 million	10	20	165	182	1,009	555	640
250,000 to 500,000	7	15	122	142	1,045	550	468
100,000 to 250,000	6	11	73	151	871	556	353
50,000 to 100,000	4	8	49	85	675	492	297
25,000 to 50,000	3	6	33	71	562	443	212
10,000 to 25,000	2	6	19	67	462	309	141
Under 10,000	2	5	12	62	369	236	99
Rural	4	9	10	58	308	176	51
Suburban area	3	10	28	66	545	359	160
All places	5	12	61	107	605	420	251

SOURCE: "UCR," 1965, table 1, p. 51 and table 6, p. 94.

percent.[95] The increase in the cities and their suburbs since 1960 alone has been about 10 percent.[96] Because of the higher crime rates in and around the larger cities, this trend toward urbanization has a considerable effect on the national rate for most Index crimes. Commission studies show that if metropolitan, small city, and rural crime rates for 1960 had remained constant through 1965, the increase that could have been expected due to

[94] See Andrew F. Henry and James F. Short, Jr., *Suicide and Homicide* (Glencoe, Ill.: The Free Press, 1954), pp. 90–91; Edwin H. Sutherland, *Principles of Criminology* (3d rev. ed., Chicago: J. P. Lippincott, 1939), p. 135; and Marshall B. Clinard, *Sociology of Deviant Behavior* (rev. ed., New York: Holt, Rinehart and Winston, 1963), pp. 78–80.

[95] U.S. Bureau of the Census, *U.S. Census of Population, 1960: Characteristics of the Population, Number of Inhabitants* (Washington: U.S. Government Printing Office), vol. I, part A.

[96] *Ibid.*

urbanization would have been about 7 to 8 percent of the increase reported by the UCR.[97]

Increased Affluence

Another change that may result in more crime is increasing affluence. There are more goods around to be stolen. National wealth and all categories of merchandise have increased in terms of constant dollars more than fourfold since 1940[98]—significantly more than the population or the rate of reported theft.

Increased affluence may also have meant that property is now protected less well than formerly. More than 40 percent of all auto thefts involve cars with the keys inside or the switch left open.[99] A substantial percentage of residential burglaries occur in unlocked houses.[100] Bicycles, whose theft constitutes 15 percent of all reported larcenies, are frequently left lying around. Larceny of goods and accessories from cars accounts for another 40 percent of all reported larceny.[101]

Some increased business theft seems directly due to less protection. The recent rise in bank robbery seems due in large part to the development of small, poorly protected branch banks in the suburbs.

In retail establishments, managers choose to tolerate a high percentage of shoplifting rather than pay for additional clerks.[102] Discount stores, for

---

[97] The following table illustrates the method used for estimating the percent of increase in reported rates for Index crimes due to urbanization between 1960 and 1965. (The place-specific rates and number of observed offenses are from UCR, 1960, p. 33, and UCR, 1965, p. 51).

Place	1960 population in millions	1960 place specific rates per 100,000 persons	1965 population in millions	1965 expected offenses*	1965 observed offenses
SMSA's	113,861	1327.9	129,796	1,723,561	2,312,351
Other cities	23,629	728.8	24,338	177,375	242,345
Rural	41,832	423.2	39,684	167,943	225,319
Total	179,323		193,818	2,068,879	2,780,015
Overall rate		1037.9		1067.4	1434.3
Increase over 1960				29.5	396.4

Percent of increase due to changing urbanization = 29.5/396.4 = 7.4.

* (Rates/100,000 persons) × 1965 population = expected offenses.

    ·   ·   ·   ·   ·

[98] U.S. Bureau of the Census, *Statistical Abstract of the United States: 1966* (87th ed., Washington: U.S. Government Printing Office, 1966), table 490, p. 346.

[99] UCR, 1963, p. 23.

[100] UCR, 1963, p. 17.

[101] UCR, 1965, table 14, p. 105.

[102] See generally *supra* note 68, chapter 3, "The Economic Impact of Crime," particularly at notes 64–67.

example, experience an inventory loss rate almost double that of the conventional department store. Studies indicate that there is in general more public tolerance for theft of property and goods from large organizations than from small ones, from big corporations or utilities than from small neighborhood establishments. Restraints on conduct that were effective in a more personal rural society do not seem as effective in an impersonal society of large organizations.

Inflation has also had an impact on some property crimes. Larceny, for example, is any stealing that does not involve force or fraud. The test of the seriousness of larceny is the value of the property stolen. The dividing line between "grand" and "petty" larceny for national reporting purposes is $50. Larceny of $50 and over is the Index offense that has increased the most over the history of the UCR, more than 550 percent since 1933. Because the purchasing power of the dollar today is only 40 percent of what it was in 1933,[103] many thefts that would have been under $50 then are over $50 now. UCR figures on the value of property stolen, for example, indicate that the average value of a larceny has risen from $26 in 1940 to $84 in 1965.[104]

Changes in the Distribution of Crime—a 30-Year History

Because of the problems of reporting discussed earlier, any discussion of change in the distribution of crime is hazardous, particularly over long periods of time. While the impact of reporting changes on national trends can be corrected to some extent,[105] there is no way to correct their distorting effect on the crime pattern of the Nation because they occur in different places at different times. The Task Force has nevertheless attempted to discover the main outlines of change, for it is only through identification of such changes that the causes of change can be understood and used in the development of sound prevention and control programs for the future.

While there have been many changes in the pattern of crime throughout the country over the past 30 years, the most important changes are those involving (1) the decline of the South as a region of very high crime relative to the rest of the Nation, (2) the evolution of the West as the region

[103] U.S. Bureau of Labor Statistics, Consumer Price Index.

[104] UCR, January 1941, p. 197; and UCR, 1965, table 14, p. 105.

[105] See *supra* note 68, appendix E, "Uniform Crime Reporting Trends—FBI Procedures." The method used prior to 1958 is discussed in UCR, 1958, Special Issue, pp. 33–38. The "chain index" method of adjustment is based on the assumption that changes in the rate of crime of the city undergoing a change in reporting methods is the same as that of other cities of the same size in the same State or in the case of very large cities of other cities of the same size regionally or nationally. One alternative assumption would be that the entire difference between the old level of reporting (the 3-year average for the years prior to the change, for example) and the new level of reporting (the amount of crime reported in the year after the change had been made) was due to the change in reporting methods. Under this assumption the percentage increase between 1960 and 1965 both for Index crimes against the person and Index crimes against property would have been less.

of highest crime for both persons and property, and (3) the increase in reported crime in the larger cities.

Changes by Region and State

Sharp regional differences in crime have been reported in many countries of the world since man first began to study crime.[106] They have been apparent in the United States throughout its history. The frontier was from its earliest days noted for its lawlessness and Appalachia for the feuds of the Hatfields and the McCoys. Organized crime, while a national problem, is heavily concentrated in the cities of the East and Northeast.[107] What regional patterns of crime there are, why they exist, and how they are changing are important parts of the national picture of crime.

Table 9 shows the regional pattern for Index crimes for 1965. Reported rates are lowest in New England for crimes against the person and in the East South Central States of Alabama, Mississippi, Tennessee, and Ken-

Table 9—Index Crime Rates, by Region and by Offense, 1965

[Rates per 100,000 population]

	Crimes against the person				Total against person
	Murder	Forcible rape	Robbery	Aggravated assault	
United States	5.1	11.6	61.4	106.6	184.7
New England	2.1	5.0	26.6	43.6	77.3
Middle Atlantic	4.0	9.6	57.1	97.4	168.1
East North Central	4.0	12.9	90.4	93.7	201.0
West North Central	3.1	9.3	43.7	61.0	117.1
South Atlantic	8.4	11.5	56.3	165.8	242.0
East South Central	8.4	9.1	28.1	108.0	153.6
West South Central	7.0	10.9	41.3	123.9	183.1
Mountain	3.9	13.2	42.6	84.0	143.7
Pacific	4.3	18.5	94.4	122.9	240.1

	Crimes against property			Total. against property
	Burglary	Larceny $50 and over	Motor vehicle theft	
United States	605.3	393.3	251.0	1,249.6
New England	520.2	303.8	354.0	1,178.0
Middle Atlantic	514.6	419.9	264.8	1,199.3
East North Central	529.3	336.3	272.8	1,138.4
West North Central	509.5	299.1	176.4	985.0
South Atlantic	588.1	365.1	194.0	1,147.2
East South Central	445.0	270.9	130.6	846.5
West South Central	571.4	324.2	178.5	1,074.1
Mountain	642.5	507.5	235.9	1,385.9
Pacific	1,078.9	658.6	388.3	2,125.8

SOURCE: "UCR, 1965," pp. 52–55.

[106] See, for example, Walter C. Reckless, *The Crime Problem* (New York: Appleton-Century-Crofts, Inc., 1961), pp. 49–72; Terrence Morris, *The Criminal Area* (London: Routledge & Kegan Paul, 1957), pp. 37–64.

[107] President's Commission on Law Enforcement and Administration of Justice, *The Challenge of Crime in a Free Society* (Washington: U.S. Government Printing Office, 1967), p. 192. See also the Commission's *Task Force Report: Organized Crime, p. 7.*

tucky for Index property crimes. Overall rates for Index crimes against both persons and property are highest on the Pacific coast. Rates for robbery, forcible rape and for each individual Index property offense are also highest in the Pacific region. Robbery is also high in the North Central States centered around Illinois, and murder and aggravated assault is highest in the South Atlantic States.

Analysis by region of the NORC survey of victimization, which includes both reported and unreported crime, confirms the existence of sharp regional differences for rates of crime.

For crimes such as forcible rape, burglary, and larceny over $50, the regional patterns found by the survey, as indicated by Table 10, are about the same as those reported in the police statistics, even though the survey

Table 10—UCR and NORC Survey Index Crime Rates Compared, by Region, 1965

[Rates per 100,000 population]

Crimes	Northeast		North Central		South		West	
	NORC	UCR	NORC	UCR	NORC	UCR	NORC	UCR
ıl homicide_____	0	3. 6	0	3. 7	10	8. 0	0	4. 2
ble rape_____	25	8. 5	42	11. 8	48	10. 8	57	17. 2
ery [1]_____	139	49. 9	85	76. 6	48	45. 6	133	81. 9
ıvated assault_____	164	84. 7	233	84. 1	173	140. 6	361	113. 5
ʹary [1]_____	746	515. 9	987	523. 5	866	552. 4	1, 348	1, 078. 5
ʹny ($50 and over) [1]___	480	392. 6	594	325. 4	596	332. 4	855	622. 2
r vehicle theft [1]_____	278	285. 8	170	244. 5	96	175. 7	380	351. 5
Against the person___	328	146. 7	360	176. 2	279	205. 0	551	216. 8
Against property_____	1, 504	1, 194. 3	1, 751	1, 093. 4	1, 558	1, 060. 5	2, 583	2, 052. 2

ɔRC figures are for individuals only; UCR figures are not adjusted and reflect all offenses known to the police, not just those for individuals.
rce: "UCR, 1965," pp. 52–53; NORC survey, p. 21.

rates are higher. For robbery and aggravated assault, however, the patterns are quite different. In the police statistics robbery is highest in the Western States, followed by the North Central region. The NORC survey, however, found the Northeast region to have the highest rates for robbery. The more accurate methods of reporting now in use in New York City should narrow this sharp discrepancy between the survey results and the police statistics but will probably not be enough to eliminate it.[108] Whether this means that there is still more under-reporting in the Northeast region than elsewhere or whether it indicates some defect in the survey method is not clear.

The differences in the rates for aggravated assault are more striking and harder to explain. In the police statistics, the rate for the South is substantially higher than that for the West or the North Central region. In the NORC victimization survey, however, the rate for the South is less than that for either of these regions. NORC rates for the regions outside the South show rates of aggravated assault from 2 to 3 times those in the police statistics. The South shows much less difference—only about 20 percent.

The high Southern rates in the police statistics have a long history. The

[108] UCR, *Preliminary Report for 1966*, March 15, 1967.

South also has a long record of high rates for homicide. The statistics for homicide are much better and correlate strongly with those for aggravated assault.[109] When the NORC regional figures are broken down by metropolitan center city, metropolitan suburban and nonmetropolitan, in every region except the South the rates are much higher in the metropolitan center city areas. In the South, however, the metropolitan center city rates are less than one-third of the rate for the suburbs.[110] This may mean that the problems which the survey noted in getting accurate responses from Negroes were concentrated in the South.[111] It seems highly unlikely that the rates for the other regions are overstated. The individual city surveys in selected precincts of Washington, Boston, and Chicago all found unreported amounts of aggravated assault well in excess of those indicated by the NORC survey.[112]

Table 11—Regional Differences in Non-Index Crimes

[Rates per 100,000 population]

Crimes	Northeast	North Central	South	West
Simple assault	265	425	375	570
Larceny (under $50)	1,289	1,380	1,356	2,051
Malicious mischief	1,176	1,189	731	1,310
Counterfeiting or forgery	38	32	38	76
Consumer fraud	114	85	96	247
Other fraud (bad checks, swindling, etc.)	139	202	298	418
Sex offenses (other than forcible rape)	126	127	125	228
Family crimes (desertion, nonsupport, etc.)	177	308	231	342

SOURCE: NORC survey.

There are no regional statistics on offenses known to the police for non-Index offenses. The NORC results, shown in Table 11, indicate generally higher rates in the West for every offense.

Both the NORC victimization survey and the current police statistics indicate regional distributions of crime somewhat different from those shown by police statistics in earlier years. Prior to 1958, State and regional rates did not include rural areas. Comparisons can consequently be made only for city areas through 1957. Rates for city areas since 1958 are on a slightly different basis but are roughly comparable to the earlier rates.[113]

[109] See, for example, David J. Pittman and William Handy, *supra* note 10.

[110] NORC survey, *supra* note 41, pp. 24–30.

[111] *Id.* at p. 102.

[112] See Reiss studies, *supra* note 43, and BSSR survey, *supra* note 42.

[113] The UCR has published neither rates for cities nor the volume of offenses by State since 1957. The volume of offenses has been published, however, for Standard Metropolitan Statistical Areas and for "other cities." Taken together these categories are the same as the previous category for cities except for the inclusion in the Standard Metropolitan Statistical Areas of urban counties. The Task Force calculated rates for these two categories together by State in order to make comparisons with years prior to 1958. In doing so it was not possible to take into account the various changes in reporting systems which are corrected in the overall national statistics.

In the thirties and early forties, cities in the South had the highest rates for Index crimes against the person and were second only to cities in the Pacific and Mountain States for Index crimes against property.[114] New England cities had the lowest rates for crimes against the person and together with cities in the New York, New Jersey, Pennsylvania (Middle Atlantic) area had the lowest rates for crime against property.[115] Cities in the Pacific and Mountain States had the highest rates for crimes against property while those of the East North Central States had the second highest rates for crimes against persons.[116]

Today both the cities in the West and the Western States as a whole have taken over the highest position for crimes against persons as well as maintaining their position for crimes against property. While rates have gone up slightly in the South, the region no longer has the highest rate for crimes against persons, and rates in the cities for crimes against property have increased less than in most other regions. Including both urban and rural areas, the greatest percentage increases in crimes against the person in the last decade have come in New England, but the region has nevertheless continued to occupy the lowest position for crimes against the person.[117] Both New England and the Middle Atlantic States have moved up in property crimes, and the Northeast States as a whole are now second only to the West.[118]

Since 1935 willful homicide has declined generally throughout the Nation except in New England, . . . [where it] increased slightly.[119] Robbery rates have increased in the Pacific and Middle Atlantic States and declined in most other places.[120] Prior to 1958, rates for aggravated assault advanced more rapidly in the West than elsewhere but for the last few years have gone up at about the same pace as the rest of the Nation. Data for forcible rape are available only for the most recent years. Although rates are

[114] One study of patterns of crime in 86 cities in 1940 and 1946 by Southern and non-Southern pairs found the Southern cities higher both for personal and property crimes in the South. See Austin L. Porterfield and Robert H. Talbert, *Crime, Suicide and Social Well-Being in your State and City* (Fort Worth: Stafford-Lowdon Co., 1948), pp. 39–76.

[115] Rates for burglary and larceny increased considerably between 1935 and 1940 for the Middle Atlantic States, but the overall rate for Index property crimes remained low relative to the rest of the Nation.

[116] Stuart Lottier, "Distribution of Criminal Offenses in Sectional Regions," *Journal of Criminal Law and Criminology*, 29:329–344, September-October 1938, found a series of regular gradients for certain Index crimes. Except for willful homicide and aggravated assault, these seem to have been statistical artifacts rather than matters of substance. See also appendix A, President's Commission on Law Enforcement and Administration of Justice, Judith A. Wilks, particularly the section "Regional Differentiations."

[117] The increase in rates from 1958 has been 102.3 percent as compared with 43.6 percent nationally.

[118] This is partly due to changes in reporting.

[119] From 1.2 per 100,000 population in 1935 to 2.1 in 1965.

[120] Between 1935 and 1965 all regions decreased except in Pacific, New England, and Middle Atlantic.

relatively high, they have risen much more slowly in the West than elsewhere.[121]

Burglary has increased nearly 4 times in the Middle Atlantic States since 1935 but by a greater absolute amount in the Pacific States. During the same period auto theft has declined in the South, the Mountain States and the West North Central States. It has increased most in the Northeast. The greatest increase since 1958 in auto theft was in the East North Central area (110 percent) and in New England (105 percent). The Boston area was chiefly responsible for the New England increase. Auto theft increased less than 10 percent in the West South Central States during this same time. Larceny rates prior to 1958 are not comparable with those since. Increases since 1958 have been fairly uniform throughout the country.

. . . . .

Crime in the Cities

Reported rates have increased to some extent in almost all cities, at least for some crimes. By far the greatest proportion of whatever increase there has been in Index-type crimes in America within the last 30 years, however, has taken place in the larger cities. . . . Except for burglary, for which reported rates have been rising generally, the reported level of crime for the smaller cities—despite increases in recent years—is not greatly different today from what it was 30 years ago. Robbery has even declined in the smallest cities and towns.

In the larger cities, however, the picture is very different. In cities over 250,000 the rate for burglary has increased by about 150 percent since 1940, aggravated assault by almost 300 percent. Robbery, while increasing only 15 percent over 1933, has increased 140 percent since 1940. To a substantial extent these huge increases come from the highly unrealistic rates of crime that these cities were reporting earlier. In 1935, for example, the cities over 250,000 were reporting rates of burglary that were less than those in towns of 25,000 to 50,000 and only three-fourths the rate reported by cities between 100,000 and 250,000 population. . . . The rate for aggravated assault for 1964 is particularly affected because of changes in classification, and is substantially less for all size cities than that shown in the figure for that year.[122]

Changes in rates for some individual cities in the over-250,000-population group over the last 30 years are staggering. Homicide, which has generally been reported reliably throughout the period and which declined nationally, increased about four times in Newark and Boston, three times in St.

---

[121] The 1958–1965 change in rates was from 11.1 to 13.2 per 100,000 population in the Mountain States and 16.8 to 18.5 in the Pacific States.
[122] UCR, 1965.

Louis, and twice in Cleveland, Detroit and New York.[123] Reported changes
for other crimes for individual cities are less certain because of changes in
reporting systems but are equally large.

Reported rates for robbery have increased by four to six times for at least
nine cities while rates for aggravated assault have gone up as much as 25 to
30 times for a few cities. Only two cities with populations today totaling
more than 250,000 reported decreases in the overall rate for Index crimes
against the person and not a single city reported a decline in either burglary, larceny, auto theft or the overall rate of Index crimes against
property.

The major cities with declining overall rates for Index crimes against the
person were Memphis and Louisville. The decline was greatest in the case
of Memphis where the rates in 1940 were by far the highest among the
country's larger cities; showing 25 murders, 580 aggravated assaults, and
209 robberies, and an overall rate of 814 crimes against the person per
100,000 population. This compares with 7 murders, 80 aggravated assaults,
and 57 robberies for a total of 144 Index crimes against the person per
100,000 population in 1965, a decline of enormous proportions.[124]

Except for homicide, virtually all of the decline took place between 1940
and 1950. The rate has been increasing slowly since then. The overall rate
for violence decreased much more modestly in Louisville, dropping from 308
offenses per 100,000 population in 1940 to 297 in 1965.

Rates for homicide, in line with the national trend, dropped in a great
number of places, particularly among the Southern cities where the 1940
rates were highest but also in such other places as Cincinnati, Phoenix,
Tulsa, Pittsburgh, San Jose, and El Paso. Reported robbery rates dropped
over two-thirds in Memphis, halved in Tulsa, and declined considerably in
Nashville and Atlanta. The sharpest drop in aggravated assault was in
Memphis. Declines were also registered in Birmingham, Louisville, Akron
and in one city, Omaha, where the rate was already very low.[125]

The greatest increases in burglary were in Minneapolis, where the rate
increased nearly 350 percent and Newark, where it increased more than 225
percent. The rate for larceny of $50 and over at least doubled in virtually
every large city—the largest increase being in Phoenix which increased its
rate 13 times, and Baltimore whose rate increased nearly 10 times. Cincinnati had the least increase for both burglary (3 percent) and larceny $50
and over (105 percent). Rates in Boston and Newark went up the most for
auto theft, about 4 times, while the changes in Albuquerque, Norfolk,

---

[123] The rates increased from 4.9 per 100,000 population in 1940 to 17.3 in 1965 in
Newark; 1.7 to 8.6 in Boston; 6.7 to 19.7 in St. Louis; 6.6 to 12.6 in Cleveland; 4.9 to
11.5 in Detroit; and 3.7 to 8.0 in New York.

[124] See also Andrew A. Bruce and Thomas S. Fitzgerald, "A Study of Crime in the City
of Memphis, Tennessee," *Journal of Criminal Law and Criminology*, vol. 19, No. 2, part
II, August 1928, p. 14.

[125] The rate in Omaha in 1940 was 27.3. It decreased to 8.7 in 1965, the lowest of all
cities over 250,000 in population.

Seattle, and San Diego were so small that they were essentially the same in 1965 as in 1940.[126]

Rates for a number of cities have shown increases in percentage terms but, because their rates were low initially, have not had any great increase in the actual number of reported crimes per 100,000 population. Cities in this category include Honolulu, Milwaukee, and San Jose for Index crimes against the person and San Diego, Milwaukee, and Cincinnati for Index crimes against property.

The dramatic and turbulent changes which America's cities have been undergoing throughout this period are well known. They were bound to have an impact on the amount of crime in the city. One of the most significant facts has been the simple one of growth. The metropolitan areas of the cities have been getting larger—growing more than 70 percent between 1940 and 1965.[127] More than two-thirds of this increase, however, has not come within the political boundaries of the city, but in the surrounding suburbs. In most metropolitan areas this has meant that the center city high crime rate areas . . . now occupy a larger percentage of the city itself while a larger percentage of the outlying low crime rate areas are in the suburbs.

.   .   .   .   .

. . . [C]omparing city crime rates of today with those of earlier years is to some extent like comparing the rates for a high crime district with those for the whole city. Changes in rate depend in part on the extent to which the city has absorbed its suburbs. Finding comparable units is difficult, however. Greater metropolitan areas of today are not necessarily urbanized

Table 12—Robbery Rates

[Per 100,000 population]

	1940 city	1965 metropolitan	1965 city
Chicago	170.8	244.3	420.8
Newark	77.0	109.4	379.8
Washington	137.7	153.2	358.8
Miami	131.3	164.2	241.2
Los Angeles	144.2	189.1	293.4
Cleveland	102.2	101.1	213.3
Houston	81.4	95.5	135.3
Dayton	37.0	55.2	129.6

[126] The Boston rates, which at 420.9 offenses per 100,000 in 1940 were already third highest among the Nation's larger cities, increased to 1956.7 offenses per 100,000 population in 1965. The Newark rates increased from 304.1 to 1127.5 per 100,000 population. The rates for Albuquerque, Norfolk, Seattle, and San Diego were 372.4, 367.2, 322.3, 287.2 per 100,000 population in 1940 and 377.5, 380.6, 337.0, and 277.3 in 1965.

[127] The population in Standard Metropolitan Statistical Areas in 1940 was 72,576,000; in 1965 it had risen to 123,813,000. The population in central cities rose from 45,473,000 to 59,612,000; in the suburbs from 27,103,000 to 64,201,000.

to the same extent as the city of 30 years ago, but they do provide a crude approximation. Table 12 compares the 1965 rate of robbery per 100,000 population for the greater metropolitan areas of several cities with the rates for the city proper in 1940 and 1965. Given some bias toward higher reporting today, the rates are quite comparable.

For other offenses, the 1965 rates for metropolitan areas are not as close to those of the 1940 city. Metropolitan auto theft rates for 1965 tend to fall midway between the 1940 and 1965 city rates while the 1965 metropolitan burglary rates are in many instances only slightly lower than those of the 1965 city.

Trends in the Solution of Crime and the Prosecution and Conviction of Offenders

No subject is more fraught with controversy than that of the extent to which the persons who commit crimes are apprehended, prosecuted, and convicted. This controversy is as old as the criminal justice system itself. It received considerable attention in the city, State and national crime commission studies of the 1920's and 30's.[128] Nevertheless, it still remains that there are many difficulties in discussing these subjects on the basis of available statistics, primarily because there is no reliable way of connecting up the number of offenses committed with the number of offenders processed at each stage. These proportions vary considerably, and for most of the Index crimes at least they are quite low.

What data there are suggest that some individual was ultimately convicted or sent to juvenile court in about 40 percent of the cases of homicide known to the police, but that the likelihood that an individual will be apprehended and convicted or referred to juvenile court in thefts known to the police is less than 15 percent.[129] What data there are available cover only 1,657 cities in 1965 with an estimated population of 57 million.[130] If

---

[128] For a useful summary description and analysis of the meaning of criminal justice "mortality table" statistics, the term coined during the Cleveland Survey to describe the dropping of cases through the progressive stages of the criminal justice process, see National Commission on Law Observance and Enforcement, *Report on Prosecution* (Washington: U.S. Government Printing Office, 1931), pp. 52–72. For the initial use of such tables see Roscoe Pound and Felix Frankfurter, eds., *Criminal Justice in Cleveland* (Cleveland: The Cleveland Foundation, 1922), pp. 91–96.

[129] These percentages are based on UCR, 1965, table 12, p. 103. They are subject to at least two sources of error. Several persons may be charged for the same offense, or one person may have been responsible for a number of offenses. With the available data it is not possible to correct for these types of errors in arriving at a reliable figure, and it is not known to what extent the errors may cancel each other out. In addition, it should be noted that the offenses known to the police are reported for the calendar year in which they occurred, while many of those convicted undoubtedly committed their offenses in earlier years. The clearance tables reported by the UCR reflect agency actions within the calendar year and are not based on the follow-up of a cohort of offenses or offenders through the system.

[130] UCR, 1965, table 12, p. 103.

account is taken of the number of crimes that are never reported to the police, percentages become even smaller.

The greatest difficulty lies in catching the offender in the first instance. For offenses such as murder, forcible rape, or aggravated assault where the victim is likely either to have been acquainted with the offender or to be able to identify him, the police are able to solve or "clear" a high percentage of the cases, from 90 percent in 1965 in the case of homicide to 64 percent in the case of forcible rape.[131] Where the offense is one of theft in which the police can identify the offender only through investigation or apprehension during the act, they are able to solve a much smaller percentage of the cases, ranging from 25 percent in the case of burglary and auto theft to 20 percent in the case of larceny. The clearance rate for robbery (38 percent) is somewhere in the middle of those for property crimes and the other crimes against the person. Its victims are less often acquainted with the offender than in the case of other personal crimes.

Not all of the persons arrested for crime are charged and prosecuted, however. In 1965, the percentage charged varied from about 60 percent for homicide to over 80 percent for burglary. Of the adults who are charged, about 70 percent are usually convicted of the crime charged or some lesser offense.[132]

The reasons why a suspect who has been arrested may not ultimately be convicted are many. The case may involve a juvenile who is handled through some process less formal than that of the juvenile court. The police who "cleared" the case may not have been able to secure enough evidence to prove the charge. The complaining witness may, as often happens in cases of aggravated assault, refuse to press charges or cooperate with the prosecution. The offense may be a borderline one that the prosecuting officer uses his discretion to dismiss. The court may decide that no offense was committed in the first instance, or that the suspected offender was not guilty.

Measuring the trend over time of the solution of crime and the prosecution and conviction of offenders is even more difficult than that of measuring the trend of crime. Computation of clearance rates, for example, involves not only the number of offenses known to the police, but also the number of arrests, the number of persons charged, and the number of exceptional cases where an offense is considered solved even though some sets of circumstances, such as suicide of the offender, prevent an arrest from being made.[133] While the concepts involved seem clear cut, studies have shown that in practice they are not.

.   .   .   .   .

Because the clearance rate is itself a measure of police effectiveness, there

[131] *Ibid.*
[132] *Ibid.*
[133] Federal Bureau of Investigation, *UCR Handbook,* p. 48.

are also pressures at some times to manipulate the clearance rate.[134] It is quite clear, moreover, that concepts as to how offenses should be cleared have changed from time to time.[135]

Caution must also be exercised in evaluating clearance rates because of the way that they are developed, particularly for the property crimes. When a burglar is caught for a single offense, it is common to question him concerning other offenses. One arrest will in some instances clear up as many as 30 or 40 offenses. In many cases such "clearances" will reflect what actually occurred. In other cases, however, they will merely reflect the desire of the suspect to cooperate with the police in hopes of getting a

Table 13—Percentages of Offenses Known to Police Cleared, by Arrest for Selected Years, 1935–1966

	Willful homicide	Forcible rape	Rob- bery	Aggra- vated assault	Bur- glary	Larceny	Motor vehicle theft
1935	85.6	----------	41.5	70.7	31.6	26.2	16.7
1940	88.7	----------	41.8	73.7	33.1	23.4	23.8
1945	86.9	----------	36.2	76.2	31.3	22.8	26.4
1950	93.8	----------	43.5	76.6	29.0	22.1	25.6
1955	92.7	----------	42.8	77.4	32.1	21.0	29.2
1959	92.7	73.6	42.5	78.9	30.7	20.9	26.2
1960	92.3	72.5	38.5	75.8	29.5	20.1	25.7
1961	93.1	72.6	41.6	78.7	30.0	20.8	27.8
1962	93.1	66.5	38.4	75.5	27.7	20.3	25.3
1963	91.2	69.4	38.6	76.1	26.9	19.9	26.2
1964	90.2	66.9	37.0	74.3	25.1	19.4	26.3
1965	90.5	64.0	37.6	72.9	24.7	19.6	25.2
1966	89.0	65.0	35.0	72.0	23.0	----------	25.0

SOURCE: "UCR." 1966 figures from "UCR, Preliminary Report, 1966." Percentages for rape not comparable prior to 1958 and are omitted.

lighter sentence. Since he is often not charged with the additional offenses, he may have little to lose in confessing to them.

.   .   .   .   .

These limitations on the data are compounded by the fact that in past years the number of jurisdictions reporting clearances to the UCR has been low and that the jurisdictions reporting have changed frequently.[136] In view of all these limitations, it is quite surprising to find a remarkable degree of stability in the clearance rates reported over the years. As Table 13 shows, the clearance rate for willful homicide is today slightly higher than it was in 1935 but the rates for it, forcible rape, robbery, aggravated assault, and motor vehicle theft have varied only a few percentage points over most of

[134] *Id.* at pp. 188–191.
[135] *Id.* at p. 189. See also Courtland C. Van Vechten, "Differential Criminal Case Mortality in Selected Jurisdictions," *American Sociological Review*, 7:833–39, December 1942. California shows a relatively steady drop in clearance rates from 1960 to 1965, for example. See *Crime in California*, table 1–3, p. 18.
[136] The number has varied from 51 to 2,351 cities, UCRB, 1958, p. 21; UCR, 1960, p. 83.

the reporting period. Rates for burglary and larceny have declined some-what during the past decade.

Trends regarding the percentage of persons arrested who are charged by the police can be evaluated only in conjunction with trends in the rate of arrest and clearance by the police. Otherwise, changes in arrest procedures could affect what happens subsequently. If the police, for example, were to limit arrests to cases in which there was conclusive evidence of guilt, the percentage of persons charged would rise as would the percentage of persons found guilty. The net result, however, might be that fewer guilty persons were convicted than when the arrest rate was higher, and the percentage of persons charged and convicted was lower.

Table 14—Trend in Prosecutions and Convictions, by Offense, 1962–1965

[In percents]

	Willful homi-cide	Forc-ible rape	Rob-bery	Aggra-vated assault	Bur-glary	Larceny	Motor vehicle theft
1962							
Clearances_____	92.8	71.5	40.4	76.8	28.0	20.2	27.1
Charged (percent of arrests)_	79.1	79.2	80.4	83.3	85.2	84.7	86.9
Guilty (percent of charged)__	67.0	47.4	54.3	51.7	41.9	46.7	30.6
Referred to juvenile court (percent of charged)_____	3.9	17.8	28.1	13.8	48.8	41.7	57.3
1965							
Clearances_____	89.9	65.6	38.4	72.8	25.6	18.8	25.3
Charged (percent of arrests)_	62.5	71.8	70.6	74.8	84.1	81.7	81.0
Guilty (percent of charged)__	62.9	44.1	46.7	50.3	32.3	41.9	27.7
Referred to juvenile court (percent of charged)_____	7.0	23.4	34.2	14.8	51.4	45.1	60.6

SOURCE: "UCR, 1962," p. 87; "UCR, 1965," p. 103.

Note: Table 14 is derived from data involving two different groups of jurisdictions for each year.

Table 14 indicates the trend from 1962 through 1965. As in the case of the solution of crime, the picture does not appear to have changed significantly. Figures for earlier years are not comparable. The percentage of referrals to juvenile court has been increasing during the 1960's, probably indicating the growing percentage of juvenile crime that could be expected from the population figures.

The rates of clearance, charging, and conviction vary not only from time to time but from place to place. Undoubtedly this is in part due to different conceptions but the subject is one that has received little attention. Because of its importance, it should be studied much more thoroughly than it has been to date. Why Chicago, for example, should have a clearance rate for burglary that is twice that of Los Angeles and a clearance rate for willful homicide that is 10 percent greater is a question that could have important implications for law enforcement.[137]

[137] Chicago Police Department, *Annual Report, 1965,* p. 10; Los Angeles Police Department, *Statistical Digest, 1965,* pp. 11, 13.

Other Countries

Crime is a worldwide problem. For most offenses it is difficult to compare directly the rates between countries because of great differences in the definitions of crime and in reporting practices. It is clear, however, that there are great differences in the rates of crime among the various countries and in the crime problems that they face. These differences are illustrated to some extent by the homicide rates for a number of countries shown in Table 15. The comparisons show only the general range of difference, as defini-

Table 15—Homicide Rates for Selected Countries

[Per 100,000 population]

Country	Rate	Year reported
Colombia	36. 5	1962
Mexico	31. 9	1960
South Africa	21. 8	1960
United States	4. 8	1962
Japan	1. 5	1962
France	1. 5	1962
Canada	1. 4	1962
Federal Republic of Germany	1. 2	1961
England/Wales	. 7	1962
Ireland	. 4	1962

SOURCE: "Demographic Yearbook," 15th issue, United Nations Publication, 1963, pp. 594–611.

tions and reporting even of homicide vary to some extent. In the years covered by the table, Colombia had the highest rate for all countries and Ireland the lowest.

A comparison between crime rates in 1964 in West Germany and the North Central United States, prepared by the FBI, indicates that the Federal Republic, including West Berlin, had a crime rate of 0.8 murders per 100,000 inhabitants, 10.6 rapes, 12.4 robberies, 1,628.2 larcenies, and 78.2 auto thefts, as opposed to 3.5 murders per 100,000 inhabitants for North Central United States, 10.5 rapes, 76.2 robberies, 1,337.3 larcenies, and 234.7 auto thefts.[138]

Commission and other studies of crime trends indicate that in most other countries officially reported rates for property offenses are rising rapidly, as they are in the United States, but that there is no definite pattern in the trend of crimes of violence in other countries.[139] Since 1955 property crime rates have increased more than 200 percent in West Germany, the Netherlands, Sweden, and Finland, and over 100 percent in France, England and

[138] "Crime Is a Worldwide Problem," *FBI Law Enforcement Bulletin,* December 1966, p. 9.

[139] *Id.* at pp. 7–10. See also Karl O. Christiansen, *Report on the Post-War Trends of Crime in Selected European Countries,* a report to the President's Commission on Law Enforcement and Administration of Justice, 1966 (mimeo).

Wales, Italy, and Norway. Of the countries studied, property crime rates in Denmark, Belgium, and Switzerland remained relatively stable.

Crimes of violence could be studied in only a few countries. Rates declined in Belgium, Denmark, Norway, and Switzerland, but rose more than 150 percent in England and Wales between 1955 and 1964. Sexual offenses, which are usually kept as a separate statistic in Europe, also showed a mixed trend.

Assessing the Amount and Trend of Crime

Because of the grave public concern about the crime problem in America today, the Commission has made a special effort to understand the amount and trend of crime and has reached the following conclusions:

1. The number of offenses—crimes of violence, crimes against property, and most others as well—has been increasing. Naturally, population growth is one of the significant contributing factors in the total amount of crime.

2. Most forms of crime—especially crimes against property—are increasing faster than population growth. This means that the risk of victimization to the individual citizen for these crimes is increasing, although it is not possible to ascertain precisely the extent of the increase. All the economic and social factors discussed above support, and indeed lead to, this conclusion.

The Commission found it very difficult to make accurate measurements of crime trends by relying solely on official figures, since it is likely that each year police agencies are to some degree dipping deeper into the vast reservoir of unreported crime. People are probably reporting more to the police as a reflection of higher expectations and greater confidence, and the police in turn are reflecting this in their statistics. In this sense more efficient policing may be leading to higher rates of reported crime. The diligence of the FBI in promoting more complete and accurate reporting through the development of professional police reporting procedures has clearly had an important effect on the completeness of reporting, but while this task of upgrading local reporting is under way, the FBI is faced with the problem, in computing national trends, of omitting for a time the places undergoing changes in reporting methods and estimating the amount of crime that occurred in those places in prior years.

3. Although the Commission concluded that there has been an increase in the volume and rate of crime in America, it has been unable to decide whether individual Americans today are more criminal than their counterparts 5, 10, or 25 years ago. To answer this question it would be necessary to make comparisons between persons of the same age, sex, race, place of residence, economic status, and other factors at the different times; in other words, to decide whether the 15-year-old slum dweller or the 50-year-old businessman is inherently more criminal now than the 15-year-old slum

dweller or the 50-year-old businessman in the past. Because of the many rapid and turbulent changes over these years in society as a whole and in the myriad conditions of life which affect crime, it was not possible for the Commission to make such a comparison. Nor do the data exist to make even simple comparisons of the incidence of crime among persons of the same age, sex, race, and place of residence at these different years.

4. There is a great deal of crime in America, some of it very serious, that is not reported to the police, or in some instances by the police. The national survey revealed that people are generally more likely to report serious crimes to the police, but the percent who indicated they did report to the police ranged from 10 percent for consumer fraud to 89 percent for auto theft. Estimates of the rate of victimization for Index offenses ranged from 2 per 100 persons in the national survey to 10 to 20 per 100 persons in the individual districts surveyed in 3 cities. The surveys produced rates of victimization that were from 2 to 10 times greater than the official rates for certain crimes.

5. What is needed to answer questions about the volume and trend of crime satisfactorily are a number of different crime indicators showing trends over a period of time to supplement the improved reporting by police agencies. The Commission experimented with the development of public surveys of victims of crime and feels this can become a useful supplementary yardstick. Further development of the procedure is needed to improve the reliability and accuracy of the findings. However, the Commission found these initial experiments produced useful results that justify more intensive efforts to gather such information on a regular basis. They should also be supplemented by new types of surveys and censuses which would provide better information about crime in areas where good information is lacking such as crimes by or against business and other organizations. The Commission also believes that an improved and greatly expanded procedure for the collection of arrest statistics would be of immense benefit in the assessment of the problem of juvenile delinquency.

6. Throughout its work the Commission has noted repeatedly the sharp differences in the amount and trends of reported crimes against property as compared with crimes against persons. It has noted that while property crimes are far more numerous than crimes against the person, and so dominate any reported trends, there is much public concern about crimes against persons. The more recent reports of the UCR have moved far toward separating the reporting of these two classes of crime altogether.

The Commission in its General Report recommended that the present Index of reported crime should be broken into two wholly separate parts, one for crimes of violence and the other for crimes against property.

The Commission also recommended, in principle, the development of additional indices to indicate the volume and trend of such other important crime problems as embezzlement, fraud, and other crimes against trust, crimes of vice that are associated with organized crime, and perhaps others.

The Commission urged that consideration be given to practical methods for developing such indices.

The Commission also urged that the public media and others concerned with crime be careful to keep separate the various crime problems and not to deal with them as a unitary phenomenon. Whenever possible, crime should be reported relative to population as well as by the number of offenses, so as to provide a more accurate picture of risks of victimization in any particular locality.

7. The Commission believes that age, urbanization, and other shifts in the population already under way will likely operate over the next 5 to 10 years to increase the volume of offenses faster than population growth. Further dipping into the reservoirs of unreported crime will likely combine with this real increase in crime to produce even greater increases in reported crime rates. Many of the basic social forces that tend to increase the amount of real crime are already taking effect and are for the most part irreversible. If society is to be successful in its desire to reduce the amount of real crime, it must find new ways to create the kinds of conditions and inducements—social, environmental, and psychological—that will bring about a greater commitment to law-abiding conduct and respect for the law on the part of all Americans and a better understanding of the great stake that all men have in being able to trust in the honesty and integrity of their fellow citizens.

[*The President's Commission on Law Enforcement and Administration of Justice*, Task Force Report: Crime and Its Impact—An Assessment (*Washington: U.S. Government Printing Office, 1967*), pp. 14–30, 35, 37–40.]

3 Criminal statistics
—an urgently needed resource*

Over 30 years ago a distinguished Commission appointed by the President of the United States to study crime and propose measures for its control reported serious deficiencies in essential information at the national level. Calling "accurate data * * * the beginning of wisdom," the Wickersham Commission recommended development of a "comprehensive plan" for a "complete body of statistics covering crime, criminals, criminal justice, and penal treatment" at the Federal, State, and local levels and the entrusting of this plan at the Federal level to a single agency.[1]

Had this recommendation been adopted, the present Commission would not have been forced in 1967 to rely so often on incomplete information or to conclude so frequently that important questions could not be answered.

Given the importance of sound data to both crime control and public understanding, it is hard to believe that such basic facts as the trend of juvenile delinquency, the percent of crimes committed by professional criminals, or the likelihood of recidivism are beyond the capacity of our present statistical resources. In some respects the present system is not as good as that used in some European countries 100 years ago. There are no national and almost no State or local statistics at all in a number of important areas: the courts, probation, sentencing, and the jails.[2] There are important deficiencies in those statistics which are collected. There is no reliable measure of the extent of organized crime and no satisfactory test for police performance. In short, the United States is today, in the era of the high speed computer, trying to keep track of crime and criminals with a system that was less than adequate in the days of the horse and buggy.

In other areas our society has not been so cavalier about the

* This chapter was prepared in conjunction with the Task Force on Science and Technology.
[1] U.S. National Commission on Law Observance and Enforcement, *Report on Criminal Justice* (Washington: U.S. Government Printing Office, 1931), pp. 3, 6 (hereinafter cited as Wickersham Statistics Report).
[2] The Administrative Office of the Courts publishes statistics for the Federal courts and for Federal probation, and some individual States have good statistics regarding some parts of the criminal justice system.

need to obtain the information basic to the solution of social problems. Millions of dollars and hundreds of highly trained statistical personnel are employed annually in the collection of information about the population, the economy, the Nation's health, education, and various other facets of our society. Budget estimates for 1967 for current major Federal statistical programs total $124 million; 1967 estimates for the Bureau of the Census and the Bureau of Labor Statistics alone total over $15 million each, while 12 other Federal statistical programs each spend more than $2 million annually.[3] This dwarfs completely the present Federal expenditures for criminal statistics totaling less than $800,000 annually.[4]

Adequate statistical programs are of enormous importance. Without the highly sophisticated and detailed system of economic statistics now available, the striking progress of the last few years in the management and control of the economy would not have been possible. Newly developed statistical programs for health ($9.3 million)[5] and education ($7.6 million) are expected to contribute significantly to the accomplishment of national goals in those areas.

If a serious effort to control crime is to be made, a serious effort must be made to obtain the facts about crime. Safe streets require knowledge of what is happening in our streets, who is causing the trouble, what happened there before, and many other facts. A much improved national criminal statistical program is urgently needed today in order to:

1. Inform the public and responsible governmental officials as to the nature of the crime problem, its magnitude, and its trend over time.
2. Measure the effects of prevention and deterrence programs, ranging from community action to police patrol.
3. Find out who commits crimes, by age, sex, family status, income,

[3] Office of Statistical Standards, Bureau of the Budget, *Statistical Reporter*, December 1966, pp. 93–100. This total includes both current programs and current expenditures for periodic programs such as the census. Census expenditures go up sharply in the decennial years.

[4] The principal Federal expenditure for crime statistics is that involved in the Uniform Crime Reports. Expenditures for fiscal year 1966 totaled $573,000. Personnel involved include 4 special agents and 73 clerks. The Children's Bureau of the Department of Health, Education, and Welfare spends about $65,000 annually and employs approximately six persons in the collection of statistics concerning delinquency. The Department of Justice centrally, the Bureau of Prisons, and the Bureau of the Census all collect modest amounts of crime data, but the activity is too small to be accounted for separately and is included in general expenditures. About seven persons are employed by the Administrative Office of the Courts in its statistical program, but no figures are available concerning expenditures and these personnel spent only part time on criminal as opposed to other court statistics. Overall, it seems clear that less than $800,000 is expended annually in the Federal criminal statistics program.

[5] Department of Health, Education, and Welfare, *Origin, Program and Operation of the U.S. National Health Survey* (Washington: U.S. Government Printing Office, 1965), Series 1, No. 1.

ethnic and residential background, and other social attributes in order to find the proper focus of crime prevention programs.

4. Measure the workload and effectiveness of the police, the courts, and the other agencies of the criminal justice system, both individually and as an integrated system.

5. Analyze the factors contributing to success and failure of probation, parole, and other correctional alternatives for various kinds of offenders.

6. Provide criminal justice agencies with comparative norms of performance.

7. Furnish baseline data for research.

8. Compute the costs of crime in terms of economic injury inflicted upon communities and individuals, as well as assess the direct public expenditures by criminal justice agencies.

9. Project expected crime rates and their consequences into the future for more enlightened government planning.

10. Assess the societal and other causes of crime and develop theories of criminal behavior.

A National Criminal Statistics Program

Answers to these and other important questions require strong criminal statistical programs at all levels of government—local, State and national. While State and local needs are in many ways the most important, the quickest and the surest way to promote such data is through a strong national program. Moreover, there is a very strong need for national data in itself.

The need for national data was recognized as long ago as 1870 when the Congress made it the duty of the Attorney General to collect statistics of crime from the States.[6] While this program and those begun by the Federal Government in 1907 and 1933[7] to collect criminal judicial statistics failed

[6] Section 12, Act of June 22, 1870, ch. 150, 16 Stat. 164, states: "That it shall be the duty of the Attorney General to make an annual report to Congress, including the statistics of crime under the laws of the United States, and, as far as practicable, under the laws of several States." The portion of this section concerning the statistics of crimes involving State laws was deleted by the Act of March 3, 1873, ch. 238, sec. 1, 17 Stat. 578. The Act of June 11, 1930, ch. 455, 46 Stat. 554, 5 U.S.C. 340, provides the authority under which the Federal Bureau of Investigation publishes the Uniform Crime Reports. Some data concerning crime or criminals were included in the census from 1850 on. State statistics "of crime, of prosecution and of penal treatment go back in New York to 1829 and in Massachusetts to 1832." Wickersham Statistics Report, p. 8. The very first meeting of the National Police Association in 1871 adopted a resolution declaring the necessity to "procure and digest statistics for the use of police departments." See also Louis Robinson, *History and Organization of Criminal Statistics in the United States* (Boston: Houghton Mifflin, 1911); Louis Robinson, "History of Criminal Statistics, 1908–1933," *Journal of Criminal Law and Criminology*, 24:125–139, May–June, 1933.

[7] Harry Alpert, "National Series on State Judicial Criminal Statistics Discontinued," *Journal of Criminal Law and Criminology*, 34:181–188, July–August 1948.

because of the inability to secure the necessary cooperation from the State and local agencies, the need which they were established to fill remains.[8]

Including the Wickersham Commission study of 1931 and the study of Professor Lejins for this Commission,[9] at least four major governmental studies of national criminal statistical needs have been made in the last 35 years.[10] Each of these studies concluded that there was a critical need for a strong, effective Federal statistical program.

All four of these studies of criminal statistical needs concluded that an effective program required the establishment of a single Federal criminal statistical agency which would bear the main responsibility for the program.

The Wickersham Commission offered three reasons for its recommendation of a single agency: (1) that it was necessary to secure unity of treatment throughout the whole criminal justice system; (2) that a single agency was more likely to bring about improvements in methods of gathering, compiling, organizing, and interpreting data; and (3) that a single agency would be more economical.[11]

Experience has demonstrated the soundness of these arguments. The present system under which each of a number of different Federal agencies collect some information from the State or local agencies most closely related to it has not secured unity of treatment. It has failed to provide coverage of many of the most important criminal justice agencies. It has even failed to provide intelligent treatment of statistics concerning Federal crimes. In short, it has not worked well and is unlikely to do so. For the future it promises the least return for the greatest expense, particularly as its operation would be on a scale insufficient to take maximum advantage of modern high speed equipment.[12] Without the benefit of any overall direction, it encourages the continued collection of information after it is no longer needed, and delays the development of new information as it is required.

[8] For a review of previous Federal collection efforts, see Ronald H. Beattie, "Problems of Criminal Statistics in the United States," *Journal of Criminal Law and Criminology*, 46:178–186, July–August 1955. For a general history of the criminal statistics, see Thorsten Sellin and Marvin E. Wolfgang, *The Measurement of Delinquency* (New York: John Wiley & Sons, 1964), pp. 7–70.

[9] See Peter Lejins, *National Crime Data Reporting System: Proposal for a Model*, appendix C of President's Commission on Law Enforcement and Administration of Justice, *Task Force Report*.

[10] Committee on Government Statistics and Information Services, *Federal Collection of Criminal Statistics*, prepared in 1934 for the Attorney General; and Harry Shulman, *The Reporting of Criminal Statistics in the United States*, a 1964 study for the Bureau of the Budget. Also see generally Ronald H. Beattie, "Sources of Statistics on Crime and Correction," *Journal of the American Statistical Association*, 54:582–592, Sept. 1959; Donald R. Cressy, "The State of Criminal Statistics," *National Probation and Parole Association Journal*, 3:230–241, July 1957.

[11] *Wickersham Statistics Report*, pp. 14–15.

[12] See, for example, the *Report of the Task Force on the Storage of and Access to Government Statistics*, Carl Kaysen, Chairman (Bureau of the Budget, mimeo, October 1966), pp. 2–13.

However it might be improved, continuation of the present decentralized system is therefore the least desirable of all the possible alternatives for developing a Federal statistical program.

Whether a central Federal statistical agency should have sole responsibility for criminal statistics at the national level or should share this responsibility to some degree with other Federal agencies depends at least in part upon whether the Federal Government should collect State and local data directly from operating agencies or only from a State statistical bureau which has checked and can vouch for their accuracy.

Each State is responsible for crime control within its own borders—defining crimes, setting up penalties, and establishing its own administrative structure for the enforcement of criminal law. Accurate information on the full extent of crime in the United States must therefore come from 50 highly independent and separate systems of criminal justice, in addition to the District of Columbia and the Federal jurisdictions.

For the most part this information must be obtained voluntarily. A local agency may withhold data because its record would compare unfavorably with other agencies or simply because it does not care to file. Even where the local agency is cooperative, it often does not keep the records desired itself or lacks adequate resources to file the necessary reports. If the reports are filed they may or may not be accurate and are sometimes deliberately misleading.

The difficulties inherent in dealing with thousands of different agencies over which there is no Federal control led the Wickersham Commission to recommend that the Federal Government deal only with State statistical bureaus.[13] Because of their position within the State criminal justice structure, these bureaus could, it was felt, require the maintenance of necessary records and could through training and the monitoring of programs insure the quality of the information reported.

On paper this looks like an excellent system. The success which the California Bureau of Criminal Statistics has had in producing uniform, high quality statistics is a good indication of its potential. Except for California, however, the State statistical bureaus upon which such a system depends do not exist.

While almost all States collect some criminal statistics, this collection is usually fragmented among various agencies whose statistics are not compatible with each other. More importantly, in most States there is no systematic method of monitoring or improving the quality of data received from operating agencies.

It seems clear that any State which is serious about limiting crime and improving its criminal justice system should establish a centralized criminal statistics bureau with the funds and authority necessary for it to be effective. The Uniform Criminal Statistics Act, promulgated by the Commission-

[13] *Wickersham Statistics Report,* pp. 7, 88.

ers on Uniform State Laws in 1946 [14] but adopted to date only in California,[15] is one effective way of beginning this. The Federal Government should do all it can to promote and encourage such development, including the providing of funds and expert assistance. Even with increased Federal funding, however, it seems unlikely, in the absence of some step such as requiring an effective statistics bureau as a condition of Federal assistance, that a large number of such bureaus will come into being any time soon.

This poses sharp problems for the development of the Federal statistical program. National statistics must either wait until there is operating in every State a bureau which can collect and check the local statistics or the Federal Government must itself attempt to perform these functions, knowing that this is likely to be less effective. The need is too great, however, to delay development for the length of time necessary to create a fully operating system of State bureaus. Federal collection should not be limited to State statistical bureaus. It should make use of such bureaus where they exist, and work for the development of new ones, but rely in the meantime on development of alternative methods of collecting and monitoring statistics directly from the operating agencies.[16]

Paralleling its recommendation that statistics be collected only from State bureaus which could vouch for their accuracy, the Wickersham Commission recommended that the central Federal agency for criminal statistics be solely responsible for all statistical operations and that it be divorced from all operating responsibilities. In conjunction with the recommendation concerning State statistical bureaus, this recommendation was designed to eliminate completely the possibility of statistical manipulation, which the

---

[14] The Uniform Criminal Statistics Act is contained in 9 *Uniform Laws Annotated* (1957). It was approved by the American Bar Association as well as the Uniform Commissioners on Uniform State Laws. A prior act was promulgated in 1937 but was withdrawn in 1943 as obsolete. It had been adopted by South Dakota. The present act contains 6 sections: Par. 1 establishes the bureau. Par. 2 establishes the position of director, requiring that he have "statistical training and experience" and a "knowledge of criminal law enforcement and administration and of penal and correctional institutions and methods." Par. 3 directs the bureau to collect data, prescribe records to be kept by operating agencies, tabulate and analyze data, and cooperate with Federal statistical programs. Par. 4 requires officials of all operating agencies to maintain records as prescribed, furnish data as required, and allow inspections. Par. 5 requires the bureau to furnish the governor with an annual written report. And Par. 6 authorizes the director to withhold the salary of any State or local official refusing to supply information to the bureau. See also Thorsten Sellin, "The Uniform Criminal Statistics Act," *Journal of Criminal Law and Criminology*, 40:679–700, March–April 1950.

[15] California Penal Code secs. 13,000–13,030. This act is a modified form of the Uniform Act.

[16] Two of the foremost authorities, Ronald H. Beattie, Chief, Bureau of Criminal Statistics, California Department of Justice, and Thorsten Sellin, Professor of Sociology, University of Pennsylvania, asked to comment on the Task Force proposal, indicated the view that there would never be an adequate national statistical system until the States establish criminal statistical bureaus. Even where State bureaus exist, it may still be necessary to have direct reporting from local units in order to meet publication deadlines. This does not mean, however, completely bypassing the State bureau.

Wickersham Commission had observed frequently at the State and local levels, particularly among the police agencies.[17]

In the absence, however, of State statistical bureaus with [which] . . . such a central agency could deal, it seems undesirable to centralize all Federal collection in a single agency. Collection from State and local agencies can in some instances be better made by the Federal agency most often in touch with such agencies. In the absence of some new collection technique centralization would be particularly unwise for those Federal collection programs which are already established and which depend upon relationships between Federal and State agencies which have taken many years to develop.

A National Criminal Justice Statistics Center

A National Criminal Justice Statistics Center should have clear statutory and executive branch authority to oversee and coordinate all Federal criminal statistical programs, including both the collection of statistics from the States and the collection of data relating specifically to Federal crimes.[18] This authority should be formalized in such a way—through budget review powers or otherwise—as to insure that it exists in fact as well as in theory.

Insofar as existing Federal programs of collection from the States are operating satisfactorily or could be brought up to a satisfactory performance by improvements, the Center should continue the present arrangements. Where an existing Federal program requires a major overhaul, however, the Center should be free to take over responsibility for collecting information in the hands of State and local agencies itself, if that appears desirable. Individual Federal agencies with collection programs would continue to disseminate information in accordance with the needs of the criminal justice agencies which they serve. The Center would have free access to all data collected by other agencies, including terminal linkups, and would coordinate data storage as well as collection and dissemination. The Center would itself be expected to publish comprehensive statistics covering the whole criminal justice system.

The desirability of divorcing statistical programs from operating agencies and the clear need for relating crime statistics to demographic data and statistics concerning other social problems, such as mental health, poverty,

[17] *Wickersham Statistics Report,* pp. 36–39, 52–57. See also Sam Bass Warner, "Crimes Known to the Police—An Index of Crime?" *Harvard Law Review,* 45:307–334, December 1931.
[18] The Safe Streets and Crime Control Act of 1967, S. 917, 90th Cong., 1st. sess., sec. 405 provides that "the Attorney General is authorized * * * (b) to collect, evaluate, publish, and disseminate statistics and other information on the condition and progress of law enforcement and criminal justice in the several States." The National Health Survey Act is set forth in 42 U.S.C. sec. 304. Neither of these Federal acts provides powers as strong as the Uniform Criminal Statistics Act, see note 14 *supra.*

education, and housing, might argue for creating the National Criminal Justice Statistics Center in the Bureau of the Census or as an independent agency.[19]

There are more advantages to having such a Center located within the Department of Justice, however. There through full integration with Federal programs of assistance to States and localities, it could take maximum advantage of the inducement that these programs offer local agencies to cooperate with its collection program and could at the same time offer the maximum aid to the planning process required for effective crime control. Because many of the Federal agencies with which the Center will need to work are located within the Department of Justice, location there will also be helpful in securing the cooperation necessary for an effective program. Mere creation of the Center will not itself, however, bring about the degree of cooperation needed at all levels of government. That will require strong support from the Attorney General, particularly during the formative period of the Center. In establishing the Center, care should of course be taken to insure the proper degree of independence from operating responsibility and from any taint of manipulation for political or ideological purposes.

To assist the Center in the exercise of its leadership role and in achieving necessary coordination there should be a Criminal Statistics Council chaired by the director of the Center and composed of representatives of those Federal agencies which collect criminal statistics, those agencies which are major users of criminal statistics, and other Federal statistical agencies, such as the Bureau of the Census, with which the work of the Center should be closely meshed.

The Center should also have a strong advisory group of nongovernment experts and representatives of State and local criminal justice and statistical agencies to provide advice and communication and to serve as a sounding board for Center plans.

The Center and the national criminal information system discussed in chapter 11 of the Commission's general report and chapter 6 of the Science and Technology Task Force Report should cooperate fully with each other but be entirely separate organizations. The information system will be at the heart of operations, answering questions such as whether a particular car is stolen or a particular offender wanted. The statistical system, on the other hand, should for the most part be divorced from operations so that it may assist in evaluating how operations are being conducted and may give an unbiased view as to what the real crime situation is.

The principal responsibilities of a National Criminal Justice Statistics Center should be:

---

[19] See, for example, the *Wickersham Statistics Report,* pp. 17, 89. Professor Peter Lejins also indicates some of the reasons for not locating the Center within the Bureau of the Census in appendix C of President's Commission on Law Enforcement and Administration of Justice, *Task Force Report: Crime and Its Impact—An Assessment* (Washington: U.S. Government Printing Office, 1967).

☐ To insure the collection of adequate statistics from the various agencies of the criminal justice system, Federal, State, and local, including both those for which such statistics are now collected and those for which new series must be begun;

☐ To work for improvement in the accuracy, completeness, and usefulness in these agency statistics;

☐ To promote and assist in the development of adequate statistical systems at the State and local levels;

☐ To conduct surveys, censuses, and special studies in areas not covered by agency statistics or where some independent check of agency statistics is desirable;

☐ To evaluate and disseminate the statistics collected; and

☐ To investigate on a continuing or a periodic basis the need for various kinds of criminal statistics and establish an overall plan for their collection, analysis, and dissemination. This function would include the development where necessary of new statistical indicators and standards, designed to bring into better focus the various crime problems and the work of the various agencies of the law enforcement and criminal justice system.

In order to promote comprehensive planning for the system as a whole, the Center should be organized along functional lines rather than around the various agencies of the criminal justice system (police, courts, etc.). Thus, the Center might have four operating divisions:

1. An agency statistics division to collect agency statistics from other Federal agencies and from local and State agencies where the Center was the primary collection agent;
2. A technical assistance division to give aid to State and local systems;
3. A survey, planning, and analysis division to perform those functions;
4. A public dissemination division.

Inventory of Needed Data

Crime statistics provide operational information for the agencies which produce them, inform governmental officials and the public concerning crime, provide raw material for research, provide indicators of the social health of the society, and serve numerous other purposes.

No statistical system can hope to answer regularly all the questions which might legitimately be asked either about crime or about the criminal justice system. Some priorities must therefore be established as to the questions which are most important and the kinds of data needed to answer these questions.

Areas which are particularly important at the national level are those which bear on the public understanding of crime, especially as developed by the mass media; those which relate to crime problems, such as organized crime, which are clearly national in scope; and those which are necessary to make comparisons between various regions and localities. Research is another area which requires a broad statistical base. Much of the information necessary for research must of course come from special studies and compilations. Research of necessity, however, relies on regular statistical series for insights as to profitable areas for exploration, for data to compare time periods longer or geographic areas wider than those covered by any particular study and for many other purposes. Many present and past research efforts, particularly at the national level, have failed because of incomplete or faulty statistical resources.[20]

Studies of the Commission and others have identified many different kinds of data needs. The Commission has not, however, made a survey of present and potential users of data. This should be done before any final inventory of data needs is compiled. Such a survey should include the agencies of the criminal justice system, Federal, State, and local; legislators and other governmental officials; and nongovernmental users such as the press, scholars, and librarians, etc. Particular attention should be paid to the needs of government and nongovernment officials who are responsible for crime prevention and crime-prevention related programs. Respondents would be asked to indicate the items of information they regard as the most important and how often such items were needed.

Based upon the survey and the Center's own study, information requirements would be classified as to the frequency of need: (1) annually or more often, (2) every 3 years, (3) every 10 years (to be collected through decennial census), or (4) one-time collection or no fixed time. Information should also be classified as to whether it is already being collected or not and, if not, whether it could be obtained by modifying an existing program, by a sample survey, or by establishing a new, comprehensive statistical series. Because modern techniques often make it possible to secure greater accuracy and detail at lower cost through sampling than through universal collection, particular attention would be paid to information which could be obtained by sampling.

Data Concerning the Criminal Justice System

There are many data needs concerning the criminal justice system. Each of the agencies of the system is itself a vital institution in our society with its own functions, problems, and statistical needs. Data is needed to under-

---

[20] Statistical correlation, for example, of crime rates for cities or States with social characteristics which fail to take reporting changes into account inevitably have distortion in their findings. See Ronald H. Beattie, "Criminal Statistics in the United States—1960," *Journal of Criminal Law, Criminology and Police Science,* 51:49–65, May–June 1960.

stand its workload, know the kinds of people with whom it deals, evaluate how effectively it performs its functions and to describe fully its operations. For many of the criminal justice agencies, data is also needed about the institution itself, how many and what kind of people it employs, with what kind of training, what its budget is, and many other such items.

Beyond the need for data concerning the individual criminal justice agencies and their work, there is also an urgent need for information concerning the criminal justice system as a whole. The delay involved in the criminal justice process, for example, may look quite reasonable from the viewpoint of each separate agency but wholly unreasonable from the viewpoint of the individual person forced to run through the whole system. There are, in addition, various points in the system where similar functions are performed by different agencies, parole and probation, for example. Only through knowledge of the whole system can performance regarding these kinds of functions be evaluated.

Knowledge of the whole system is particularly important insofar as the offender is concerned. Because each step in the process is critical, each step in the process is like the link of a chain. If any one is unfair or weak, the whole chain is unfair or weak. It is therefore important to be able to trace his [the offender's] path through the whole system.

From the viewpoint of fairness or of the control of crime, the ultimate question is not whether a particular institution performed its function properly and well, but how the whole system performed. If the courts convict the innocent or the correctional institutions fail to reform the guilty, the efficiency and the courtesy of the police matter a great deal less.

Two overriding problems exist insofar as the collection of statistics . . . [on] the criminal justice system [is concerned]: (1) the lack of a common method of classification among the various criminal justice agencies and jurisdictions, and (2) the need for a satisfactory method of collection.

UNIFORM CLASSIFICATION

To be useful at all statistics must involve the counting of comparable units. Today, however, when a single individual commits several offenses, the police normally count the number of offenses, and the prison the individual committed to its care. The court count, however, depends largely upon whether the prosecutor decided to bring one case or several. In California the taking of valuables from a locked car is defined as burglary but in Virginia the offense is larceny.[21] Penalties for the offense are different as are the methods of prosecution and the philosophies and organization of the institutions which will be in charge of the offender.

With these kinds of widely varying situations, it is easy to see why the

[21] Compare California Penal Code Sec. 459 with Virginia Code Secs. 18.1–86 through 18.1–89.

development of uniform definitions and methods of recording has not proceeded further. The system used in police statistics, for example, was developed only after a detailed State-by-State study that took over 2 years to complete[22] and which after more than 30 years of operation requires continual monitoring by the FBI.

The development of a uniform classification system is essential, however, both for the system as a whole and for those components of the system for which no statistical collection is now being made. The development of uniform units of measurement which will allow a single offender to be followed through the whole system is particularly important.

During the course of development, attention will also need to be paid to the development of methods for presenting information concerning the whole criminal justice system in an integrated way. California now reports some information in a way that makes the path through the criminal justice system clear. . . . It is working on a model which will allow such reporting for its entire system.[23]

Developing a national model will be considerably harder than the development of models for individual States. Without it, however, it will be difficult to make the interstate comparisons which are needed so that each State may learn from the experience of others. The illustrative model in chapter 1 of the Commission's general report represents a good beginning,[24] and with the development of uniform classification systems would be helpful in creating a national model.

COLLECTION

Many of the problems related to collection would, as discussed earlier, be solved with the development of State statistical bureaus. A major objective of the Center should therefore be the promotion of State bureaus which can be responsible for adequate statistical programs within their jurisdictions.

This promotion could take the form of Federal financial assistance, technical assistance in establishing such a bureau or merely encouragement to do so. Similar promotion of local systems and programs for individual criminal justice agencies would have important benefits both for completeness of reporting and the quality of data. In connection with these efforts the Center should consider the development of a training program for

[22] See International Association of Chiefs of Police, Committee on Uniform Crime Reports, *Uniform Crime Reporting* (New York: J. J. Little and Ives Co., 1929).

[23] State of California, Bureau of Criminal Statistics, *Crime and Delinquency in California* (Sacramento: Bureau of Criminal Statistics, 1965), pp. 13, 31–32. The criminal career record system now being established by the New York State Identification and Intelligence System will, in addition to its operational usefulness, provide some capability for following individual offenders through the system.

[24] President's Commission on Law Enforcement and Administration of Justice, *The Challenge of Crime in a Free Society* (Washington: U.S. Government Printing Office, 1967), pp. 8–9 (hereinafter cited as *President's Commission, General Report*).

statistical personnel and should do what it can to encourage the development in the universities of academic courses in criminal statistics.

These long-range efforts will eventually be very important. In the meantime the Center will be faced with the difficult, practical problems of collection and monitoring. Not very much is known about how this can best be done, and development of a good system will require much work and experimentation.

Among the best of the ideas which warrant investigation is the development of model record forms which might be supplied to agencies and which agencies would find useful in their own operations and in statistical analysis of their experience and achievement. These forms could be designed for automatic scanning by modern electronic data processing equipment, thus facilitating more precise, speedy, and economical record keeping and accounting. The development of prompt and useful feedback information has proved in other statistical programs not only to be a powerful incentive to good reporting but also an important benefit of the whole statistical program.

Payment of small Federal subsidies has been suggested to help defray the costs of collection and reporting.[25] This has proved useful in some other Federal statistical programs.[26] Conditioning Federal assistance upon the submission, on a continuing basis, of adequate statistics to the Center is another idea worthy of investigation.

In addition to the problem of securing reports in the first instance from the many thousand independent agencies which make up the criminal justice system, reliable statistics depend in large part upon a careful system for auditing and checking reports to insure conformity to the uniform classification system.[27] Where State criminal statistical bureaus which have the authority and capacity to do this exist, the Center should rely upon them. The California Bureau of Criminal Statistics has been particularly successful in this kind of activity. To the extent that this burden falls on the Center, it should attempt to develop new techniques for monitoring. Sampling for quality should be a regular procedure along with the more familiar routine of checking for accuracy and looking into those cases where a discrepancy appears from the face of the report.[28]

[25] The Wickersham Commission recommended that collection agencies be paid a small sum for each report submitted rather than have the Federal government bear the larger cost of collecting the statistics itself (*Wickersham Statistics Report*, pp. 46, 52). Professor Lejins, *supra* note 19, appendix C, suggests adequate staff support and a system of matching funds to enable the various State agencies to participate in the national statistics program.

[26] *The Wickersham Statistics Report*, pp. 44–46, discusses the development of national mortality statistics.

[27] *President's Commission, General Report*, pp. 25–27. A field staff of some sort is essential if this function is to be performed properly.

[28] Sampling for quality control is used when the expense and time involved are too great to permit each item to be checked. A sample of the data received can be checked further for accuracy and some idea of the percent of error can be derived. The St. Louis

Providing full statistical information concerning each important aspect of the criminal justice system is one of the principal functions of the Center. It will require improvement of the existing collection programs and the beginning of wholly new collection programs for some criminal justice agencies.

PRESENT DATA COLLECTION PROGRAMS

(1) *Police Statistics.* The most important single source of information concerning crime at the national level, both as to the extent of crime and the characteristics of criminals, is . . . the national police statistics compiled by the FBI and published annually as "Crime in the United States, Uniform Crime Reports."[29] Begun in 1930 this series has a history of significant improvement over time. Particularly important improvements were made in 1958 following detailed study of the entire system by a special advisory panel.[30] Commission studies suggest a number of future improvements, many of them in directions in which the Bureau has already been moving.

From the beginning, the series has been very successful in securing a high degree of reporting for offenses known to the police for cities and, since 1958, for the country as a whole. This has been entirely through voluntary cooperation, since the FBI has no compulsory jurisdiction over the local and State agencies involved.

Voluntary cooperation has worked less well in the case of arrest statistics and other data. UCR arrest statistics are useful for the data they give as to what kinds of people commit different kinds of offenses and as to the relationship between the number of offenses committed and the number solved. These statistics are much less useful than they might be, however, because they are available for only part of the country.

Since demographic information is, except for decennial census years, normally available only for the country as a whole, it is not possible to calculate offense rates by characteristics of the offender, such as age, sex, race, and the like, without an estimated national total for arrests.[31]

Without such a national total it is also difficult to calculate accurately the trend of arrests from year to year.[32] Because the number of reporting departments and the departments which submit reports change from year to year, the only way that the trend of arrests can usually be measured is by

---

police department has developed an excellent system of quality control based on an audit by independent experts. See chapter 2, note 89 *supra.* For a general discussion of quality control methods and procedure, see Clifford W. Kennedy, *Quality Control Methods* (New York: Prentice-Hall, Inc., 1948); and Statistical Research Group, Columbia University, *Sampling Inspection* (New York: McGraw-Hill, 1948). See also Herman H. Fasteau, J. Jack Ingram, and Ruth H. Mills, "Study of the Reliability of Coding of Census Returns," *Proceedings of the Social Statistics Section,* American Statistical Association Annual Meeting, September 1962, pp. 104–111.

[29] Hereinafter cited as UCR.

[30] See UCR, 1958, Special Issue.

[31] Data are sometimes available in other years for some places but not on any systematic basis.

[32] See *supra* note 19, appendix D, "The Prediction of Crime from Demographic Variables: A Methodological Note."

comparing data from those departments reporting in both years concerned. Departments representing a population of 115 million reported in both 1964 and 1965. The departments reporting in both 1960 and 1965, however, totaled only 80 million in population.[33] The trend shown for comparable places is useful information but may not always be the same as the national trend.

The kind of information which is dependent upon estimated national totals for arrests is important to an understanding of crime, including such essential matters as the number and rate of arrests, the rate of juvenile arrests, the ratio of juvenile to total arrests, the ratio of arrests to offenses known to the police, and other critical facts. Increasing the number of

Table 1—1965 Uniform Crime Reports

	Number of reporting units	Estimated population (millions)
Offenses known to the police	8,000	178.3
Arrests, number and rate, by population groups	4,062	134.1
Arrests by age	4,062	134.1
By race	4,043	125.1
By sex	4,062	134.1
Arrest trends, 1964–65	3,355	115.0
Arrest trends, 1960–65	1,882	86.2
Offenses known and percent cleared by arrest	3,404	115.6
Offenses cleared by arrest of persons under 18 years of age	3,227	104.8
Disposition of persons formally charged	1,781	57.8
Police disposition of juvenile offenders taken into custody	2,877	95.1
Offenses known, cleared, persons arrested, charged and disposed of	1,657	56.6
Offenses analysis, trends 1964–65	646	75.4
Type and value of property stolen and recovered	646	75.4
Full-time police department employees	4,767	142.0

NOTE: The estimated 1965 population for the United States as a whole was 193,818,000.

units reporting or making them representative enough through sampling to allow calculation of total national estimates is therefore a very important action.[34]

Table 1 indicates the principal items of information now collected through the UCR and the extent of places reporting usable figures for each.

The type of information indicated in Table 1 is on the whole very good. It has been supplemented within recent years by a number of highly useful

[33] UCR, 1965, pp. 110–111. See chapter 2, note 67 *supra*.

[34] By far the easiest and cheapest way to obtain a total national estimate is through sampling. It is highly likely that the present extent of reporting is more than adequate for the creation of such a sample. Investigation of this possibility should be a matter of priority. Whether a sampling system is instituted or not, however, it is desirable that there be full reporting for as many places as possible. Much of the utility of arrest data lies in the ability to compare data from one place to another. The most sensible system may well be some mixture of sampling and full reporting such as a sample for the national total and full reporting for all cities over 100,000 population. This issue was considered by the UCR Consultant Committee, UCR, 1958, Special Issue, pp. 17–18, 39–40. The Committee recognized the value of sampling but recommended that an attempt be made to secure full coverage. Since that time coverage for arrest data generally has grown from 30 to 70 percent of the population, but it seems clear that anything like full coverage is at least some years away.

special reports covering individual crimes. Some improvements in coverage or presentation suggested by Commission studies are indicated below:

☐ That arrest data be collected and presented so that it may be cross-tabulated for age, sex, place, race, and type of crime. Under the present system offenders may be compared with the place and type of crime by either age, race, or sex but not by a combination of these.[35] Changes in reporting and presentation would allow the more detailed analysis to be made.

☐ That, as recommended in chapter 2 of the General Report,[36] the present index of reported crime be broken into two wholly separate parts, one for crimes against persons and one for crimes against property, and that consideration be given to the development of other indices.

☐ That the method of counting arrests be clarified. Present methods of counting arrests confuse to some degree (1) the number of criminal events, (2) the number of criminals, and (3) the frequency of arrest for a single offender. Particular problems are posed by cases involving multiple offenders and those in which a single offender has committed a number of offenses.

☐ That further study be given to developing a definition of suburban areas that does not overlap with other classifications in the presentation.[37]

☐ That further efforts be made by both the UCR and the Census Bureau to bring UCR and census classifications into accord with each other or that some easy method of translating one into the other be developed.[38]

☐ That the UCR undertake to publish either as a regular feature or by special supplement the revisions which it makes annually in many of its critical historical figures.[39]

☐ That the UCR indicate the number, kind, and percentage of reporting units each year which it must omit from the national trends.[40]

☐ That, in addition to the rate of offenses per 100,000 of the total population now published, the UCR regularly publish rates for specified types of offenders (juveniles, males, etc.) and that the difference between victim and offender rates be clearly labeled.[41]

☐ That the UCR publish each year some data ranking cities by the rate of crime for various individual crimes.[42] While there is some danger that such rankings would create overreaction in high crime

[35] See generally *supra* note 19, appendix D.
[36] See *President's Commission, General Report*, p. 31.
[37] See UCR, 1965, table 6, pp. 94–95, particularly note 1.
[38] Some of the classification problems are discussed in appendix D, *supra* note 35. Other such problems also exist.
[39] *Ibid.* See also *supra* note 19, appendix E.
[40] *Ibid.*
[41] See "New Ways of Looking at Crime," discussed below.
[42] Rankings might be published both for cities and Standard Metropolitan Statistical Areas. For most purposes, metropolitan areas are a preferable statistical unit. The rate of crime, however, is often reported more consistently within a single police jurisdiction.

areas, such rankings would almost certainly create useful additional pressures on high crime areas to reduce the amount of crime, encourage research into the causes of differences in crime rates among cities, and promote the development of more sophisticated measures of comparing crime rates among cities, and promote the development of more sophisticated measures of comparing crime among areas. Because it would also create danger of statistical manipulation by high crime rate cities, it would increase the need for rigorous monitoring of the statistics reported. Readers should continue to be cautioned, as now, about the many factors involved in crime rate variations, particularly about the fallacy of attributing all such differences to the police.

(2) *Prison Statistics.* These are collected by the Bureau of Prisons of the Department of Justice and published annually as the *National Prisoner Statistics*. This series was begun in 1926 and was handled by the Bureau of the Census until 1950.[43] It is a voluntary reporting program which has achieved complete coverage. Information covered now includes the number of persons handled by State and Federal prisons and correctional institutions but does not include information concerning jail or other short-term penal institutions. While this is an excellent series in many respects, it could be improved by an increase in staff and funds. Several types of information, such as prison personnel and types of crimes committed by the inmates, have had to be dropped from the series because their inclusion caused time delays in the publication of the series.

Coverage should be extended to provide more complete information on the prior history of the inmates, their sentences and their crimes, the correctional programs in different correctional institutions, the length of actual incarceration versus the length of sentence, any crimes or major disciplinary actions taken with respect to an inmate while incarcerated, transfers from one security level institution to another, and termination of custody either by completion of the sentence or by parole.

One major problem with the present series is that it now includes much data that are not comparable. Because some States send misdemeanants to prison while others send only felons, the types of prisoners which the series include are different from State to State. Further work is obviously needed to establish a better method of uniform classification. The Children's Bureau of the Department of Health, Education, and Welfare publishes annual statistics on juvenile institutions and from time to time publishes special reports.[44] A new classification system needs to be developed for these statistics also.

[43] From 1926 to 1947, the series was known as *Prisoners in State and Federal Prisons and Reformatories*.

[44] Department of Health, Education, and Welfare, Children's Bureau, *Institutions Serving Delinquent Children* (Children's Bureau Statistical Series, Washington: U.S. Government Printing Office, annual publication); see also the Children's Bureau, *Personnel and Personnel Practices in Public Institutions for Delinquent Children, 1958–1965* (Washington: U.S. Government Printing Office, 1966).

(3) *Juvenile Court Statistics.* These are collected by the Children's Bureau and published as *Juvenile Court Statistics.* Begun in 1940 this series covers the number of delinquency cases, of dependency and neglect cases, and of special proceedings. Delinquency cases are classified by sex and place of occurrence and to some degree by reason for referral, manner of handling, and disposition. Some traffic offense information is also included. The series is based in part on a national sample of juvenile courts (494 out of an estimated 2,700 having jurisdiction in juvenile matters in 1965[45]) and in part on special reports from selected localities. Because many cases of delinquency are not referred to court, this series cannot properly be used as an index of delinquency.

While the information which is included within these reports is useful in a very modest way, the reports lack the detail and completeness required for the serious study of delinquency. There are no data at all regarding the age or race of the delinquents. Most of the detailed information in the report does not come from the national sample, apparently because it is not maintained by the reporting units. Of the country's 30 largest cities asked to submit data on reasons for referral and disposition, only 19 responded in usable form in 1965. Missing were such cities as New York, Chicago, and Philadelphia. The maximum age limits of the courts which did report varied considerably, from 16-year-olds to 21-year-olds.[46]

Needs include (1) a better system of classification, (2) an expansion of information conveyed, (3) an increase in the percentage of reporting from solicited units, and (4) more developed reporting on the part of many local units. A great deal more information with regard to the courts themselves is also needed, such as the number and background of judges (for example, half now lack college degrees), and the extent to which the courts have access to psychiatric help.

NEW DATA COLLECTION PROGRAMS

While decisions concerning format, coverage, and frequency of collection should await completion of the inventory, Commission studies indicate that, at a minimum, some type of program should be started in the following areas:

(1) *Pretrial Statistics.* While the work of the courts is subjected to constant scrutiny, the decisions of the charging authorities are almost never evaluated except in ad hoc cases of great notoriety. Yet the number of persons arrested but released without being charged by the police, or charged by the police but released by the prosecuting authorities, exceeds

---

[45] Department of Health, Education, and Welfare, Children's Bureau, *Juvenile Court Statistics—1965,* Children's Bureau Statistical Series, No. 85. (Washington: U.S. Government Printing Office, 1966), p. 7; and information supplied by the Children's Bureau.

[46] *Ibid.*

by far the number of persons who are released by the courts.[47] These decisions may have enormous effects on crime in the community. Without statistical information, however, it is impossible even for the authorities to know what the effects are. And without such information, the community is often in the dark even about such matters as what the policies of the authorities are.

Statistics concerning the pretrial aspects of the criminal justice system are therefore a significant gap in our present knowledge which should be filled by the development of a more complete statistical program. These statistics should cover: (1) the work of prosecuting attorneys, (2) grand juries, (3) bail, and (4) detention. Where the police are the charging authority, this aspect of their work should also be included. Few of these statistics are now maintained even at the local level. The chief problems in attempting their collection are the number of different agencies involved—the prosecutor, the grand jury, the courts, and the jails; and the fact that these institutions are generally very small units. Data from prosecuting attorneys are particularly important.

(2) *Court Statistics.* The criminal court is a central institution to our system of justice, for it is charged with determining whether there was an offense, what kind of an offense, and whether the person charged was the offender. There are today, however, no national criminal judicial statistics, the series begun in 1932 by the Bureau of the Census having been discontinued in 1946.[48] Such statistics are essential for any real understanding as to how well the criminal court system is working. In addition to pretrial information, they should cover the number of offenders standing trial, the charges, the plea, the type of trial, the type of representation and disposition. They should also cover the sentencing process, including the use of presentence reports. A special section should be devoted to the delay involved in the judicial process from time of arrest. The statistics should cover misdemeanors as well as felonies.

(3) *Probation Statistics.* In modern correctional systems the best risks among offenders are often given suspended sentences or placed on probation rather than sent to prison. There is a continuing need to know how well this type of treatment protects the public and rehabilitates the criminal, as opposed to other types of treatment. Information needed includes the

---

[47] See, e.g., President's Commission on Law Enforcement and Administration of Justice, *Task Force Report: The Courts* (Washington: U.S. Government Printing Office, 1967), p. 132, table 4; State of California, Bureau of Criminal Statistics, *Crime and Delinquency in California* (Sacramento: Bureau of Criminal Statistics, 1965), pp. 24 (table 1–6), 53–55.

[48] See Harry Alpert, "National Series on State Judicial Criminal Statistics Discontinued," *Journal of Criminal Law and Criminology*, 34:181–188, July–August 1948. The European countries have long published extensive court statistics. See, e.g., Home Office, *Criminal Statistics, England and Wales, 1965* (London: Her Majesty's Stationery Office, 1966).

number of offenders placed on probation; their characteristics, including their prior criminal history; the time or length of probation; the conditions and the extent of supervision; the number of revocations because of the commission of other crimes; and the number of violations of other probation conditions. While collecting this type of information may be difficult because many probation officers are attached to individual courts, it is, nevertheless, very important. Some beginnings toward a uniform reporting system are already being made.[49]

(4) *Jail Statistics.* Jail often plays an important role in the beginning of a serious criminal career. Many more people are exposed to it than to any other type of penal or correctional institution. Yet, jails are the most antiquated and the least rationally operated part of the entire system. Except for the limited amount of information provided by the census,[50] virtually no information regarding jails is collected at either the local, State, or national level. Information which is needed includes the number of prisoners, the sentences under which they serve, and the type of treatment they receive. If modernization is to take place, information is also needed about the institutions themselves, the facilities they provide and the kinds of people who staff them.

Jail statistics are also needed as a part of pretrial statistics because persons awaiting trial are sometimes held there, too often in contact with convicted offenders. The statistics should indicate whether those being detained for trial are held separately or not.[51]

(5) *Parole Statistics.* Parole is a critical stage in the correctional process. Nationally, the number of persons on parole during 1965 was roughly 173,000.[52] Good decisions regarding who should be paroled, the effectiveness of the parole system, the workload involved and other important questions depend upon adequate statistical information. Studies show that even within a single system previous experience factors rapidly become obsolete and that there is therefore a need for continuous information feedback.[53] One of the greatest problems in effective parole decisionmaking has been the lack of reliable statistical information. To remedy this defect the National Parole Institutes conducted a feasibility study of a uniform parole reporting system for the President's Committee on Juvenile Delinquency and Youth Crime under a grant from the Office of Juvenile Delin-

---

[49] See Peter Lejins, *supra* note 19, appendix C.

[50] U.S. Census of Population: 1960, *Inmates of Institutions* (PC(2)–8A). This gives social and economic data for inmates by area and type of institution. See also Louis Robinson, *History and Organization of Criminal Statistics in the United States* (Boston: Houghton Mifflin, 1911), pp. 12–37.

[51] See *President's Commission, General Report*, pp. 178–179.

[52] National Council on Crime and Delinquency, *Correction in the United States,* President's Commission on Law Enforcement and Administration of Justice, *Task Force Report: Corrections* (Washington: U.S. Government Printing Office, 1967), appendix A, p. 60.

[53] Peters Lejins, *supra* note 19, appendix C.

quency and Youth Development. This study demonstrated that a uniform system is both feasible and desirable. Thirty-three States are now participating on a voluntary basis in further development under a 3-year grant from the National Institutes of Mental Health.[54] Emphasis is being placed on formulation of procedures, standardization of definitions, and collection of cohort statistics.

(6) *Juvenile Statistics.* Whether criminal statistics concerning juveniles should be handled separately as juvenile statistics or jointly with adult statistics as a part of the overall work of the criminal justice agency concerned is not an easy problem. The UCR deals with both adult and juvenile statistics. *Juvenile Court Statistics,* on the other hand, deals only with juvenile statistics. Perhaps the best answer is to cover juveniles both ways. Statistics relating strictly to juveniles could then be processed by the Department of Health, Education, and Welfare, which under the proposed "Juvenile Delinquency Prevention Act of 1967" would be given authority "to collect, evaluate, publish, and disseminate information and materials relating * * * to prevention or treatment of delinquency or provision of rehabilitative services for delinquent youths."[55]

Other statistics would be handled by the Center or some other criminal justice agency. The Center would exercise its general coordinating authority to prevent duplication and work out a reporting scheme under which one report from State and local units would suffice for both juvenile and general statistical needs. The Center should have the same general powers with regard to juvenile delinquency statistics as with other criminal justice statistics.

Developing adequate statistics concerning juveniles poses many special problems. Many acts which are considered delinquent are not criminal. Many of the actions of the police, courts, and corrections institutions are either unofficial or indeterminate, and agencies differ widely from one jurisdiction to the next in the extent to which this is so. The UCR, for example, shows that the percentage of juveniles handled within the department and released by the police varies from 29.6 to 56.3 percent.[56] Much of the information needed is kept highly confidential. If solutions are to be found for the delinquency problem, however, ways must be found to overcome these difficulties. With proper planning and effort, it should be possible to develop methods that record the necessary information but do not interfere with the degree of flexibility which is desirable in the system.

In addition to data concerning the amount and trend of delinquency, much more data is needed regarding the characteristics of delinquents, the types of treatment offered, and the results of treatment.

---

[54] *Ibid.;* also information supplied by the National Parole Institute, May 1967.
[55] S. 1248, 90th Cong., 1st Sess., March 10, 1967, sec. 203.
[56] UCR, 1965, p. 104.

(7) *Federal Statistics.* What Federal statistics there are about crime are today scattered throughout numerous publications. Some of these are informative, but for the most part they cannot be compared either with each other or with similar data from the States. The chief publications are: *Annual Report of the Attorney General,* which covers prosecutions by the Department of Justice; *Administrative Office of the United States Courts: Annual Report of the Director,* which covers the work of the courts and probation; *National Prisoner Statistics,* which covers the Federal as well as the State prisons; and *Traffic in Opium and Other Dangerous Drugs,* which covers the work of the Bureau of Narcotics. The UCR covers Federal offenses only to the extent that they are reported by local police.

There should be a consolidated report covering all Federal criminal statistics. It should cover all facets of crime and the criminal justice system under Federal law, including data that are now reported in some form and those which are not reported at all. In particular it should cover the work of the Federal agencies with police powers [57] and the military criminal justice system. It should be descriptive enough so that it is possible to tell what part of the crime problem is being handled by the States and what part by the Federal Government. Several excellent studies indicate generally what needs to be done and how it might be accomplished.[58]

New Kinds of Statistics

Statistics derived from the criminal justice system are necessary and important in dealing with crime. Modern statistical methods are not limited, however, to collecting data from official agencies. New methods of collection, new types of indicators of crime and of the effectiveness of the criminal justice agencies, new ways of looking at crime, special statistical studies, and in general a great deal more innovation in statistical efforts are all required if headway is to be made against crime. The Center should be the leader in these innovations.

VICTIM SURVEYS

There is much important information about crime that either cannot be obtained from the agencies of law enforcement or criminal justice at all or that can only be obtained imperfectly. In terms of the system as a whole two of the most basic questions are how much of the various crimes there is and whether these amounts of crimes are going up or down. At various

---

[57] *The Wickersham Statistics Report,* pp. 158–165, reviews the work of some of the Federal agencies with police authority.

[58] *Wickersham Statistics Report,* pp. 153–205; Committee on Government Statistics and Information Services, *Federal Collection of Criminal Statistics,* prepared in 1934 for the Attorney General; and Harry Shulman, *The Reporting of Criminal Statistics in the United States,* a 1964 study for the Bureau of the Budget.

times attempts have been made to answer these questions with court data, such as prosecutions or convictions, or with arrest statistics. At the present time, the best measure is considered to be statistics of offenses known to the police.[59] It has always been known that there was a great deal of unreported crime, however, and given the changing nature of police forces and community expectations, there is every reason to believe that the ratio of reported to unreported crime, at least for some offenses, has been changing.[60]

To see if some new technique might be developed which would assist in answering these questions more satisfactorily, the Commission . . . sponsored the first wide-scale survey of crime victimization ever undertaken. While it is clear that more work needs to be done to develop the methodology of this kind of survey, the results were promising enough for the Commission to encourage its further use.[61] The Center is the logical agency to develop this methodology further and to be responsible for new surveys at the national level.

In addition to improving the results, further development should also reduce survey costs. While there is probably no need for an annual survey nationally, such surveys should be conducted often enough to provide data against which other indicators might be compared. Since only one national survey has been conducted to date, it is particularly important that another be undertaken within the next few years for this purpose.

Surveys can also be useful in individual localities when some independent check of agency statistics is desirable. They should be particularly helpful in evaluating new crime prevention or control programs. New police patrol techniques, for example, often uncover crime that has previously gone unreported, making evaluation in terms of crimes known to the police difficult. A victim survey in the area before the new technique was introduced and after it had had a trial run would provide the police with a much more accurate way of testing effectiveness. Surveys could be used similarly in testing delinquency prevention and other broad community-type prevention programs.

RECIDIVISM DATA

About 380,000 persons who have been convicted of felony crimes are released into society each year as a result of probation, parole, or termination of sentence.[62] More than $1 billion is spent annually in operating institutions which have as one of their primary purposes the rehabilitation of those who are released so that they will not commit further crimes

---

[59] See Thorsten Sellin, "The Basis of a Crime Index," *Journal of Criminal Law and Criminology,* 22:335–356, September–October 1931.

[60] See *President's Commission, General Report,* p. 25.

[61] *Id.* at pp. 20–22.

[62] Bureau of Prisons, *National Prisoner Statistics, 1965,* p. 12. President's Commission on Law Enforcement and Administration of Justice, *Task Force Report: Corrections* (Washington: U.S. Government Printing Office, 1967), p. 174.

against society. Present statistical systems, however, are incapable of indicating how well the system works. There is no way of knowing, for example, how many of those offenders released into society in 1960 have since been convicted for new crimes. One result of this is that if an institution today developed a new and dramatically successful rehabilitation technique, it would have a hard time showing that its record was any better than that of any other institution.

There is some information concerning the incidence of recidivism within single States. This information is not worth a great deal, however, because offenders are so mobile. More than 45 percent of the 130,000 offenders contained in a special FBI 3-year study of Careers in Crime had arrests in two States and nearly half of these had arrests in three States or more.[63] This means that anything like comprehensive data concerning post-release criminal violations can be collected only at the national level. Although the nature of the sample involved raises real questions as to the meaning of the data collected, the FBI study encompasses a far larger sample of offenders than any previous data concerning recidivism and clearly indicates the usefulness of such collection for a properly drawn sample of offenders. It also indicates the need for the collection process to be continuous and maintained over a substantial period of time.

The cost of securing adequate data on recidivism under present methods of data storage and retrieval is extremely high. The index (directory) of offenders to be maintained at the national level, recommended by the Commisson and discussed in its Science and Technology Task Force Report,[64] however, offers the first real opportunity for development of adequate data on recidivism, particularly information that is based on new convictions rather than on arrest data. Because this directory will be computerized, the kind of information needed to keep track of recidivism can be obtained without prohibitive cost. With the directory in operation sampling could be much more useful than at present and some data could perhaps be maintained for the whole correctional system. Information could be analyzed by the institution or correctional policy concerned, and the Center would be able to compile and analyze statistics on all aspects of the life careers of offenders. Judges would be able to see how well their decisions on probation had worked out. Correctional systems would be better able to see the result of parole.

The Center should probably not be responsible for maintaining the directory but should have full access to its information, with the exception of names, for statistical purposes. As the directory becomes machine-coded, the Center should be directly linked to its terminal. The Center should also have full access to the registries maintained at the State levels in order to do

---

[63] UCR, 1965, pp. 27–28.

[64] *Supra* note 19, chapter 6, pp. 68–79. See also *President's Commission, General Report,* pp. 266–269.

in-depth analysis for particular types of recidivism problems. Adequate protection for privacy should, of course, be maintained.

How an institution performs depends in part on the kind of offender it receives in the first place. In turn, whether an institution receives good, medium, or bad risks depends largely on how the agencies earlier in the criminal justice system chain handled their work. If the court, for example, places the best risks on probation, the prison receives only the bad risks.

Evaluation of any one agency therefore requires that its record be compared to the extent possible either with other agencies handling the same type of population or by some standardized part of its population. Parole effectiveness, for example, might be tested by comparing the recidivism rates of persons discharged, those released conditionally, and those paroled, matched by duration of imprisonment prior to release, offense, prior criminal record, and perhaps age among other possible variables. Effectiveness of the whole system would be measured by the cumulative results of all agencies.[65]

NEW INDICATORS FOR CRIME PROBLEMS

Many crime problems do not now receive the kinds of attention they should because no regular statistical information is available about them. Identifying these problems and developing indicators that will focus attention on them in the right way should be one of the Center's most important functions.[66] The importance of having good indicators goes well beyond that of keeping users adequately informed. The existence of a meaningful indicator often affects the internal incentive structure of the various organizations concerned with the problem. If the indicator is present, there is a far

[65] For example, "if area A with 1,000 felons in a given period granted probation to only 100 and sent 900 to prison, subsequent felony convictions might be incurred by only 10 percent of its probationers and 30 percent of its prisoners, for a total of 280 recidivists. If area B, also with 1,000 felons, granted probation to 700 and sent 300 to prison, it might find subsequent felony convictions for 20 percent of its probationers and 40 percent of its prisoners, but these would comprise only 260 recidivists, less than the total in area A. Thus, area B, with higher failure rates on both probation and parole, would actually have more effective crime control from its correctional program than area A (and, incidentally, at much less cost, since probation costs only about one-tenth the cost of imprisonment)." Daniel Glaser, "National Goals and Indicators for the Reduction of Crime and Delinquents," *Annals of the American Academy of Political and Social Science,* May 1967. A comprehensive plan for compiling statistics on recidivism, proposed by the same author in 1957, is described by Daniel Glaser, "Released Offender Statistics: A Proposal for a National Program," *American Journal of Correction,* 19:15–25, 1957.

[66] The need for adequate indicators and the problem of insuring that indicators in use relate to current rather than bygone problems are discussed in Albert D. Biderman, "Social Indicators and Goals," in Raymond A. Bauer, ed., *Social Indicators* (Cambridge, Mass.: M.I.T. Press, 1966), pp. 68–153, particularly at pp. 79–112. A number of measures of effectiveness in the correctional area are discussed in Daniel Glaser, *The Effectiveness of a Prison and Parole System* (Indianapolis: Bobbs-Merrill, 1964). See particularly the discussion of prediction and "base expectancy" tables in evaluating various correctional alternatives (pp. 289–310).

greater likelihood that performance will be judged by the indicator and therefore that something will be done about the problem.

Organized Crime

Organized crime thrives on invisibility. One reason that so widespread and insidious an evil has been able to lurk so often beneath the level of national concern has been the lack of a reliable indicator as to its magnitude or character. No one knows whether it is getting bigger or smaller, employing fewer or more criminals or corrupting more or less officials. Development of a reliable statistical measure would in itself be an important step in bringing it under control.

Indicators are needed at both the national and local levels. Neither arrest nor any other police statistics can fulfill this function. Arrest statistics are now collected for some offenses related to organized crime, but they are among the least reliably reported of all police statistics and not at all indicative of the magnitude of the problem. They make no distinctions between the bookie or the bettor, the prostitute or the customer, etc. They are better indicators of police activity than of crime.

Some indicators such as the number of gang murders or the number of syndicate families would be useful and should be regularly published but are too general or too specialized to answer the larger questions about organized crime. Other indicators such as the number of officials corrupted or the total number of persons involved in the syndicate would go a long way toward answering these questions but are impossible to obtain.

The most promising indicator in terms of both usefulness and availability is the gross amount of profit that the syndicate derives from gambling, loan sharking, narcotics, and its other illegal activities. This information cannot be estimated from data available to the police or prosecutors. It should be possible to obtain, however, through use of surveys. The Commission attempted through its national survey of households to determine the amount of illegal gambling that goes on. While this proved unsuccessful, showing far less gambling than independent and more reliable indicators suggested,[67] there was nothing in the results to indicate that a better designed survey would not be successful. Such a survey should cover not only gambling, but also loan sharking, narcotics, prostitution, extortion, and other syndicate activities. To be successful it will probably have to offer strict anonymity, particularly for those activities which are crimes for the purchaser as well as the seller.

Given the importance of the problem and the difficulty of obtaining information through other means, development of an effective survey method and institution of a regular series concerning the incidence of organized crime should be a priority matter for the Center.

---

[67] See chapter 3, note 111 *supra*.

"Professional" or Habitual Criminals

In virtually every large community and many smaller ones there is a group of hardened, habitual, or "professional" criminals. Commission and other studies show that these criminals commit a disproportionate part of all offenses but that they rarely get caught.[68] At present, however, there is no indicator either for the community or for law enforcement as to how well this group of criminals is being controlled. Such an indicator is required and could be developed by the Center. Such an indicator would serve two very necessary functions: (1) it would indicate to law enforcement and the public just how important this problem is, and (2) it would serve as a powerful incentive to find means for control. Development of such a measure requires, among other things, a method of identifying those crimes which are committed by habitual criminals and those offenders who are professional criminals.

Street Crime

No problem is more critical or needful of police and community attention than that of crime in the streets. Yet there is no regular indicator, either at the national or the local level, as to what the incidence of street crime is. Even the most sophisticated police departments do not regularly use this kind of statistic as an internal control figure. Street crime may need to be broken down even further to be as sensitive an indicator as is called for. Indicators should not mix apples and oranges. The high proportion of the Index crimes against the person which take place between relatives and acquaintances are largely different in their causes and in the controls which have any effect from the kind of violent street crime that is committed by robbers and other strangers.

Police Effectiveness

The most commonly used measure of police effectiveness is that of the clearance rate—that is, the number of offenses that can be accounted for by the arrest and charging of a suspected offender.[69] For some purposes this is a satisfactory indicator of effectiveness. There is an urgent need, however, for the development of more sophisticated indicators. A simple clearance rate can place a premium on catching the petty offender who can be readily caught while letting the hardened offender get away. The detective who is

[68] See generally chapter 7, "Professional Crime."

[69] Federal Bureau of Investigation, *Uniform Crime Reporting Handbook* (February 1965), p. 48. See generally Bruce Smith, *Police Systems in the United States* (2d, ed., New York: Harper & Bros., 1960), pp. 38–39. The present system of reporting clearances would be improved if the published clearance rates indicated the number of offenders connected with the offenses reported as cleared. (More than one offense may be cleared by the arrest of a single offender, and the arrest of several offenders may clear only one offense.)

expected to maintain a satisfactory record of solutions can hardly be blamed for spending the bulk of his time trying to solve the five little cases instead of the one big one. While clearly wrong, it is also understandable why the police may sometimes be willing to record the shoplifting case referred by the department store when the offender has already been caught, but not the petty larceny where there is never any hope of catching the thief.

New indicators are also needed for a variety of other problems, such as white-collar crime, police-community relations, and fraud.

NEW WAYS OF LOOKING AT CRIME

The Center could also help to clarify the various ways of looking at the crime problem. Traditionally crime has been measured either in terms of the number of crimes (volume) or the number of crimes in relation to population (rate). Both of these ways of looking at crime are valid for certain purposes. For other purposes other ways of measuring crime are required. The search for a single index to answer all questions about crime has been a blind alley. There is no such thing.

The volume of offenses is important to the police and other agencies as a measure of their workload and the resources needed to cope with the problem. The rate of offenses per 100,000 population is a rough measure of the risk of victimization for the population as a whole. Other rates of victimization could and should be calculated for parts of the population which run specific risks: rape victimization rates for females, robbery rates for liquor stores, etc.[70]

The question of whether the population or various parts of it are becoming more crime-prone can only be measured by a wholly different kind of rate. For example, the number of crimes committed by 18-year-olds per 100,000 18-year-olds (age-specific rate) would give a general measure of the crime-proneness of that age group. Similar rates can be calculated for various other attributes of the population, such as sex, race, place of residence, or income. These rates are particularly important but in most instances cannot now be calculated on a national basis because the necessary arrest data are not available.[71]

Measures of volume, victimization risk, and crime-proneness are all useful. Each serves a different purpose. Each poses its own particular kinds of problems and possible misuses. The amount of police work may go up

[70] Albert J. Reiss, Jr., *Studies in Crime and Law Enforcement in Major Metropolitan Areas* (Field Surveys III, vol. 1, sec. 1, President's Commission on Law Enforcement and Administration of Justice, Washington: U.S. Government Printing Office, 1967), pp. 1–17.

[71] Even with arrest data available, calculation of crime-proneness rates depends upon the unproven assumption that the characteristics of those who escape arrest are the same as those who are arrested. In the case of offenses like burglary in which the clearance rate is below 30 percent, this is a very significant assumption.

whether the risk of victimization or the trait-specific rates do or not. If the relationships between these measures are not made clear, however, people will conclude that the risk of victimization and the crime-proneness of the population are increasing too.

Other measures may also occasionally be useful. When rates are calculated for more than one type of crime, for instance, the resulting rate does not usually take into account the fact that some crimes are more serious than others. Thus, one aggravated assault and one murder constitute two "crimes against the person." To remedy this obvious difference in the degree of severity of various crimes, Professors Sellin and Wolfgang have developed an index of seriousness.[72]

Other measures are usually stated as a ratio between the number of criminal events taking place and the number of units exposed to the risk of crime. One measure of crime in terms of the opportunity for crime, for example, is the ratio between the number of burglaries and the number of buildings in the area.

SPECIAL STUDIES

The Center would also be charged with conducting special statistical studies either through survey techniques, as add-ons to existing collection programs (as the FBI and the Bureau of Prisons have done) or in other ways. The economic costs of crime is one area in particular where the Center could be useful in this way. Special studies could also be helpful in examining the underlying reasons behind differences in the reporting of crime such as the degree to which one community will report crimes that another will not, and the differences in ways that different criminal justice agencies, particularly the police, undertake their work.[73] They might also examine possible new sources of information such as selective service registration questions which have been used successfully in at least one other country to obtain information concerning the criminal histories of whole groups of persons of the same age.[74]

Considering the widespread losses that private businesses and institutions suffer from crime and the large amounts of money they expend to protect themselves from crime, it is surprising that information about business crime is no more available than it is. Trade associations, in-house protective services, and commercial security firms have only scratched the surface of

[72] Thorsten Sellin and Marvin E. Wolfgang, *The Management of Delinquency* (New York: John Wiley & Sons, 1964), particularly appendix F, pp. 401–412. Attitude studies to examine community norms regarding the seriousness of various types of acts defined as crimes might provide helpful guidance to legislators, police officials, and judges who must sentence offenders.

[73] See Stanton Wheeler, "Criminal Statistics: A Reformulation of the Problem," *Journal of Criminal Law, Criminology and Police Science,* 1967.

[74] Nils Christie, *et al.,* "A Study of Self-Reported Crime," in Karl O. Christiansen, ed., *Scandinavian Studies in Criminology* (Oslo: Scandinavian University Books, 1965), pp. 86–116.

what could be done to produce useful statistical information. Some information has never been collected at all, and that information which has been collected is too seldom readily accessible. In addition to special studies in the areas of greatest need, the Center should undertake to promote the further development of private statistical services on crime problems.

Another area of need concerns the design of law enforcement information systems and the assessment of their effectiveness. Studies of stolen property and autos recovered and wanted persons arrested, broken down to indicate whether the recovery or the arrest took place in the originating jurisdiction, the State in which the originating jurisdiction is located, or some other State, would be particularly helpful.

Research would not be a primary activity of the Center, at least initially, other than necessary research into statistical techniques. The Center would, however, maintain close ties with any criminal research institutes founded with Federal funds.[75] No hard and fast line would be drawn between the functions of the Center and any such institutes, but every effort would be made on the part of both institutions to insure that each did not duplicate the work of the other. The general line of division for the Center would be that of conducting surveys, censuses, and statistical analyses. The research institute's primary purpose would be to do more basic research, but it would be free to conduct surveys, censuses, etc. when its purposes so required, especially in areas where government sponsorship might raise problems.

Technical Assistance

Perhaps the most important use of criminal statistics is that made by the agencies of criminal justice to improve their own operations, to employ their resources better, to locate and catch criminals, to deter criminal activity, to make optimum decisions regarding sentencing, treatment, and release of prisoners, etc. These decisions are basically made at the local level, and the kinds of statistics required are basically local statistics.[76]

A National Criminal Justice Statistics Center could serve as a resource for the strengthening of these State and local systems. In addition to the

[75] *President's Commission, General Report,* pp. 273–277.

[76] "Crime patterns in any area in almost any city are relatively constant month after month and year after year.

"If you took a map of Chicago, for instance, and spotted on it all the armed robberies that occurred between 9 P.M. and 1 A.M. in the year 1960, and then did the same for 1961, you would find the patterns identical. That would also be true of assaults, rape, burglaries—any kind of crime you'd like to name—even traffic accidents.

"Then, if your records are good enough—and we have them here now—you can determine where crime is going to be committed, and when it's going to be committed— not only the hour of the day, but the day of the week. So with the knowledge, you can place policemen where the criminal is most likely to be." ("What to Do About Crime in the Big Cities," interview with Orlando W. Wilson, Chicago's Police Superintendent, *U.S. News and World Report,* Mar. 12, 1962, p. 85.)

benefits to the national collection system already discussed, such a program could have a very powerful effect on crime prevention and control at the local level. Local police forces not only require the kind of assistance which the FBI has long provided for the development of strong central complaint systems but also require assistance in developing statistical programs for operational use.[77] Some few cities such as Chicago, St. Louis, and Los Angeles have already developed detailed information and statistical programs which are computerized and capable of giving up-to-date analyses of crime fluctuations throughout the city and during different periods of time. St. Louis has been experimenting with a computerized crime map that is capable of pinpointing the densities of various kinds of crimes. These developments are by and large relatively recent, however, and many departments lag far behind this practice.[78] Moreover, as technology develops, most departments, and particularly the smaller ones, will lack the knowledge and expertise to know what has proved useful elsewhere.

State and local statistics are also necessary for planning at the State and local levels. Analysis of the situation, the establishment of priorities, and many other facets of the planning process all require considerable statistical information. Adequate evaluation likewise requires reliable statistics. Providing for this data should be part of every planning process. This may require, in addition to other things, a survey of crime victimization at the outset of the planning period to determine the relationship between reported and unreported crime. Such surveys should be eligible for funding under the Federal program and may need to be repeated later as one measure of progress under the plan.

Dissemination

No great purpose is served by the collection of statistics unless they are disseminated and used. Publication of regular statistical series and special studies is the beginning of a good dissemination program. It will never be possible, however, to publish all the statistical information available in all the various ways that it could be useful to different types of users. The Center should therefore be equipped to provide a great deal of additional information free of charge and to perform on a fee basis special tabulating, analysis, computer runs, and other similar services.

The lack of this kind of service is one of the greatest defects of the present system. This kind of service would be particularly useful to State and local governments, academic and other nonprofit users, and business users. Such services should be easily procured and their availability widely

[77] *President's Commission, General Report,* pp. 25–26; Federal Bureau of Investigation, *Uniform Crime Reporting Handbook* (1965), pp. 1–3.

[78] *President's Commission, General Report; Task Force Report: Science and Technology,* chapter 6 and appendix F, pp. 266–269.

known. The Center should make a particular point of developing external working relationships with the agencies making up the criminal justice system and the academic community.

Future Data Needs

While it should be possible to establish the data needs of the present, it is very difficult to establish those of the future. As society changes, as new technology and new ideas take hold, the problems of law enforcement and the criminal justice system change too. New problems require new kinds of information. Keeping abreast of changing requirements should be one of the major on-going functions of the Center. This will require periodic user surveys, the use of special studies, the development of new indicators for new crime problems, and the development of better methods of presentation.

Beginning Center Operations

Aside from organizational questions the most immediate tasks facing the Center at the outset would seem to be: (1) completion of the user survey and development of the inventory of needed information, (2) setting in motion the process to develop the uniform system of classification upon which meaningful statistics for many criminal justice agencies and the system as a whole depend, and (3) working with existing collection agencies to make immediate improvements in existing series.

Some such series of priorities is necessary because the Center will not be able to get all its functions under way at once. The user survey and the inventory of needed information are critical items around which much of the remainder of the program must be built. The sooner they can be completed, the sooner other plans can become final. An early attack on the uniform classification problem is needed because it is apt to be a lengthy process and much of the system depends upon it. Some early work on existing collection systems is also warranted because of the immediately valuable results that can be attained for relatively little input.

These tasks and others which the Center must perform necessarily overlap each other to some extent. They should not and cannot be kept wholly separate. Decisions as to what new statistical series, if any, for the criminal justice system should be begun will necessarily depend in part upon the results of the user survey and the inventory, in part on what common classifications can be reached and in part on other factors. Completion of 'the classification process, however, will be difficult until some decision is made as to which series will be undertaken and which collection system will be responsible for items of information that overlap several agencies. Because of these interrelationships, all three tasks should go forward simultaneously with an effort made to coordinate at the various stages of completion.

The most involved of the early actions which the Center must undertake is the task of uniform classification. Perhaps the best way to proceed with this task would be through the appointment of (1) a task force for each major criminal justice agency, including those for which statistics are already collected, to identify and work out whatever classification problems exist; and (2) a task force on overall classification to work on the problem of integrating the whole system. All task forces would be composed of governmental and nongovernmental experts and would use the user survey and the inventory to the extent available and possible. Initial task force reports would be made widely available for study and comment, and a conference of users and interested persons might be convened to discuss the initial proposals. Following this the task forces would consider the comments, revise the initial reports, fully integrate all the task force comments with each other, and again make the whole package available for comment.

This chapter has tried to make clear the need for a National Criminal Justice Statistics Center and to outline a framework for its most effective operation. The technical aspects of collecting, analyzing, and disseminating crime statistics are by nature a complex subject, in a sense unexciting when compared with the great substantive issues with which the criminal justice system must contend: the impact of court decisions, the relative merits of rehabilitation and punishment, the deterrent effects of capital punishment, the need for stop-and-frisk laws or wiretapping, and the like. If the heated debates which these issues generate are to be anything other than the sterile disputations of rival philosophies, however, they must be based on the facts of the situation. As this chapter and other portions of this report have tried to show, the facts of the situation are at the present time all too often simply not available.

. . . . .

[*The President's Commission Report on Law Enforcement and The Administration of Justice,* Task Force Report: Crime and Its Impact—An Assessment (*Washington: U.S. Government Printing Office, 1967*), *pp. 123–137.*]

4 *The etiology of crime*

Even simple crimes such as an assault or theft reflect the complex interaction and influence of many different persons and conditions. To understand different types of crime we need to know a great deal about different aspects of the situations within which crimes typically occur. Of central importance is greater knowledge of the characteristics of offenders. . . . Much can be learned from the statistics now collected independently about offenders . . . for various administrative purposes. However, lack of knowledge of their interrelationships prohibits the development of more informative and useful statistical reconstructions of criminal events. This type of information must be secured more systematically if greater understanding of the different conditions under which crimes occur is to be achieved.

Characteristics of Offenders

There is a common belief that the general population consists of a large group of law-abiding people and a small body of criminals. However, studies have shown that most people, when they are asked, remember having committed offenses for which they might have been sentenced if they had been apprehended.[1]

[1] The following studies are representative of the different populations surveyed in these "self-report" studies and of the different types of methods used to get the information: Austin L. Porterfield and Stanley C. Clifton, *Youth in Trouble* (Fort Worth: Leo Potishman Foundation, 1946); Fred J. Murphy, Mary M. Shirley, and Helen L. Witmer, "The Incidence of Hidden Delinquency," *American Journal of Orthopsychiatry*, 16:686–696, October 1946; James F. Short, Jr., "A Report on Incidence of Criminal Behavior, Arrests and Convictions in Selected Groups," *Research Studies of State College of Washington*, 22:110–118, June 1954; F. Ivan Nye, James F. Short, and Virgil J. Olson, "Socioeconomic Status and Delinquent Behavior," *American Journal of Sociology*, 63:381–389, January 1958; Robert Dentler and Lawrence J. Monroe, "Early Adolescent Theft," *American Sociological Review*, 26:733–743, October 1961; John P. Clark and Eugene P. Wenninger, "Socio-Economic Class and Area as Correlates of Illegal Behavior Among Juveniles," *American Sociological Review*, 27:826–834, December 1962; Maynard L. Erickson and LaMar T. Empey, "Class Position, Peers, and Delinquency," *Sociology and Social Research*, 268–282, April 1965; Martin Gold, "Undetected Delinquent Behavior," *The Journal of Research*

These studies of "self-reported" crime have generally been of juveniles or young adults, mostly college and high school students. They uniformly show that delinquent or criminal acts are committed by people at all levels of society.[2] Most people admit to relatively petty delinquent acts, but many report larcenies, auto thefts, burglaries, and assaults of a more serious nature.

One of the few studies of this type dealing with criminal behavior by adults was of a sample of almost 1,700 persons, most of them from the State of New York.[3] In this study, 1,020 males and 678 females were asked which of 49 offenses they had committed. The list included felonies and misdemeanors, other than traffic offenses, for which they might have been sentenced under the adult criminal code.

Ninety-nine percent of the respondents admitted they had committed one or more offenses for which they might have received jail or prison sentences. Thirteen percent of the males admitted to grand larceny, 26 percent to auto theft, and 17 percent to burglary. Sixty-four percent of the males and 29 percent of the females committed at least one felony for which they had not been apprehended. Although some of these offenses may have been reported to the police by the victims and would thus appear in official statistics as "crimes known to the police," these offenders would not show up in official arrest statistics.

Such persons are part of the "hidden" offender group. They evidently at one time or another found themselves in situations that led them to violate the criminal law. However, most people do not persist in committing offenses. For many the risk of arrest and prosecution is deterrence enough, while others develop a stake in a law-abiding way of life in which their youthful "indiscretions" no longer have a place.

What is known today about offenders is confined almost wholly to those

---

on *Crime and Delinquency,* 3:27–46, January 1966. Similar results have also been discovered in extensive studies with the "self-report" technique in Norway and Sweden. See Nils Christie, Johs. Andenaes, and Sigurd Skirbekk, "A Study of Self-Reported Crime," and also Kerstlin Elmhorn, "Study in Self-Reported Delinquency Among School Children in Stockholm," in Karl O. Christiansen, ed., *Scandinavian Studies in Criminology,* vol. 1, 86–146 (London: Tavistock Publications, 1965).

[2] In reviewing the results of his own and earlier studies, Martin Gold ("Undetected Delinquent Behavior," *The Journal of Research on Crime and Delinquency,* 3:27–46, January 1966) notes that more frequent and serious delinquencies are reported by lower class youngsters; but this result, which accords with official police records, is found primarily in those studies which have used interviews rather than anonymous questionnaires to secure the self-reports. The questionnaire studies have shown only slight or insignificant relationships between social class and educational level and crime. Gold tried a new technique for validating the interview method. He checked the responses of his subjects against the independently obtained reports of the subject's friends about his delinquencies. He then classified his subject as follows: truthtellers (72 percent); questionables (11 percent); and concealers (17 percent). The interview method seems to offer the best chance to correct for overreporting, but may possibly induce greater concealment.

[3] James S. Wallerstein and Clement J. Wyle, "Our Law-Abiding Law-Breakers," *Probation,* 25:107–112, March–April 1947.

who have been arrested, tried, and sentenced. The criminal justice process may be viewed as a large-scale screening system. At each stage it tries to sort out the better risks to return to the general population. The further along in the process that a sample of offenders is selected, the more likely they are to show major social and personal problems.[4]

From arrest records, probation reports, and prison statistics a "portrait" of the offender emerges that progressively highlights the disadvantaged character of his life. The offender at the end of the road in prison is likely to be a member of the lowest social and economic groups in the country, poorly educated and unemployed, unmarried, reared in a broken home, and to have a prior criminal record. This is a formidable list of personal and social problems that must be overcome in order to restore offenders to law-abiding existence. Not all offenders, of course, fit this composite profile, as a more detailed examination of the arrest, probation, and prison data reveals.

Arrest Data on Offenders

National arrest statistics, based on unpublished estimates for the total population, show that when all offenses are considered together the majority of offenders arrested are white, male, and over 24 years of age.[5] Offenders over 24 make up the great majority of persons arrested for fraud, embezzlement, gambling, drunkenness, offenses against the family, and vagrancy. For many other crimes, the peak age of criminality occurs below 24.

The 15-to-17-year-old group is the highest for burglaries, larcenies and auto theft. For these three offenses, 15-year-olds are arrested more often than persons of any other age with 16-year-olds a close second. For the three common property offenses the rate of arrest per 100,000 persons 15 to 17 in 1965 was 2,467 as compared to a rate of 55 for every 100,000 persons 50 years old and over. For crimes of violence the peak years are those from 18 to 20, followed closely by the 21 to 24 group. Rates for these groups are 300 and 297 as compared with 24 for the 50-year-old and over group.

One of the sharpest contrasts of all in the arrest statistics on offenders is that between males and females. Males are arrested nearly seven times as

---

[4] For a discussion of the selection process as it occurs in juvenile court, see Robert D. Vintner, "The Juvenile Court as an Institution," in *Task Force Report: Juvenile Delinquence and Youth Crime*, President's Commission on Law Enforcement and Administration of Justice (Washington: U.S. Government Printing Office, 1967), appendix C. Nathan Goldman, *The Differential Selection of Juvenile Offenders for Court Appearance* (New York: National Council on Crime and Delinquence, 1963); Martin Gold, *Status Forces in Delinquent Boys* (Ann Arbor: University of Michigan, Institute for Social Research, 1963). For a discussion of the sorting-out process among adult criminals, see Edwin H. Sutherland and Donald R. Cressey, *Principles of Criminology* (7th ed., Philadelphia: Lippincott Co., 1966), pp. 411–416; 429–441; 484–487.

[5] The data for the 1965 arrest rates were derived from *Uniform Crime Reports for the United States, 1965* (Washington: U.S. Department of Justice, Federal Bureau of Investigation, 1966), pp. 107–145.

frequently as females for index offenses plus larceny under $50. The rate for males is 1,097 per 100,000 population and the corresponding rate for females is 164. The difference is even greater when all offenses are considered.

The differences in the risks of arrest for males and females are diminishing, however. Since 1960 the rate of arrest for females has been increasing faster than the rate for males. In 1960 the male arrest rate for index offenses plus larceny under $50 was 926 per 100,000 and in 1965 it was 1,097, an increase in the rate of 18 percent. However, the female rate increased by 62 percent during this same period, from 101 per 100,000 females to 164. Most of the increase was due to the greatly increased rate of arrest of women for larcenies. The larceny arrest rate for women increased 81 percent during this same period in marked contrast to an increase of 4 percent for aggravated assault, the next highest category of arrest for women among these offenses.

The factor of race is almost as important as that of sex in determining whether a person is likely to be arrested and imprisoned for an offense. Many more whites than Negroes are arrested every year but Negroes have a significantly higher rate of arrest in every offense category except certain offenses against public order and morals. For index offenses plus larceny under $50 the rate per 100,000 Negroes in 1965 was four times as great as that for whites (1,696 to 419).

In general, the disparity of rates for offenses of violence is much greater than the differences between the races for offenses against property. For instance, the Negro arrest rate for murder is 24.1 compared to 2.5 for whites, or almost 10 times as high. This is in contrast to the difference between Negroes and whites for crimes against property. For example, the rate of Negro arrest (378) for burglary is only about 3½ times as high as that for whites (107). The statistics also show that the difference between the white and Negro arrest rates is generally greater for those over 18 years of age than for those under 18. Negroes over 18 are arrested about five times as often as whites (1,684 to 325). In contrast, the ratio for those under 18 is approximately three to one (1,689 to 591).

The differences between the Negro and white arrest rates for certain crimes of violence have been growing smaller between 1960 and 1965. During that period, considering together the crimes of murder, rape, and aggravated assault, the rate for Negroes increased 5 percent while the rate for whites increased 27 percent. In the case of robbery, however, the white rate increased 3 percent while the Negro rate increased 24 percent. For the crimes of burglary, larceny, and auto theft the Negro rate increased 33 percent while the white rate increased 24 percent.

Many studies have been made seeking to account for these differences in arrest rates for Negroes and whites.[6] They have found that the differences

[6] For a discussion on the differential administration of justice as it pertains to Negro-white differences, see R. R. Korn and L. W. McKorkle, *Criminology and Penology* (New

become very small when comparisons are made between the rates for whites and Negroes living under similar conditions.[7] However, it has proved difficult to make such comparisons, since Negroes generally encounter more barriers to economic and social advancement than whites do. Even when Negroes and whites live in the same area the Negroes are likely to have poorer housing, lower incomes, and fewer job prospects.[8] The Task Force is of the view that if conditions of equal opportunity prevailed, the large differences now found between the Negro and white arrest rates would disappear.

Probation Data on Offenders

Arrest statistics supply only a limited amount of information about offenders. More detailed descriptions can be obtained from the probation records maintained by the courts. An illustration of what such records reveal is provided in a report by the Stanford Research Institute to the President's Commission on Crime in the District of Columbia.[9] The study examined the background characteristics contained in the probation records of a sample of 932 felons convicted during the years 1964 and 1965 in Washington, D.C.

Among those offenders for whom income information was available, 90 percent had incomes of less than $5,000. At the time of the 1960 census, 56

York: Henry Holt & Co., 1959). For the effects of urbanization, see H. D. Sheldon, "A Comparative Study of the Non-White and White Institutional Population in the United States," *The Journal of Negro Education*, 22:355–362, Summer 1953; H. Mannheim, "American Criminology Impressions of a European Criminologist," *British Journal of Delinquency*, 5:293–308, December 1954. For the effects of family structure on the racial differences in crime rates, see J. Toby, "The Differential Impact of Family Disorganization," *American Sociological Review*, 22:505–512, October 1957; T. P. Monahan, "Family Status and the Delinquent Child: A Reappraisal and Some New Findings," *Social Forces*, 35:250–258, March 1957. For a discussion of economic factors, see B. Fleischer, *The Economics of Delinquency* (Chicago: Quadrangle Books, 1966); Earl R. Moses, "Differential in Crime Rates Between Negroes and Whites, Based on Comparisons of Four Socio-Economically Equated Areas," *American Sociological Review*, 12:411–420, August 1947. For an extensive review of the literature in this area, see Leonard Savitz, "Crime and the American Negro" (unpublished manuscript, Department of Sociology, Temple University, Philadelphia, Pennsylvania).

[7] See especially Henry D. McKay and Solomon Kobrin, "Nationality and Delinquency: A Study of Variation in Rates of Delinquency in Nativity, Nationality, and Racial Groups Among Types of Areas in Chicago" (unpublished manuscript, Institute for Juvenile Research, Department of Mental Health, State of Illinois), pp. 101–194.

[8] *Id.* at pp. 88–96.

[9] *Report of the President's Commission in the District of Columbia* (Washington: U.S. Government Printing Office, 1966), hereinafter referred to as the *D.C. Crime Commission Report*. Further detail is contained in a study by Irving A. Wallach, "A Description of Active Juvenile Offenders and Convicted Adult Felons in the District of Columbia—Volume II: Adult Felons," in appendix volume, *D.C. Crime Commission Report*, pp. 453–645.

percent of the adult population in Washington earned less than $5,000.[10] The highest median incomes were found among those who had been convicted of forgery, fraud, and embezzlement.[11] Of the sample, 78 percent were Negro, as contrasted with an estimated 61 percent of Negroes in the population of Washington.[12] The median age of arrest was 29.2 years, and approximately three-fourths of the sample was between 18 and 34 years, a proportion very much higher than that for the same age group in the general population of the District.[13] Adult criminal records were found in 80 percent of the cases.[14] More than half, 52 percent, had six or more prior arrests and 65 percent had previously been confined in some type of juvenile or adult institution.[15]

The picture that emerges from this data is of a group of young adult males who come from disorganized families, who have had limited access to educational and occupational opportunities, and who have been frequently involved in difficulties with the police and the courts, both as juveniles and adults.

Prison Data on Offenders

An even more disadvantaged population can be identified from the characteristics of prisoners tabulated in the 1960 U.S. Census of Population.[16] Every 10 years, the census lists the characteristics of persons in custodial institutions, including Federal and State prisons and local jails and workhouses. These tabulations show the median years of school completed for the State and Federal prison and reformatory population is 8.6 years, in contrast to 10.6 years for the general population in the country. It also shows that 23.9 percent of the offenders were laborers, compared to 5.1 percent in the total population. Only 5.8 percent of the offender population engaged in high status occupations, such as professional, technical work, manager, official, proprietor, and similar groupings, compared to 20.6 percent of the general population. Prisoners are also much more likely to be unmarried than other males 14 or over in the general population. Only 31.1 percent of the prisoners are married compared to 69.1 percent of males generally. The comparable rates for single status are 43.7 percent and 25.1 percent, and for separated, widowed and divorced, 24.6 and 7.2.

[10] *Id.* at p. 130.
[11] *Id.* at p. 119.
[12] *Id.* at p. 118.
[13] *Id.* at pp. 119–120.
[14] *Id.* at p. 119.
[15] *Ibid.*
[16] Material for this section comes from *1960 Census of Population: Inmates of Institutions* (Washington: U.S. Government Printing Office, 1964), p. 24, and *1960 Census of Population—Volume I: Characteristics of the Population; Part I. United States Summary* (Washington: U.S. Government Printing Office, 1964), pp. 1–207.

Recidivism

The most striking fact about offenders who have been convicted of the common serious crimes of violence and theft is how often how many of them continue committing crimes. Arrest, court, and prison records furnish insistent testimony to the fact that these repeated offenders constitute the hard core of the crime problem. One of the longest and most painstaking followup studies was conducted by Sheldon and Eleanor Glueck on a sample of 510 Massachusetts reformatory inmates released between 1911 and 1922.[17] It showed that 32 percent of the men who could be followed over a 15-year period repeatedly committed serious crimes during this period, and many others did so intermittently.

A recent study of adults granted probation by 56 of the 58 county courts in California from 1956 to 1958 showed that by the end of 1962, 28 percent of the more than 11,000 probationers had been taken off probation because almost half of them had committed new offenses, and others had absconded or would not comply with regulations.[18] Because judges select the better risks for probation, one would expect that men discharged or paroled from prison would be more likely to commit further crimes, and the facts show that they do. A California study of parolees released from 1946 through 1949 found that 43 percent had been reimprisoned by the end of 1952; almost half for committing further felonies and the rest (almost one-third of whom were thought also to have committed further felonies) for other parole violations.[19]

A review of a number of such studies in the various States and in the Federal prison system leads to the conclusion that despite considerable variation among jurisdictions, roughly a third of the offenders released from prison will be reimprisoned, usually for committing new offenses, within a 5-year period.[20] The most frequent recidivists are those who commit such property crimes as burglary, auto theft, forgery, or larceny, but robbers and narcotics offenders also repeat frequently. Those who are least likely to commit new crimes after release are persons convicted of serious crimes of violence—murder, rape, and aggravated assault.[21]

These findings are based on the crimes of released offenders that officials learn about. Undoubtedly many new offenses are not discovered. Furthermore, released offenders continue to come to the attention of the police,

[17] Sheldon and Eleanor T. Glueck, *Criminal Careers in Retrospect* (New York: The Commonwealth Fund, 1943), p. 121.

[18] George F. Davis, "A Study of Adult Probation Violation Rates by Means of the Cohort Approach," *Journal of Criminal Law, Criminology and Police Science*, 55:70–85, March 1964.

[19] California Director of Corrections and Adult Authority, *California Male Prisoners Released on Parole*, 1946–1949.

[20] Daniel Glaser, *The Effectiveness of a Prison and Parole System* (Indianapolis: The Bobbs-Merrill Co., Inc., 1964), pp. 15–24.

[21] *Id.* at pp. 41–44.

even though not always charged or convicted for new offenses. A 2½-year followup by the UCR of the arrest records of 13,198 offenders released by the Federal courts, parole, or correctional authorities during the calendar year 1963 shows that 57 percent had been arrested for new offenses by June 30, 1966. Figures on the percent convicted are not available.[22]

Studies made of the careers of adult offenders regularly show the importance of juvenile delinquency as a forerunner of adult crime. They support the conclusions that the earlier a juvenile is arrested or brought to court for an offense, the more likely he is to carry on criminal activity into adult life; that the more serious the first offense for which a juvenile is arrested, the more likely he is to continue to commit serious crimes, especially in the case of major crimes against property; and that the more frequently and extensively a juvenile is processed by the police, court, and correctional system the more likely he is to be arrested, charged, convicted, and imprisoned as an adult. These studies also show that the most frequent pattern among adult offenders is one that starts with petty stealing and progresses to much more serious property offenses.[23]

.   .   .   .   .

[*The President's Commission on Law Enforcement and Administration of Justice,* Task Force Report: Crime and Its Impact—An Assessment (*Washington: U.S. Government Printing Office, 1967*), *pp. 77–80.*]

Focusing Prevention

In the last analysis, the most promising and so the most important method of dealing with crime is by preventing it—by ameliorating the conditions of life that drive people to commit crimes and that undermine the restraining rules and institutions erected by society against antisocial conduct. The Commission doubts that even a vastly improved criminal justice system can

[22] Federal Bureau of Investigation, U.S. Department of Justice, press release, April 25, 1967.

[23] Clifford R. Shaw, *The Jack Roller* (Chicago: University of Chicago Press, 1930) (republished with a new Introduction by Howard S. Becker as a Phoenix Book, University of Chicago Press, 1966); Clifford R. Shaw, *The Natural History of a Delinquent Career* (Chicago: University of Chicago Press, 1931); Harold S. Frum, "Adult Criminal Offense Trends Following Juvenile Delinquency," *Journal of Criminal Law, Criminology and Police Science,* 49:29–49, May–June 1958; Henry D. McKay, "Subsequent Arrests, Convictions and Commitments Among Former Juvenile Delinquents," President's Commission on Law Enforcement and Administration of Justice, *Selected Consultants' Papers* (Washington: U.S. Government Printing Office, 1967). A summary version of McKay's paper appears in Henry D. McKay, "Report on the Criminal Careers of Male Delinquents in Chicago," in *Task Force Report: Juvenile Delinquency and Youth Crime, supra* note 4, appendix E. For further data and discussion on this process of escalation to more serious criminal careers, see the *President's Commission, General Report,* pp. 265–266.

substantially reduce crime if society fails to make it possible for each of its citizens to feel a personal stake in it—in the good life that it can provide and in the law and order that are prerequisite to such a life. That sense of stake, of something that can be gained or lost, can come only through real opportunity for full participation in society's life and growth.[24] It is insuring opportunity that is the basic goal of prevention programs.

Our system of justice holds both juveniles and adults who violate the law responsible for their misconduct and imposes sanctions on them accordingly, even though the level of responsibility may be lower for juveniles than for adults. Society thereby obligates itself to equip juveniles with the means—the educational and social and cultural background, the personal and economic security—to understand and accept responsibility.

Clearly it is with young people that prevention efforts are most needed and hold the greatest promise. It is simply more critical that young people be kept from crime, for they are the Nation's future, and their conduct will affect society for a long time to come. They are not yet set in their ways; they are still developing, still subject to the influence of the socializing institutions that structure—however skeletally—their environment: Family, school, gang, recreation program, job market. But that influence, to do the most good, must come before the youth has become involved in the formal criminal justice system.[25]

> *Once a juvenile is apprehended by the police and referred to the Juvenile Court, the community has already failed; subsequent rehabilitation services, no matter how skilled, have far less potential for success than if they had been applied before the youth's overt defiance of the law.* Report of the President's Commission on Crime in the District of Columbia (1966), p. 733.

One way of looking at delinquency is in the context of the "teenage culture"[26] that has developed in America since the end of the Second World

---

[24] See generally Clark, *Dark Ghetto* (1965); Cloward and Ohlin, *Delinquency and Opportunity* (1960); Cohen, *Delinquent Boys: The Culture of the Gang* (1955).

[25] Studies have shown that the further a juvenile becomes involved in the juvenile justice system, the greater are his chances of subsequent arrest. McKay, *Report on the Criminal Careers of Male Delinquents in Chicago,* published as an appendix to President's Commission on Law Enforcement and Administration of Justice, *Task Force Report: Juvenile Delinquency and Youth Crime* (Washington: U.S. Government Printing Office, 1967). And see the *Report of the Commission's Task Force on Corrections,* chapter 2, especially at 22, on noncriminal treatment, and chapter 4 on alternatives to traditional corrections methods.

[26] For a discussion of the context and implications of "teenage culture," see Wolfgang, *The Culture of Youth* (U.S. Department of Health, Education and Welfare Juvenile Delinquency Publication No. 9003, 1967), reprinted as an appendix to President's Commission on Law Enforcement and Administration of Justice; *Task Force Report: Juvenile Delinquency and Youth Crime* (Washington: U.S. Government Printing Office, 1967); Kenniston, "Social Change and Youth in America," in Erikson, ed., *The Challenge of Youth* (1965); Cohen and Short, "Research in Delinquent Subcultures," *Journal of Social Issues,* 1958, 14:20.

War. In America in the 1960's, to perhaps a greater extent than in any other place or time, adolescents live in a distinct society of their own. It is not an easy society to understand, to describe, or, for that matter, to live in. In some ways it is an intensely materialistic society; its members, perhaps in unconscious imitation of their elders, are preoccupied with physical objects like clothes and cars, and indeed have been encouraged in this preoccupation by manufacturers and merchants who have discovered how profitable the adolescent market is. In some ways it is an intensely sensual society; its members are preoccupied with the sensations they can obtain from surfing or drag racing or music or drugs. In some ways it is an intensely moralistic society; its members are preoccupied with independence and honesty and equality and courage. On the whole it is a rebellious, oppositional society, dedicated to the proposition that the grownup world is a sham. At the same time it is a conforming society; being inexperienced, unsure of themselves, and, in fact, relatively powerless as individuals, adolescents to a far greater extent than their elders conform to common standards of dress and hair style and speech, and act jointly, in groups—or gangs.

Adolescents everywhere, from every walk of life, are often dangerous to themselves and to others. It may be a short step from distrusting authority to taking the law into one's own hands, from self-absorption to contempt for the rights of others, from group loyalty to gang warfare, from getting "kicks" to rampaging through the streets, from coveting material goods to stealing them, from feelings of rebellion to acts of destruction. Every suburban parent knows of parties that have turned into near riots. Every doctor knows how many young unmarried girls become pregnant. Every insurance company executive knows how dangerously adolescent boys drive. Every high school principal is concerned about the use of marihuana or pep pills by his students. Every newspaper reader knows how often bands of young people of all kinds commit destructive and dangerous acts.

Other than that it appears to be increasing, little is known as yet about delinquency among the well to do.[27] Its causes, to the extent that they are

[27] Middle-class delinquency has received less attention from the analysts and theorists than the lower-class delinquency, and empirical studies of its incidence are less frequent even than theories about it. One field study found a small (5 percent) group of middle-class students whose aggressive delinquent acts compared in seriousness and frequency with those of lower-class students. Shanley, Lefever, and Rice, "The Aggressive Middle Class Delinquent," 57 *Journal of Criminal Law and Police Science* 145 (1966).

For examples of largely theoretical writing on middle-class delinquency, see paper by Albert Cohen, "Middle Class Delinquency and the Social Structure," American Sociological Association meeting (1957); Bohlke, "Social Mobility, Stratification Inconsistency and Middle Class Delinquency," 8 Social Problems (1961). Martin Gold in *Status Forces in Delinquent Boys* (Inter-City Program on Children, Youth, and Family Life, Institute for Social Research, University of Michigan, 1963) examines delinquency rates in a small city in the light of the social class and status concepts. For a discussion of the broad social forces that produce delinquency and other troublesome adaptations in youth of all social classes, see Coleman, *Growing Up Absurd* (1966). See generally Empey and Erikson, "Hidden Delinquency and Social Status," 44

understood, are of a kind that is difficult to eliminate by any program of social action that has yet been devised. The weakening of the family as an agent of social control; the prolongation of education with its side effect of prolonging childhood; the increasing impersonality of a technological, corporate, bureaucratic society; the radical changes in moral standards in regard to such matters as sex and drug use—all these are phenomena with which the Nation has not yet found the means to cope.

Delinquency in the slums, which, as has been shown, is a disproportionately high percentage of all delinquency and includes a disproportionately high number of dangerous acts, is associated with these phenomena, of course. Both figures and observation clearly demonstrate, however, that it is also associated with undesirable conditions of life. Among the many compelling reasons for changing the circumstances of inner-city existence, one of the most compelling is that it will prevent crime.

The inner city has always been hard on whoever is living in it. The studies by Shaw and McKay . . . show dramatically that it is in the inner city that delinquency rates have traditionally been highest, decade after decade and regardless of what population group is there. And besides delinquency rates, the other familiar statistical signs of trouble—truancy, high unemployment, mental disorder, infant mortality, tuberculosis, families on relief—are also highest in the inner city. Life is grim and uncompromising in the center of the city, better on the outskirts. As the members of each population group gain greater access to the city's legitimate social and economic opportunities and the group moves outward, rents are higher, more families own their own homes, the rates of disease and dependency—and delinquency—drop.

But in the inner city, now occupied by a different group, the rate of delinquency remains roughly the same, regardless of race, religion, or nationality. That strikingly persistent correlation, coupled with the fact that the inner city is for its present Negro inhabitants more of a trap than a way station, emphasizes the urgency of intensifying efforts to improve in the inner city the institutions that elsewhere serve to prevent delinquency.

Attempts to concentrate prevention efforts on those individuals most seriously in need of them has led to increased interest in methods for predicting who will become a delinquent.[28] Some attempts have been at least partly successful, and such attempts should certainly be pursued. It

---

Social Forces, 1966, 44:546; Greely and Casey, "An Upper Middle Class Deviant 'Gang,'" 24 *Catholic Sociological Review* 33 (1963); Porterfield, "Delinquency and Its Outcome in Court and College," 49 *American Journal of Sociology,* 199 (1963); Wallerstein and Wyle, "Our Law-Abiding Law-Breakers," 25 *Probation* 107 (1947).

[28] See, e.g., Glueck, "Efforts to Identify Delinquents," *Federal Proceedings,* 1960, 24:49; Wilkins, *Social Deviance* (1965); Bureau of Research, Wisconsin Department of Welfare, "Juvenile Base Expectancies—Wisconsin School for Boys, First Releases (1959–1960)," *Research Bulletin C–7* (1964); Warren, *An Experiment in Alternatives to Incarcerations for Delinquent Youth: Recent Findings on the Community Treatment Project,* California Board of Corrections Mono. No. 4 (1964).

may eventually prove possible to predict delinquency specifically with a high degree of accuracy and to design programs that can prevent the predictions from coming true. But if we could now predict with accuracy who would be delinquent, our present knowledge and experience still would not carry us far in designing effective preventive programs for individuals. And inherent in the process of seeking to identify potential delinquents are certain serious risks—most notably that of the self-fulfilling prophecy.[29]

Even if we could identify in advance and deal with those individuals most likely to become delinquent, that would hardly be a sufficient substitute for general shoring up of socializing institutions in the slums. For the fact of the matter is that, whether or not the result in any given case is delinquency, society is failing slum youth. Their families are failing. The schools are failing. The social institutions generally relied on to guide and control people in their individual and mutual existence simply are not operating effectively in the inner city. Instead of turning out men and women who conform to the American norm at least overtly, at least enough to stay out of jail, the slums are producing the highest rates of crime, vice, and financial dependence. By failing these men and women and, most important these young people, society wounds itself in many ways. There is the sheer cost of crime—billions of dollars every year spent on apprehending and adjudicating and treating offenders. There are the lives forfeited, the personal injuries suffered, the inconveniencing and sometimes irremediable loss and destruction of property. But all of those together are less significant than the loss of individual initiative, of productivity, of a basis for pride in and a sense of participation in society. And whether or not society is tangibly injured by crime, inevitably it is diminished by the loss of a member's potential contribution.

Perhaps we cannot be sure that it is the slum family that is failing to instill the values accepted by society, or the slum school that is failing to impart the capabilities for livelihood. But it is on such institutions that we depend, and so it is to them we turn when we wish to change the way people live their lives. And because of our dependence on these social institutions to shape individuals and, through individuals, the face of the Nation, we must ask even more of the slum's institutions than of their middle- and upper-class counterparts. The family must instill strength against the larger society's harshness. The school must reach out and rescue those lacking families. Job skills must be developed and employment opportunities broadened.

[29] See, e.g., Kahn, "Public Policy and Delinquent Predictions: The Case of the Premature Claims," *Crime and Delinquency* 1965, 11:217; Toby, "An Evaluation of Early Identification and Intensive Treatment Programs for Predelinquents," *Social Problems* 1965, 13:100; Gottfredson, "Assessment and Prediction Methods in Crime and Delinquency," published as an appendix to President's Commission on Law Enforcement and Administration of Justice, *Task Force Report: Juvenile Delinquency and Youth Crime* (Washington: U.S. Government Printing Office, 1967).

In sum, our society has for too long neglected the conditions of life in the inner-city slum. The past several years have seen unprecedented recognition of the gravity of those conditions and commitment of resources to their amelioration. But if we fail to devote, in the future, even more money and people and energy and concern to the problems of our inner cities, we must be willing to pay the price—a price already high and mounting.

Crime is only part of that price. But the importance of ameliorating social conditions in order to prevent crime is not to be minimized. Each day additional law-abiding citizens turn their backs on the city; fear for personal safety—fear of crime—is a major reason. As they leave, the city changes; the quality of city life deteriorates; the crime problem worsens, hurting people not only by forcing them to narrow their lives out of apprehensiveness but also by the most direct and incompensable of injuries to their person and property—the circle continues around.

It is neither appropriate nor possible for this Commission to specify or select among the many possible ways of helping to break that circle. The time has been much too short; the Commission's experience cannot compare with that of the dedicated educators, social scientists, community workers, program planners already struggling with these discouragingly complex and intractable concerns. What is imperative is for this Commission to make clear its strong conviction that, before this Nation can hope to reduce crime significantly or lastingly, it must mount and maintain a massive attack against the conditions of life that underlie it.

Slums and Slum Dwellers

The slums of virtually every American city harbor, in alarming amounts, not only physical deprivation and spiritual despair but also doubt and downright cynicism about the relevance of the outside world's institutions and the sincerity of efforts to close the gap. Far from ignoring or rejecting the goals and values espoused by more fortunate segments of society, the slum dweller wants the same material and intangible things for himself and his children as those more privileged. Indeed, the very similarity of his wishes sharpens the poignancy and frustration of felt discrepancies in opportunity for fulfillment. The slum dweller may not respect a law that he believes draws differences between his rights and another's, or a police force that applies laws so as to draw such differences; he does recognize the law's duty to deal with lawbreakers, and he respects the policeman who does so with businesslike skill and impartiality. Living as he does in a neighborhood likely to be among the city's highest in rates of crime, he worries about and wants police protection even more than people living in the same city's safer regions. He may not have much formal education himself, or many books in his house, and he may hesitate to visit teachers or attend school functions, but studies show that he too, like his college-graduate counterpart, is vitally interested in his children's education.[30] And while some inner-city residents, like some people everywhere, may not be eager to change their unemployed status, it is also true that many more of them toil day after day at the dullest and most backbreaking of society's tasks, traveling long distances for menial jobs without hope of advancement. Very likely his parents (or he himself) left home—the deep South, or Appalachia, or Mexico, or Puerto Rico—looking for a better life, only to be absorbed into the yet more binding dependency and isolation of the inner city.

> *The children of these disillusioned colored pioneers inherited the total lot of their parents—the disappointments, the anger. To add to their misery, they had little hope of deliverance. For where does one run to when he's already in the promised land?* Claude Brown, *Manchild in the Promised Land* (1965), p. 8.

A sketch[31] drawn from the limited information available shows that disproportionately the delinquent is a child of the slums, from a neighborhood that is low on the socioeconomic scale of the community and harsh in many ways for those who live there. He is 15 or 16 years old (younger than his counterpart of a few years ago), one of numerous children—perhaps representing several different fathers—who live with their mother in a home that the sociologists call female-centered. It may be broken; it may never have had a resident father; it may have a nominal male head who is often drunk or in jail or in and out of the house (welfare regulations prohibiting payment where there is a "man in the house" may militate against his continuous presence). He may never have known a grownup man well enough to identify with or imagine emulating him. From the adults and older children in charge of him he has had leniency, sternness, affection, perhaps indifference, in erratic and unpredictable succession. All his life he has had considerable independence, and by now his mother has little control over his comings and goings, little way of knowing what he is up to until a policeman brings him home or a summons from court comes in the mail.

He may well have dropped out of school. He is probably unemployed, and has little to offer an employer. The offenses he and his friends commit are much more frequently thefts than crimes of personal violence, and they rarely commit them alone. Indeed, they rarely do anything alone, preferring

---

[30] See especially Coleman, *Equality of Educational Opportunity* (1966); see also Cloward and Jones, "Social Class: Educational Attitudes and Participation," in Passow, ed., *Education in Depressed Areas* (1963). Concerning the effects of conflicting values on young people in the slums, see Muller, "Lower Class Culture as a Generating Milieu of Gang Delinquency," *Journal of Social Issues* 1958, 11:5–19; Kobrin, "The Conflict of Values in Delinquency Areas," *American Sociological Review* 1951, p. 653–661.

[31] See, e.g. President's Commission on Crime in the District of Columbia, *Report 120* (1966).

to congregate and operate in a group, staking out their own "turf"—a special street corner or candy store or poolroom—and adopting their own flamboyant title and distinctive hair style or way of dressing or talking or walking, to signal their membership in the group and show that they are "tough" and not to be meddled with. Their clear belligerence toward authority does indeed earn them the fearful deference of both adult and child, as well as the watchful suspicion of the neighborhood policeman.[32] Although the common conception of the gang member is of a teenager, in fact the lower class juvenile begins his gang career much earlier and usually in search not of co-conspirators in crime but of companionship. But it is all too easy for them to drift into minor and then major violations of the law.[33]

That is not to suggest that his mother has not tried to guide him, or his father if he has one or an uncle or older brother. But their influence is diluted and undermined by the endless task of making ends meet in the face of debilitating poverty; by the constant presence of temptation—drugs, drinking, gambling, petty thievery, prostitution; by the visible contrast of relative affluence on the other side of town.[34]

The Physical Environment

It is in the inner city that the most overcrowding, the most substandard housing, the lowest rentals are found. Farther out in the city, more families own their own homes; presumably more families are intact and stable enough to live in those homes and more fathers are employed and able to buy them. The inevitable influence of slum living conditions on juvenile behavior[35] need not be translated into sociological measurements to be obvious to the assaulted senses of the most casual visitor to the slum. Nor

[32] See Block and Niederhoffer, *The Gang* (1958); Matza, *Delinquency and Drift* (1964); Short and Strodtbeck, *Group Process and Gang Delinquency* (1965); Yablonsky, *The Violent Gang* (1962). See also Werthman, "The Function of Social Definitions in the Development of Delinquent Careers," published as an appendix to President's Commission on Law Enforcement and Administration of Justice, *Task Force Report: Juvenile Delinquency and Youth Crime* (Washington: U.S. Government Printing Office, 1967); Cicourel, *Social Class, Family Structure and the Administration of Juvenile Justice* (Office of Juvenile Delinquency and Youth Development, U.S. Department of Health, Education and Welfare, Grant No. 62224, 1963); Piliavin and Briar, *Police Encounters with Juveniles* (Office of Juvenile Delinquency and Youth Development, U.S. Department of Health, Education and Welfare, Grant No. 62224, 1963).

[33] Among recent writings arguing against the idea of the hard-core single-track delinquent are Matza, *op. cit. supra* note 32, and Lerman, "Issues in Subcultural Delinquency" (unpublished thesis, Columbia University School of Social Work).

[34] See Toby, "Affluence and Adolescent Crime," published as an appendix to President's Commission on Law Enforcement and Administration of Justice, *Task Force Report: Juvenile Delinquency and Youth Crime.*

[35] For a discussion of the effects of slum conditions on behavior, see Schorr, *Slums and Social Security* (1963).

does the child who lives there fail to recognize—and reject—the squalor of his surroundings:

> *Well, the neighborhood is pretty bad, you know. Trash around the street, stuff like that and the movies got trash all in the bathroom, dirty all over the floors. Places you go in for recreation they aren't clean like they should be, and some of the children that go to school wear clothes that aren't clean as they should be. Some of them, you know, don't take baths as often as they should. Well, my opinion is * * * it's not clean as it should be and if I had a chance, if my mother would move, I would rather move to a better neighborhood.* [16-year-old boy.][36]

> *It's sort of small. * * * It's something like a slum. Slum is a place where people hang out and jest messy, streets are messy, alleys are messes and a lot of dirty children hang around there. I would say it is a filthy place.* [12-year-old boy.]

What the inner-city child calls home is often a set of rooms shared by a shifting group of relatives and acquaintances—furniture shabby and sparse, many children in one bed, plumbing failing, plaster falling, roaches in the corners and sometimes rats, hallways dark or dimly lighted, stairways littered, air dank and foul. Inadequate, unsanitary facilities complicate keeping clean. Disrepair discourages neatness. Insufficient heating, multiple use of bathrooms and kitchens, crowded sleeping arrangements spread and multiply respiratory infections and communicable diseases. Rickety, shadowy stairways and bad electrical connections take their accidental toll. Rat bites are not infrequent and sometimes, especially for infants, fatal. Care of one's own and respect for others' possessions can hardly be inculcated in such surroundings. More important, home has little holding power for the child—it is not physically pleasant or attractive; it is not a place to bring his friends; it is not even very much the reassuring gathering place of his own family. The loss of parental control and diminishing adult supervision that occur so early in the slum child's life must thus be laid at least partly at the door of his home.

The physical environment of the neighborhood is no better. In the alley are broken bottles and snoring winos—homeless, broken men, drunk every day on cheap wine. (*"There are a whole lot of winos who hang around back in the alley there. Men who drink and lay around there dirty, smell bad. Cook stuff maybe. Chase you * * *."* [13-year-old.]) Yards, if there are any, are littered and dirty. (*"* * * and the yard ain't right. Bottles broke in the yard, plaster, bricks, baby carriages all broken up, whole lot of stuff in*

---

[36] This and the following quotations from inner-city children are from Fine, *Neighbors of the President,* President's Commission on Juvenile Delinquency and Youth Crime, 1963.

people's yards." [14-year-old describing his home.]) The buildings are massive sooty tenements or sagging row houses. (*"I don't like the way those houses built. They curve * * * I don't like the way they look * * *. They make the street look bad."* [13-year-old.])

On some stoops, apparently able-bodied men sit passing away the time. On others children scamper around a grandmother's knees; they have been on the streets since early morning, will still be there at dusk. The nearest playground may be blocks away across busy streets, a dusty grassless plot. (*"There ain't no recreation around. There was a big recreation right across the street and they tore it down. * * * [T]hey just closed it up—instead of building a road they put up a parking lot. * * * There ain't enough playgrounds, and if you go down to the railroad station, there is a big yard down there, * * * cops come and chase us off. * * *"* [14-year-old boy.]) Harlem, for example, although it borders on and contains several major parks,

> *is generally lacking in play space * * * [A]bout 10 percent of the area consists of parks and playgrounds, compared to over 16 percent for New York City as a whole. The total acreage of 14 parks and playgrounds is not only inadequate, but all the parks are esthetically and functionally inadequate as well. * * * For many of the children, then, the streets become play areas, and this, coupled with the heavy flow of traffic through the community, results in a substantially higher rate of deaths due to motor vehicles among persons under 25 (6.9 per 100,000 compared to 4.2 per 100,000 for all of New York City).* Youth in the Ghetto *(Harlem Youth Opportunities Unlimited, Inc., 1964), pp. 100–101.*

In addition to actual dangerousness, lack of recreation facilities has been shown to be linked to negative attitudes toward the neighborhood and those attitudes in turn to repeated acts of delinquency.[37]

Overcrowding alone is an obstacle to decent life in the slum. In central Harlem, the population density is approximately 66,000 people for every square mile—a rate at which all the people in the Nation's 12 largest cities would fit inside the city limits of New York. Even apart from its effects on the soul, such packing has obvious implications for the crime rate. Some crime is a kind of collision; when so many people are living and moving in so small a space, the probability of collisions can only increase. Crowding has a harmful effect on study habits, attitudes toward sex, parents' ability to meet needs of individual children; clearly, crowding intensifies the fatigue and irritability that contribute to erratic or irrational discipline.

Many of the people and activities that bring slum streets and buildings to life are unsavory at best. Violence is commonplace:

> *When I first started living around here it was really bad, but I have gotten used to it now. Been here 2 years. People getting shot and*

[37] Gold, *Status Forces in Delinquent Boys* (1963), pp. 107–122.

*stuff. Lots of people getting hurt. People getting beat up * * *. Gee, there's a lot of violence around here. You see it all the time * * *.* [14-year-old boy.]

Fighting and drunkenness are everyday matters:

*Sometime where I live at people be hitting each other, fighting next door. Then when they stop fighting then you can get some sleep * * *.* [15-year-old boy.]

Drinking, cussing, stabbing people, having policemen running all around mostly every day in the summertime. [14-year-old.]

Drug addiction and prostitution are familiar. The occupying-army aspects of predominantly white store ownership and police patrol in predominantly Negro neighborhoods have been many times remarked; the actual extent of the alienation thereby enforced and symbolized is only now being generally conceded.[38]

The Family

Too frequently the combination of deprivation and hazard that characterizes the slums—a test by fire for the most cohesive of families—must be confronted in the slum by a family that lacks even minimal material and intangible supports.

The family is the first and most basic institution in our society for developing the child's potential, in all its many aspects: emotional, intellectual, moral, and spiritual, as well as physical and social. Other influences do not even enter the child's life until after the first few highly formative years. It is within the family that the child must learn to curb his desires and to accept rules that define the time, place, and circumstances under which highly personal needs may be satisfied in socially acceptable ways. This early training—management of emotion, confrontation with rules and authority, development of responsiveness to others—has been repeatedly related to the presence or absence of delinquency in later years. But cause-and-effect relationships have proved bewilderingly complex and require much more clinical experience and systematic research.[39]

Research findings, however, while far from conclusive, point to the principle that whatever in the organization of the family, the contacts among its

[38] See, e.g., Fine, *op. cit. supra* note 36, at p. 126; surveys cited in *Report of the Commission's Task Force on Police,* chapter 6, "The Police and the Community."

[39] See Toby, "Affluence and Adolescent Crime," published as an appendix to President's Commission on Law Enforcement and Administration of Justice, *Task Force Report: Juvenile Delinquency and Youth Crime* (Washington: U.S. Government Printing Office, 1967), for a discussion of the interrelationships among individual, family, and neighborhood factors in connection with predicting the occurrence of delinquent acts. See generally Erikson, *Childhood and Society* (2nd ed., 1962).

members, or its relationships to the surrounding community diminishes the moral and emotional authority of the family in the life of the young person also increases the likelihood of delinquency.

The following discussion draws upon the extensive—though not by any means exhaustive—work already done by numerous researchers.

Family Membership

If one parent (especially the father of a son) is absent,[40] if there are many children,[41] if a child is in the middle in age among several siblings[42]—such family arrangements tend to reduce parental control and authority over children and consequently increase vulnerability to influences toward delinquent behavior.

Besides the basic membership of the family, relations among the members also appear significant in determining the strength of familial influence. It has been shown that deep unhappiness between parents increases the likelihood that the children will commit delinquent acts and that children reared in happy homes are less delinquent than those from unhappy homes. Apparently marital discord tends to expose the child to delinquent influences, perhaps by outright rejection or neglect or by undercutting his respect for his parents and so the force of their authority.[43]

Discipline

The discipline associated with the loose organization and female focus that characterize many inner-city families has also been related by social scientists to the development of what has been termed "premature auton-

[40] See, e.g., Glueck and Glueck, *Unraveling Juvenile Delinquency* (1950); Monahan, "Family Status and the Delinquent Child," *Social Forces* 1957, 35:250; Browning, "Differential Impact of Family Disorganization on Male Adolescents," *Social Problems* 37, 1960, 11:37; see also Toby, "The Differential Impact of Family Disorganization," *American Sociological Review* 1957, 22:451 (effects of child's age on his reaction to a broken home). See also *The Negro Family: The Case for National Action* (U.S. Department of Labor, Office of Policy Planning and Research, 1965) (Moynihan Report).

[41] For studies relating family size to various types of delinquency, see Barker and Adams, "Glue Sniffers," *Sociology and Social Research*, 1963, 47:298 Reiss, "Social Correlates of Psychological Types of Delinquency," *American Sociological Review*, 1952, 17:710.

[42] See Lees and Newson, "Family or Sibship Position and Some Aspects of Juvenile Delinquency," *British Journal of Delinquency*, 1954, 5:46; Nye, *Family Relationships and Delinquent Behavior* (1958); Glueck and Glueck, *Unraveling Juvenile Delinquency* (1950).

[43] See Nye, *op. cit. supra* note 42; Browning, *supra* note 40; Glueck and Glueck, *Unraveling Juvenile Delinquency* (1950); Dentler and Monroe, "Social Correlates of Early Adolescent Theft," *American Sociological Review*, 1961, 26:733; Slocum and Stone, "Family Culture Patterns and Delinquent-Type Behavior," *Marriage and Family Living*, 1963, 25:202.

omy"[44] and to consequent resentment of authority figures such as policemen and teachers. Often child-rearing practices are either very permissive or very stern—the latter reinforced physically. In the first instance, the child is on his own, in charge of his own affairs, from an early age. He becomes accustomed to making decisions for himself and reacts to the direction or demands of a teacher or other adult as to a challenge to his established independence.[45] Strictness is not objectionable in itself, when it is seen as fairminded and well meant. But where strictness amounts simply to control by force, the child harbors resentment until the day when he can successfully assert physical mastery himself; rather than a learning and shaping process, discipline for him is a matter of muscle:

> *My father don't get smart with me no more. He used to whup me, throw me downstairs, until I got big enough to beat him. The last time he touch me, he was coming downstairs talking some noise about something. I don't know what. He had a drink, and he always make something up when he start drinking. He was trying to get smart with me, so he swung at me and missed. I just got tired of it. I snatched him and threw him up against the wall, and then we started fighting. My sister grabbed him around the neck and started choking him. So I started hitting him in the nose and everything, and around the mouth. Then he pushed my mother and I hit him again. Then he quit, and I carried him back upstairs. Next morning he jump up saying, "What happened last night? My leg hurts." He made like he don't know what had happened. And ever since then, you know, he don't say nothing to me.[46]*

An inconsistent mixture of permissiveness and strictness has also been found in the backgrounds of many delinquents.[47] Many inner-city parents express at once a desire to keep track of their children, and keep them out of trouble, and a resignation to their inability to do so.

> *(How do you handle Melvin when he gets into trouble?) Well, we figure that weekends are the main times he looks forward to—parties and going out. So we'd say, "You can't go out tonight." You know, we'd try to keep him from something he really wanted to do. But he usually goes out anyway. Like one night we was watching TV, and Melvin said he was tired and went to bed. So then I get a phone call from a lady who wants to know if Melvin is here because her son is with him. I said, "No, he has gone to bed already." She says, "Are you*

[44] Werthman, *supra* note 32.
[45] *Ibid.*
[46] *Ibid.*
[47] See, e.g., Glueck and Glueck, *Unraveling Juvenile Delinquency* (1950); Nye, *op. cit. supra* note 42; Stanfield, "The Interaction of Family Variables and Gang Variables in the Aetiology of Delinquency," *Social Problems,* 1966, 13:411; McCord and McCord, "The Effects of Parental Role Model in Criminality," in *Readings in Juvenile Delinquency* (Cavan, ed., 1964).

> sure?" I said, "I'm pretty sure." So I went downstairs and I peeked in
> and saw a lump in the bed but I didn't see his head. So I took a look
> and he was gone. He came home about 12:30, and we talked for a
> while. (What did you do?) Well, I told him he was wrong going
> against his parents like that, but he keeps sneaking out anyway.
> (What does your husband do about it?) Well, he don't do much. I'm
> the one who gets upset. My husband, he'll say something to Mel and
> then he'll just relax and forget about it. (Husband and wife laugh
> together.) There's little we can do, you know. It's hard to talk to him
> cause he just go ahead and do what he wants anyway.[48]

Such vacillations may be virtually inevitable where the man of the house is
sometimes or frequently absent, intoxicated, or replaced by another; where
coping with everyday life with too many children and too little money
leaves little time or energy for discipline; or where children have arrived so
early and unbidden that parents are too immature not to prefer their own
pleasure to a child's needs. Nevertheless, erratic discipline may engender
anxiety, uncertainty, and ultimately rebellion in the child.

Parental Affection or Rejection

More crucial even than mode of discipline is the degree of parental
affection or rejection of the child. Perhaps the most important factor in the
lives of many boys who become delinquent is their failure to win the
affection of their fathers.[49] It has been suggested that delinquency correlates
more with the consistency of the affection the child receives from both
parents than with the consistency of the discipline.[50] It has also been found
that a disproportionately large number of aggressive delinquents have been
denied the opportunity to express their feelings of dependence on their
parents.[51]

Identification Between Father and Son

Several recent studies focusing on identification between a boy and his
father have tried to determine the conditions under which a boy is more

[48] Werthman, *supra* note 32.

[49] See Glueck and Glueck, *Unraveling Juvenile Delinquency* (1950), reporting that
affection between father and son appeared particularly significant in their studies of
delinquents and nondelinquents. See also Andry, "Faulty Paternal and Maternal–Child
Relationships, Affection and Delinquency," *British Journal of Delinquency*, 1957, 9:3;
McCord et al., "Some Effects of Paternal Absence on Male Children," *Journal of Ab-
normal and Social Psychology*, 1962, 64:361; Slocum and Stone, *supra* note 43; Stanfield, "The Interaction of Family Variables and Gang Variables on the Aetiology of
Delinquency," *Social Problems*, 1966, 13:411.

[50] For a discussion of relationships between affection and parental discipline, see
McCord and McCord, *supra* note 47.

[51] See Bandura and Walters, *Adolescent Aggression* (1959); Bettelheim, *Children
Who Hate;* Bandura and Walters, "Dependency Conflicts in Aggressive Delinquents,"
Social Issues, 1958, 52:14.

likely to be attracted to his father, on the assumption that such attraction provides a basis upon which parental discipline can inculcate youthful self-control. Unemployment has been found to weaken a father's authority with his family, especially over adolescent children for whom he is unable to provide expected support.[52] Children also appear less likely to identify with fathers if their discipline is perceived as unfair.[53] The strong influence of the father over his son, for good or for ill, is also very significant. When father-son and mother-son relationships are compared, the father-son relationships appear more determinative in whether or not delinquent behavior develops.[54]

Family Status in the Community

The capacity of parents to maintain moral authority over the conduct of their children is affected not only by the family's internal structure and operation but also by the relationships that the family maintains with the community and the role of the family itself in modern life.[55] There seems to be a direct relationship between the prestige of the family in the community and the kind of bond that develops between father and son. Respected family status increases the strength of parental authority and seems to help insulate the child from delinquency.[56]

In inner-city families one or more of the detrimental factors discussed above is particularly likely to be present. Many families are large. Many (over 40 percent according to some estimates) are fatherless, always or intermittently, or involve a marital relationship in which the parties have and communicate to their offspring but little sense of permanence. And the histories of delinquents frequently include a large lower class family broken in some way.[57]

.   .   .   .   .

Youth in the Community

The typical delinquent operates in the company of his peers, and delinquency thrives on group support. It has been estimated that between 60 and

[52] Brenfenbrenner, "Some Familial Antecedents of Responsibility and Leadership in Adolescents," in Petrullo and Bass, *Leadership and Interpersonal Behavior* (1961).

[53] See Nye, *op. cit. supra* note 42.

[54] See studies cited in note 49.

[55] Studies dealing with the effect of neighborhood on the family include Lander, *Toward an Understanding of Juvenile Delinquency* (1954); Maccoby, Johnson and Church, "Community Integration and the Social Control of Juvenile Delinquency," *Journal of Social Issues*, 1958, 14:38; Polk, "Juvenile Delinquency and Social Areas," *Social Problems*, 1957–1958, 5:214.

[56] See Gold, *Status Forces in Delinquent Boys* (Inter-City Program on Children, Youth, and Family Life, Institute for Social Research, University of Michigan, 1963).

[57] See, e.g., President's Commission on Crime in the District of Columbia, *Report* 122, 125 (1966).

90 percent of all delinquent acts are committed with companions.[58] That fact alone makes youth groups of central concern in consideration of delinquency prevention.

It is clear that youth groups are playing a more and more important part in the transition between childhood and adulthood. For young people today that transition is a long period of waiting, during which they are expected to be seriously preparing themselves for participation at some future date in a society that meanwhile provides no role for them and withholds both the toleration accorded children and the responsibilities of adults.[59] Some young people, however, lack the resources for becoming prepared; they see the goal but have not the means to reach it. Others are resentful and impatient with the failure of their stodgy elders to appreciate the contributions they feel ready to make. Many, slum dwellers and suburbanites both, feel victimized by the moral absolutes of the adult society—unexplained injunctions about right and wrong that seem to have little relevance in a complex world controlled by people employing multiple and shifting standards. Youth today accuse those ahead of them of phoniness and of failure to define how to live both honorably and successfully in a world that is changing too rapidly for anyone to comprehend.[60]

The very rapidity of that change is making it ever more difficult for young people to envision the type of work they might wish to commit themselves to, more difficult for them to find stable adult models with whom to identify.[61] To fill the vacuum, they turn increasingly to their own age mates. But the models of dress and ideal and behavior that youth subcultures furnish may lead them into conflict with their parents' values and efforts to assert control. It has been suggested that, besides being more dependent on each other, youth today are also more independent of adults; parents and their young adolescents increasingly seem to live in different and at times antagonistic worlds. That antagonism sometimes explodes in antisocial acts.

Most of the youngsters who rebel at home and at school seek security and recognition among their fellows on the street. Together they form tightly knit groups in the decisions of which they are able to participate and the authority of which they accept as virtually absolute. Their attitudes, dress, tastes, ambitions, behavior, pastimes are those of the group.[62]

While the members are still young—before and during their early teens—such groups engage with apparent abandon and indifference in whatever seems like fun, delinquent and nondelinquent. Only some of what they do is seriously violent or destructive. Frequently, however, adults see

[58] For a summary of the evidence, see Empey, "Peer Group Influences in Correctional Programs" (Consultant's Paper submitted to President's Commission on Law Enforcement and Administration of Justice, 1966).

[59] See Wolfgang, *op. cit. supra* note 26.

[60] See Goodman, *Growing Up Absurd* (1956); Matza, *op. cit. supra* note 32.

[61] See Block and Niederhoffer, *op. cit. supra* note 32, for discussion of gang behavior in connection with transitions of adolescence.

[62] See generally Cohen, *op. cit. supra* note 24; Whyte, *Street Corner Society* (1955); Yablonsky, *op. cit. supra* note 32.

even their minor misdeeds as malicious and defiant and label the actors troublemakers. The affixing of that label can be a momentous occurrence in a youngster's life. Thereafter he may be watched; he may be suspect; his every misstep may be seen as further evidence of his delinquent nature. He may be excluded more and more from legitimate activities and opportunities. Soon he may be designated and dealt with as a delinquent and will find it very difficult to move onto a law-abiding path even if he can overcome his own belligerent reaction and negative self-image and seeks to do so.[63]

Being labeled a troublemaker is a danger of growing up in suburbia as well as in the slums, but the suburbs are more likely to provide parental intervention and psychiatrists, pastors, family counselors to help the youth abandon his undesirable identity. It is much harder for the inner-city youth to find alternatives to a rebel role. Thus it is in the slums that youth gangs are most likely to drift from minor and haphazard into serious, repeated, purposeful delinquency.

It is in the slums, too, that young people are most likely to be exposed to the example of the successful career criminal as a person of prestige in the community.[64] To a population denied access to traditional positions of status and achievement, a successful criminal may be a highly visible model of power and affluence and a center of training and recruitment for criminal enterprise.

> *Johnny D.* * * * *was about the hippest cat on Eighth Avenue* * * *. He was a man* * * *21* * * *. Johnny D. had been in jail since he was 17* * * *. Johnny did everything. He used to sell all the horse[heroin] in the neighborhood* * * *. Everybody used to listen when he said something. It made sense to listen—he was doing some of everything, so he must have known what he was talking about* * * *. He sure seemed to know a lot of things. Johnny just about raised a lot of the cats around there* * * *.* Claude Brown, *Manchild in the Promised Land* (1965), pp. 104, 108–109.

Delinquent gangs are commonly blamed for much of the street crime that presently alarms the Nation. In fact, however, according to a detailed 2-year study, recently completed, of the 700 members of 21 delinquent gangs, gang violence against persons is less frequent, less violent, and less uncontrolled than is generally believed. Only 17 percent of all the offenses recorded by observers included an element of violence, and about half of

[63] Among the growing number of studies of the effects of labeling on the development of delinquent behavior patterns, see Werthman, *supra* note 32; Becker, *Outsiders: Studies in the Sociology of Deviance* (1963); Kitsuse, "Societal Reaction to Deviant Behavior," in Becker, ed., *The Other Side, Perspectives on Deviance* (1964); Cicourel, *The Social Organization of Juvenile Justice* (in press); Chwast, "Value Conflicts in Law Enforcement," *American Sociological Review*, 1965, 30:1; Vinter and Sarri, "Malperformance in the Public School: A Group Work Approach," *Social Work*, 1965, 10:3; Piliavin and Briar, *op. cit. supra* note 32.

[64] See Spergel, *Street Gang Work* (1960); Shaw, *The Jack Roller* (1930); Sutherland and Cressy, *Principles of Criminology* (4th ed., 1955), pp. 76–80.

the violent offenses were committed against rival gang members. Much gang violence, in other words, appears to occur not against strangers but in attempts to achieve or preserve individual or gang status or territory.[65]

Many cities have sent youth workers into the streets to befriend gang boys and dissuade them from fighting. Street workers have often succeeded in their immediate objective of averting gang violence, but, with little more permanent to offer than bus trips and ball games, they have rarely managed to convert boys from total gang involvement to more socially acceptable pursuits.[66] Indeed, there are indications that street work has in some places had negative effects by creating a vacuum too likely to be filled by such destructive activities as using narcotics. Yet even the hard core delinquent whose gang is his life continues to share the conventional American belief that work and education are the right ways to get ahead in the world.[67]

.   .   .   .   .

Delinquency and the School

The complex relationship between the school and the child varies greatly from one school system to another. The process of education is dramatically different in the slum than in the middle-class suburb. The child and the problems he brings to school are different. The support for learning that he receives at home and in his neighborhood is different. The school systems themselves are very different. The slum school faces the greatest obstacles with the least resources, the least qualified personnel, the least adequate capability for effective education.

The school, unlike the family, is a public instrument for training young people. It is, therefore, more directly accessible to change through the development of new resources and policies. And since it is the principal public institution for the development of a basic commitment by young people to the goals and values of our society, it is imperative that it be provided with the resources to compete with illegitimate attractions for young people's allegiance. Anything less would be a serious failure to discharge our Nation's responsibility to its youth.

The Commission recognizes that many in the field of education have identified the shortcomings of slum schools. The Commission recognizes too that in many places efforts are being made to improve various aspects of

[65] Yablonsky, *op. cit. supra* note 32; Klein and Meyerhoff, eds., *Juvenile Gangs in Context, Theory, Research and Action* (1964); Miller, "Violent Crimes in City Gangs," *The Annals* 364:96 (Wolfgang, ed., 1966); Short and Strodtbeck, "Why Gang Fights," *Trans-Action* Sept.–Oct. 1964, pp. 25–29.

[66] This was the experience, for example, of street workers with the New York City Youth Board during the gang wars of the 1950's.

[67] Gordon, Short, Cartwright, and Strodtbeck, "Values and Gang Delinquency: A Study of Street-Corner Groups," *American Journal of Sociology*, 1963, 69:109–128; Karacki and Toby, The Uncommitted Adolescent: Candidate for Gang Delinquency and Anomie," in Clinard, ed., *Anomie and Deviant Behavior* (1964).

schools. But as a general matter our society has not yet been willing to devote resources sufficient for the radical changes necessary.

Recent research has related instances of delinquent conduct to the school-child relationship and to problems either created or complicated by schools themselves. First, in its own methods and practices, the school may simply be too passive to fulfill its obligations as one of the last social institutions with an opportunity to rescue the child from other forces, in himself and in his environment, which are pushing him toward delinquency. Second, there is considerable evidence that some schools may have an indirect effect on delinquency by the use of methods that create the conditions of failure for certain students. Mishandling by the school can lower the child's motivation to learn. It can aggravate his difficulty in accepting authority and generate or intensify hostility and alienation. It can sap the child's confidence, dampen his initiative, and lead him to negative definitions of himself as a failure or an "unacceptable" person.

Some schools, particularly in the poorest areas, are unable to deal with children who are neither ready nor able to learn. Asserting demands for performance that the child cannot meet, the frustrated teacher may become hostile and the child indifferent, apathetic, or hostile in turn. If the child is also rebelling at home, the effect is more immediate and the confrontation becomes intolerable to all. The too-usual result is that the child turns to other things that have nothing to do with academic learning, and the school finds a way to ignore him or push him out so the rest of its work can continue.

The following discussion attempts to identify ways in which some schools may be contributing directly or indirectly to the behavior problems of children and to assess the capacity of schools to prevent and manage such problems. In formulating its recommendations, the Commission has had the benefit of advice and assistance from the Office of Education in the Department of Health, Education, and Welfare.[68]

The Educationally Handicapped Child

Children enter the school system already shaped by their earlier experiences—many of them already handicapped in their potential for educational achievement.[69] The educational handicaps that seem most closely related to delinquency appear in the slum child.

[68] See Office of Education, U.S. Department of Health, Education and Welfare, *Delinquency and the Schools,* published as an appendix to the President's Commission on Law Enforcement and Administration of Justice, *Task Force Report: Juvenile Delinquency and Youth Crime* (Washington: U.S. Government Printing Office, 1967). And see Schafer and Polk, *Delinquency and the Schools,* also appended to the same report.

[69] For an annotated bibliography of the literature on cultural deprivation in children, see Silverman, "Bibliography," in Bloom, Davis, and Hess, *Compensatory Education for Cultural Deprivation* (1965).

He comes from a home in which books and other artifacts of intellectual accomplishment are rare. His parents, while they care about his education, are themselves too poorly schooled to give him the help and encouragement he needs. They have not had the time—even had they the knowledge—to teach him basic skills that are milestones painlessly passed by most middle-class youngsters: telling time, counting, saying the alphabet, learning colors, using crayons and paper and paint. He is unaccustomed to verbalizing concepts or ideas. Written communication may be rare in his experience.

It is sometimes assumed that the parents of children in slum neighborhoods do not value education. In fact, there is persuasive evidence of their commitment to an adequate education for their children.[70] Similarly, the youngsters themselves care a great deal about education. Indeed, there are indications that Negro and lower income students place a higher value on education than do white and higher income ones.[71]

But whether he and his parents value education or not, the tide of life soon begins to run against success in school for the child from the ghetto. Sordid surroundings, harsh or missing discipline, having to fight for what he wants, and taking over (far too soon) control of his own comings and goings—all adversely affect the odds against him. To some extent, of course, these problems are also encountered in the middle-class school, but there they are usually less extreme, and there is a greater likelihood of useful assistance through counseling, guidance, special tutoring, or some other form of individual help.

The Slum School

The manner in which the school system responds to the educational problems that the child brings with him is of extraordinary importance. It must be able to recognize these problems and to direct a battery of resources toward them.

Stimulated by the poverty program, recent and extensive studies have been made of the educational problems of children reared in slum communities. It has been clearly demonstrated that the educational system in the slums is less well equipped than its nonslum counterpart to deal with the built-in learning problems of the children who come to it. Schools in the slums have the most outdated and dilapidated buildings, the fewest texts and library books, the least experienced full-time teachers, the least qualified substitute teachers, the most overcrowded classrooms, and the least developed counseling and guidance services in the Nation.[72]

---

[70] Coleman, *op. cit. supra* note 30; Cloward and Jones, *supra* note 30 at p. 60.
[71] See Cloward and Jones, *supra* note 30; Vinter and Sarri, *supra* note 63.
[72] Among the studies that document this situation are Eddy, *Urban Education and the Child of the Slum* (Hunter College Project TRUE, 1965); Havighurst, *The Public Schools of Chicago* (1963); Sexton, *Education and Income* (1960); *Education in Deprived Areas, op. cit. supra* note 30; Riessman and Hannah, "Teachers of the Poor," *PTA Magazine*, November 1964.

The inadequacies of facilities and teaching resources are aggravated by the slum school's increasing segregation, both racial and economic. Despite efforts to combat and prevent segregation, central cities are growing increasingly nonwhite and poor, suburban areas increasingly white and affluent. Educational achievement is generally lower among nonwhite lower income students, and so racial and economic segregation in the schools has the circular effect of exposing nonwhite lower income students to inferior examples of educational achievement. There is substantial evidence that the achievements and aspirations of students are strongly related to the educational backgrounds and performances of other students in their school,[73] and that nonwhite lower income students do better when placed in mixed or middle-class schools. Chief Justice Warren enunciated one destructive effect of racial segregation in *Brown* v. *Board of Education of Topeka,* the landmark school desegregation decision:

> *To separate them from others of similar age and qualifications solely because of their race generates a feeling of inferiority as to their status in the community that may affect their hearts and minds in a way unlikely ever to be undone. Social and economic separation compound the educational obstacles of racial segregation in many schools today.*

The deficiencies of the slum school are further aggravated by a widespread belief that the intellectual capability of most slum children is too limited to allow much education. As a result standards are lowered to meet the level the child is assumed to occupy. Frequently the chance to stimulate latent curiosity and excitement about learning is irretrievably lost, and the self-fulfilling prophecy of apathy and failure comes true.[74]

It is increasingly apparent that grouping procedures often operate in this way. Children with educationally deprived backgrounds are often grouped on the basis of achievement of "ability" tests with built-in cultural biases.[75] The assumption is then made that these children lack ability, and standards are lowered accordingly. Thus, while grouping methods are designed to

[73] This is the major finding of the Coleman report. This factor accounted for more variation in student achievement than any other school condition. See also Reiss and Rhodes, *A Sociopsychological Study of Adolescent Conformity and Deviation* (U.S. Office of Education Cooperative Research Project No. 507, 1959), relating school segregation and student performances to delinquency rates.

[74] See Davidson and Lang, "Children's Perceptions of Their Teacher's Feelings Toward Them Related to Self-Perception, School Achievement and Behavior," *Journal of Experimental Education,* 1960, p. 114; "Harlem Youth Opportunities Unlimited," *Youth in the Ghetto* (1964), p. 227; Ravitz, "The Role of the School in the Urban Setting," in *Education in Depressed Areas, op. cit. supra* note 30; Gottlieb, "Teaching and Students: The Views of Negro and White Students," *Sociology of Education,* 1964, p. 345; Clark, *Dark Ghetto* (1965), p. 139.

[75] See, e.g., Eels, "Some Implications for School Practices of the Chicago Studies of Cultural Bias in Intelligence Tests," 1963, *Harvard Educational Review* 223:284. Vernon, "Coaching for All Advised," *The London Times Education Supplement,* Feb. 1, 1952 and Dec. 12, 1952, on changing IQ scores by intense coaching.

help tailor curriculum to individual needs and abilities, and while such methods could be valuable in channeling efforts to help educationally deprived children make up for lack of preparation, too frequently they are administered with a rigidity and oversimplification that intensify rather than ameliorate the slum child's learning problems.[76]

These problems are further reinforced by the lack of relationship between the instructional material usually provided by slum schools and the social, economic and political conditions of living in the slums.[77] To the youngster, the instruction seems light years away from the circumstances and facts of life that surround him every day. The following comments of a former delinquent are illuminating:

> *It wasn't interesting to me, I liked the science books but I didn't dig that other stuff. Dick and Jane went up the hill to fetch a pail of water and all that crap. Mary had a little lamb. Spot jumped over the fence. See Spot jump over the fence. * * * I say, ain't this the cutest little story. And I took the book one day and shoved it straight back to the teacher and said I ain't going to read that stuff.*

> *When I took the test I think I was four point something so I was real low in English, but I mostly got all my English listening in the streets, from listening to people. I didn't pick up my English mostly from school. (Can you read now?) I can read something that I am really interested in.*

> *(Going back to junior high, what kind of things would you have liked to read, that would have made you interested?) Well, I could see Dick and Jane when I was in elementary school, but in junior high school I was ready to know about life, about how it really is out there. In elementary school it's painted like it is beautiful, everything is beautiful. (In a sing-song.) Get your education and you can go somewhere. I didn't want to hear that no more, because I had seen my brother go through the same thing. He quit school, he ain't making it. So I wanted to know, okay how can I get somewhere if I go to school. How is life in general? How is the government ran? What's in the government right now that makes it hard for young people that graduate from high school to get somewhere? Why is it that people are fighting each other in the United States? Why is it that people can't communicate with each other? Society in general—what is it*

[76] See, e.g., Conant, *Slums and Suburbs* (1961); Harrington, *The Other America* (1962); House Commission on Education and Labor, *A Task Force Study of the Public Schools in the District of Columbia as it Relates to the War on Poverty* (1966); Sexton, *op. cit. supra* note 72, at p. 43; Schafer, "High School Curriculum Placement: A Study of Educational Selection," paper before Annual Meeting of the Pacific Sociological Association, Vancouver, B.C., April 1966.

[77] See, e.g., Klineberg, "Life Is Fun in a Smiling, Fair-Skinned World," *The Saturday Review*, 1965, 46:75; Bullock and Singleton, "The Minority Child and the Schools," in Gowan and Demos, eds., *The Disadvantaged and Potential Dropout* (1956).

that society has said that we have to follow? How is the police structure set up? Why is the police hard on youth?

These are all the things I would have loved to learn in school. (Is that the way you think now or the way you thought then?) I used to want to know about the government. How it was structured. I wanted to learn how it was run—really. Back then I didn't know people were marching for their rights. I didn't know about that. (When did you find out?) In the streets.[78]

The slum child often feels a similar lack of relationship between school and his future in the adult world:

(What kind of school program were you doing? Vocational education?) Yeah, vocational training. (Did that prepare you for a job?) It was supposed to prepare me for a job but it didn't. (Did you try to get a job?) Yeah, I tried to get a job. The men said I wasn't qualified. (Did you think while you were in school that you would get a job?) That's right—that's why I stayed in school so I could get a job upon completion of high school because they put so much emphasis on getting a high school diploma. "If you get a high school diploma, you can do this and you can do this, without it you can't do this." And I got one and I still can't do nothing. I can't get a job or nothing after I got one. [Ex-delinquent.][79]

There is evidence that many students become disillusioned earlier than this young man. Many students who are not taking college preparatory work seem to believe that regardless of their efforts or achievement, the system will not come through with anything but low status, low paying jobs after high school.[80] Present tasks and demands of the school therefore have little meaning or payoff. That problem, to be sure, lies not only in the schools' failure to prepare students adequately for the future, but also in the absence of adequate and equal employment opportunity. The U.S. Department of Labor[81] has shown that a Negro high school graduate has a greater chance of being unemployed than a white high school dropout—a subject dealt with in greater detail below.

Too often, as a result of the virtual absence of relation between it and the life he is living or will live, the school cannot hold the slum child's interest. It is boring, dull, and apparently useless, to be endured for a while and then abandoned as a bad deal.

[78] Interview by Commission staff members with members of Rebels With a Cause, youth group in Washington, D.C.

[79] *Ibid.*

[80] See Stinchcombe, *Rebellion in a High School* (1965), relating to perceived irrelevancy of education and delinquency. See also Elliot, "Delinquency and Perceived Opportunity," *Sociological Inquiry*, 1962, pp. 216–222.

[81] U.S. Department of Labor, *The Negro in the Economy* (1961).

Failure in School and Delinquency:
The Downward Spiral of Failure

When the school system is not adequately equipped to meet the early learning problems a child brings to school with him, a cycle of deterioration and failure may be set in motion. As the youngster is "promoted" from grade to grade to keep him with his age mates but before he has really mastered his tasks, failure becomes cumulative. While he may have been only half a year behind the average in fourth grade, for example, recent evidence shows that the achievement gap may widen to three-quarters of a year by sixth grade and to one-and-one-quarter years by eighth grade.[82]

The school failure, especially if he has developed a tough, indifferent façade, may give the impression that he does not care about his conspicuous failure to "make out" in school. In fact he probably cares a great deal, and even if the academic failure itself does not much matter to him, the loss of others' esteem does. He finds himself labeled a slow learner or a "goof-off." The school typically reacts to his failure with measures that reinforce his rejection: by assigning him to a special class for slow students, by excluding him from participation in extracurricular activities, by overlooking him in assigning prestigious school tasks and responsibilities.[83]

The child, in self-defense, reacts against the school, perhaps openly rebelling against its demands.[84] He and others like him seek each other out. Unable to succeed in being educated, they cannot afford to admit that education is important. Unwilling to accept the school's humiliating evaluation of them, they begin to flaunt its standards and reject its long-range goals in favor of conduct more immediately gratifying.

That conduct may not at first be seriously delinquent, but it represents a push toward more destructive and criminal patterns of behavior. Moreover, it takes forms, such as repeated truancy, that end hope of improved academic achievement. It may lead to dropping out of school.

There is mounting evidence that delinquency and failure in school are correlated. For example, in comparison of a group of "A" and "B" students with a group of "C" and "D" ones (both working and middle class), the "C" and "D" ones were seven times more likely to be delinquent; boys from blue-collar backgrounds who failed in school have been found to be delinquent almost seven times more often than those who did not fail.[85]

[82] Sexton, *op. cit. supra* note 72.

[83] See Vinter and Sarri, *op. cit. supra* note 63, on how different schools define and emphasize behavior problems in children and how the school's response, as well as the child's personality, play a part in adjustment to school. See also Polk and Richmond, *Those Who Fail* (Lane County Youth Project, Eugene, Oregon, 1966); Wilkerson, "Prevailing and Needed Emphasis in Research on the Education of Disadvantaged Children and Youth," *Journal of Negro Education Yearbook,* 1964, 33.

[84] See Werthman, *supra* note 44; Bertrand and Smith, "Environmental Factors and School Attendance," *Louisiana State University Bulletin* No. 533 (1960).

[85] Polk and Richmond, *supra* note 83. Also see Gold, *Status Forces in Delinquent Boys* (Inter-City Program on Children, Youth, and Family Life, Institute for Social Research,

It is of course difficult if not impossible to separate the part played by some schools from the innumerable other forces that may be related to the development of delinquent behavior. But both common sense and data such as these support the view that the high degree of correlation between delinquency and failure in school is more than accidental.

School Response to Behavior Problems

Student misbehavior is a real and urgent problem in many slum schools. Much youthful obstreperousness is best understood as a process of "testing" those in authority and demonstrating—partly for the benefit of peers—one's toughness and masculinity.[86] For many inner-city children, the teacher represents the first real challenge to their independence. While middle-class children, accustomed to the close supervision of parents or parent substitutes, defer almost automatically to the authority of the teacher, the slum child arrives at school in the habit of being his own master and is not about to surrender his autonomy upon demand.

The way in which the school responds to early signs of misbehavior may have a profound influence in either diverting the youngster from or propelling him along the path to a delinquent career. Not all teachers have trouble with "difficult" youngsters. Some, especially sensitive to what lies behind insolence and disobedience, adopt a firm but positive attitude that allows the task of learning to be carried on, if not always under placid conditions.

. . . . .

Other teachers simply submit, ignoring as best they can commotions and disruptions of classroom routine—an alternative that avoids head-on conflict with autonomy-seeking youth but at the same time deprives them of instruction even when they choose to accept it.

. . . . .

Many teachers, on the other hand, assume a right to unquestioning obedience. There results a sometimes ceaseless conflict between teacher and child. The child's assertions of autonomy are dealt with by the teacher, and eventually the school administration, as misbehavior, and sanctioned in a variety of ways. By labeling the youth a troublemaker and excluding him from legitimate activities and sources of achievement, the sanctions may reinforce his tendency to rebel and resist the school's authority. Nor is it easy for him to reform; grades lowered for misconduct, the stigma of assignment to a special class, and records of misbehavior passed on both

University of Michigan, 1963), pp. 154, 161; and Short, "Gang Delinquency and Anomie" in *Anomie and Deviant Behavior, op. cit. supra* note 67.

[86] See Werthman, *The Function of Social Definitions in the Development of Delinquent Careers,* published as an appendix to President's Commission on Law Enforcement and Administration of Justice, *Task Force Report: Juvenile Delinquency and Youth Crime* (Washington: U.S. Government Printing Office, 1967); Reissman and Hannah, *supra* note 72.

formally and informally from teacher to teacher make his past difficult to live down. The conception he forms of himself as an outsider, a nonconformer, is of particular importance. With no other source of public recognition, such negative self-images become attractive to some young people,[87] and they begin to adapt their behavior to fit the labels applied to them. A process of defining and communicating a public character occurs, and some young people in a sense cooperate in actually becoming the delinquents they are said to be.

．　　　．　　　．　　　．　　　．

Delinquency and Employment

Growing up properly is difficult at best, but manageable with help at times of critical need. To become a fully functional adult male, one prerequisite is essential: a job. In our society a person's occupation determines more than anything else what life he will lead and how others will regard him. Of course other important factors—family, wealth, race, age—exert significant influence on his future. But for most young men, it is securing jobs consistent with their aspirations that is crucial, that provides a stake in the law-abiding world and a vestibule to an expanding series of opportunities: to marry, to raise a family, to participate in civic affairs, to advance economically and socially and intellectually.

Getting a good job is harder than it used to be for those without preparation. To be a Negro, an 18-year-old, a school dropout in the slums of a large city is to have many times more chance of being unemployed than has a white 18-year-old high school graduate living a few blocks away. Poorly educated, untrained youth from 16 to 21 years of age are becoming the Nation's most stubborn employment problem, especially in the large cities. Our current economy simply does not need the skills and personal attributes they have to offer.

Youth and the Labor Market of the Future.[88]

Between 1960 and 1970 the available labor force is expected to rise by more than 1.5 million persons a year, an average annual increase nearly 50 percent greater than that which occurred during the first half of the 1960's and almost double that of the 1950's. Young workers, aged 14 to 24, will constitute nearly half (about 45 percent) of this increase.

One sign of greater difficulties ahead is the rising ratio of nonwhite workers joining the labor force—the workers who suffer most from lack of

---

[87] See, on the formation of a negative identity during adolescence, the writings of Erik Erikson, e.g., "Identity and the Life Cycle," *Psychological Issues,* 1959, 1:1.

[88] The statistics in this section are from *Profile of Youth,* a report prepared for the Subcommittee on Employment, Manpower, and Poverty of the Commission of Labor and Public Welfare, U.S. Senate, 1966.

adequate education and training, shortage of unskilled jobs, and discriminatory barriers to employment. Between 1965 and 1970, the number of non-white youth reaching 18 will increase by 20 percent over the 1965 level. During the same period, the white population in the same age group will actually decrease, and will not regain the 1965 figure of 3.3 million until 1970. During the 5-year period after that, the number of nonwhite 18-year-olds will again increase by 20 percent while the number of white 18-year-olds will increase by only 10 percent.

And young people compose the category of workers with the highest unemployment rate. In 1965 the average unemployment rates for youth between 16 and 24 decreased somewhat from the peak reached in 1963. But the unemployment rate of youth aged 16 to 21 was over 12.5 percent, two and one-half times that for all workers. The 1.1 million young people unemployed represented, therefore, one-third of the jobless workers in the country, and for them the familiar syndrome—minority group member, school dropout, unemployed—holds stubbornly true. Of the 26 million young people who will enter the labor force during the 1960's, an estimated 25 percent will not have completed high school. Only 45 percent will be high school graduates. Only 26 percent will have graduated from or even attended college.

Employment and Employability

Any young person meets a number of problems when he sets out to find a job. He must learn where and how to look, decide what to look for and, finally, make himself acceptable. If he is a school dropout or has a delinquency record, those problems are significantly more serious.

It is commonplace today to observe that educational preparation is increasingly required for getting and holding a steady job. One would expect, therefore, that dropping out of school and being unemployed might be related to each other. Undereducated youngsters are eligible only for unskilled jobs; it is hard for them to get information about the local job market; they lack prior work experience.[89] Most of them, consequently, do not in any real sense choose a job. Rather, they drift into one. And since such jobs rarely meet the aspirations that applicants bring with them, frustration typically results.

The search for a job may be even more discouraging when the young person has a delinquency record. There is evidence that many employers make improper use of records. A juvenile's adjudication record is required by the law of most jurisdictions to be private and confidential; in practice

[89] See *Getting Hired and Getting Fired,* a report prepared by the National Committee on Employment of Youth (U.S. Department of Health, Education and Welfare, 1965), describing the importance of information systems and work experience in finding employment. See also Boodish, "Automation and School Dropouts," *Social Studies,* 1964, 55:67–70; Ellington, "Unemployment and Unfilled Jobs: A Dropout Paradox," *Minnesota Journal of Education,* 1963, 44:9–10.

the confidentiality of these records is often violated. The employment application may require the applicant to state whether he was ever arrested or taken into custody, or employers may ask juvenile applicants to sign waivers permitting the court to release otherwise confidential information.

Many employers also inquire as to all arrests, whether or not a conviction resulted. About 75 percent of the employment agencies sampled in a recent study of employment practices in the New York City area stated that they ask applicants about arrest records and, as a matter of regular procedure, do not refer any applicant with a record, regardless of whether the arrest was followed by conviction.[90] The standard U.S. Government employment application form (Form 57) has just recently been modified to ask for information concerning only those arrests that were followed by conviction, rather than all arrests as previously. The fact that the majority of slum males (estimates vary from 50 to 90 percent) have some sort of arrest record indicates the magnitude of this problem.

The delinquency label may preclude membership in labor unions or participation in apprenticeship training. Licensing requirements for some occupations, such as barbering and food service, may act as a bar to entry for those with a record of delinquent conduct.

The Effect of Unemployment

It does not take the slum youth long to discover the gap between what he had hoped for and thought he was entitled to as an American and what actually awaits him; and it is a bitter as well as an oft repeated experience. So he looks for some other way out.

The career decisions of these youths, and the reasons for them, are varied; many are not really decisions at all. Some find their way back to school or into a job training program. Some drift among low paying jobs. Those who have good connections with organized criminal enterprises may feel few restraints against following a career that, although illegitimate, is relatively safe and lucrative; they have seen many others thrive on the proceeds of vice, and it will not be hard for them to persuade themselves that the steady demand for illicit goods and services justifies providing them. Others try theft; some become good enough at it to make it their regular livelihood; others lack aptitude or connections and become failures in the illegal as well as the legal world—habitués of our jails and prisons. Finally, there are those who give up, retreat from conventional society, and search for a better world in the private fantasies they can command from drink and drugs.[91]

---

[90] Sparer, *Employability and the Juvenile Arrest Rate* (New York University Center for the Study of Unemployed Youth, 1966).

[91] Cloward and Ohlin, *Delinquency and Opportunity,* argue that delinquent behavior is a response to the availability or paucity of opportunities. Also see Fleisher, *The Economics of Delinquency* (1966) (data linking school dropout status, unemployment, and delinquency).

The Transmission of Poverty from One
Generation to the Next

Lack of educational preparation, an economy that does not need the young, availability of illicit "jobs," the effect of having an arrest record—all these decrease the slum youth's employment opportunities and increase his chances of becoming or continuing delinquent. Basic to the economics of delinquency is the transmission of poverty across the generations. Today, for the 18-year-old, employment is hard to find. What chance has a slum-dwelling 6-year-old to break out of the cycle of poverty? Individual initiative may be important in determining an individual's destiny, but it is the economic and social forces shaping the way children are brought up, their preparation for adulthood by public institutions, their chances for self-improvement that perpetuate poverty.

The neighborhood in which the 6-year-old has been growing up is disorganized and has a high rate of delinquency. His father may be struggling to support a large family on a low wage or, jobless, may have left or deserted his family. Chronic dependency of families is further reinforced by the failure of welfare laws to provide economic incentives for fathers to remain in the home.

The 6-year-old now enters school. Although his parents value education, they realistically enough have little expectation that he will advance very far, and they have neither time nor skill to aid him. The slum school, as discussed above, is incapable of picking up the burden. He leaves school, or is pushed out at age 16, educationally unprepared, often already with an arrest record. He marries early or fathers illegitimate children. The cycle continues.

In earlier times, when muscle power was enough to earn a living, his slum-dwelling predecessors could with less difficulty break out of the cycle of poverty. A better job meant a chance to move into a better neighborhood. The better neighborhood was less crowded, had better schools, better social services. The poverty circle was broken, and, as shown by studies like McKay's, . . . delinquency rates were concomitantly reduced. The new American "immigrants" have much greater difficulty escaping the city's high-delinquency areas. They are confined there by the new economics of the job market and the old coin of racial prejudice. The ghettos expand, the citizen fears crime, the summer brings riots, and no less than the future of America's cities is threatened.

[*The President's Commission on Law Enforcement and Administration of Justice,* Task Force Report: Juvenile Delinquency and Youth Crime (*Washington: U.S. Government Printing Office,* 1967), Chap. 2, pp. 41–51, 54–55.]

5 The ecology of crime

Patterns of Crime Variation in City Areas

The first systematic and sustained effort to investigate the regularities in the variation of crime within a large city in the United States started in Chicago in 1921.[1] This analysis of the delinquency areas of Chicago by Clifford Shaw and his associates set off a wave of studies in other cities and a spirited debate about the interpretation of the findings, which is still being fed by new studies using different techniques, different measures, and competing theories. This development has been greatly aided by the growth and increasing sophistication of the field of human ecology which involves the study of the relationship of human individuals and groups to their physical, social, and cultural environment by geographers, demographers, and other social scientists.[2]

The National Commission on Law Observance and Enforcement published the second major ecological study of the Institute of Juvenile Research in Chicago in 1931.[3] This study was of particular significance since it demonstrated that the characteristic patterns for delinquency rates in Chicago could also be found in Philadelphia, Richmond, Cleveland, Birmingham, Denver, and Seattle. Three of their major findings about the distribution of delinquency rates have been repeatedly borne out in subsequent studies, subject only to local and usually accountable variations:

1. *Juvenile delinquents are not distributed uniformly over the City of Chicago but tend to be concentrated in areas adjacent to the central business district and to heavy industrial areas.*

2. *There are wide variations in the rates of delinquents between areas in Chicago.*

.   .   .   .   .

[1] Clifford R. Shaw, *Delinquency Areas* (Chicago: The University of Chicago Press, 1929), p. ix.
[2] Amos H. Hawley, *Human Ecology* (New York: The Ronald Press, 1950).
[3] Clifford R. Shaw and Henry D. McKay, *Social Factors in Juvenile Delinquency, Report on the Causes of Crime* (Washington: National Commission on Law Observance and Enforcement, 1931), pp. 2, 13.

3. *The rates of delinquents tend to vary inversely with distance from the center of the City.*[4]

.   .   .   .   .

These patterns in the distribution of delinquency rates have stood up remarkably well under tests in many cities throughout the country and have also been found in Mexico City and Honolulu.[5] Most studies have concerned themselves with delinquency rather than adult crime patterns and have only rarely plotted the distribution of separate offenses.

. . . [O]ccasionally the distribution of particular offenses are compared. For example, the study in Honolulu found that the distribution of arrests for vice followed most closely the distribution for delinquency court cases while suicide cases were much more widely dispersed than the other two series.[6]

A much more intensive and detailed study of the distribution of different offenses known to the police and the residences of arrested persons has recently been completed in Seattle.[7] The offenses known to the police were analyzed for the 3-year period 1949–51, and a second series based on persons arrested by the police was drawn for the 2-year period 1950–51.

When the crime rates for the various census tracts of the city were correlated with each other, certain offenses could be grouped together because they showed very similar patterns of distribution in the city. The closest degree of correspondence (intercorrelations over 0.90) was found in the spatial distribution of drunkenness, disorderly conduct, vagrancy, lewdness, petty larcenies and robbery (highway and car). Another closely related clustering of offenses (intercorrelations over 0.87) was found for burglary of residence by day and night and check fraud.[8]

Most of the offenses showed a varying degree of positive correlation with one another, indicating a tendency to follow somewhat similar patterns. However, bicycle theft showed negative correlations with most crimes studied and positive correlations only with indecent exposure and nonresidence burglary. The results of further study of the bicycle theft pattern illustrates the way in which the existence of special criminal opportunities can shape the distribution of crime rates.

.   .   .   .   .

. . . [T]he risk of victimization for all crimes except bicycle theft is greatest for those who visit or reside in the central segment of the city. The

---

[4] *Id.* at pp. 383–385.

[5] Andrew W. Lind, "Some Ecological Patterns of Community Disorganization in Honolulu," *American Journal of Sociology*, September 1930, 36:206–220; Norman S. Hayner, "Criminogenic Zones in Mexico City," *American Sociological Review*, August 1940, 11:428–438.

[6] Andrew W. Lind, *id.* at p. 212.

[7] Calvin F. Schmid, "Urban Crime Areas: Part I," *American Sociological Review*, August 1960, 25:527–542, and Calvin F. Schmid, "Urban Crime Areas: Part II," *American Sociological Review*, October 1960, 25:655–678.

[8] *Id.* at pp. 529–534.

difference in risk ranges all the way from 27 times greater in "theft from the person" to less than a third greater in the offenses of "peeping tom" or "obscene phone calls." These differences also are found in those types of offenses which citizens say they report most often to the police, such as robbery. For all of the types of robbery . . . the risk is almost nine times greater in the central segment. To some extent, of course, these differences are exaggerated because the rates are based on resident population, and many persons who become victims of crime in the central segment are transients who would not be represented in the resident population count.

. . . Of all types of offenses known to the police the central segment contributes the largest proportion of all types of fraud (65 percent) and all types of robbery (63 percent) including purse snatching and nonresidential robbery. Some of the offenses for which the central segment accounts for more than half of those known to the police are assaults (60 percent), felonious homicide (52 percent), miscellaneous forms of robbery (88 percent), residential robbery (79 percent), and highway robbery (67 percent), while the remainder of the city absorbs a greater percentage of such crimes as various types of burglary and sex violations, except sexual perversions. . . .

When the city is divided into six 1-mile zones radiating out from the city center, the usual pattern of high rates in the central zones and low rates on the outskirts is shown for most crimes.[9] As one might expect, this is most pronounced for the crime of embezzlement since the rates are based on place of occurrence of offense. The rate of embezzlement is 18.3 for zone I and 0.03 for zone VI. Bicycle theft is the only offense which runs counter to this pattern, showing a rate of 65.3 in zone I and 149.5 in zone VI. It should be noted, however, that the differences between the inner and outer zones for such offenses as peeping tom, obscene telephone calls, indecent liberties, and carnal knowledge are relatively small.[10]

. . . . .

Trends in the Crime and Delinquency Rates of City Areas

As we have seen, the studies of different types of crime and delinquency rates have established that these rates follow a fairly consistent pattern in their distribution throughout the geographical areas of the city, and that this pattern shows a considerable amount of similarity among American cities. A further question concerns the stability of this pattern of crime rates from one time period to another. Do these rates show any trends? Do changes in the area rates alter the relative standing of these areas in the total crime distribution pattern of the city? Do the higher crime rate areas remain the higher crime rate areas?

[9] *Id*. at p. 666.
[10] *Id*. at p. 666.

The pace of change is swift in American cities. Commerce and light industry invade the less intensively utilized land spaces. Old slums are torn down and replaced by high-rise apartment units. Older migrants to the city are displaced by more recent arrivals competing for low-cost housing and ethnic enclaves of immigrants, creating new physical boundaries to movement and community identity. In all this incessant turmoil, growth, and change what happens to the geographic patterns of crime and delinquency rates which existed before?

The answer appears to be that the general pattern of distribution of crime and delinquency rates among the various areas of the city remains the same, even though some of these rates may change drastically in a few areas where major shifts in land use and population composition have occurred. This conclusion rests, however, on relatively few studies that have been carried out in the same fashion, for the same city, and at different time periods. In the recent study of Seattle, for example, a special effort was made to collect comparable data on the area crime rates in the years 1939–41 to compare with the 1949–51 series.[11] Though the *actual* or *absolute* rates for different crimes were not the same in the two time periods, due partly to changes in definition and classification of crimes, the same pattern of *relative* variation from the central to the outer zones of the city remained the same. The similarity of the patterns of distribution of crime rates among city areas for the two periods varied somewhat. For example, the patterns for highway robbery for these periods showed a correlation with each other of 0.94, nonresidential burglary 0.93, nonresidential robbery 0.81, and residential burglary 0.65.

The most fully developed time series of the geographic distribution of crime and delinquency rates in a city are those assembled for Chicago.[12] Table 1 shows the rates for different series of delinquents who were referred to the Juvenile Court of Cook County over a 40-year period from 1900 to 1940. The rates are shown for the city of Chicago, which is divided into five 2-mile concentric zones with the focal point of the zones located in the center of the central business district. Though the *absolute* sizes of the rates differ, the same *relative* tendency for the rates to be highest in zone 1 (the central district zone) and lowest in zone 5 (the outermost part of the city) holds for all series, except for the reversal of rank in zones 4 and 5 in the first series, 1900–1906. During this 40-year period Chicago experienced enormous growth in population and industrial and economic power. It also was confronted with the task of assimilating wave after wave of new immigrants with very different cultural values and expectations. In the light of this ceaseless turmoil of change and new development, the relative stability of the relationships between the zonal rates is impressive.

Though the comparison of rates by city zones is useful to demonstrate the

[11] Schmid, *supra* note 7, pp. 669–670.
[12] For the most current statement on these studies see Henry D. McKay and Solomon Kobrin, *Nationality and Delinquency* (Chicago: Institute of Juvenile Research, Department of Mental Health, State of Illinois, 1966).

stability of relationships between delinquency areas, it also obscures important changes in neighborhood rates of delinquency as the result of social and economic change. We need much more detailed study of the way in which the changing character of life in the city affects the rates of delinquency and crime in the many different geographical areas of the city. It will require more intensive study of the trends in rates in the same areas in relation to the various physical, demographic, economic, and cultural changes which may have occurred. Such studies should also take account of the effects of changes in the organization, policies, and practices of the

Table 1—Rates of Delinquents Per 100 Males, 10–17 Years of Age, in Chicago by 2-Mile Concentric Zones, for Selected Time Periods, 1900–40

Years	Zone				
	I	II	III	IV	V
1900–1906	16	9	6	4	6
1917–23	10	7	4	3	3
1927–33	10	7	5	3	2
1934–40	9	9	6	4	2

Source: Henry D. McKay and Solomon Kobrin, "Nationality and Delinquency" (Chicago: Institute of Juvenile Research, Department of Mental Health, State of Illinois, 1966).

criminal justice system itself. From such studies we could obtain a much clearer idea than we now possess of the way delinquency rates reflect the existing structure of life within these areas and the way they are affected by changes both inside the area and in the city as a whole.

. . . . .

Sources of Irregularity in Crime Patterns

The presentation of the distribution of crime and delinquency rates by census tracts, community areas, or concentric mile or 2-mile zones sometimes gives the impression of disjointed and abrupt breaks in the delinquency patterns. This is to some extent an artifact of the manner of presentation, reflected by the necessity to use somewhat arbitrary boundaries for areas. The general assumption that has characterized these studies is that the distribution of offenses and offenders shows a fairly continuous decreasing density from the center of the city outward to the suburban areas. Even within census tracts offenses and offenders usually show up on spot maps more heavily concentrated toward the central district side of the tract rather than the side toward the periphery of the city.[13]

This assumption of a fairly continuous decline in rates outward from the

[13] See spot-maps in Clifford R. Shaw and Henry D. McKay, *Juvenile Delinquency in Urban Areas* (Chicago: The University of Chicago Press, 1942).

city center, while apparently a generally valid description for most American cities, must allow for many exceptions. Cities are broken up by physical and social barriers which often create sharply juxtaposed contrasts in the economic and cultural characteristics of adjacent city areas. In the growth of a city the existence of physical barriers such as rivers, railroads, canals, viaducts, lakes, parks, elevated lines, and high-speed limited access highways turn and shape the flow of population so that great differences in the characteristics of adjoining areas and their population may result, which in turn find reflection in very different rates of delinquency. Such contrasts show up in nearly all of the studies. These natural or artificial barriers sometimes create the circumstances for the development of rather homogeneous settlements of racial and ethnic groups whose measures for social control may produce much lower delinquency rates than neighboring groups.[14]

However, perhaps the most common source of irregularity in the distribution of delinquency rates is the development of industrial and commercial subcenters at various points in the city, near the periphery, or in suburban areas. This was immediately noticed in the first studies undertaken in Chicago. It was noted that rates decreased as they radiated outward from the city center except toward the south, where they increased again in the commercial and industrial subcenter of South Chicago and Pullman adjacent to Lake Calumet, and in the west near the Union Stock Yards.[15] South Chicago and Pullman were originally independent cities until they were annexed to Chicago in 1889. This area still functions as a relatively independent industrial and commercial subcenter. All of the juvenile delinquency series of rates developed in Chicago showed higher rates in this area than surrounding districts.[16] Similarly the Union Stock Yards and affiliated industries in the west were incorporated into Chicago in the general annexation of 1889. This area continues to some extent to function like South Chicago as a secondary industrial and business center with its own radiating effect on delinquency rates.

A study of the Detroit metropolitan area and its surrounding region indicates that the tendency for higher rates of crime and delinquency to be associated with centers of industrial and commercial development is the prevailing pattern outside the central city as well.[17] Satellite centers of business and industry in the suburban areas and surrounding region produce slightly higher crime rates than are found in the intervening areas. This tendency holds true for the offenses analyzed (murder, rape, robbery, assault, burglary, larceny, and auto theft), but it is most evident in the case of property crimes. This type of break in the declining size of crime rates

---

[14] See discussion on cultural enclaves, *infra.*
[15] Shaw, *Delinquency Areas, supra* note 1.
[16] Shaw and McKay, *Juvenile Delinquency in Urban Areas, supra* note 13.
[17] Stuart Lottier, "Distribution of Criminal Offenses in Metropolitan Regions," *Journal of Criminal Law and Criminology,* May–June 1938, 29:37–50.

from the city center confirms the general conclusion of these ecological studies; areas which show intensive commercial and industrial development also are the places where most crimes occur, since they offer more opportunities for most types of crime and are usually areas with highly transient populations and weak social controls.

The Relation of Crime To Other Social Indicators

. . . The studies in Chicago found a high degree of relationship between delinquency rates and the existence of other social problems in urban areas, such as school truancy (0.89), infant mortality (0.64), tuberculosis (0.93), and mental disorder (0.72).[18] In addition to showing that areas having high rates of crime also show high rates for other social or health problems, indicators were developed on the physical and economic status of these areas and the composition of the population. The concentration of delinquency in or adjacent to areas of heavy industry and commerce has already been noted. In addition, high crime rate areas tend to show the following characteristics: decreasing population (a correlation of 0.52 for one series of rates and 0.69 with another), a high percentage of families on relief (0.89), low monthly rents (−0.61), low rates of home ownership (−0.49), and a high percentage of foreign-born or Negro heads of family (0.60).[19]

These findings were based on studies in Chicago, and studies in other cities have not only generally confirmed these relationships but have often identified additional variables, such as: in Philadelphia high rates of demolition of residences (0.72);[20] in Indianapolis a high percentage of land used for business purposes (0.56) and low per capita contributions to the Community Fund (−0.60);[21] and in Baltimore a low average education (−0.51), low proportion of owner-occupied dwelling units (−0.80), high proportion of nonwhite (0.70), and a high proportion of overcrowded and substandard dwelling units (0.73). . . .[22]

---

[18] Shaw and McKay, *Juvenile Delinquency in Urban Areas, supra* note 13, pp. 86–101.

[19] *Id.* at pp. 134–163.

[20] *Id.* at p. 203.

[21] Clyde R. White, "The Relation of Felonies to Environmental Factors in Indianapolis," *Social Forces*, May 1932, 10:504.

[22] Bernard Lander, *Toward an Understanding of Juvenile Delinquency* (New York: Columbia University Press, 1954). Several other studies have used additional variables reporting a close relation to crime and delinquency rates, though no zero order correlations are given. In Seattle Schmid found the following factors had close association with certain types of offenses; high percentage of males, high percentage 60 years old and over, low percentage married, low number of children per 1000 females, low median income, low number of dwelling units with television, high percentage of females in the labor force, high percentage of males unemployed, high mobility, and high percentage of old housing (Schmid, *supra* note 7, p. 530). In Detroit Bordua found a high percentage of unrelated individuals was a useful indicator: David J. Bordua, "Juvenile Delinquency and 'Anomie': An Attempt at Replication," *Social Problems*, Winter 1958–1959, 6:230–238. In Indianapolis Chilton successfully used high number of persons per household, high percentage of wage workers, low percentage of couples with own household, high proportion of service workers, high percentage of old homes and low per-

In general, there has been a considerable amount of agreement among the various studies as to the social and demographic characteristics of areas which are most closely associated with crime. In part, this agreement is attributable to the fact that correlations have been made with total rates of crime or delinquency based on the offender's residence. When the crime rates are based on offenses known to police, rather than on arrests or court appearance, the factor of opportunity at the place of occurrence of the crime comes more into focus, and somewhat different area characteristics emerge as most important.

.   .   .   .   .

Important differences also can be seen when crimes against property are treated separately from crimes against the person. These differences can be illustrated from data collected in Atlanta, Ga.[23] . . . Victimization by crimes against the person is much more concentrated in the low income areas than crimes against property. The rate of crimes against the person is over eight times as great in the lowest income areas as compared to the highest, while for crimes against property it is less than twice as great. The high rates for the downtown area reflect the opportunity factor and are inflated by the high transient and low resident population of the area.

.   .   .   .   .

Many of the variables which are highly associated with crime rates have also been shown to be highly associated with each other. In recent years a number of attempts have been made to coalesce these diverse indicators into simpler sets of variables which could be used to characterize more directly the basic features of the urban areas relevant to crime. The mathematical techniques of factor analysis make it possible to manipulate the statistical interrelationships between these various indicators to identify the ones which best hang together. These efforts have yielded anywhere from two to eight basic factors depending in part on the number and types of variables introduced.

One of the most recent studies of this type also reanalyzed two previous studies and showed that all three reached a remarkable degree of agreement despite the fact that they were done in different cities for different time periods, in Baltimore, Detroit, and Indianapolis.[24] The results suggest that a basic socioeconomic factor is at work in the production of high delinquency rates based on residence of offenders that can be indicated best by such variables as overcrowded housing, the percentage of unrelated individuals, and mobility which is negatively represented by the "proportion of persons reporting that they did not move during the preceding year." In the final analysis of the Indianapolis data the factor most closely related

centage of new homes: Roland J. Chilton, "Continuity in Delinquency Area Research: A Comparison of Studies for Baltimore, Detroit, and Indianapolis," *American Sociological Review*, February 1964, 29:71–83.

[23] Atlanta Commission on Crime and Juvenile Delinquency, *Opportunity for Urban Excellence*, February 1966.

[24] Chilton, *supra* note 22.

to delinquency also showed close relationships to overcrowded and substandard housing and high mobility. It also showed moderately close relationships to low education, low income, low percentage of owner-occupied dwelling units, and low percentage of married men.[25]

To be most useful these techniques need to be applied to the distribution of different types of offenses in relation to area characteristics. An attempt to do this with 20 offenses, using the Seattle data, produced eight basic factors which brought together different groupings of offenses with such descriptive variables of the areas as low occupational status, low family status, low economic status, high or low mobility, and race.[26] An indication of the potential usefulness of this technique is evident in the clarity with which the "Skid Road" syndrome of characteristics emerged. This factor rejected "a social pattern characterized by large proportions of unmarried and unemployed males."[27] Significant relationships emerged for percentage of the population classified as male (0.782), percentage unemployed (0.647), and low proportion of the population married (−0.375). The crime pattern showed very close relationships for common drunkenness, vagrancy, drunkenness, lewdness, petty larceny, fighting, and robbery (highway and car).

This study goes on to develop profiles for individual census tracts based on the relative applicability of the eight basic factors to each tract.[28] Many of the profiles of the individual tracts on these factors were very similar and others very different. This opens up the possibility that a smaller set of typical crime pattern profiles can be developed for classifying the criminal potential of city areas in a more precise, distinctive, and useful way. Tracts could then be grouped together because of the similarity of their social, economic, or demographic characteristics and their crime patterns without regard to where they were located in the city. This would free the analysis from the restriction of geographic location and avoid the averaging out of very different types of areas, a tendency for which the zonal approach has been constantly criticized.

Studies to achieve this objective have recently been undertaken under the heading of "social area" analysis. The goal is to identify a set of census variables which will make it possible to classify the various social areas of the city into as distinctive types as possible. One can then use these groupings to study the distribution of social problems or to make other useful comparisons. The basic problem is to derive a set of variables that will yield the most distinctive and useful groupings for a variety of purposes. Tryon solved this by using a technique of cluster analysis on census data for San Francisco and the East Bay area.[29] Shevky and his associates developed a typology based on an analysis of previous ecological and social

[25] *Id.* at pp. 80–81.
[26] Schmid, *supra* note 7, pp. 535–539.
[27] *Id.* at p. 538.
[28] *Id.* at pp. 539–541.
[29] Robert C. Tryon, *Identification of Social Areas by Cluster Analysis* (Berkeley and Los Angeles: University of California Press, 1955).

studies and tested it for the Los Angeles Area and the San Francisco Bay Region.[30] The Shevky-Bell typology has been used most frequently in analyzing the distribution of crime and delinquency. This typology contains three dimensions. The first is called economic status and is based on measures of occupational status (total number of craftsmen, operatives, and laborers per 1,000 employed persons), and educational level (number of persons who have completed no more than grade school per 1,000 persons 25 years old and over).[31] The second is named family status and is based on the fertility ratio (number of children under 5 years per 1,000 females age 15 through 44), women in the labor force ratio (number of females in the labor force per 1,000 females 14 years old and over), and single family detached dwelling units ratio (number of single-family dwelling units per 1,000 dwelling units of all types). The third dimension is called ethnic status and is based on race and nativity (high proportion of non-native-born white persons in total population of tract).

Only a few studies have been made using these typologies, but the results, particularly in studies of delinquency, show promise. In Seattle it was found that the two typologies yielded very similar results in that the comparable dimensions showed high intercorrelations.[32] It was also discovered that for certain crime patterns, particularly the "Skid Road" variety, single indexes, such as percent male or percent male unemployed, frequently showed higher correlations than did the typologies.[33]

One of the most informative applications of the Shevky-Bell typology occurred in the study of crime and delinquency rates in Lexington, Ky.[34] The distribution of the crime rates showed little relationship to family status (-0.16) but a closer relationship to economic status (-0.52) and racial status (0.47) of the areas. The delinquency rates, however, showed a relationship to all three (-0.35, -0.38, and -0.48, respectively).[35]

One of the interesting results involved the computation of the ratio of juvenile to adult arrest rates. It was found that the proportion of delinquency to adult crime *increases* as family status (-0.53) and racial status (-0.28) of areas *decrease*. However, the proportion of delinquency to adult crime *increases* with an *increase* in the economic status (0.40) of social areas. Putting these relationships together shows the proportion of delinquency to adult crime will be greatest when high economic status is

---

[30] Eshref Shevky and Wendell Bell, *Social Area Analysis* (Stanford: Stanford University Press, 1955). See also references to earlier explorative work by Shevky and his associates.

[31] In this presentation the alternative typological designations suggested by Bell have been used instead of the original designations, which were social rank for economic status, urbanization for family status, and segregation for ethnic status. See Wendell Bell, "The Utility of the Shevky Typology for the Design of Urban Sub-Area Field Studies," *Journal of Social Psychology*, February 1958, 47:71–83.

[32] Schmid, *supra* note 7, p. 672.

[33] *Id.* at pp. 672–673.

[34] Richard Quinney, "Crime, Delinquency and Social Areas," *The Journal of Research in Crime and Delinquency*, July 1954, 1:149–154.

[35] *Id.* at table 1, p. 151.

combined with low family status, as can be seen from the following progression in the delinquency crime ratio: low economic–low family status, 22.0; low economic–high family status, 28.1; high economic–high family status, 33.5; high economic–low family status, 62.2.[36] One possible interpretation of this finding is that high economic status areas show fewer adult arrests, and a condition of low family status tends to be associated with more delinquency. Thus, the combined interactive effect of these two tendencies becomes evident in a sharp increase in the proportion of delinquency to adult crime for areas characterized as high economic–low family status areas.

Several significant relationships are obtained between the social areas variables and crime and delinquency rates for specific age, sex, race, and offense categories.[37] For example, nonwhite delinquency shows no relation to economic status (0.05) or racial status (0.03) of census tracts but is significantly related to low family status (–0.49). The nonwhite adult crime rate shows mildly negative relationships to all three factors in the social areas typology, but it is the only category that shows the crime rate increasing as the percent nonwhite in the area decreases. The association of the family status variable is primarily with youth delinquency, though it seems to be more closely related to male delinquency (−0.38) than female delinquency (−0.12). The young adult age group 18 to 24 contributes heavily to the crime totals, and here the high association with economic status (−0.58) and racial status (0.63) and the lack of association with family status (−0.03) are particularly striking. With respect to the offense categories, racial status shows especially high associations with juvenile (0.68) and adult (0.59) sex offenses, criminal homicide, and assault (0.67), but very little relationship with juvenile homicide and assault (0.18).

These studies using social area analysis have raised many issues that are unresolved, such as the relative value of the typologies versus single variables for different problems and the applicability of social area analysis to offense as compared to offender data. However, further exploration of the usefulness of these typologies in revealing the significant dimensions of social areas for the crime problem is clearly indicated.

The Relationships of Nationality and Race with Crime and Delinquency by City Areas

The greatest contribution of data for public consideration of this problem was made through the series of studies in Chicago.[38] The use of ecological methods permitted them to go beyond the simple relationship between crime rates and nationality. It enabled them to demonstrate the operation of

---

[36] *Id.* at table 2, p. 152.

[37] The following results are drawn from Quinney, *ibid.*, table 4, p. 153.

[38] See Shaw and McKay, *Juvenile Delinquency in Urban Areas, supra* note 13; also see McKay and Kobrin, *supra* note 12.

a relatively effective process of assimilation of these different nationality groups into the mainstream of American economic and social life. With this assimilation the high rates of crime and delinquency as well as a number of other social problems disappeared. It enabled them to focus public attention on the conditions of life, and on cultural and social change, rather than on inherent criminality as a function of national origin.

The problem of public stereotyping of certain nationality groups at that time as inherently criminal is not unlike the criminal stereotyping of the Negro and other minority groups today. These early studies did not attempt to refute the clearly demonstrable fact that the crime rates of certain nationality groups were disproportionately high. Instead, they amassed evidence to show that while this fact was attributable, in some measure, to the social and cultural traditions of these groups, mainly it was a consequence of the socially disorganized nature of the conditions under which they were forced to live. The overwhelming thrust of the evidence was that the high rates of crime were not a consequence of being German, Irish, Scandanavian, Polish, Italian, or Slavic, but a consequence of their life situation.

Three types of data were assembled for studying the relation of race, nationality, and nativity with crime and delinquency rates. These data related to

(1) The succession of nationality groups in the high-rate areas over a period of years;
(2) Changes in the national and racial backgrounds of children appearing in the Juvenile Court; and
(3) Rates of delinquents for particular racial, nativity, or nationality groups in different types of areas at any given moment.[39]

Marked changes were noted in the composition of the population inhabiting the high delinquency and crime rate areas near the central district over a period of many years. The Germans, Irish, English-Scotch, and Scandinavians in Chicago were gradually replaced by the Italians, Polish, and persons from Slavic countries. Despite the change in population the rates remained high relative to other areas in the city. Nor were those families left behind by each nationality group the most delinquent. They actually produced fewer delinquents than their proportion in the population of the area would lead one to expect.[40]

As the older immigrant group moved out, their children appeared proportionately less often in the Juvenile Court, and the court intake reflected instead the disproportionate appearance of the new arrivals. Nor did the children of the disappearing nationality groups raise the court intake in their new areas either for foreign-born or native-born children.[41]

[39] Shaw and McKay, *id.* at p. 149.
[40] *Id.* at pp. 151–152.
[41] *Id.* at p. 152.

Comparison of the rates for whites and Negroes, native and foreign-born, and old and new immigrants, classified by the area rates for white delinquents, shows that all of these groups have rates that range from high to low. Each racial and nationality group shows a considerable range in rates. At the same time these different groups produce much the same rate when they live in the same areas.[42]

There is some difficulty in comparing the rates for different groups at any one time because of the concentration of the new groups in the high rate areas. Nevertheless, when tracts are compared that are closely comparable in living conditions, very similar rates are revealed. In more recent comparisons of the rates for Negro and white delinquents in Chicago, considerable difficulty was encountered in identifying comparable areas for the two groups. Even in the same tracts the whites were found to occupy the better quarters and were, of course, not subject to the same discrimination in access to employment and other opportunities.[43] In the last major sample in the Chicago studies, the 1934–40 Juvenile Court Series, application of a method of statistical standardization for partially equating the population distribution of white and Negro males yielded a standardized delinquency rate of 4.41 per 100 white youth age 10–17 and 14.55 per 100 Negro youth.[44] Despite this difference the study concludes,

> All of the materials in this study indicate that if situations could be found where Negro and white children had equal opportunities in all meaningful aspects of life, the widely observed differences in rates of delinquents would be greatly reduced and perhaps would disappear.[45]

This limitation in the ecological method, the difficulty of locating comparable living conditions for the comparison of the experience of different population groups, was explored in some detail in a study in Baltimore.[46] Two white and two Negro areas were selected so as to permit as full an equating as possible of the conditions of life and the demographic characteristics of the population between each pair of matched Negro and white areas. Because of the segregation each area was quite racially homogeneous. Furthermore, the paired areas had about the same size population, similar age and sex differences, predominantly lower occupational levels, the same low levels of education, comparable size households, generally low health status though somewhat lower in the Negro areas, and general comparability on such indices as condition of dwellings, homes with radios, refrigeration equipment, and presence of central heating unit. The chief differences were that the white populations, predominantly of foreign-born

---

[42] *Id.* at pp. 152–153.
[43] McKay and Kobrin, *supra* note 12.
[44] *Id.* at table 57.
[45] *Id.* at p. 125.
[46] Earl R. Moses, "Differentials in Crime Rates Between Negroes and Whites," *American Sociological Review,* August 1947, 12:411–420.

extraction, were a settled population of long residence in their areas, while the Negro populations had sizeable groups of new migrants. Home ownership was much greater among the whites, the Negroes being primarily renters. The Negroes also paid higher rents for comparable dwelling units. The whites were "one step up the occupation ladder above Negroes."[47]

The results showed considerably higher rates of felons convicted in 1940 in the Negro as compared to the matched white areas. The white rates for males were 2.36 and 2.21, while the rates for the respectively paired Negro areas were 15.11 and 12.47.[48] The juvenile delinquency rates, however, per 1000 population, age 6–17, for the years 1939–42 were much closer. The white rates were 14.4 and 22.0, while the Negro area rates were 26.7 and 28.4.[49]

The discrepancy in the crime rates might have been anticipated since, as we have already seen in other studies, the differences which did exist between the Negro and white areas are ones which show high associations with crime rates, such as the high percentage of home ownership in the white area, a stable white population and a mobile Negro population and somewhat higher occupational status in the white area, that is, more craftsmen, foremen, and kindred workers as contrasted with laborers and domestic service workers among the Negro population. What is surprising is the relatively close correspondence in delinquency rates despite these differences. Nevertheless, the study does indicate the grave difficulties in locating truly equated areas for such controlled comparisons.

The basic findings in the Chicago studies of the spatial distribution of nationally and racial delinquency rates have not gone unchallenged. The primary objection is that the concern with documenting the effects of the process of assimilation on the delinquency rates within each nationality group led to the neglect of significant differences in the crime and delinquency rates of nationality groups arising from different tolerances in their own cultural and historical tradition for various forms of deviance.[50] Reference has been made to the low rates of delinquency and crime in areas of Oriental settlement, to significant differences in the delinquency of children of Russian Jewish immigrants and Italian immigrants in New York City though they entered at much the same time, and to the high rates of arrest of Jewish boys for violating street peddling laws.[51] It seems to be generally conceded that these cultural differences can influence significantly the *actual* or *absolute* size of the delinquency rate.[52] However, the main propo-

---

[47] *Id.* at p. 417.

[48] *Id.* at table V, p. 418.

[49] *Id.* at p. 418.

[50] Christen T. Jonassen, "A Re-evaluation and Critique of the Logic and Some Methods of Shaw and McKay," *American Sociological Review,* October 1949, 14:608–614. Also see rejoinder by Shaw and McKay, pp. 614–617.

[51] Sophia M. Robison, *Can Delinquency be Measured?* (New York: Columbia University Press, 1936), pp. 187 and 122.

[52] Shaw and McKay, *supra* note 50, p. 615.

sitions of the Chicago studies rest not so much on the actual size of the rates but the relationship between these rates. It is the *relative* difference between area rates for the same or different nationality groups depending on their length of residence in the city and the amount of movement toward the better integrated, more comfortable and settled areas toward the periphery of the city that supports the principal findings.[53]

The Cultural Enclave

One of the most significant findings of the ecological studies has been the identification of enclaves of culturally different insulated groups who have maintained low rates of crime and delinquency despite exposure to poverty, discrimination, exploitation, and disadvantageous conditions. Perhaps the most striking capacity to do this has been observed in areas of Oriental settlement in large cities. In Seattle a school district comprised of 90 percent Japanese boys showed a low delinquency rate of 5.7 despite the fact that the rate for the rest of the area was 27.7.[54] This district was located in a very deteriorated section of town with "the highest concentration of homicides, houses of prostitution, unidentified suicides, and cheap lodging-houses in Seattle."[55] Of the 710 boys who were sent to the Parental School (a boy's reform school) from 1919 to 1930 from Seattle, only three were Japanese, and the cases of these three indicated that they had lost "vital contact with the racial colony."[56]

This same type of situation was observed and studied in Vancouver. In an 8-year period (1928–36) a total of 4,814 delinquents appeared in the Vancouver Juvenile Court.[57] Only 19 were Orientals. During this period the delinquency rate for the whites was 15.65 per 1,000 and for the Orientals 1.0 per 1,000.[58]

Further investigation revealed that the Oriental children in Vancouver resided in areas of high delinquency and they attended schools with bad delinquency records. Furthermore the status of the Oriental was low. He experienced discrimination and was often the object of active hostility. The explanation seems to be that strenuous efforts were made to maintain family discipline and loyalty, to sustain a common concept and respect for their national origin, and to promote actively the pursuit and study of the Oriental religion, language, and culture.[59]

How long can this type of insularity maintain itself under the pressures

---

[53] *Ibid.*

[54] Norman S. Hayner, "Delinquency Areas in the Puget Sound Region," *American Journal of Sociology*, November 1933, 39:319.

[55] *Ibid.*

[56] *Ibid.*

[57] Helen G. MacGill, "The Oriental Delinquent in the Vancouver, B.C., Juvenile Court," *Sociology and Social Research*, May–June 1938, 22:430.

[58] *Ibid.*

[59] *Id.* at pp. 432–438.

for participation in modern life? There are historical examples to indicate that this is very difficult. A study of a Russian colony of immigrants in Los Angeles reported in 1930 that 5 percent of the children appeared before the juvenile court in the first 5 years of residence in a highly delinquent area. In the second 5 years of residence 46 percent were referred to the court, and in the next 10 years 83 percent were referred to the court.[60] Similarly, in Honolulu it was discovered that the Orientals who became involved in serious delinquency were most likely to be those who had previous associations with members of other groups.[61]

No one seriously suggests that it is easier to maintain control over the behavior of children in a high as compared to a low delinquency area but the fact is that many succeed. A recent study in New Haven suggests that the proper kind of family and school climate can provide a certain amount of insulation from highly delinquent surroundings and secure commitment to conventional goals.[62] The study included a sample of all youth born in Greater New Haven in 1942–44 whose supervising relative was on the Aid to Dependent Children rolls in 1950. Records were examined for the years between the sixth birthday and the 19th. Data came primarily from welfare, school, and police records. By 1962, a total of 34 percent had become known to the police or the juvenile court, compared to a delinquency rate of 18 percent for a control group of youth of the same age, sex, type of neighborhood, school performance, and lowest class level. However, the ADC group did show twice as many living in public housing, twice the number moving three or more times over an 11-year period, three times as many Negroes, and over ten times more broken homes.[63]

The delinquency rates among the ADC group varied markedly by race, sex, and school performance, all the way from no delinquency cases among 75 white females who were successful in school to 71 percent arrested or referred to court among 38 Negro males who were failing in school.[64] Additional significant differences appear when family deviance and the nature of the neighborhood of residence are considered. A "deviant family" was defined as one in which "one or both parents are in prison or mental hospital, or the parent has had a series of marriages, separations, multiple illegitimacies, or 'cut and run' affairs."[65] Those from deviant families are more delinquent, 41 percent to 31 percent, but deviant families had twice as much effect on Negro as compared to white youth. School success seems to compensate to some extent for the effects of deviant families, since among the successful in school 33 percent from the deviant families were delin-

[60] Pauline V. Young, "Urbanization as a Factor in Juvenile Delinquency," *Publications of the American Sociological Society*, 1930, 24:162–166.

[61] Lind, *supra* note 5, p. 217.

[62] Erdman B. Palmore and Phillip E. Hammond, "Interacting Factors in Juvenile Delinquency," *American Sociological Review*, December 1964, 29:848–854.

[63] *Id.* at p. 849.

[64] *Id.* at table 1, p. 850.

[65] *Id.* at p. 850.

quent, and 27 percent of those from nondeviant families were delinquent. However, among those failing in school 71 percent from deviant families were delinquent as compared to 45 percent of those from nondeviant families.[66]

Consideration was also given to the effect of residing in a deviant neighborhood, which was defined as of the lowest class standing in social and economic characteristics and having a high delinquency rate.[67] Negro youth were more than twice as likely as white youth to live in deviant neighborhoods. The effect of the deviant neighborhood is much greater on boys than on girls since 71 percent of the boys from deviant neighborhoods were delinquent compared to 47 percent of the boys from nondeviant neighborhoods, while the comparable percentages for girls were 14 and 16 percent.[68] Here again the effect of living in a deviant neighborhood is likely to be worst for those boys failing in school. Perhaps success in school insulates the boys to some extent from complete responsiveness to delinquent influences in the neighborhood or perhaps those least involved in neighborhood life are most likely to succeed in school. Among those boys failing in school who were from deviant neighborhoods, 82 percent were delinquent compared to 53 percent of the school failures from nondeviant neighborhoods, while the comparable percentages for the school successes were 44 and 37 percent.[69]

As this study points out, some factors are additive in their effects. If one is male, Negro, and a school failure, the chances of developing a delinquent record are greater than if any of these factors were different. Other factors seem to be interactive. They have a selective and sometimes a cushioning effect. School success may offset many of the effects of deviant neighborhoods or families. Also being from nondeviant neighborhoods or families is associated with lower delinquency rates despite failure in school.

Explanations and Implications of the Distribution of Crime Rates

The prevailing explanation of those conducting the ecological studies in Chicago of the high rates in certain areas of the city was in terms of social disorganization.[70] The high rates of transiency in these areas, the inability of the poor and unskilled new migrants to rely on old habits and customs as a guide to adjustment in the urban area, and the lack of stable institutions and relationships which the new migrant could trust contributed to a highly unstable set of social and cultural conditions in which to rear a family.

[66] *Id.* at table 3, p. 851.
[67] *Id.* at p. 851.
[68] *Id.* at table 4, p. 851.
[69] *Id.* at table 5, p. 851.
[70] Shaw and McKay, *Juvenile Delinquency in Urban Areas, supra* note 13, pp. 177–183.

These problems were compounded by the tendency for illegal practices and institutions to cluster in areas where the residents were not organized or equipped to defend their territory. The more fortunate groups brought customs and institutions from the old world which helped them to build cultural enclaves in which the process of assimilation could proceed more slowly, safely, and surely. As this assimilation progressed, they could begin to participate and accept responsible roles in the economic, social, and political life of the larger society. This increased security and economic well-being permitted them to move out and undertake commitments for themselves and their children to the accepted goals of the larger society.

From this perspective the Chicago ecologists identified the development of a stable and unified community as a major goal of action programs designed to prevent and control various social problems, including crime and delinquency. They saw a need to engage local participants in the task of developing indigenous institutions which they directed and which would reflect the critical needs of the residents themselves. This perspective resulted in the development of the Chicago Area Project in the 1930's and provided a body of action experience which has aided the development of many current delinquency area and poverty prevention programs.[71]

There are three other major explanations which have been advanced to account for the distribution of crime and delinquency rates and the characteristics of high rate areas. One of these points to the selective attraction of the poorer areas for many kinds of people, the poor, the emotionally disturbed, and the criminal, among others. This idea that many people who "drift" to unstable areas are already delinquent, or inclined to be so, has been frequently advanced but rarely studied. A very limited study was made in Decatur, Ill., of persons committed to the Illinois Prison System from Decatur.[72] The backgrounds of 73 residents were finally studied. Sixty-five of the 73 residents lived in delinquency areas of Decatur, but the study concluded that from 42 to 89 percent might be regarded as having been delinquent or criminal prior to coming to Decatur, or subject to the influence of other family members who had been criminal or delinquent elsewhere. The small numbers, inadequate records, and the inability to include delinquents and misdemeanants make this study rather inconclusive and leave the issue of the relative importance of "drift" unresolved.

A third explanation stresses the importance of conditions in the high delinquency areas and particularly the effect of a frustrating gap between the goals, aspirations, or expectations of residents in the area and the existence of either legitimate or illegitimate means to achieve them. The high rates of delinquency are thus a reflection of the limited legitimate

[71] For a recent reevaluation of this project from the standpoint of a chief participant see, Solomon Kobrin, "The Chicago Area Project—A 25-Year Assessment," *The Annals of the American Academy of Political and Social Science,* March 1959, 322:19–29.

[72] Donald R. Taft, "Testing the Selective Influence of Areas of Delinquency," *American Journal of Sociology,* March 1933, 38:699–712.

opportunities. At the same time there are available more institutionalized illegitimate opportunities than are present in other less criminal and delinquent areas of the city.[73]

The fourth explanation calls attention to the social, economic, and political forces which come to bear on the city from the surrounding region and the country. The shape and distribution of the social areas of the city, the problems and opportunities, land use, and population composition are in a major way responsive to this larger network of constantly changing demands in the national process of technological, cultural, and economic growth. To understand the distribution of persons, institutions, and social problems, like crime, in the city, one must relate them to this larger social context.[74] However, just how these external forces might operate to affect the distribution of such social problems as crime, in a city has not yet been clearly conceptualized.

It is not possible on the basis of current studies to determine which of these explanations will provide the most fruitful guidelines to action. They all, to some degree, have in common a focus on the operation of the social and economic system and the particular social processes which link people to it. Inherent in the operation of this system is to be found the source of the pressures which distribute people and crime rates among the various areas of the city. The path to understanding and successful action involves learning more about how it works, how it comes to bear on those who do or do not participate in it, and what types of changes in its structure or operation will enhance its utility and limit its costs.

Though these ecological studies of the distribution of crime and delinquency rates in cities have not been specifically addressed to a search for causes of crime, they have produced many useful insights about the conditions of life with which crime and delinquency are most often associated. In calling attention to the close relation between the social and economic conditions of life and the adequacy of local institutions in meeting the needs of residents of high delinquency areas, such studies have pointed to the need for much more detailed investigation of these connections. This more intensive analysis would be greatly facilitated if police districts and the reporting of crime data coincided with the area boundaries used in reporting census data. It would also be extremely helpful if other types of social and economic data reported by public and private institutions, such as education, health, and welfare agencies, used comparable census area

[73] For an exposition of this explanation and related theories see Richard A. Cloward and Lloyd E. Ohlin, *Delinquency and Opportunity* (Glencoe, Illinois: The Free Press, 1960).

[74] Shevky and Bell, *supra* note 30, pp. 3–19. Also see the paper by Judith Wilks in appendix A of President's Commission on Law Enforcement and Administration of Justice, *Crime and Its Impact—An Assessment* (Washington: U.S. Government Printing Office, 1967). The organization ot this chapter was greatly aided by the interpretive comments in Wilks' paper pertaining to intracity variations in crime and delinquency rates.

boundaries. This failure to use comparable area units has been one of the major restraints on the full exploitatation of ecological methods for the analysis of crime problems. Nevertheless, the ecological studies have provided the beginnings of a theoretical explanation of the distribution of crime rates which justifies a broad attack on the underlying social and economic conditions which produce such heavy concentrations of both offenses and offenders in some areas of the city rather than others.

.   .   .   .   .

Riots and Crime

It is tempting to describe the riots that flared up in the ghettos of some 20 cities during the summers of 1964, 1965, and 1966 as "senseless." It is also unenlightening. To be sure, there were respects in which the riots made little sense. Few of the policemen or white passersby whom the rioters assaulted were people against whom they had specific personal grievances. The great majority of the casualties of the riots—the dead, the injured, and the arrested—were rioters.[75] Some of the property the rioters destroyed belonged to them or their neighbors; a poignant journalistic vignette from the Watts riot in Los Angeles was a description of a man woefully gazing at a gutted drycleaning establishment to which he had entrusted seven pairs of trousers. The riots changed the attitude of some Americans toward the civil rights movement from sympathy to antipathy.[76] And of course there is no sense to the idea—in the doubtful event that anyone seriously entertains it—that sporadic outbursts of frenzy and violence can solve complicated social problems.

However, to say that the riots were unplanned, undisciplined, unled, and incoherent is not to say that they expressed nothing and signified nothing.[77] They expressed the general hostility many Negroes feel toward white people. They expressed the particular hostility many Negroes feel toward the police and toward ghetto merchants and businessmen. They expressed the outrage many Negroes feel at the conditions in which they must live. They expressed the increasing refusal by Negroes to accept further delay in being granted full participation in the social, economic, and political development

[75] For example, of the 34 fatalities in the Watts riot 26 were shot by police or National Guard, indicating that they were active participants (looting, burning, running road blocks, etc.).

[76] Over a 2-year period the Gallup poll added the question "Do you think the Johnson administration is pushing integration too fast?" The percentage of respondents, in the national sample, who answered "yes" follows:

	Percent
February 1964 (before the first riot)	30
April 1965	34
August 1965	40
July 1966	46
September 1966	52

[77] Evidence of the widespread participation in the riots is cited below.

of the Nation. They expressed the increasing conviction of Negroes that legal methods of protest have not accomplished enough fast enough. They signified that the ghettos of American cities are a threat to the peace and safety of all of America. They signified that the need to abolish ghettos is urgent, and that the time is short.

Unmistakably, then, the riots were social protest of a sort—a criminal sort. Thousands of acts of assault, of arson, of theft, of vandalism are what a riot is. Putting an end to a riot is a police problem. Almost every riot was touched off by an encounter between the police and a Negro.[78] The majority of those encounters were essentially commonplace or even trivial;[79] in many of them the police were responding to a complaint by a Negro; in most of them the police acted, at least to begin with, with prudence and propriety. In short, an integral element in every riot was strain between the police and members of the Negro community. Finally, it cannot be a coincidence that riots take place in just those neighborhoods where there is the greatest amount of everyday crime.[80] This is not to say, of course, that rioters and everyday criminals are the same people—though in some instances they may be. The point is that anger, violence, despair, and cynicism prevail in the Negro ghettos of America and these conditions contribute both to everyday crime and to protest riots.

[*The President's Commission Report on Law Enforcement and Administration of Justice,* Task Force Report: Crime and Its Impact—An Assessment (*Washington: U.S. Government Printing Office, 1967*), *pp. 60–61, 63–64, 67–76, 116.*]

[78] The two Chicago riots of 1965 are among the few not started by a police-citizen incident.

[79] Although in a few cases (Harlem 1964, Cleveland, Atlanta, San Francisco 1966) the precipitating incident was serious—a Negro boy shot by a patrolman—the majority of precipitating incidents were routine police actions. For example, in Philadelphia in 1964 the incident was an attempt by the police to remove an intoxicated woman from a vehicle blocking an intersection.

[80] Precise arrest rate figures comparing the riot areas with other Negro and white areas are not available. All of the riot areas, however, were Negro ghettos and had crime rates much higher than the city as a whole.

6 *Professional crime*

. . . . .

Existing information about professional crime is fragmentary, and much of it may be outdated. A primary source is Edwin H. Sutherland's classic description of theft as a way of life, "The Professional Thief," but that work, though helpful, was published in 1937 and describes the life of a thief in the period between 1905 and 1925. Other books published since have focused on particular types of criminal activity normally engaged in by professionals including confidence game operations,[1] pickpocketing,[2] professional robbery and burglary,[3] and receiving stolen goods.[4] These few studies provide the basic information on professional crime available in the literature. Although differences in emphasis and coverage exist among them, they present a reasonably coherent, though necessarily incomplete, description of certain types of professional criminal activity.

In order to supplement this material, the Commission sponsored a pilot field research study in four cities—Atlanta, Chicago, New York, and San Francisco—during the summer of 1966.[5] The study differed from previous research in that it used police and prosecutors as well as professional criminals as primary informants. Each consultant spent approximately half of his field time, or about 10 days, conferring with police and district attorneys on the problems of professional crime in their cities. In addition, some of the consultants observed the police in action and examined relevant materials in the files of special intelligence units. Law enforcement agents provided most of the leads to professional criminals.[6]

[1] D. W. Maurer, *The Big Con* (New York: Pocketbooks, Inc., 1949).
[2] D. W. Maurer, *Whiz Mob* (New Haven: College and University Press, 1955).
[3] J. B. Martin, *My Life in Crime* (New York: Harper, 1952).
[4] See J. Hall, *Theft, Law, and Society* (2nd ed., Indianapolis: Bobbs-Merrill, 1952).
[5] The Office of Law Enforcement Assistance, Justice Department, funded the project. Brandeis University administered the project grant. The project's coordinator was Professor Leroy Gould of Yale University. He was assisted by 5 field consultants, 2 advisors, and 1 research assistant.
[6] Some of those contacted through the police referred the staff to other professional criminals.

The consultants spent the balance of their time in the field (about 10 to 15 days each) locating and talking with professional criminals. The number of criminals interviewed varied from a low of eight in one city (Chicago) to 19 in another (San Francisco), with a total of 50 being interviewed. About two-thirds of the total number were in jail or prison at the time of their interviews. Although compared with prior studies the combined samples amounted to a relatively large number of informants, it is obvious that such a survey, conducted under such tight time limitations, could not result in a detailed comprehensive picture of professional crime in the United States. But the data collected are useful for obtaining some insights about professional criminals and the life they lead. Combined with relevant data from previous studies, they provide the basis for the material in this chapter.

For purposes of the Commission-sponsored study, professional crime was defined as: "Crime committed for personal economic gain by individuals whose major source of income is from criminal pursuits and who spend the majority of their working time in illegal enterprises." Organized crime and white-collar crime were specifically excluded. And while the definition was comprehensive enough to cover a variety of crimes such as killing or strong-arming for hire, professional arson and even prostitution, the principal emphasis of the Commission's study, following the pattern of earlier studies, was on essentially predatory crimes where the victim does not consent and where the actors usually function not as employees but as entrepreneurs. This approach tends to focus on theft and theft-related offenses, including such crimes as receiving stolen goods, shoplifting, pickpocketing, auto theft, burglary, forgery, confidence games, and various kinds of fraud.

This definition differs from traditional definitions in that it does not include any requirement that professionals have specially developed skills or that they have any particularly close association with other professionals. In Sutherland's classic study, the professional thief was described as having "a complex of abilities and skills * * * developed * * * by education" which "can be secured only in association with professional thieves."[7] Obviously this difference in definition affected the characteristics found to be associated with professional criminals. Thus prior studies found that professional criminals were often highly specialized, and that they tended to be quite loyal to members of their professional groups. The Commission-sponsored study, on the other hand, found that professional criminals tended to be generalists, to operate in a variety of loose associations with other professionals, and to exhibit no particular loyalty to their fellows. There is no way of knowing whether these different findings reflect only the difference in definition, or whether they reflect in addition changes in the character of professional crime.

· · · · ·

[7] E. H. Sutherland, *The Professional Thief* (Chicago: University of Chicago Press, 1937), pp. 197–198.

The Extent of Professional Crime

There are no accurate statistics on the amount of professional crime. Published studies contain only estimates of career earnings of individual professional criminals, illustrative "touches," estimated average weekly earnings of various types of professional mobs, and other data of this order.[8]

The lack of accurate data on professional crime is in part a reflection of the general absence of adequate statistics on crime. . . . But there are particular difficulties in measuring professional crime. The professional and nonprofessional often engage in the same type of criminal activity. Even if crime reporting improves, it will still be difficult to distinguish the professional's work from that of the amateur. The task is complicated by the fact that the kinds of crimes committed by professionals change over a period of time.

Nevertheless, there is reason to believe that professional criminals are responsible for a large proportion of all property crimes committed and probably an even larger proportion of total property loss through such crimes. Available information indicates, for example, that there are a large number of professional criminals, all of whom, by definition, work at crime on a relatively full-time basis, and some of whom are reported to have very high incomes, sometimes exceeding $100,000. And it is apparent that thefts involving the loss of large amounts of valuable merchandise require the sorts of contacts with fences and commercial establishments that professionals develop.

There is evidence that the more successful professionals tend to spend substantial portions of their working time in developing lucrative opportunities and planning their criminal activity. A week, month, or even longer period may be spent in preparing for a particularly promising venture. As a result, "scores" tend to be good and the risk of apprehension low. The run-of-the-mill professional criminal, on the other hand, finds it necessary to spend more time in actual stealing to meet expenses and maintain himself at a comfortable and free-spending standard of living. Members of rackets, such as picking pockets and other forms of low-paying larceny, spend virtually all of their time this way.

The Commission's study produced some vivid descriptions of the day-to-day life of the typical professional, the flavor of which is captured by the term "hustling."[9] For the small-time professional criminal, hustling means

[8] For example, Martin's professional burglar estimated that he was in on $250,000 worth of thieving over a 4-year period. Martin, *supra* note 3, p. 139. This contrasts with the "scores" made by big con-men which during the 1920's were reported to run to $375,000. Maurer, *The Big Con, supra* note 1, pp. 26–30. At the other extreme, $15,000 is said to be a better than average income for a pickpocket, as of 1955. Maurer, p. 38.

[9] This term was often encountered in Atlanta and San Francisco, where it is most likely to be used to describe the activities of run-of-the-mill professionals, rather than the more successful ones.

moving around the bars and being seen; it means asking "what's up." It means "connecting" in the morning with two others who have a burglary set up for the evening, calling a man you know to see if he wants to buy 10 stolen alpaca sweaters at $5 each, and scouting the streets for an easy victim. It means being versatile: passing checks, rolling a drunk, driving for a stickup, boosting a car, burglarizing a store. It is a planless kind of existence, but with a purpose—to make as much money as can be made each day, no holds barred. While the more successful professional criminals hustle to some extent, they can afford to be much more purposeful and choosy in their criminal activities.

The Commission's study revealed that run-of-the-mill professionals regularly gather at certain bars and restaurants which in effect function as criminal job placement centers. These centers do for the professional criminal what want ads, employment offices, and businessmen's luncheons do for legitimate business. Through contact with other criminals, professionals learn of jobs to be pulled and of openings in groups planning to pull them. Contacts of this type also enable the professional to keep abreast of the latest techniques, and to gather information regarding criminal opportunities. These centers tend to attract the low-status professional criminal; apparently the successful practitioner in crime does not go to the employment office.

Characteristics of Professional Crime

Skills

Sutherland drew a sharp distinction between the professional and the amateur thief based upon their relative skills. Under his classification, a person might steal as a full-time occupation, but he would not be a professional if he lacked the comprehensive complex of technical skills, personal contacts, and knowledge necessary in order to make a good living at crime in comparative safety. Sutherland's professional thief was contemptuous of the amateur's crude techniques, low income, and inability to avoid arrest. He therefore avoided association with amateurs and excluded them from the complex of reciprocal expectations and services which characterized his own way of life. But even under this definition, the professional criminal's skills vary significantly in kind[10] and degree. The big-time jewel thief and the "ropers" and "insidemen" who contrive to extract thousands of dollars from wealthy victims in the big con game are at one end of the spectrum. At the other are petty thieves, short con operators, and pickpockets who, though technically competent, lack the techniques needed to make big scores consistently.

---

[10] A classification frequently encountered is the distinction between the "light" rackets in which stealing is accomplished by stealth or by manipulating the victim, and the "heavy" rackets in which force, or its threat, is used.

Clearly there is an even greater range in skills when all persons who work at crime on a relatively full-time basis are classified as professionals. Nevertheless even this group is, as a whole, a relatively competent one. Many of its members possess, in addition to particular skills, the ability to plan and carry out detailed operations, to manipulate people, to analyze problems and implement solutions. It is clear that professional crime represents the loss to society of the potential contributions of a capable group of people, as well as the channeling of their energies into destructive activities.

Specialization

There is evidence that some individual professional criminals tend to specialize in a limited number of related rackets. Many exclude certain kinds of activities: thus some of the professional criminals who were interviewed in the course of the Commission's study said that they would not use violence. But in general the Commission's study indicated that professionals in the middle and lower status levels tend to be versatile.[11] Even the better professional criminal is not always free to follow his preferred line of work, since it may not be either profitable or safe at all times. Under these circumstances he may undertake activities at which he is not especially skilled.

Group Activity

Earlier studies described the relationship between professional criminals as relatively structured. Sutherland, in describing the professional thief of 40 years ago, and Maurer, in his treatment of professional confidence men and pickpockets, stressed the idea that professional criminals enjoy a sense of identity and solidarity and work within a set of well-defined norms and codes of loyalty, helpfulness, and honesty in dealing with one another.

The Commission-sponsored study, directed at a broader group of criminals, found that only the more successful members of this group could be so characterized. It found that the associations or gangs which run-of-the-mill professionals form to commit their crimes tend to be unstable, and that this instability results in part from the diversity of their activities. Different crimes require different kinds of personnel, amounts of financial backing, and types of fencing operations. Consequently, groupings and relations with loan sharks and fences may change from operation to operation. Even the few relatively stable groups which the consultants heard about brought in other professional criminals for certain jobs, and some members of the group might hire out from time to time on other jobs.

The shifting, transitory pattern of most professional criminals' working

[11] A notable exception are pickpockets who are relatively unsuccessful members of the professional crime group, and yet are highly specialized.

relationships was found to be accompanied by the absence of any strong ethical codes. Few of the professional criminals interviewed, for example, seemed to feel bound by any "no ratting" rule. Typically they appeared to take it for granted that others would do whatever necessary to protect themselves—to avoid imprisonment or reduce a sentence—and that they, therefore, should do likewise. As one professional criminal commented: "The one who gets his story told first gets the lightest sentence." There was little resentment expressed about this. It was treated like the weather—a fact of life. Further, criminals expected to be cheated by their colleagues, or by most colleagues. Many of those interviewed reported having been cheated by fences and even by their partners in a particular venture. Victimization of one professional group by another is apparently also fairly common, limited only by fear of reprisal.

There were exceptions to this general pattern, however. Some professional criminals stated that they had worked with certain individuals whom they trusted completely. And relative stability was found among the really successful professional criminals in New York and Chicago. In Chicago, for example, there is a group of between 50 and 200 "heavy" professional thieves who concentrate on such criminal activities as burglary, robbery, and cartage theft. It is said that this group, or at least the core members of the group, are quite stable and quite highly organized, and apparently they exert a considerable amount of control over their own regular members, as well as over persons who work with them only on occasional jobs.

Changing Criminal Opportunities

As conditions in society change, certain criminal occupations become relatively unprofitable, and other opportunities develop. The nature of crime will tend to change accordingly. Criminal activity like legitimate business activity may respond to the market, to supply and demand curves, and to technological developments. Professional crime, guided by the profit motive, can be expected to be particularly responsive to such factors. One example is the reported decline in safecracking. This is apparently due in part to such factors as increased law enforcement surveillance and mobility, and improvements in the design of safes. Undoubtedly the fact that safes no longer play as important a role has also contributed to the decline—modern economic transactions involve the transfer of credits much more than the transfer of cash. Thus it may have become both more difficult and riskier to rob safes, and also less profitable. At the same time, more promising opportunities for crime have arisen. One of these is check-passing. The Commission's study learned that nearly every burglar nowadays is also in the check business. One professional burglar said that in one period of several weeks between burglaries he passed over $20,000 of stolen checks. A generation ago burglars did not even look for checks to steal.

A good illustration of the effect of the development of a new market is auto theft and crimes relating to the automobile, such as auto stripping and auto "boosting" (stealing goods from parked cars), activities which are reported to be thriving in the cities surveyed. The Commission's study found also that there has been a rapid rise in recent years in home improvement and related frauds, a rise which corresponds roughly to the increase in privately owned homes. Some law enforcement officials think that in many cities these frauds currently constitute the most profitable source of income for professional criminals.

Professional criminals are also reported to be turning from robbing banks, picking pockets, and operating confidence games to other opportunities, but documentation for such new trends is scanty.

Careful research into changes in the general patterns of crimes committed by professionals and the factors that caused such changes would provide us with more insight into the nature of professional criminality and might provide a basis for designing better methods of crime prevention and control. It might also make it possible to begin to anticipate and plan for such changes.

Key Aspects of Professional Crime

The services of the fence and the loan shark appear to be essential to the operations of many professional criminals. Since a great many professionals may depend on a very few such figures, they may constitute a particularly vulnerable aspect of professional crime. The "fix" appears to be of similar importance to the success of professional criminality.

The Fence

Nearly all professional theft is undertaken with the aim of selling the goods thereafter. Although the thief himself may retail his stolen merchandise,[12] he probably will prefer to sell to a fence. He thereby increases his safety by reducing the risk that he will be arrested with the goods in his possession, or that they will be stolen in turn from him. He also avoids the dangers associated with the disposal process itself. In addition, large quantities of goods which may be perishable or otherwise quickly lose their value, or for which there is a specialized demand, will require a division of labor and level of organization beyond the capacity of an individual thief operating as his own retailer. The professional thief thus needs a "middleman" in the same way and for some of the same reasons as the farmer, manufacturer, or other producer.

---

[12] Most professional shoplifters are thought to bypass fences and sell directly to the public. See Mary O. Cameron, *The Booster and the Snitch* (Glencoe, Ill.: The Free Press, 1964), p. 57. Martin's burglar had considerable experience retailing the goods he had stolen (*supra* note 3).

The types of thefts recorded by the Commission study staff in New York and Chicago suggest the presence of big-time fences who can handle large quantities of specialized goods. For example, in Chicago there recently occurred a cartage theft of $250,000 worth of merchandise and Green Stamps from a Sperry and Hutchinson warehouse and another cartage theft of copper metal valued at over $400,000. To dispose of such quantities of specialized goods requires connections with commercial firms. Most likely a highly accomplished fence served as a middleman between the thieves and the eventual buyers.[13]

As an illustration of the level of efficiency which may be attained by professionals working in cooperation with fences, the Commission's study learned from the New York City police that, within the space of approximately 1 month following the recent increase in that city's cigarette sales tax, an entire system for distributing bootlegged cigarettes had been set up and was operating smoothly. The out-of-state suppliers, the truckers, and both the wholesale and retail distributors had been organized, and the system was operating on a scale capable of handling full truckloads of untaxed cigarettes shipped in from the South.

Some fences engage in fencing as a supplement to their legitimate businesses, often on a more or less regular basis. The consultants learned of clothing and appliance dealers who regularly serve as outlets for stolen goods. The major outlets for stolen jewels in one of the cities studied were reported to be legitimate jewelry merchants. Other fences deal primarily or wholly in stolen goods, and are therefore professional criminals themselves.

Some narcotics pushers act as fences, taking stolen goods instead of cash for narcotics. While dealing with addicts is generally regarded as more dangerous than dealing with nonaddicts, it is also more profitable. The addict in need of a "fix" does not bargain well.

Little research has been done on fencing,[14] despite its central role in professional crime. More information is needed about the nature of the market for illicit goods and the extent to which demand for various types of goods affects the incidence of theft. More should also be learned about the relationship of legitimate and illegitimate markets. Little is known about the pattern of distribution of stolen goods. When stolen automobiles are excluded, only a very small proportion of the total amount of goods stolen is returned to its owners. The redistribution of goods through theft and resale might constitute a significant subsidy to certain groups in our society; its curtailment might have significant side effects which should be explored.

[13] See also John F. Lyons, "Lucrative Looting," *Wall Street Journal,* July 28, 1965, for an analysis of the role played by fences in the theft and distribution of large quantities of mercury and synthetic rubber.

[14] Jerome Hall's report, *supra* note 4, is the only systematic study of fencing published. Sutherland, Maurer, and Martin, however, provide some additional descriptive and analytic material (*supra* notes 7, 1, and 3).

Finally, it would be desirable to have more information about the organization and operations of large-scale fencing operations, to aid in the development of better methods of law enforcement.

The Loan Shark

The loan shark also performs a key function by providing professional criminals with capital and emergency funds. The literature of professional crime contains few references to loan shark activity. Both Sutherland and Maurer[15] describe a practice whereby members of a professional criminal gang establish their own emergency fund. Each member of the gang contributes an equal share to the fund which he may receive back if he leaves the gang. If he is arrested while working with the gang, he has access to as much of the fund as he needs for a bail bond, legal fees, or related expenses. This sort of arrangement appears to be an extension of the natural interdependence of a closely knit group and tends to reinforce the solidarity of the group.

The loan shark functions quite differently. He may meet professional criminals' needs for cash in emergencies, but his activity often has secondary effects which tend to be detrimental to his clients.

Professional criminals may turn to the loan shark to finance crimes which require extra amounts of capital—to buy the tools, or whatever may be needed for the operation, or to bribe public officials. The professional criminal may be willing to pay usurious interest rates (sometimes reported to be as high as 100 percent per week for highly risky loans) if he expects his activities to be particularly lucrative. He may also need emergency financing when apprehended, to pay bail and legal costs. To repay the money borrowed plus interest upon his release, the criminal will often engage in further criminal activities, often more risky than those he ordinarily undertakes. If rearrested, he must post bond again and incur additional legal fees. This pattern may be repeated a number of times before he is finally brought to trial. The high interest charged by the loan shark may thus itelf precipitate criminal activity.

The interaction between loan sharking and professional crime doubtless is far more complicated than was discovered during the course of the Commission's brief study. The study staff was told that some "legitimate" businessmen provide loans to criminals occasionally. And there was some evidence that professional criminals regard loan sharking as a relatively safe and profitable racket, and that those who make a big score or otherwise accumulate enough capital frequently set themselves up as loan sharks. But further study is needed on these as well as other facets of the relationship between professional crime and the loan shark.

[15] Sutherland, *supra* note 7, pp. 31, 35–36, 111; Maurer, *Whiz Mob, supra* note 2, pp. 137–138.

The Fix

There is evidence that the professional criminal frequently bribes public officials to increase his security against law enforcement activity.[16] The fix may be applied in advance to forestall intervention by the police and thereby reduce a major occupational hazard of his profession. Or it may be used after the fact to alleviate the usual consequences of apprehension—to obtain reduced charges or a lighter sentence, or to arrange for preferential treatment. In some communities the professional must himself deal directly with the appropriate officials. In others there may be a local "fixer" who has connections with the party in power and who may be tied in with organized crime. Here the professional criminal need only deal with the fixer as a middleman.[17] Maurer reports that in some cities there are several fixers, each handling the fix for a different type of a racket. Specialization attaches even in the world of bribery.

Attorneys, bondsmen, politicians, and other ostensibly legitimate persons may be fixers. A fixer may also be a fence, the insideman in a big con game, or a member of organized crime. Cash is the usual commodity used to purchase immunity, but sometimes a case may be fixed for credit or as a favor.

The extent of fixing today is difficult to document. The Commission's study, which did not focus on this aspect of professional crime, encountered little evidence of the sort of fixing described here. The fact that police, judges, and prosecutors probably are better paid and trained today may mean that individually they are less susceptible to bribery. The increased bureaucratization of police operations and personnel practices may also make policemen less subject to corruption from above. And the decline of the big city political machine may have contributed to a decline in organized fixing. On the other hand, professional criminals still operate with considerable success, and it seems likely that they need some protection to do so.

Relations with Organized Crime

Professional crime may or may not be carried on in structured groups. In some ways it can be loosely analogized to legitimate business activity. But its essence is not business; it is outright theft or theft-related conduct. Organized crime, on the other hand, tends to bear a closer resemblance to the operations of business. It involves thousands of criminals working in

[16] See generally, Maurer, *The Big Con, supra* note 1, pp. 216–251; Sutherland, *supra* note 7, pp. 118, 210–222.

[17] Martin's professional burglar found that: "With the exception of shooting the Mayor or the President, there isn't anything he can't straighten out. For money, lots of money." Martin, *supra* note 3, p. 247. However, it is also reported that "right towns" in which complete immunity can be purchased are becoming increasingly scarce.

well-organized, highly structured operations engaged in activities involving the supplying of illegal goods and services—such as gambling, narcotics, and prostitution—to cooperative customers; it often involves infiltration into legitimate businesses and labor unions.

Regrettably, little is known of the nature and extent of the relationship between professional and organized crime. This is hardly surprising given the limited facts known about either activity. But it is apparent that a variety of working arrangements exist between professional criminals and organized crime, which are of substantial significance for both categories of crime. There is some evidence, for example, that the fences and loan sharks with whom professional criminals deal are frequently part of the organized crime operation. And there is some indication that organized crime exerts significant power and control over professional crime. The Commission's study staff was informed, for example, that in Chicago the syndicate occasionally provides the services of an arbitrator to settle disputes among the members of a large theft gang. And the syndicate apparently hires professional criminals, on occasion, to do particular jobs such as homicide. But organized crime may also be victimized by professionals. Martin's professional criminal frequently hijacked syndicate trucks and distilleries.

Conclusion

The professional criminal's energy and talents are devoted not merely to committing profitable crimes, but to avoiding the legal consequences of such activity. His methods range from simply taking full advantage of all rights accorded him by the system of criminal justice to actual corruption of the system. It is obvious that sophisticated methods of law enforcement are necessary to deal with the phenomenon of professional crime. A more sophisticated understanding of professional crime is a clear prerequisite.

Present knowledge about professional crime is clearly inadequate. The literature is limited in scope and may be outdated. The Commission's pilot study could obviously do little more than touch on issues deserving of further exploration. But even this brief study gave some indication of the potential that further research has for improved methods of law enforcement.

Some similarities, for example, have been noted between professional crime and ordinary business activity. Further study may lead to the application of the techniques of economic analysis, business, and marketing to the problem of diverting and channeling professional criminal activity. More information about the direction of future change in the types of crimes professionals tend to commit would help planners to build crime prevention components into new business devices and law enforcement agencies to allocate their resources more efficiently. Greater concentration on key figures such as the loan shark or fence may provide a greater return per law enforcement dollar and greatly inhibit professional criminal activity. Further research may produce sufficient information to justify allocation of a larger proportion of law enforcement resources to dealing with professional crime.

The development of more information about the skills and versatility of the professional criminal may also be of direct use to law enforcement and correctional agencies. Correctional programs might take more account of the competence exhibited by the typical professional—with the purpose of channeling his existing capabilities into legitimate fields. The apparent versatility exhibited by professional criminals suggests that the traditional organization of police agencies into specialized squads—such as robbery, burglary, auto theft, and bunco—requires reconsideration. It suggests also the need for a much greater degree of communication between law enforcement agents with information on professional criminals. Detectives tend to be too reluctant to share their information sources with other detectives, or to supply information to any centralized intelligence unit which may exist. Also the traditional complaint orientation of police departments is not appropriate for dealing with persons who are engaged continuously, rather than episodically, in criminal activities.

Chicago provides one exception to the traditional pattern of police organization in relation to the problem of professional crime. In 1963 the Chicago Police Department established an intelligence unit, locally referred to as the C.I.U., which has the responsibility for gathering, and disseminating to other detectives, information about persons in the Chicago area who are known to be, or are highly suspected of being, regularly engaged in big-time professional crime. The members of this unit concentrate not on crimes, but on criminals. When a crime is committed that appears likely to have been committed by someone on whom they have a file, the C.I.U. tries to link their suspects to the crime. There is a different intelligence unit assigned to organized crime.

Other cities should experiment with the development of a similar intelligence function. By developing and sharing knowledge about the operations of professional criminals among different jurisdictions, it is likely that far greater success can be achieved in controlling professional crime.

[*The President's Commission Report on Law Enforcement and Administration of Justice,* Task Force Report: Crime and Its Impact—An Assessment (*Washington: U.S. Government Printing Office, 1967*), Chap. 7, pp. 96–101.]

7   *White-collar crime*

. . . . .

The term white-collar crime was first popularized by Edwin H. Sutherland in 1939. Until the publication in 1949 of his pioneering study. *White Collar Crime,*[1] virtually all criminological literature dealt with ordinary crimes—crimes most prevalent among persons in the lower socioeconomic classes. Donald R. Cressey, in his introduction to the 1961 edition of *White Collar Crime,* observed that "the lasting merit of this book * * * is its demonstration that a pattern of crime can be found to exist outside both the focus of popular preoccupation with crime and the focus of scientific investigation of crime and criminality."[2]

Sutherland defined white-collar crime as "crime committed by a person of respectability and high social status in the course of his occupation."[3] But the term white-collar crime has generally come to include crimes such as tax fraud, which are not necessarily committed either in connection with an occupation or by persons of "high" social status, but are as a general matter committed by the relatively well-to-do. This definition excludes so-called street crimes, such as burglary, robbery or aggravated assault, which are occasionally, but not generally, committed by persons of means.

As applied to regulatory offenses, the scope of white-collar criminality has expanded in recent years. Until the late 19th century, the economic life of this country was largely unregulated, but over the years it became clear that business enterprise had to be regulated in order to protect both the public and business itself—to maintain standards of health and safety, to assist the poor and ignorant, to obtain decent housing and other necessities, and to maintain the economy at a high level of production. Today virtually every aspect of business life is regulated in some way. There are antitrust laws, food and drug laws, safety and health laws, licensing systems for different kinds of

[1] Sutherland, *White Collar Crime* (Dryden Press, Inc., 1949).
[2] Donald R. Cressey, "Foreword," in Sutherland, *White Collar Crime* (New York: Holt, Rinehart & Winston, 1961), p. xii.
[3] Address to the American Sociological Society, 1939.

business, housing codes, and a multitude of other regulatory statutes. Many of these regulatory laws are enforced, at least in part, by criminal sanctions.

As compared to the offenders described in Chapters 4 and 5 of this volume, white-collar offenders, by definition, have enjoyed a variety of social and economic advantages. They have received better educations and are better equipped to earn their livings legitimately. Perhaps over-simplifying the distinctive characteristics of such offenders, Sutherland wrote in "Crimes of Corporations" in 1956:

> it is very clear that the criminal behavior of businessmen cannot be explained by poverty, in the usual sense, or by bad housing or lack of recreational facilities or feeble-mindedness or emotional instability. Business leaders are capable, emotionally balanced, and in no sense pathological.[4]

At the outset it is important to recognize the imprecision of the white-collar crime label both as applied to offenders and offenses. Crimes such as employee theft range from pilfering by truck drivers, stock-room personnel or retail salespeople to embezzlement by top executives. Cheating the government can include failure to report tips or other cash receipts and major tax or government contract frauds. And just as burglars range from the relatively successful professional in his 30's or 40's to the 13-year-old amateur from the slums, white-collar offenders include many different types of people.

. . . . .

The Impact of White-Collar Crime

Extent and Scope

There is little systematic data available regarding the incidence of white-collar crime. There are, for example, no consolidated statistics comparable to the FBI's Uniform Crime Reports in the area of traditional crime. Many white-collar crimes are of relatively recent origin. Moreover, it is very difficult to obtain statistics about some types of white-collar crime. . . . [I]t is extremely difficult to discover the existence of such crimes as antitrust violations and tax frauds.[5]

Such information as is available, though not systematically compiled, indicates that white-collar crime is pervasive in our society and causes enormous economic and social harm. Congressional investigations have

[4] Edwin H. Sutherland, "Crimes of Corporations," in Albert K. Cohen, Alfred Lindesmith, and Karl F. Schuessler, *The Sutherland Papers* (Bloomington: Indiana University Press, 1956), p. 96.

[5] President's Commission on Law Enforcement and Administration of Justice, *Task Force Report: Crime and Its Impact—An Assessment* (Washington: U.S. Government Printing Office, 1967), Attachment A, p. 111, Attachment B, p. 113.

turned up indications of widespread unethical and illegal behavior in various industries. Popular accounts tell of dishonest and unethical practices in the medical and legal professions, the television industry, and among morticians, drug companies and other businesses and professions.

These are corroborated by the few scientific surveys which have been undertaken. Sutherland's investigation of 70 of our largest corporations, published in 1948, suggests that law violation is prevalent in our large business enterprises. He examined the decisions of courts and regulatory commissions under the antitrust, false advertising, patent, copyright, and labor laws as they applied to corporations. During a 45-year period, he found that 980 adverse decisions had been rendered, of which 779 indicated that crimes had been committed. Every one of the 70 corporations had a decision against it and the average number was 14.0. Ninety-eight percent of the 70 corporations had at least four adverse decisions. About 60 percent of the 70 corporations had been convicted by criminal courts. They averaged approximately four convictions each.[6] A study of blackmarket violations during World War II revealed that approximately one in every 15 of the three million business concerns in the country had been punished for serious violations of price regulations. The evidence showed that the total number of violations was much larger than indicated by officially imposed sanctions.[7]

The *Reader's Digest* staff in 1941 sought to document by experimentation the level of white-collar crime in a study of automobile garages, radio repair shops and watch repair shops. Investigators for the magazine disconnected a coil wire in an automobile, a relatively easily diagnosed problem, and then took the automobile to 347 garages in 48 states. Of these, 129 immediately noted the trouble, and either charged nothing or a nominal fee for the work. The remainder—63 percent of the garages—overcharged, inserted unnecessary parts, charged for work not done or for parts not needed, or took other similar action. Similarly, a radio in excellent working condition was taken to repair shops after one of the tubes had been loosened. Of 304 shops, 109 honestly identified the obvious difficulty, but the rest (almost two-thirds) treated it as a substantial repair problem. And, finally, the investigators loosened the small screw that fastens the winding wheel on a watch, and then requested a number of shops to repair it. In almost half of the cases the jewelers charged for cleaning work not performed, and for parts not needed or used.[8]

Commissioner Cohen provided some insight into the amount of tax fraud

[6] Sutherland, *White Collar Crime, supra* note 1, chapter II.

[7] Clinard, *The Black Market* (New York: Rinehart, 1952), p. 36. See also Hartung, "White Collar Offenses in the Wholesale Meat Industry in Detroit," *American Journal of Sociology,* 1950, 56:25. But see Lane, "Why Businessmen Violate the Law," *Journal of Criminal Law, Criminology, and Police Science,* 1953, 44:151, which found relatively low rates of violation.

[8] These findings, first reported in the *Reader's Digest,* are presented in Riis and Pattie, *The Repairman Will Get You If You Don't Watch Out* (Doubleday, Doran & Co., Inc., 1942), pp. 53–184.

by noting that in 1964, with the inauguration of dividend and interest reporting by banks and corporations to the taxpayer, there was a 45 percent increase in this type of income reflected on tax forms, and that 28 percent more income was collected from these sources.[9] Of course there is no way to determine how much of the unreported income in earlier years was merely overlooked and how much deliberately ignored on the assumption that the Government would be unlikely to discover the omission.

The most comprehensive survey of attitudes by business executives toward management and corporate practices showed that many believed that unethical conduct and criminal activities are widespread. The sample consisted of executives subscribing to the Harvard Business Review. Almost half of the respondents agreed with the statement: "The American business executive tends to ignore the great ethical laws as they apply immediately to his work. He is preoccupied chiefly with gains." Four out of seven believed that businessmen "would violate a code of ethics whenever they thought they could avoid detection."[10]

Costs

White-collar crime may cause several different types of harm. First, it may and often does cause serious financial losses, sometimes to a single individual or business and sometimes to the entire business community or consumer public. The exact financial loss to the Government caused by tax fraud is difficult to determine but undoubtedly enormous. Estimates of the amount of reportable income that goes unreported each year range from $25 to $40 billion.[11] Some of this is inadvertent, but undoubtedly a sizable amount is deliberate, criminal evasion. The financial loss to the public caused by a single conspiracy in restraint of trade may be untold millions in extra costs paid ultimately by the buying public. It is estimated that the cost to the public annually of securities frauds, while impossible to quantify with any certainty, is probably in the $500 million to $1 billion range. A conservative estimate is that nearly $500 million is spent annually on worthless or extravagantly misrepresented drugs and therapeutic devices. Fraudulent and deceptive practices in the home repair and improvement field are said to result in $500 million to $1 billion losses annually; and in the automobile repair field alone, fraudulent practices have been estimated

[9] Sheldon S. Cohen, "Morality and the American Tax System," *George Washington Law Review*, 1966, 35:839, 840. Since January 1, 1962, $6 million in previously unreported taxes has been realized from taxpayers who specifically indicated that they were paying because of fear of detection by the automatic data processing system. This system was not instituted nationwide for individual tax returns until January 1, 1967, but it received publicity prior to that time. Commissioner of Internal Revenue, *Annual Report, 1966,* p. 20.

[10] Raymond C. Baumhart, "How Ethical Are Businessmen?" *Harvard Business Review* July–August 1961, 39:6–19, 156–176.

[11] See *supra* note 5, Attachment B, note 3. See also chapter 3, note 103.

to cost $100 million annually.[12] Individual white-collar criminals are sometimes responsible for losses that are quite beyond the scale of most traditional crime. Billy Sol Estes' $30 million fertilizer swindle and De Angelis' $125–$175 million vegetable oil scandal are two notable examples.

While no reliable estimates can be made of the financial burdens produced by white-collar crime, they probably are far greater than those produced by traditional common law theft offenses—robbery, larceny and burglary. Such a simple comparison, of course, does not take into account the attendant evils usually related to the traditional offenses—the risk, threat, or occurrence of physical injury or psychological trauma.

But white-collar crime may also result in physical harm, or the risk of such harm. Death or serious injury may result from tainted products merchandised in violation of the Pure Food and Drug Act or local health laws, or from misconduct by doctors.[13] Building code violations may cause fire or other serious health hazards. Although offenses involving such risks constitute a small proportion of the total amount of white-collar crime, the potential number of victims of such conduct may be very high.

White-collar crime also does serious damage to our social and economic institutions—although it is extremely difficult to determine the extent of these harms. Thus crimes such as bribery and violation of conflict-of-interest statutes strike deeply at responsible, impartial government. And the damage done by a case such as the celebrated conspiracy of 29 electrical equipment companies to fix prices is not limited to the extra costs paid by their unsuspecting buyers and ultimately the general public. As Judge T. Cullen Ganey declared in sentencing the defendants: "This is a shocking indictment of a vast section of our economy, for what is really at stake here is the survival of the kind of economy under which America has grown to greatness, the free enterprise system."[14]

More broadly, white-collar crime affects the whole moral climate of our society. Derelictions by corporations and their managers, who usually occupy leadership positions in their communities, establish an example which tends to erode the moral base of the law and provide an opportunity for other kinds of offenders to rationalize their misconduct.

The President's Committee on Consumer Interests found that one in 30 of the letters it received from consumers throughout the country conveyed "an attitude of frustration, anger, and displeasure with 'the system.' "

> The most striking feature, in our opinion, is not the allegations of criminal fraud that occasionally have been made to us by correspondents. Rather, it is the sense of unfairness, of disregard of the individ-

[12] For these figures, see generally *supra* note 5, chapter 3, which discusses the economic impact of crime.

[13] See Howard Whitman, "Why Some Doctors Should be in Jail." *Collier's* Oct. 30, 1953, 132:23–27.

[14] Judge Ganey quoted in Herling, *The Great Price Conspiracy* (New York: Van Rees Press, 1962), p. 195.

ual by the organized business community, of lack of effective recourse, and of a feeling that the marketplace is unethical.[15]

Such frustration and discontent with abusive practices may be an important factor underlying some forms of violent crime. The report of the McCone Commission, the Commission appointed by the governor to investigate the Watts riot, included the following:

> The Commission heard recurrent testimony of alleged consumer exploitation in south central Los Angeles: of higher prices being charged for food there than in other parts of town, of spoiled meat or produce or old bread being sold at the same price as fresh, of high interest rates on furniture and clothing purchases, of shoddy materials at high prices. Complaints were also registered to the effect that there is a bias against the curfew area in the practices of insurance companies and institutional lenders. In a related vein, a number of witnesses advanced the view that there was a vengeance pattern to the destruction of stores in the curfew area, that it was a retribution on merchants who were guilty of consumer exploitation, and particularly on Caucasians who were said to "take from the area but put nothing back into it * * *"[16]

White-Collar Crime and the Criminal Process

Effectiveness of Criminal Sanctions

. . . [M]ost persons convicted of common law crimes are likely to be young and to have serious educational and vocational lacks which rehabilitation programs can help meet. Presumably such programs are far less significant and will often be irrevelant for the white-collar offender.

Furthermore, with respect to many kinds of white-collar offenders long periods of incarceration or supervision are not needed to protect society from further criminality. For example, there appears to be only a negligible amount of recidivism among those convicted of certain white-collar crimes. Thus of the 1,186 persons convicted of criminal tax fraud in 1963 and 1964, only 2 persons were repeat offenders.[17] On the other hand, among some classes of white-collar offenders, such as those guilty of cheating consumers, recidivism may be a serious problem.

There is, unfortunately, no hard evidence available regarding the deterrent effect of criminal sanctions. This was vividly illustrated when in a 1964

[15] Letter from Mrs. Esther Peterson, Special Assistant to the President for Consumer Affairs, to James Vorenberg, Executive Director of the President's Commission on Law Enforcement and Administration of Justice, Mar. 25, 1966.

[16] Governor's Commission on the Los Angeles Riots, *Violence in the City—An End or a Beginning?* (Los Angeles: Office of the Governor, 1965), p. 62.

[17] Attachment B, p. 115. See also Robert E. Lane, "Why Businessmen Violate the Law," *Journal of Criminal Law, Criminology and Police Science*, 1953, 44:151.

tax case the Justice Department was asked to submit a memorandum to the court justifying imposition of a 4-month jail term and a $10,000 fine as a deterrent. The only significant data produced were figures indicating that recidivism among tax violators was minimal, and a case study from Israel which indicated that since 1956, when the government had adopted a program of criminal prosecutions for tax evasion, there had been a graphic increase in the amount of income declared for taxation.[18] There is a clear need for further research into the effectiveness of criminal sanctions in this area. We need to know, for example, more about the comparative deterrent effects of prosecution, publicity, a jail sentence, a criminal fine, and civil damages. To this end, the IRS and the Justice Department recently engaged the National Opinion Research Center of the University of Chicago to conduct a survey of public attitudes toward the administration, enforcement and infringement of the tax laws.

Despite the lack of hard evidence, common sense notions about how people behave support the thesis that the condemnatory and deterrent aspects of criminal sanctions are likely to be peculiarly effective in the white-collar area. Persons who have standing and roots in a community and are prepared for and engaged in legitimate occupations can be expected to be particularly susceptible to the threat of criminal prosecution. Criminal proceedings and the imposition of sanctions have a much sharper impact upon those who have not been hardened by previous contact with the criminal justice system. Moreover, white-collar crimes as a class are more likely than common law crimes to be preceded by some deliberation; there is therefore more often an opportunity to calculate the risk objectively.

It appears further that jail sentences, however short, would constitute particularly significant deterrents for white-collar crime. The imposition of jail sentences may be the only way adequately to symbolize society's condemnation of the behavior in question, particularly where it is not on its face brutal or repulsive. And jail may be the only sanction available which will serve as an adequate deterrent.

These impressions are supported by the opinions of those who have had experience with the enforcement of the tax and antitrust laws.

> No one in direct contact with the living reality of business conduct in the United States is unaware of the effect the imprisonment of seven high officials in the Electrical Machinery Industry in 1960 had on the conspiratorial price fixing in many areas of our economy; similar sentences in a few cases each decade would almost completely cleanse our economy of the cancer of collusive price fixing and the mere prospect of such sentences is itself the strongest available deterrent to such activities.[19]

[18] Government brief, *United States v. Dugan* (District Court, Massachusetts, 1964), U.S. Department of Justice files 5–36–2843.

[19] Spivack (Director of Operations, Antitrust Division, U.S. Department of Justice), "Antitrust Enforcement, A Primer," *Connecticut Bar Journal,* 1963, 375, 382.

The Department of Justice believes that imprisonment may often be the appropriate penalty for a clear-cut antitrust violation, such as price fixing. . . . [C]riminal fines or civil damages may be inadequate for a number of reasons: present statutory maximums often make criminal fines trivial for corporations[20] in proportion both to their ability to pay and to the profits resulting from the criminal violations; in a number of states corporate executives may be lawfully reimbursed by the corporation for fines imposed on them; and since discovery of criminal violations of the antitrust laws is very difficult, even substantial civil penalties may not constitute adequate deterrents.[21]

Significantly, the Antitrust Division does not feel that lengthy prison sentences are ordinarily called for. It "rarely recommends jail sentences greater than 6 months—recommendations of 30-day imprisonment are most frequent."[22]

In tax cases, the Justice Department also considers criminal sanctions, and jail sentences in particular, of significant value as deterrents. It is the Tax Division's policy to recommend jail sentences for all defendants convicted of tax fraud whenever the court requests a recommendation.[23] James V. Bennett, former Director of the Federal Bureau of Prisons, has taken the position that the effort to deter misconduct by imposing relatively harsh penalties, while often a feeble thing in regard to traditional crime, "has had a most benign effect on those who do not like to pay taxes."[24]

But it is clear that the criminal law is not an appropriate means of dealing with all kinds of white-collar misconduct. Since white-collar misconduct usually does not involve an act which, like robbery, burglary or rape, is of a simple and dramatic predatory nature, it is inevitable that one of the critical and difficult issues is determining when the violation is clear-cut enough to warrant use of society's ultimate method of control. A great deal of business is now subject to regulations whose interpretation is not at all clear. The language of the Sherman Act, for example, is extremely broad and abstract, and has been subject to varying administrative and judicial interpretations. . . . [T]he Antitrust Division's solution has been to seek criminal sanctions only where there has been an intentional violation of clear and established rules of law. Where misconduct does not constitute such a violation, the Antitrust Division pursues civil remedies in place of criminal sanctions.

[20] Between 1890 and 1955 the Sherman Act provided for a fine not to exceed $5,000. This amount was raised to $50,000 in 1955.
[21] See President's Commission on Law Enforcement and Administration of Justice, *Task Force Report: Crime and Its Impact—An Assessment* (Washington: U.S. Government Printing Office, 1967), attachment A, p. 112. See also Alan M. Dershowitz, "Increasing Community Control Over Corporate Crime: A Problem in the Law of Sanctions," *Yale Law Journal*, 1961, 71:280.
[22] See *supra* note 5, Attachment A, p. 112.
[23] See *supra* note 5, Attachment B, p. 14.
[24] James V. Bennett, "After Sentence—What?" *Journal of Criminal Law, Criminology, and Police Science*, 1955, 45:537.

But the law is often adequately unambiguous. The offenders in the *Electrical Equipment* cases were, for example, quite aware that their activities were in violation of the law. As one of the violators testified:

> [I]t was considered discreet to not be too obvious and to minimize telephone calls, to use plain envelopes if mailing material to each other, not to be seen together traveling, and so forth ° ° ° not leave wastepaper, of which there was a lot, strewn around a room when leaving.[25]

The list of executives in attendance at meetings was referred to as the "Christmas card list," and the meetings as "choir practice."[26] The executives filed false travel vouchers in order to conceal their visits to the cities in which meetings were held.[27]

Aside from the question of ambiguity of the violation, it is important to recognize that a decision to use criminal sanctions involves costs and disadvantages which must be analyzed against the gains to be achieved and the alternative methods available to seek compliance. As discussed above, against many types of white-collar offenders application of criminal sanctions is likely to be highly effective in terms of deterrence. But this "economy" of sanction does not argue for an indiscriminate increase in the use of criminal sanctions. Among the economic and social costs involved in using criminal sanctions are the loss of services or serious curtailment of the usefulness of highly productive members of society, and the danger that greatly increased use of the criminal law would dilute its condemnatory effect. And there are many situations in which use of criminal sanctions may not be the most effective means of obtaining compliance with the law. Thus it is apparent that use of the withholding tax scheme has proved an extraordinarily efficient and effective method of preventing tax fraud. This is of course true in other areas of the law as well. Increased use of locks may be far more effective in reducing burglary and auto theft than an increase in police patrol. But the threat of criminal sanctions will often be an economical way to obtain compliance. In the tax area, for example, 80 million income tax returns are filed annually. It would be impractical to audit all of these and investigate all cases in which there was some reason for suspicion. The Tax Division audits only 4 percent of all returns filed.[28] And the withholding tax scheme, while highly effective, can only ensure that income earned in the course of some regular employment is reported. The Government must therefore depend to a great extent on the deterrent effect of the threat of criminal sanctions.

---

[25] U.S. Senate Subcommittee on Antitrust and Monopoly, Committee on the Judiciary, 87th Congress, 1st session, 1961, "Administered Price Hearings," part 28, p. 17395 (hereinafter cited as *Hearings*).

[26] *Id.* at part 27, p. 17100.

[27] *Id.* at part 27, p. 16760.

[28] See *supra* note 5, Attachment B, p. 114.

Careful thought must be given to determining those areas in which use of criminal sanctions is appropriate and in which other means of enforcement will suffice. And sound prosecutorial discretion must be exercised in deciding which cases, among those that might technically involve criminal violations, should be selected for prosecution.

Practical Problems with the Use of Criminal Sanctions

There are practical obstacles to enforcement of the laws relating to white-collar crime because of factors peculiar to this kind of criminality.

As noted previously, it is often extremely difficult even to discover the existence of white-collar crimes; it is similarly difficult to secure evidence of criminal guilt. White-collar crime may not stand out as unusual conduct when committed as would, for example, theft, burglary or assault. It may involve acts of omission rather than commission, which are less likely to be observed or noticed. It is often committed in the privacy of a business office or home. In addition, there may be no single victim or group of victims to complain to law enforcement authorities. Or victims may be unaware at the time of the offense that they have been victimized. Victims of consumer fraud are but one example. Moreover, the crime itself may be difficult to identify. It is often committed in the course of ordinary business activity and may not be significantly distinguishable from noncriminal business conduct. Especially where financial offenses are involved, the crime may be so technical that discovery is possible only after detailed and lengthy audit or economic analysis by specially trained law enforcement personnel with expertise in fields such as accounting and economics. Careful scrutiny of a huge mass of data for weeks or months may be necessary to produce the required evidence of criminality. A complicated security fraud investigation, for example, may involve several years of investigation by a team of law enforcement personnel.

A pervasive problem affecting enforcement is the fact that white-collar crime is often business crime and business crime is often corporate crime. Where corporate defendants are involved, the only criminal sanction available is the fine. As noted previously, fines may be inadequate as deterrents for a variety of reasons. There are also serious practical problems in imposing sanctions upon corporate employees. It is very difficult to obtain the conviction of the true policy formulators in large, complex corporations. The top executives do not ordinarily carry out the overt criminal acts—it is the lower or middle management officials who, for example, attend price-fixing meetings. Under traditional doctrines of complicity, to hold a superior responsible he must be shown actually to have participated in his subordinate's criminal activities, as by ordering the conduct or encouraging or aiding in its performance. It is very difficult to obtain evidence of such participation. Difficulties of proof have prevented the prosecution of top management in many Sherman Act cases.[29]

Resistance to the Use of Criminal Sanctions

As important as the practical obstacles to effective law enforcement is society's reluctance to impose criminal sanctions upon the white-collar offender. Thus despite the apparent effect of the *Electrical Equipment* cases, in which seven individual executives received and served jail sentences, since that case no antitrust defendant has been imprisoned. In seven cases since then, involving 45 individual defendants, prison sentences were imposed, but in each case the sentence was suspended. During this time the Government has recommended that, out of 58 cases in which individual defendants were charged with criminal violations, prison sentences be imposed but suspended in seven cases, and imposed and served in 27 cases. The recommendations covered 105 individual defendants.[30] Similarly, Marshall Clinard's study of a variety of rationing and other controls during the second World War revealed that the sentences imposed on OPA violators after conviction were relatively mild.[31]

While little is known of the public attitude toward white-collar crime, it is apparent that the present concern with crime is not directed at white-collar crime but at "crime on the streets." As one executive convicted and sentenced to jail in the *Electrical Equipment* conspiracy said:

> [O]n the bright side for me personally have been the letters and calls from people all over the country, the community, the shops and offices here, expressing confidence in me and support. This demonstration has been a warm and humbling experience for me.[32]

But one attempt to measure public reactions to a form of white-collar crime—violations of the Federal Food, Drug and Cosmetic Act—indicated that the public would treat offenders more severely than the courts, although not as severely as persons guilty of such crimes as larceny and burglary. Consumers were asked to judge cases of food law violation in terms of how they would punish the offender. Six actual cases were selected, representing three types of violation—misbranding, distasteful but not physically harmful adulteration, and physically harmful adulteration.

[29] Dershowitz has recommended imposing upon corporate executives a duty, enforceable by criminal sanctions, to exercise reasonable care in preventing acquisitive crime within the area of corporate business under their control. Alan M. Dershowitz, *supra* note 21.

[30] See *supra* note 5, Attachment A, p. 112 and note 35.

[31] Marshall Clinard, "Criminological Theories of Violations of Wartime Regulations," *American Sociological Review*, 1946, 11:258, 261.

[32] *Schenectady & Union-Star*, Feb. 10, 1961.

Fifty-eight percent of the consumers felt that penalties should have been more severe than the actual court decisions, and yet within the maximum penalty provided by the Federal law, a one-year prison sentence on first conviction. Twenty-two percent of the sample chose penalties equal to or less harsh than the one actually imposed, while almost 20 percent felt that the violators should receive a prison term longer than a year.[33]

The very characteristics which make white-collar criminals particularly deterrable may make it difficult to obtain the sanctions necessary to deter. They generally have families, an established place in the community, and a spotless record. They often occupy managerial or executive roles in their business and a leadership position in their community.

In the *Electrical Equipment* cases the defendants included several vice presidents of the General Electric Corporation and the Westinghouse Electric Corporation. They were described by a newspaper reporter as "typical business men in appearance, men who would never be taken for lawbreakers."[34] Several were deacons or vestrymen of their churches. One was president of his local Chamber of Commerce, another a hospital board member, another chief fund raiser for the Community Chest, another a bank director, another director of the taxpayer's association, another organizer of the local Little League.

The highest paid executive to be given a jail sentence was a General Electric vice president, earning $135,000 a year. He was married, and the father of three children. He had served in the Navy during the second World War, rising to the rank of lieutenant commander, was director of the Schenectady Boy's Club, on the board of trustees of a girls' finishing school, and was a member of the Governor's Temporary State Committee on Economic Expansion in New York.

Obviously there is resistance to subjecting defendants who are performing useful functions in society to criminal sanctions and especially to prison sentences. Clinard's study of OPA violators found that one reason for the light sentences imposed was "the fact that the offenders seldom had a criminal past or other circumstances which would warrant a severe sentence. As the judges on occasion stated from the bench, they 'would not make criminals of reputable businessmen.' "[35] On the other hand Judge Skelly Wright, in considering the question of whether an income tax violator ought to be sentenced to jail, took the position that "the only real purpose of an income tax sentence is its deterrent value. Unless we use the income tax sentence as a deterrent, we are overlooking one of our responsibilities as judges."[36]

[33] Donald J. Newman, "Public Attitudes Toward a Form of White Collar Crime," *Social Problems,* January 1967, 4:228, 230, 231.

[34] *New York Times,* Feb. 7, 1961, p. 1, p. 26, col. 3.

[35] Marshall Clinard, "Criminological Theories of Violations of Wartime Regulations," 11 *American Sociological Review,* 1946, 11:258, 263.

[36] Wright, "Sentencing the Income Tax Violator, Statement of the Basic Problem," delivered before the Sentencing Institute for the Fifth Circuit, 30 F.R.D., 1962, 30:185, 302, 304–305.

In addition to the standing of the offenders, there are a number of aspects of white-collar offenses that may encourage public and official reluctance to use criminal sanctions, as well as provide rationalizations for the violators themselves. Thus Cressey's study of embezzlement found rationalization to be an important factor in offender's patterns of misconduct. They distinguished embezzlement sharply from robbery or theft. He found, for example, that independent businessmen who converted "deposits" which had been entrusted to them because of their business positions, convinced themselves "either (a) that they were merely borrowing the money which they converted, or (b) that the funds entrusted to them were really theirs."[37] It has been argued that use of criminal sanctions to enforce much of the law in this area is inappropriate because the conduct proscribed is "morally neutral."[38] The soundness of some of the regulatory laws that have grown up in recent decades is a subject of continuing debate. And the very fact that they are so recent in comparison with the laws prohibiting such conduct as larceny and assault makes it unlikely that they will enjoy similar acceptance for some time. Many of the defendants in the *Electrical Equipment* cases argued that their behavior, while technically criminal, had really served a worthwhile purpose by "stabilizing prices." They frequently combined this altruistic interpretation with an attempted distinction among illegal, criminal, and immoral acts, expressing the view that what they had done might have been designated by the statutes as criminal, but either they were unaware of such a designation or they thought it unreasonable that acts with admirable consequences should be considered criminal. The fact that the line between legitimate and illegitimate behavior is sometimes fuzzy and seems occasionally arbitrary does not help in obtaining popular support for the law. Thus the fine line between legal tax avoidance and illegal evasion may make it hard for the violator himself or others to accept the appropriateness of criminal sanctions even where the violation is not close to the line.

But most white-collar crime is not at all morally neutral. Most fraud involves preying upon the weak and ignorant; violation of food and drug laws may cause death or serious injury; embezzlement is, very simply, a form of theft; tax fraud involves cheating the Government and, indirectly, other taxpayers.

Reluctance to see criminal sanctions used in the white-collar area derives also from the fact that there is often no particular victim, or group of victims. The harm is not as apparent, and certainly not as dramatic. Where loss is spread throughout society, the harm to any particular individual is minimal. As Sanford H. Kadish has pointed out,

> it is possible to reason convincingly that the harm done to the
> economic order by violations of many of these regulatory laws are of a

---

[37] Cressey, *Other People's Money* (Glencoe, Ill.: The Free Press, 1953), p. 102.

[38] Sanford H. Kadish, "Some Observations on the Use of Criminal Sanctions in Enforcing Economic Regulations," *University of Chicago Law Review*, 1963, 30:423, 435.

magnitude that dwarf in significance the lower class property offenses. But the point is that these perceptions require distinguishing and reasoning processes that are not the normal governors of the passion of moral disapproval, and are not dramatically obvious to a public long conditioned to responding approvingly to the production of profit through business shrewdness, especially in the absence of live and visible victims.[39]

Moreover, where corporate misconduct is involved, the offenders—and particularly the offenders against whom evidence of guilt can be obtained—act as part of a corporate hierarchy and, ordinarily, follow a pattern of corporate behavior. Individual responsibility is therefore reduced—the offenders are often following orders from above, either explicit or implicit. Moreover, the fact that acts are performed to further the interests of the corporation, and not merely the offenders' personal interests, helps to rationalize misconduct. Thus in the *Electrical Equipment* cases, personal explanations for the acts were, for the most part, sought in the structure of corporate pressures. The defendants almost invariably testified that they came new to a job, found price-fixing an established way of life, and simply entered into it as they did into other aspects of their job. This is illustrative of a pattern that Senator Everett Dirksen of Illinois, during the subcommittee hearings, labeled "imbued fraud."[40] There was testimony that, if one employee refused to engage in price-fixing, the responsibility would simply be delegated to another. Prior to imposing sentence in the *Electrical Equipment* cases, Judge T. Cullen Ganey criticized the corporations as the major culprits, but he did not excuse the offenders:

> they were torn between conscience and an approved corporate policy, with the rewarding objectives of promotion, comfortable security, and large salaries. They were the organization or company men, the conformist who goes along with his superiors and finds balm for his conscience in additional comforts and security of his place in the corporate setup.[41]

And in his study of embezzlement Cressey found that offenders rationalized on the basis "that 'everyone' in business in some way or other converts or misapplies deposits so that it is not entirely wrong."[42] Criminal conduct that accords with such an accepted "system" and is in response to such pressures is not unique to white-collar offenders, as the Commission's work on juvenile delinquency, organized crime and professional crime indicates.

There is strong evidence that many white-collar offenders do not think of themselves as criminals. Cameron's study of middle-class shoplifters who

[39] *Id.* at 436.
[40] *Hearings,* pt. 27, p. 16773.
[41] *New York Times,* Feb. 7, 1961, p. 26.
[42] Cressey, *supra* note 37 at p. 102.

had stolen from a large department store in Chicago gave some indication of the potential educative effect of the use of criminal sanctions. Shoplifters generally do not think of themselves as thieves, Cameron points out, and "even when arrested, they resist strongly being pushed to admit their behavior is theft. Again and again store people explain to pilferers that they are under arrest as thieves, that they will, in the normal course of events, be taken in a police van to jail, held in jail until bond is raised, and tried in a court before a judge and sentenced." Interrogation procedures at the store are directed specifically and consciously toward breaking down any illusion that the shoplifter may possess that his behavior is merely regarded as "naughty" or "bad."

> In the course of this investigation, it becomes increasingly clear to the pilferer that he is considered a thief and is in imminent danger of being hauled into court and publicly exhibited as such. This realization is often accompanied by a dramatic change in attitude and by severe emotional disturbance.[43]
>
> * * * * *
>
> Because the adult pilferer does not think of himself, prior to his arrest, as a thief and can conceive of no in-group support for himself in that role, his arrest forces him to reject the role * * * [and] is in itself sufficient to cause him to redefine his situation.[44]

And Cressey found that "among the violators interviewed, the accountants, bankers, business executives and independent businessmen all reported that the possibility of stealing or robbing to obtain the needed funds never occurred to them, although many objective opportunities for such crimes were present."[45]

Application of criminal sanctions in this area raises some of the most delicate and perplexing problems confronting the criminal justice system. The sensitivity of successful members of society to the threat of criminal prosecution is indicative not only of the potential success of criminal sanctions in deterring misconduct, but of their potentially destructive effect upon the offenders. Criminal sanctions may help to educate the public to realize the seriousness of misconduct which is not on its face abhorrent, yet their indiscriminate use in areas where public opinion has not crystallized may seriously weaken the condemnatory effect of the criminal law. Imprisonment may be unnecessary for purposes of rehabilitation and incapacitation, although very effective as a deterrent.

Our goal should be to achieve an "economical" level of criminal sanctions, recognizing that, in establishing such a level, account must be taken of such intangibles as strengthening public support for the regulatory,

---

[43] Mary Cameron, *The Booster and The Snitch* (New York: The Free Press, 1965), p. 162.

[44] *Id.* at p. 165.

[45] Cressey, *supra* note 37 at p. 140.

revenue, or other underlying legislative purpose sought without weakening the criminal law; balancing the effectiveness of criminal sanctions against alternative methods of social control; and maintaining some sense of fair treatment among different classes of offenders touched by the criminal system.

This chapter is not an assessment of white-collar crime in America. The data to make such an assessment are not available today, and procedures to develop such data have not been developed. Furthermore, white-collar crime as a conceptual classification does not permit close, searching analysis. It includes too many different types of offenders and offenses.

Here as elsewhere our present system operates to a great extent in the dark in seeking improvements. We rely largely on our basic notions of fairness and commonsense expectations about how certain classes of people will react to the threat of criminal penalties. The enormous stake our society has in the fair and effective operation of its tax system has led to some close analysis of what results in compliance, but even here there is no general agreement about what the levels and form of enforcement should be. Rather than dealing with a single concept of white-collar crime, we need to study different kinds of offenders and offenses separately to see what they do and do not have in common with each other. We need to know whether an apparently permissive approach to business crimes in fact encourages street crime through disrespect for law, desire for revenge, or other motives, since no valid determination of the economical level of enforcement can be made without such information on secondary effects. We need enlightenment on such crucial questions as the extent to which a criminal conviction unaccompanied by jail is likely to be an effective deterrent. On the basis of such information it will become possible for public officials and the public itself to confront, as they have not yet done, the perplexing issues in dealing with this group of crimes and offenders.

[*The President's Commission Report on Law Enforcement and Administration of Justice,* Task Force Report: Crime and Its Impact—An Assessment (*Washington: U.S. Government Printing Office, 1967*), pp. 102–109.]

8 *Organized crime*

Organized crime is a society that seeks to operate outside the control of the American people and their governments. It involves thousands of criminals, working within structures as complex as those of any large corporation, subject to laws more rigidly enforced than those of legitimate governments. Its actions are not impulsive but rather the result of intricate conspiracies, carried on over many years and aimed at gaining control over whole fields of activity in order to amass huge profits.[1]

The core of organized crime activity is the supplying of illegal goods and services—gambling, loan sharking, narcotics, and other forms of vice—to countless numbers of citizen customers.[2]

---

[1] The Kefauver committee found that

"1. There is a Nationwide crime syndicate known as the Mafia, whose tentacles are found in many large cities. It has international ramifications which appear most clearly in connection with the narcotics traffic.

"2. Its leaders are usually found in control of the most lucrative rackets of their cities.

"3. There are indications of a centralized direction and control of these rackets, but leadership appears to be in a group rather than in a single individual.

"4. The Mafia is the cement that helps to bind the Costello-Adonis-Lansky syndicate of New York and the Accardo-Guzik-Fischetti syndicate of Chicago as well as smaller criminal gangs and individual criminals throughout the country. These groups have kept in touch with Luciano since his deportation from this country.

"5. The domination of the Mafia is based fundamentally on 'muscle' and 'murder.' The Mafia is a secret conspiracy against law and order which will ruthlessly eliminate anyone who stands in the way of its success in any criminal enterprise in which it is interested. It will destroy anyone who betrays its secrets. It will use any means available—political influence, bribery, intimidation, etc., to defeat any attempt on the part of law-enforcement to touch its top figures or to interfere with its operations." Senate Special Committee to investigate Organized Crime in Interstate Commerce (hereinafter cited as *Kefauver Committee*), *3rd Interim Report, Senate Report No. 307*, 82nd Congress, 1st Session, p. 150, 1951. See also Office of the New York Counsel to the Governor, *Combating Organized Crime—A Report of the 1965 Oyster Bay, New York, Conferences on Combating Organized Crime*, 1966.

[2] Johnson, "Organized Crime: Challenge to the American Legal System," parts 1–3, *Journal of Criminal Law, Criminology, and Police Science*, 1963, 53:399, 402–404, 1962; 54:1, 127.

But organized crime is also extensively and deeply involved in legitimate business and in labor unions.[3] Here it employs illegitimate methods— monopolization, terrorism, extortion, tax evasion—to drive out or control lawful ownership and leadership and to exact illegal profits from the public.[4] And to carry on its many activities secure from governmental interference, organized crime corrupts public officials.[5]

.   .   .   .   .

Organized crime affects the lives of millions of Americans, but because it desperately preserves its invisibility many, perhaps most, Americans are not aware how they are affected, or even that they are affected at all. The price of a loaf of bread may go up one cent as the result of an organized crime conspiracy, but a housewife has no way of knowing why she is paying more.[6] If organized criminals paid income tax on every cent of their vast earnings everybody's tax bill would go down, but no one knows how much.[7]

.   .   .   .   .

Sometimes organized crime's activities do not directly affect individuals at all. Smuggled cigarettes in a vending machine cost consumers no more than tax-paid cigarettes, but they enrich the leaders of organized crime. Sometimes these activities actually reduce prices for a short period of time, as can happen when organized crime, in an attempt to take over an industry, starts a price war against legitimate businessmen. Even when

[3] See generally *Senate Select Committee on Improper Activities in the Labor or Management Field* (hereinafter cited as *McClellan Labor-Management Reports*); *1st Interim Report, Senate Report No. 1417,* 85th Congress, 2nd Session, 1958; *2nd Interim Report,* parts 1 and 2; *Senate Report No. 621,* 86th Congress 1st Session, 1959; *Final Report,* parts 1–4, *Senate Report No. 1139,* 86th Congress, 2nd Session, 1960; *Index to Reports,* 86th Congress, 2nd Session, 1960.

[4] "A gangster or racketeer in a legitimate business does not suddenly become respectable. . . . [E]vidence was produced before the committee concerning the use of unscrupulous and discriminatory business practices, extortion, bombing and other forms of violence to eliminate competitors and to compel customers to take articles sold by the mobsters." *Kefauver Committee, 3rd Interim Report, Senate Report No. 307, 82nd* Congress, 1st Session, 1951, at p. 170.

[5] Johnson, *supra* note 2 at pp. 412–414, 419–422; *Kefauver Committee, 3rd Interim Report, Senate Report No. 307,* 82nd Congress, 1st Session, 1951, pp. 181–186.

[6] *Kefauver Committee, 3rd Interim Report, Senate Report No. 307,* 82nd Congress, 1st Session, 1951, pp. 170–171: "There can be little doubt that the public suffers from gangster penetration into legitimate business. It suffers because higher prices must be paid for articles and services which it must buy . . . The public suffers because it may have to put up with shoddy and inferior merchandise in fields where gangsters have been able to obtain a monopoly."

[7] One indication of the amount of tax revenue lost is found in the testimony of Commissioner of Internal Revenue Sheldon S. Cohen before the Senate Subcommittee on Administrative Practice and Procedure on July 13, 1965. He stated that during the period between February 1961 and March 13, 1965, more than $219 million in taxes and penalties had been recommended for assessment against subjects of the Federal organized crime drive. *Hearings Before the Subcommittee on Administrative Practice and Procedure of the Senate Committee on the Judiciary* (hereinafter cited as *Long Committee Hearings*), 89th Congress, 1st Session, 1965, part 3 at p. 1119.

organized crime engages in a large transaction, individuals may not be directly affected. A large sum of money may be diverted from a union pension fund to finance a business venture without immediate and direct effect upon the individual members of the union.[8]

It is organized crime's accumulation of money, not the individual transactions by which the money is accumulated, that has a great and threatening impact on America. A quarter in a jukebox means nothing and results in nothing. But millions of quarters in thousands of jukeboxes can provide both a strong motive for murder and the means to commit murder with impunity.[9] Organized crime exists by virtue of the power it purchases with its money. The millions of dollars it can invest in narcotics or use for layoff money give it power over the lives of thousands of people and over the quality of life in whole neighborhoods.[10] The millions of dollars it can throw into the legitimate economic system give it power to manipulate the price of shares on the stock market,[11] to raise or lower the price of retail merchandise, to determine whether entire industries are union or nonunion, to make it easier or harder for businessmen to continue in business.[12]

The millions of dollars it can spend on corrupting public officials may give it power to maim or murder people inside or outside the organization with impunity; to extort money from businessmen; to conduct businesses in such fields as liquor, meat, or drugs without regard to administrative regulations; to avoid payment of income taxes or to secure public works contracts without competitive bidding.[13]

The purpose of organized crime is not competition with visible, legal government but nullification of it. When organized crime places an official in public office, it nullifies the political process. When it bribes a police official, it nullifies law enforcement.

There is another, more subtle way in which organized crime has an impact on American life. Consider the former way of life of Frank Costello, a man who has repeatedly been called a leader of organized crime. He lived in an expensive apartment on the corner of 72d Street and Central Park

[8] Such bootlegging activities cost the city and State of New York about $40 million a year in lost tax revenues. *New York Times,* February 2, 1947, p. 21.

For a discussion of the problems of cigarette smuggling in New York State, see Weintraub, "A Report on Bootlegging of Cigarettes in the City and State of New York," prepared for Cigarette Merchandisers' Association, Inc., New York, N.Y., January 1966; Weintraub and Kaufman, "Bootlegged Cigarettes," prepared for Wholesale Tobacco Distributors of New York, Inc., New York, N.Y., October 1966.

[9] Peterson, "Chicago: Shades of Capone," *Annals,* May 1963, p. 30.

[10] *Kefauver Committee, 3rd Interim Report, Senate Report No. 307,* 82nd Congress, 1st Session, 1951, p. 171.

[11] See Lefkowitz, "New York: Criminal Infiltration of the Securities Industry," *Annals,* May 1963, p. 51. See also excerpt from Porter, "On Wall Street," *New York Post,* August 3–7, 1959, in Tyler, ed., *Organized Crime in America,* 1962, p. 298.

[12] Johnson, *supra* note 2 at p. 406.

[13] *Kefauver Committee, 3rd Interim Report, Senate Report No. 307,* 82nd Congress 1st Session, 1951, pp. 30–144.

West in New York. He was often seen dining in well-known restaurants in the company of judges, public officials, and prominent businessmen. Every morning he was shaved in the barbershop of the Waldorf Astoria Hotel. On many weekends he played golf at a country club on the fashionable North Shore of Long Island. In short, though his reputation was common knowledge, he moved around New York conspicuously and unashamedly, perhaps ostracized by some people but more often accepted, greeted by journalists, recognized by children, accorded all the freedoms of a prosperous and successful man. On a society that treats such a man in such a manner, organized crime has had an impact.

And yet the public remains indifferent. Few Americans seem to comprehend how the phenomenon of organized crime affects their lives. They do not see how gambling with bookmakers, or borrowing money from loan sharks, forwards the interests of great criminal cartels.[14] Businessmen looking for labor harmony or nonunion status through irregular channels rationalize away any suspicions that organized crime is thereby spreading its influence. When an ambitious political candidate accepts substantial cash contributions from unknown sources, he suspects but dismisses the fact that organized crime will dictate some of his actions when he assumes office.[15]

President Johnson asked the Commission to determine why organized crime has been expanding despite the Nation's best efforts to prevent it. The Commission drew upon the small group of enforcement personnel and other knowledgeable persons who deal with organized crime. Federal agencies provided extensive material. But because so little study and research have been done in this field, we also secured the assistance of sociologists, systems analysts, political scientists, economists, and lawyers.[16] America's limited response to organized crime is illustrated by the fact that, for several of these disciplines, our call for assistance resulted in their first concentrated examination of organized crime.

The Types of Organized Criminal Activities

Catering to Public Demands

Organized criminal groups participate in any illegal activity that offers maximum profit at minimum risk of law enforcement interference. They offer goods and services that millions of Americans desire even though declared illegal by their legislatures.

[14] See generally Cook, *The Two Dollar Bet Means Murder* (1961).

[15] For an excellent discussion of the influences of underworld money in politics, see Heard, *The Costs of Democracy* (1960), pp. 154–168.

[16] Selected papers of consultants appear in the appendices to President's Commission on Law Enforcement and Administration of Justice, *Task Force Report: Organized Crime* (Washington: U.S. Government Printing Office).

GAMBLING[17]

Law enforcement officials agree almost unanimously that gambling is the greatest source of revenue for organized crime.[18] It ranges from lotteries, such as "numbers" or "bolita," to off-track horse betting, bets on sporting events, large dice games and illegal casinos. In large cities where organized criminal groups exist, very few of the gambling operators are independent of a large organization.[19] Anyone whose independent operation becomes successful is likely to receive a visit from an organization representative who convinces the independent, through fear or promise of greater profit, to share his revenue with the organization.[20]

Most large-city gambling is established or controlled by organized crime members through elaborate hierarchies.[21] Money is filtered from the small operator who takes the customer's bet, through persons who pick up money and slips, to second-echelon figures in charge of particular districts, and then into one of several main offices.[22] The profits that eventually accrue to organization leaders move through channels so complex that even persons who work in the betting operation do not know or cannot prove the identity of the leader. Increasing use of the telephone for lottery and sports betting

[17] See generally Permanent Subcommittee on Investigations of the Senate Committee on Government Operations, *Gambling and Organized Crime* (hereinafter cited as *McClelland, Gambling Report*), *Senate Report No. 1310*, 87th Congress, 2nd Session, 1962. See also New York Temporary Commission of Investigation, *Syndicated Gambling in New York State*, 1961.

[18] "Gambling is the principal source of income for organized criminal gangs in the country." *Kefauver Committee, 2nd Interim Report, Senate Report No. 141*, 82nd Congress 1st Session 1951, p. 11.

"According to major Federal, State and local law enforcement officials who have made studies and who are known to the subcommittee staff, organized crime in the United States is primarily dependent upon illicit gambling, a multibillion dollar market, for the necessary funds to operate other criminal and illegal activities." *McClellan, Gambling Report, Senate Report No. 1310*, 87th Congress, 2nd Session, 1962, p. 43.

[19] Information submitted to President's Commission on Law Enforcement and Administration of Justice by a Federal agency.

[20] Statement by then Deputy Inspector Arthur C. Grubert, New York City Police Department In-Service Training Program, April 19, 1965, New York, N.Y.

[21] "Number gambling follows the general pattern of organization of all large-scale vice and crime. This pattern consists of four basic elements: (1) "an elaborate hierarchical organization of personnel, (2) a spatial organization in which a wide territory is controlled from a central metropolitan area, (3) the "fix," in which public officials, principally police and politicians, are drawn into and made a part of the organization, (4) legal aid in which members of the legal profession become the advisors and consultants of the organization." Carlson, "Numbers Gambling, A Study of a Culture Complex" (unpublished Ph.D. dissertation, University of Michigan Department of Sociology, 1940), p. 68.

[22] It was reported, for example, that in Detroit there were almost 100 positions involved in the operation of one lottery enterprise. Bet slips were delivered by 50 "pick up" men to substations where they were tabulated. After a "bookkeeper" determined the winning slips, the proceeds were taken to a "section chief" who passed a portion up through the hierarchy. *McClellan, Narcotics Hearings*, 88th Congress, 1st Session, 1963, part 2 at pp. 460–462.

has facilitated systems in which the bookmaker may not know the identity of the second-echelon person to whom he calls in the day's bets. Organization not only creates greater efficiency and enlarges markets;[23] it also provides a systematized method of corrupting the law enforcement process by centralizing procedures for the payment of graft.[24]

.   .   .   .   .

There is no accurate way of ascertaining organized crime's gross revenue from gambling in the United States. Estimates of the annual intake have varied from $7 to $50 billion.[25] Legal betting at racetracks reaches a gross annual figure of almost $5 billion, and most enforcement officials believe that illegal wagering on horse races, lotteries, and sporting events totals at least $20 billion each year. Analysis of organized criminal betting operations indicates that the profit is as high as one-third of gross revenue—or $6 to $7 billion each year. While the Commission cannot judge the accuracy of these figures, even the most conservative estimates place substantial capital in the hands of organized crime leaders.[26]

LOAN SHARKING[27]

In the view of most law enforcement officials loan sharking, the lending of money at higher rates than the legally prescribed limit, is the second

[23] In his statement in the Temporary Commission of Investigation of the State of New York on April 22, 1960, Charles R. Thom, Commissioner of Police of Suffolk County (Eastern Long Island), N.Y., said: "The *advantages* of syndicate operation to the previously independent bookie included: (1) unlimited resources with absolute backing which eliminated the need to lay off, thus permitting vast expansion, and the average bookie quickly discovered he was making a bigger net on a 50–50 basis than he formerly made when he controlled the entire operation; (2) New York City telephone numbers could be passed along to regular bettors and players, which made the bookie merely a collector of money, credited on the books of the syndicate through an efficient bookkeeping system, and adding the tremendous factor that use of telephones was thus changed, greatly reducing the efficiency of telephone taps; and (3) the syndicate agreed to provide 'stand-up men' where feasible." Mimeo, p. 2.

[24] "It is somewhat startling to learn that the syndicates are particularly happy with the consolidation of the nine police departments into the Suffolk County Police Department, as they feel that protection is easier to arrange through one agency than through many. The intensive campaign against gamblers instituted by this Department commencing January 1st had the astounding side effect of solving the recruiting problem of the syndicate, as our drive successfully stampeded the independents into the arms of the syndicate for protection, and the syndicate can now pick and choose those operators which they wish to admit." *Ibid.*

[25] "[G]ambling is the leading source of organization revenue, accounting for probably half of organization profits. It has been estimated that illegal gambling grosses from seven to twenty billion dollars annually." Johnson, *supra* note 2 at p. 402. For some estimates on the volume of illegal gambling, see *id.* at p. 402 note 22.

[26] "Gambling profits are the principal support of big-time racketeering and gangsterism. These profits provide the financial resources whereby ordinary criminals are converted into big-time racketeers, political bosses, pseudo businessmen, and alleged philanthropists." *Kefauver Committee, 3rd Interim Report,* Senate Report No. 307, 82nd Congress, 1st Session, 1961, p. 2.

[27] For an excellent treatment of the subject in New York State, see New York Temporary Commission of Investigation, *The Loan Shark Racket* (1965).

largest source of revenue for organized crime.[28] Gambling profits provide the initial capital for loan-shark operations.[29]

No comprehensive analysis has ever been made of what kinds of customers loan sharks have, or of how much or how often each kind borrows. Enforcement officials and other investigators do have some information. Gamblers borrow to pay gambling losses;[30] narcotics users borrow to purchase heroin. Some small businessmen borrow from loan sharks when legitimate credit channels are closed.[31] The same men who take bets from employees in mass employment industries also serve at times as loan sharks, whose money enables the employees to pay off their gambling debts or meet household needs.[32]

Interest rates vary from 1 to 150 percent a week, according to the relationship between the lender and borrower, the intended use of the money, the size of the loan, and the repayment potential.[33] The classic "6-for-5" loan, 20 percent a week, is common with small borrowers. Payments may be due by a certain hour on a certain day, and even a few

[28] "[S]hylocking . . . represents a substantial portion of the multibillion dollar take of organized crime." Johnson, *supra* note 2 at p. 403.

[29] Permanent Subcommittee on Investigations of the Senate Committee on Government Operations, *Organized Crime and Illicit Traffic in Narcotics* (hereinafter cited as *McClellan, Narcotics Report*), Senate Report No. 72, 89th Congress, 1st Session, 1965, p. 18; testimony of J. Edgar Hoover, *Hearings Before the Subcommittee on Departments of State, Justice, and Commerce, the Judiciary, and Related Agencies Appropriations of the House Committee on Appropriations,* 89th Congress, 2nd Session, 1966.

[30] In his statement to the Temporary Commission of Investigation of the State of New York on April 22, 1960, Commissioner Charles R. Thom described how loan sharking provided the means for organizing previously independent bookmakers:

"Speaking generally, prior to 1958, professional gambling in Suffolk County was conducted primarily by independent operators. There was no known pattern of organized gambling beyond the usual facilities for laying off, and no reported rackets or collateral criminal activities.

"About two years ago, representatives of one or more syndicates began approaching these independent gambling operations with a view to incorporating them into syndicated operations. By and large, these independent gamblers refused to be so organized, and the syndicates withdrew their efforts without resort to rough tactics. The syndicates then commenced an insidious campaign of infiltration, wherein the principal M.O. was *finance.* With open pocketbook the syndicate recruited a number of independent operators, by financing their operations until these bookies were hooked. Part of this system included the notorious 6 for 5 plus 5 percent per week, which meant simply that they financed the bookies on the basis that the gambling operator had to return $6.00 for every $5.00 borrowed, plus the staggering interest of 5 per cent per week. It follows that a bookie who had a couple of bad weeks was completely hooked and fell under the control of the syndicate. Most of these independent bookies were small businessmen, including the typical barber, candy store operator and the like, without the financial resources to withstand this squeeze, which was effectively accomplished by the money men of the syndicate. Once hooked, the bookies now worked for the syndicate on a 50–50 basis."

[31] New York Temporary Commission of Investigation, *The Loan Shark Report* (1965).

[32] Information submitted to President's Commission on Law Enforcement and Administration of Justice, *Task Force Report: Organized Crime* (Washington: U.S. Government Printing Office, 1967) by a Federal agency.

[33] See *McClellan, Labor-Management Reports, Final Report,* Senate Report No. 1139, 86th Congress, 2nd Session, 1960, part 2 at p. 772.

minutes' default may result in a rise in interest rates. The lender is more interested in perpetuating interest payments than collecting principal; and force, or threats of force of the most brutal kind, are used to effect interest collection, eliminate protest when interest rates are raised, and prevent the beleaguered borrower from reporting the activity to enforcement officials.[34] No reliable estimates exist of the gross revenue from organized loan sharking, but profit margins are higher than for gambling operations, and many officials classify the business in the multi-billion-dollar range.[35]

NARCOTICS[36]

The sale of narcotics is organized like a legitimate importing-wholesaling-retailing business. The distribution of heroin, for example, requires movement of the drug through four or five levels between the importer and the street peddler.[37] Many enforcement officials believe that the severity of mandatory Federal narcotics penalties has caused organized criminals to restrict their activities to importing and wholesale distribution.[38] They stay away from smaller-scale wholesale transactions or dealing at the retail level. Transactions with addicts are handled by independent narcotics pushers using drugs imported by organized crime.[39]

The large amounts of cash and the international connections necessary for large, long-term heroin supplies can be provided only by organized crime. Conservative estimates of the number of addicts in the Nation and the average daily expenditure for heroin indicate that the gross heroin trade is $350 million annually,[40] of which $21 million are probably profits to the importer and distributor.[41] Most of this profit goes to organized crime groups in those few cities in which almost all heroin consumption occurs.

OTHER GOODS AND SERVICES

Prostitution and bootlegging play a small and declining role in organized crime's operations.[42] Production of illegal alcohol is a risky business. The

---

[34] Information submitted to President's Commission on Law Enforcement and Administration of Justice, *Task Force Report: Organized Crime* (Washington: U.S. Government Printing Office, 1967) by a Federal agency.

[35] New York Temporary Commission of Investigation, *The Loan Shark* (1965).

[36] See generally *McClellan, Narcotics Hearings,* 88th Congress, 1st Session, 1963, parts 1 and 2; 1st and 2nd Sessions, 1963–1964, parts 3 and 4; 2nd Session, 1964, part 5; *McClellan, Narcotics Report,* Senate Report No. 72, 89th Congress, 1st Session, 1965.

[37] See Cressey, *supra* note 5 at p. 35.

[38] *McClellan, Narcotics Report, Senate Report No. 72,* 89th Congress, 1st Session, 1965, p. 120.

[39] *Id.* at pp. 121–122.

[40] *Id.* at p. 120.

[41] Information submitted by a Federal agency.

[42] "Gambling has supplanted prostitution and bootlegging as the chief source of revenue for organized crime. Before the First World War, the major profits of organized criminals were obtained from prostitution. The passage of the Mann White Slave Act, the changing sexual mores, and public opinion, combined to make commercialized prostitu-

destruction of stills and supplies by law enforcement officers during the initial stages means the loss of heavy initial investment capital. Prostitution is difficult to organize and discipline is hard to maintain. Several important convictions of organized crime figures in prostitution cases in the 1930's and 1940's made the criminal executives wary of further participation.[43]

Business and Labor Interests

INFILTRATION OF LEGITIMATE BUSINESS

A legitimate business enables the racket executive to acquire respectability in the community and to establish a source of funds that appears legal and upon which just enough taxes may be paid to avoid income tax prosecution.[44] Organized crime invests the profit it has made from illegal service activities in a variety of businesses throughout the country.[45] To succeed in such ventures, it uses accountants, attorneys, and business consultants, who in some instances work exclusively on its affairs.[46] Too often, because of the reciprocal benefits involved in organized crime's dealings with the business world, or because of fear, the legitimate sector of society helps the illegitimate sector.[47] . . .

Because business ownership is so easily concealed, it is difficult to determine all the types of businesses that organized crime has penetrated.[48] Of the 75 or so racket leaders who met at Apalachin, N.Y., in 1957, at least 9 were in the coin-operated machine industry, 16 were in the garment industry, 10 owned grocery stores, 17 owned bars or restaurants, 11 were in the olive oil and cheese business, and 9 were in the construction business. Others were involved in automobile agencies, coal companies, entertain-

---

tion a less profitable and more hazardous enterprise." *Kefauver Committee, 2nd Interim Report, Senate Report No. 141,* 82nd Congress, 1st Session, 1952, p. 11.

For a recent investigation of commercialized prostitution, see New York Temporary Commission of Investigation of Law Enforcement in Buffalo, 1961.

[43] *People v. Luciano,* 277 N.Y. 348, 14 N.E.2d 433, *cert. denied sub. nom., Luciano v. New York,* 305 U.S. 620 (1938). See also Powell, *Ninety Times Guilty* (1939), and for a brief description of Charles Luciano's role in organized crime, see excerpt from Sondern, *Brotherhood of Evil* (1939) in Tyler, ed., *Organized Crime in America,* p. 302.

[44] See *Kefauver Committee, 3rd Interim Report, Senate Report No. 307,* 82nd Congress, 1st Session, 1951, p. 170.

[45] "[C]riminals and racketeers are using the profits of organized crime to buy up and operate legitimate enterprises." *Kefauver Committee, 3rd Interim Report, Senate Report No. 307,* 82nd Congress, 1st Session, 1951, p. 170.

[46] "Mobsters and racketeers have been assisted by some tax accountants and tax lawyers in defrauding the Government." *Id.* at p. 4.

[47] "In some instances legitimate businessmen have aided the interests of the underworld by awarding lucrative contracts to gangsters and mobsters in return for help in handling employees, defeating attempts at unionization, and in breaking strikes." *Id.* at p. 5.

[48] "Using dummy fronts, the real owners of a business, the men who put up the money, never have to list themselves as owners or partners or as even being involved in any way in the business." Grutzner, "Mafia Steps Up Infiltration and Looting of Businesses," *New York Times,* February 14, 1965, p. 1, col. 3; p. 65, col. 1.

ment, funeral homes, ownership of horses and race tracks, linen and laundry enterprises, trucking, waterfront activities, and bakeries.[49]

. . . . .

Control of business concerns has usually been acquired through one of four methods: (1) investing concealed profits acquired from gambling and other illegal activities; (2) accepting business interests in payment of the owner's gambling debts; (3) foreclosing on usurious loans; and (4) using various forms of extortion.[50]

. . . . .

Too little is known about the effects on the economy of organized crime's entry into the business world, but the examples above indicate the harm done to the public[51] and at least suggest how criminal cartels can undermine free competition.[52] The ordinary businessman is hard pressed to compete with a syndicate enterprise. From its gambling and other illegal revenue—on most of which no taxes are paid—the criminal group always has a ready source of cash with which to enter any business. Through union connections, the business run by organized crime either prevents unionization or secures "sweetheart" contracts from existing unions.[53]

. . . . .

The cumulative effect of the infiltration of legitimate business in America cannot be measured.[54] Law enforcement officials agree that entry into legitimate business is continually increasing and that it has not decreased organized crime's control over gambling, usury, and other profitable, low-risk criminal enterprises.

---

[49] *McClellan, Labor-Management Reports, Final Report, Senate Report No. 1139,* 86th Congress, 2nd Session, 1960, part 3 at pp. 487–488. The report of the Kefauver Committee provides a discussion of the degree of infiltration into legitimate business, including a list of 50 types of business enterprises in which organized crime is involved. *Kefauver Committee, 3rd Interim Report, Senate Report No. 307,* 82nd Congress, 1st Session, 1951, pp. 170–181.

[50] Information submitted to President's Commission on Law Enforcement and Administration of Justice by a Federal agency.

[51] "There can be little doubt that the public suffers from gangster penetration into legitimate business. It suffers because higher prices must be paid for articles and services which it must buy. . . . The public suffers because it may have to put up with shoddy and inferior merchandise in fields where gangsters have been able to obtain a monopoly." *Kefauver Committee, 3rd Interim Report, Senate Report No. 307,* 82nd Congress, 1st Session, 1951, pp. 170–171.

[52] See Johnson, "Organized Crime: Challenge to the American Legal System," part 1, *Journal of Criminal Law, Criminology, and Police Science,* 53:399, 406–407.

[53] See generally *McClellan, Labor-Management Reports, 1st Interim Report, Senate Report No. 1417,* 85th Congress, 2nd Session, 1958; *2nd Interim Report,* parts 1 and 2, *Senate Report No. 621,* 86th Congress, 1st Session, 1959; *Final Report,* parts 1 to 4, *Senate Report No. 1139,* 86th Congress, 2nd Session, 1960.

[54] For a discussion of the criminal infiltration of legitimate activities, see Woetzel, "An Overview of Organized Crime: Mores versus Morality," *Annals,* May 1963, pp. 1, 6–7. For an excellent discussion of criminal infiltration into business in Chicago, see Peterson, "Chicago: Shades of Capone," *Annals,* May 1963, pp. 30, 32–39.

LABOR RACKETEERING[55]

Control of labor supply and infiltration of labor unions by organized crime prevent unionization of some industries, provide opportunities for stealing from union funds and extorting money by threats of possible labor strife, and provide funds from the enormous union pension and welfare systems for business ventures controlled by organized criminals. Union control also may enhance other illegal activities. Trucking, construction, and waterfront shipping entrepreneurs, in return for assurance that business operations will not be interrupted by labor discord, countenance gambling, loan sharking, and pilferage on company property. Organized criminals either direct these activities or grant "concessions" to others in return for a percentage of the profits.

Some of organized crime's effects on labor union affairs, particularly in the abuse of pension and welfare funds, were disclosed in investigations by Senator John McClellan's committee. In one case almost immediately after receiving a license as an insurance broker, the son of a major organized crime figure in New York City was chosen as the broker for a number of such funds, with significant commissions to be earned and made available for distribution to "silent partners." The youthful broker's only explanation for his success was that he had advertised in the classified telephone directory.[56]

In New York City, early in 1966, the head of one organized crime group was revealed to be a partner in a labor relations consulting firm. One client of the firm, a nationally prominent builder, said he did not oppose unions but that better and cheaper houses could be built without them. The question of why a legitimate businessman would seek the services of an untrained consultant with a criminal record to handle his labor relations was not answered.

Location of Organized Crime Activities

Organized criminal groups are known to operate in all sections of the Nation. In response to a Commission survey of 71 cities, the police departments in 80 percent of the cities with over 1 million residents, in 20 percent of the cities with a population between one-half million and a million, in 20 percent of the cities with between 250,000 and 500,000 population, and in over 50 percent of the cities between 100,000 and 250,000, indicated that

[55] For a detailed examination of labor racketeering, see *McClellan, Labor-Management Reports, 1st Interim Report, Senate Report No. 1417,* 85th Congress, 2nd Session, 1958; *2nd Interim Report,* parts 1 and 2, *Senate Report No. 621,* 86th Congress, 1st Session, 1959; *Final Report,* parts 1 to 4, *Senate Report No. 1139,* 86th Congress, 2nd Session, 1960.

[56] Interview with James P. Kelly, former investigator for Senate Select Committee on Improper Activities in the Labor of Management Field, November 23, 1966.

organized criminal groups exist in their cities. In some instances Federal agency intelligence indicated the presence of organized crime where local reports denied it.[57] Of the nine cities not responding to the Commission survey,[58] six are known to Federal agencies to have extensive organized crime problems.[59] Where the existence of organized crime was acknowledged, all police departments indicated that the criminal group would continue even though a top leader died or was incarcerated.

Corruption of the Enforcement and Political Systems[60]

. . . All available data indicate that organized crime flourishes only where it has corrupted local officials.[61] As the scope and variety of organized crime's activities have expanded, its need to involve public officials at every level of local government has grown. And as government regulation expands into more and more areas of private and business activity, the power to corrupt likewise affords the corrupter more control over matters affecting the everyday life of each citizen.

. . . . .

In recent years some local governments have been dominated by criminal groups. Today, no large city is completely controlled by organized crime, but in many there is a considerable degree of corruption.[62]

Organized crime currently is directing its efforts to corrupt law enforcement at the chief or at least middle-level supervisory officials. The corrupt political executive who ties the hands of police officials who want to act against organized crime is even more effective for organized crime's pur-

---

[57] Information submitted to the President's Commission on Law Enforcement and Administration of Justice by a Federal agency. The Kefauver Committee encountered similar inconsistencies in responses of certain local law-enforcement officials: "Whether out of ignorance or indolence is not clear, but some local authorities insisted, orally and in writing, that there was no organized crime in their jurisdiction, although the subsequent testimony proved them pathetically in error." *Kefauver Committee, 2nd Interim Report, Senate Report No. 141,* 82nd Congress, 1st Session, 1951, p. 7.

[58] Buffalo, New York; Flint, Michigan; Kansas City, Kansas; Milwaukee, Wisconsin; Mobile, Alabama; Nashville, Tennessee; New Orleans, Louisiana; Oakland, California; Youngstown, Ohio.

[59] Information submitted by a Federal agency.

[60] "Finally, the public suffers because the vast economic resources that gangsters and racketeers control [enable] them to consolidate their economic and political positions. Money, and particularly ready cash, is power in any community, and over and over again this committee has found instances where racketeers' money has been used to exercise influence with Federal, State, and local officials and agencies of government . . . The money used by hoodlums to buy economic and political control is also used to induce public apathy." *Kefauver Committee, 3rd Interim Report, Senate Report No. 307,* 82nd Congress, 1st Session, 1951, p. 171.

[61] "[C]orruption by organized crime is a normal condition of American local government and politics." Moynihan, "The Private Government of Organized Crime," *The Reporter,* July 6, 1961, p. 11.

[62] Information submittel by a Federal agency.

poses.[63] To secure political power organized crime tries by bribes or political contributions to corrupt the nonoffice-holding political leaders to whom judges, mayors, prosecuting attorneys, and correctional officials may be responsive.

Membership and Organization of Criminal Cartels[64]

Some law enforcement officials define organized crime as those groups engaged in gambling, or narcotics pushing, or loan sharking, or with illegal business or labor interests. This is useful to the extent that it eliminates certain other criminal groups from consideration, such as youth gangs, pickpocket rings, and professional criminal groups who may also commit many types of crimes but whose groups are ad hoc. But when law enforcement officials focus exclusively on the crime instead of the organization, their target is likely to be the lowest-level criminals who commit the visible crimes. This has little effect on the organization.[65]

The Commission believes that before a strategy to combat organized crime's threat to America can be developed, that threat must be assessed by a close examination of organized crime's distinctive characteristics and methods of operation.

National Scope of Organized Crime

In 1951 the Kefauver Committee declared that a nationwide crime syndicate known as the Mafia operated in many large cities and that the leaders of the Mafia usually controlled the most lucrative rackets in their cities.[66]

In 1957, 20 of organized crime's top leaders were convicted (later reversed on appeal)[67] of a criminal charge arising from a meeting at Apalachin, N.Y. At the sentencing the judge stated that they had sought to corrupt and infiltrate the political mainstreams of the country, that they had led double lives of crime and respectability, and that their probation reports read "like a tale of horrors."

[63] "The largest single factor in the breakdown of law-enforcement agencies in dealing with organized crime is the corruption and connivance of many public officials." American Bar Association, *Report on Organized Crime and Law Enforcement*, 1952, p. 16.

[64] See generally Cressey, *supra* note 16, appendix A, *The Functions and Structure of Criminal Syndicates*, September 1966. For detailed information on organized crime members and their activities in various areas of the country, see McClellan, *Narcotics Hearings*, 88th Congress, 1st Session, parts 1 and 2, 1963; 1st and 2nd Sessions, parts 3 and 4, 1963–1964; 2nd Session, part 5, 1964.

[65] "Minor members . . . may be imprisoned, but the top leaders remain relatively untouched by law-enforcement agencies." American Bar Association, *op. cit. supra* note 63, at p. 13.

[66] *Kefauver Committee, 3rd Interim Report, Senate Report No. 307*, 82nd Congress, 1st Session, 1951, p. 150.

[67] *United States v. Bufalino*, 285 F. 2d 408 (2d Cir. 1960).

Today the core of organized crime in the United States consists of 24 groups operating as criminal cartels in large cities across the Nation. Their membership is exclusively men of Italian descent, they are in frequent communication with each other, and their smooth functioning is insured by a national body of overseers.[68] To date, only the Federal Bureau of Investigation has been able to document fully the national scope of these groups, and FBI intelligence indicates that the organization as a whole has changed its name from the Mafia to La Cosa Nostra.

.   .   .   .   .

In individual cities, the local core group may also be known as the "outfit," the "syndicate," or the "mob."[69] These 24 groups work with and control other racket groups, whose leaders are of various ethnic derivations. In addition, the thousands of employees who perform the street-level functions of organized crime's gambling, usury, and other illegal activities represent a cross section of the Nation's population groups.

The present confederation of organized crime groups arose after Prohibition, during which Italian, German, Irish, and Jewish groups had competed with one another in racket operations. The Italian groups were successful in switching their enterprises from prostitution and bootlegging to gambling, extortion, and other illegal activities. They consolidated their power through murder and violence.[70]

Today, members of the 24 core groups reside and are active in the states shown on the map. The scope and effect of their criminal operations and penetration of legitimate businesses vary from area to area. The wealthiest and most influential core groups operate in States including New York, New Jersey, Illinois, Florida, Louisiana, Nevada, Michigan, and Rhode Island.[71] Not shown on the map are many States in which members of core groups control criminal activity even though they do not reside there. For example, a variety of illegal activities in New England is controlled from Rhode Island.[72]

Recognition of the common ethnic tie of the 5,000 or more members of organized crime's core groups[73] is essential to understanding the structure of these groups today. Some have been concerned that past identification of Cosa Nostra's ethnic character has reflected on Italian-Americans generally. This false implication was eloquently refuted by one of the Nation's out-

[68] See testimony of J. Edgar Hoover, *supra* note 29 at pp. 272–274.

[69] See testimony of former New York City Police Commissioner Michael J. Murphy, *McClellan, Narcotics Hearings,* 88th Congress, 1st Session, 1963, part 1 at p. 63; testimony of Captain William Duffy, *id.,* part 2 at p. 506; Office of the New York Counsel to the Governor, *Combating Organized Crime: A Report of the 1965 Oyster Bay, New York, Conferences on Combating Organized Crime* (1966).

[70] See generally, Tyler, ed., *Organized Crime in America* (1962), pp. 147–224.

[71] Information submitted by a Federal Agency.

[72] *Ibid.*

[73] Testimony of J. Edgar Hoover, *Hearings Before the Subcommittee on Departments of State, Justice, and Commerce, the Judiciary, and Related Agencies Appropriations of the House Committee on Appropriations,* 89th Congress, 2nd Session, 1966, p. 273.

States in Which Organized Crime Core Group Members Both Reside and Operate

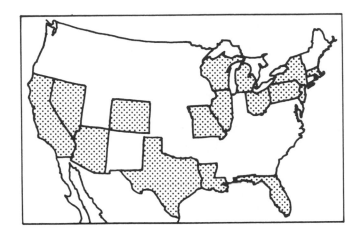

standing experts on organized crime, Sgt. Ralph Salerno of the New York City Police Department. When an Italian-American racketeer complained to him, "Why does it have to be one of your own kind that hurts you?", Sgt. Salerno answered:

> *I'm not your kind and you're not my kind. My manners, morals, and mores are not yours. The only thing we have in common is that we both spring from an Italian heritage and culture—and you are the traitor to that heritage and culture which I am proud to be part of.*[74]

Organized crime in its totality thus consists of these 24 groups allied with other racket enterprises to form a loose confederation operating in large and small cities. In the core groups, because of their permanency of form, strength of organization, and ability to control other racketeer operations, resides the power that organized crime has in America today.

Internal Structure[75]

Each of the 24 groups is known as a "family," with membership varying from as many as 700 men to as few as 20. Most cities with organized crime

[74] Grutzner, "City Police Expert on Mafia Retiring from Force," *New York Times*, January 21, 1967, p. 65, col. 3.

[75] For an extensive discussion of the internal structure of the organized crime groups, see Cressey, *The Functions and Structure of Criminal Syndicates*, September 1966, at pp. 31–40, printed as appendix A of President's Commission on Law Enforcement and Administration of Justice, *Task Force Report: Crime and Its Impact—An Assessment* (Washington: U.S. Government Printing Office, 1967). See also *McClellan, Narcotics Hearings*, 88th Congress, 1st Session, parts 1 and 2, 1963; 1st and 2nd Sessions, parts 3 and 4, 1963–1964; 2nd Session, part 5, 1961.

have only one family; New York City has five. Each family can participate in the full range of activities in which organized crime generally is known to engage. Family organization is rationally designed with an integrated set of positions geared to maximize profits. Like any large corporation, the organization functions regardless of personnel changes, and no individual—not even the leader—is indispensable. If he dies or goes to jail, business goes on.

The hierarchical structure of the families resembles that of the Mafia groups that have operated for almost a century on the island of Sicily. Each family is headed by one man, the "boss," whose primary functions are maintaining order and maximizing profits. Subject only to the possibility of being overruled by the national advisory group, which will be discussed below, his authority in all matters relating to his family is absolute.

Beneath each boss is an "underboss," the vice president or deputy director of the family. He collects information for the boss; he relays messages to him and passes his instructions down to his own underlings. In the absence of the boss, the underboss acts for him.

On the same level as the underboss, but operating in a staff capacity, is the *consigliere,* who is a counselor, or adviser. Often an elder member of the family who has partially retired from a career in crime, he gives advice to family members, including the boss and underboss, and thereby enjoys considerable influence and power.

Below the level of the underboss are the *caporegime,* some of whom serve as buffers between the top members of the family and the lower-echelon personnel. To maintain their insulation from the police, the leaders of the hierarchy (particularly the boss) avoid direct communication with the workers. All commands, information, complaints, and money flow back and forth through a trusted go-between. A *caporegime* fulfilling this buffer capacity, however, unlike the underboss, does not make decisions or assume any of the authority of his boss.

Other *caporegime* serve as chiefs of operating units. The number of men supervised in each unit varies with the size and activities of particular families. Often the *caporegima* has one or two associates who work closely with him, carrying orders, information, and money to the men who belong to his unit. From a business standpoint, the *caporegima* is analogous to plant supervisor or sales manager.

The lowest level "members" of a family are the *soldati,* the soldiers or "button" men who report to the *caporegime.* A soldier may operate a particular illicit enterprise, *e.g.,* a loan-sharking operation, a dice game, a lottery, a bookmaking operation, a smuggling operation, on a commission basis, or he may "own" the enterprise and pay a portion of its profit to the organization, in return for the right to operate. Partnerships are common between two or more soldiers and between soldiers and men higher up in the hierarchy. Some soldiers and most upper-echelon family members have interests in more than one business.

Beneath the soldiers in the hierarchy are large numbers of employees and commission agents who are not members of the family and are not necessarily of Italian descent. These are the people who do most of the actual work in the various enterprises. They have no buffers or other insulation from law enforcement. They take bets, drive trucks, answer telephones, sell narcotics, tend the stills, work in the legitimate businesses. For example, in a major lottery business that operated in Negro neighborhoods in Chicago, the workers were Negroes; the bankers for the lottery were Japanese-Americans; but the game, including the banking operation, was licensed, for a fee, by a family member.[76]

. . . . .

Organized crime groups, on the other hand, are believed to contain one or more fixed positions for "enforcers," whose duty it is to maintain organizational integrity by arranging for the maiming and killing of recalcitrant members. And there is a position for a "corrupter," whose function is to establish relationships with those public officials and other influential persons whose assistance is necessary to achieve the organization's goals.[77] By including these positions within its organization, each criminal cartel, or "family," becomes a government[78] as well as a business.

The highest ruling body of the 24 families is the "commission." This body serves as a combination legislature, supreme court, board of directors, and arbitration board; its principal functions are judicial. Family members look to the commission as the ultimate authority on organizational and jurisdictional disputes. It is composed of the bosses of the Nation's most powerful families but has authority over all 24. The composition of the commission varies from 9 to 12 men. According to current information, there are presently 9 families represented, 5 from New York City and 1 each from Philadelphia, Buffalo, Detroit, and Chicago.[79]

The commission is not a representative legislative assembly or an elected judicial body. Members of this council do not regard each other as equals. Those with long tenure on the commission and those who head large families, or possess unusual wealth, exercise greater authority and receive utmost respect. The balance of power on this nationwide council rests with the leaders of New York's 5 families. They have always served on the commission and consider New York as at least the unofficial headquarters of the entire organization.

. . . . .

[76] Information submitted to President's Commission on Law Enforcement and Administration of Justice by a Federal agency.

[77] Federal agency intelligence indicates that the *consigliere* frequently acts as the "corruptor." In this connection, the Kefauver Committee underscored the sinister influence Frank Costello exercised upon the New York County Democratic organization. *Kefauver Committee, 3rd Interim Report, Senate Report No. 307,* 82nd Congress, 1st Session, 1951, pp. 143–144.

[78] "[I]n effect organized crime constitutes a kind of private government whose power rivals and often supplants that of elected public government." Moynihan, *supra* note 61.

[79] Information submitted by a Federal agency.

As the bosses realize that they cannot handle the complicated problems of business and finance alone, their authority will be delegated. Decisionmaking will be decentralized, and individual freedom of action will tend to increase. New problems of discipline and authority may occur if greater emphasis on expertise within the ranks denies unskilled members of the families an opportunity to rise to positions of leadership. The unthinking acceptance of rank authority may be difficult to maintain when experts are placed above long-term, loyal soldiers. Primarily because of fear of infiltration by law enforcement, many of the families have not admitted new members for several years. That fact plus the increasing employment of personnel with specialized and expert functions may blur the lines between membership and nonmembership. In organized crime, internal rebellion would not take the form of strikes and picketing. It would bring a new wave of internal violence.

Code of Conduct[80]

The leaders of the various organized crime families acquire their positions of power and maintain them with the assistance of a code of conduct that, like the hierarchical structure of the families, is very similar to the Sicilian Mafia's code—and just as effective. The code stipulates that underlings should not interfere with the leader's interests and should not seek protection from the police. They should be "standup guys" who go to prison in order that the bosses may amass fortunes. The code gives the leaders exploitative authoritarian power over everyone in the organization. Loyalty, honor, respect, absolute obedience—these are inculcated in family members through ritualistic initiation and customs within the organization,[81] through material rewards, and through violence. Though underlings are forbidden to "inform" to the outside world, the family boss learns of deviance within the organization through an elaborate system of internal informants. Despite prescribed mechanisms for peaceful settlement of disputes between family members, the boss himself may order the execution of any family member for any reason.

The code not only preserves leadership authority but also makes it extremely difficult for law enforcement to cultivate informants and maintain them within the organization.

The Nation's Efforts to Control Organized Crime

Investigation and prosecution of organized criminal groups in the 20th century has seldom proceeded on a continuous, institutionalized basis.

---

[80] See Cressey, *supra* note 75, at pp. 40–50.

[81] For a description of the initiation ritual, see *McClellan, Narcotics Hearings,* 88th Congress, 1st Session, 1963, part 1 at pp. 180–185.

Public interest and demands for action have reached high levels sporadically; but, until recently, spurts of concentrated law enforcement activity have been followed by decreasing interest and application of resources.

Historical Background

. . . A few law enforcement officials became concerned with the illicit enterprises of Mafia-type groups in the United States near the close of the 19th century. Sustained efforts at investigation were abruptly terminated by the murders of two police officers, one from New Orleans and one from New York City.[82] The multimillion-dollar bootlegging business in the Prohibition era of the 1920's produced intensive investigations by the Treasury Department and the conviction of Chicago racket leader Al Capone.

In the 1930's, the special racket group of Thomas E. Dewey in New York City secured the conviction of several prominent racketeers, including the late Lucky Luciano, the syndicate leader whose organizational genius made him the father of today's confederation of organized crime families.[83] In the early 1940's, FBI investigation of a million-dollar extortion plot in the moving picture industry resulted in the conviction of several racket leaders, including the Chicago family boss who was then a member of organized crime's national council.[84]

After World War II there was little national interest in the problem until 1950, when the U.S. Attorney General convened a national conference on organized crime. This conference made several recommendations concerning investigative and prosecutive needs.[85] Several weeks later the well-publicized hearings of the Senate Special Committee under Senator Kefauver began. The Kefauver committee heard over 800 witnesses from nearly every State and temporarily aroused the concern of many communities. There was a brief series of local investigations in cities where the Senate committee had exposed organized crime operations and public corruption, but law enforcement generally failed to develop the investigative and prosecutive units necessary to root out the activities of the criminal cartels.

[82] See Cook, *The Secret Rulers* (1966), pp. 61–67.

[83] Dewey's intensive antiracketeering campaign also led to the conviction in 1941 of the notorious Louis "Lepke" Buchalter and Emmanuel "Mendy" Weiss for murder. For a description of the activities of Buchalter and Weiss, see the excerpt from Tully, *Treasury Agent* (1958), in Tyler, ed., *Organized Crime in America* (1962), p. 205.

[84] See Peterson, *supra* note 54, pp. 30–32.

[85] In a foreword to the report of the proceedings, Attorney General McGrath described the background of the Conference: "In the winter of 1949–1950 representatives of the United States Conference of Mayors, American Municipal Association, National Institute of Municipal Law Officers, National Association of Attorneys General, and others came or wrote to me expressing their alarm over the mounting problems of criminal law enforcement facing their communities, particularly the difficulties that are presented to the local communities in meeting the evils arising from organized gambling operations." U.S. Department of Justice, *The Attorney General's Conference on Crime* (1950). A key proposal by the American Municipal Association for the "development of a coordinated master plan of action on the whole system of Nation-wide rackets by Federal, State, and local governments, and citizens' groups" has never been implemented. *Id.* at p. 32.

In 1957 the discovery of the meeting in Apalachin, N.Y., of at least 75 criminal cartel leaders from every section of the Nation aroused national interest again. This interest was further stimulated by disclosures in the hearings of Senator McClellan's Select Senate Committee investigating organized crime's infiltration of labor and business.[86] A concerted Federal enforcement response developed in the 1950's, and special, institutionalized efforts on the local level have been growing slowly since that time.

Federal Law Enforcement

Following the Kefauver hearings, the Department of Justice commenced a concerted drive against the leading racket figures identified in the hearings. Federal prosecutors throughout the Nation were encouraged to initiate investigations and prosecutions of such persons. As a result, a number of high level organized crime participants were convicted of Federal law violations. Under authority of the immigration statutes, the Department was successful in effecting the deportation of other racketeers. In 1954, the Justice Department formed an Organized Crime and Racketeering (OCR) Section to encourage the continuation of these prosecutive efforts. Efforts to institutionalize an antiracketeering intelligence program were hindered by a lack of coordination and interest by some Federal investigative agencies.

In 1958, after Apalachin, an Attorney General's Special Group on Organized Crime was created in the Department of Justice with regional offices from which intelligence information was gathered and grand jury proceedings conducted, concerning the Apalachin conferees.[87] After trial and reversal of the convictions of 20 of these conferees for conspiring to obstruct justice, the group's functions were assumed by the existing OCR Section.

In September 1960, the Federal Bureau of Investigation began to supply the OCR Section with regular intelligence reports on 400 of the Nation's organized crime figures. But with only 17 attorneys and minimal intelligence information from other Federal agencies, the section could not adequately fulfill its functions, which included coordinating all Federal law enforcement activities against organized crime, accumulating and correlating all necessary data, initiating and supervising investigations, formulating general prosecutive policies, and assisting the Federal prosecuting attorneys throughout the country.

In 1961, the OCR Section expanded its organized crime program to unprecedented proportions. In the next 3 years, regular intelligence reports

---

[86] *McClellan, Labor-Management Reports, 1st Interim Report,* Senate Report No. 1417, 85th Congress, 2nd Session, 1958; *2nd Interim Report,* parts 1 and 2, *Senate Report No. 621,* 86th Congress, 1st Session, 1959; *Final Report,* parts 1 to 4, *Senate Report No. 1139,* 86th Congress, 2nd Session, 1960.

[87] The Special Group on Organized Crime in the United States was created on April 10, 1958. A detailed report analyzing Federal investigative and prosecution requirements to contain organized crime successfully was submitted to the Attorney General on February 10, 1959. See *Hearings Before Subcommittee No. 5 of the House Committee on the Judiciary,* 87th Congress, 1961, ser. 16 at pp. 102–110.

were secured from 26 separate Federal agencies, the number of attorneys was nearly quadrupled, and convictions increased.[88] Indicative of the cooperation during this enforcement effort was the pooling of information from several Federal agencies for investigative leads in income tax cases. Over 60 percent of the convictions secured between 1961 and July 1965 resulted from tax investigations conducted by the Internal Revenue Service.[89] Several high-level members of organized crime families in New York City were convicted through the efforts of the Federal Bureau of Narcotics.[90]

The FBI was responsible for convictions of organized crime figures in New York City, Chicago, and elsewhere. Enactment of statutes giving the FBI jurisdiction in interstate gambling cases[91] resulted in disruption, by investigation and prosecution, of major interstate gambling operations, including lay-off betting, which is essential to the success of local gambling businesses.

In 1965, a number of factors slowed the momentum of the organized crime drive. A Senate committee uncovered a few isolated instances of wiretapping and electronic surveillance by Treasury Department agents,[92] and some officials began to question whether special emphasis upon organized crime in tax enforcement was appropriate or fair. The Department of Justice was accused of extensively using illegal electronic surveillance in investigations of racketeer influence in Las Vegas casinos.[93] Federal prosecutors in some large cities demanded independence from OCR Section attorneys and prosecutive policies. Attacks appeared in the press on the intensity and tactics of the Federal investigative and prosecutive efforts. A high rate of turnover among OCR Section attorneys meant discontinuity of effort and reduced personnel by nearly 25 percent.

This combination of adverse circumstances apparently led the OCR Section to believe that it could no longer expect the high degree of cooperation it had received from some Federal investigative agencies, and the intensity of its efforts diminished. In May 1966, however, President Johnson directed

[88] "In 1960, before this drive began, we secured the conviction of 45 persons for racketeering crimes. In 1961, after the drive was first under way, we secured 73 convictions. In 1962 the number doubled to 138. In 1963, it doubled again to 288. And last year, it doubled once more to 546." Testimony of Attorney General Nicholas Katzenbach, *Long Committee Hearings*, 89th Congress, 1st Session, 1965, part 3 at p. 1158.

[89] *Id.* at p. 1139.

[90] These included John "Big John" Ormento, identified as a lieutenant in the Luchese family, and Carmine Galante, underboss of the Bonnano family of New York City. *McClellan, Narcotics Hearings*, 88th Congress, 1st and 2nd Sessions, 1963–1964, part 3 at p. 652 (charts F and E).

[91] Interstate and foreign travel or transportation in aid of racketeering enterprises, 75 Stat. 498, 18 U.S.C. Sec. 1953; transmission of wagering information, 75 Stat. 491, 18 U.S.C. sec. 1084, 1964.

[92] See generally *Long Committee Hearings*, 89th Congress, 1st Session, parts 1 to 3; 2nd Session, part 4; 2nd Session parts 5 to 6, 1965.

[93] *Grandi v. Central Telephone Co.*, No. A28157, 8th Judicial District Court, December 10, 1965; *Levinson & Elson*, No. A28156, 8th Judicial District Court, December 10, 1965; *Levinson v. Rogers*, No. A28155, 8th Judicial District Court, December 10, 1965.

Federal enforcement officials to review the status of the national program against organized crime. He restated his determination to continue and accelerate the program. In a White House memorandum he called upon the appropriate agencies and departments to coordinate their activities and cooperate to the utmost with the Department of Justice.[94]

State and Local Law Enforcement

The Commission made a survey of 71 cities to determine the extent of State and local law enforcement against organized crime. The survey revealed that only 12 of the 19 cities that acknowledged having organized crime have specialized units within the police department to investigate that activity. In only 6 of those 19 cities are prosecutors specially assigned to work on organized crime. Only 3 of the 43 police departments that answered that they had no organized crime in their area had created units to gather intelligence concerning the possibility of its existence. One of the three, Los Angeles, has a 55-man unit that gathers intelligence information to prevent the expansion of organized crime.[95]

[94] Memorandum from President Lyndon B. Johnson to Heads of Departments and Agencies Participating in the Federal Organized Crime Drive, May 5, 1966.

[95] "Like counterpart units in the Chicago and New York City Police Departments, the history of the Los Angeles Police Department's Intelligence Division can be traced back some years. Its current program, however, is of relatively recent date. Under the leadership of the late Chief William H. Parker, the division was created in 1950. It has responsibility for gathering information about all phases of organized crime in the Los Angeles area. The primary purpose of the division is intelligence; it has no criminal investigation responsibility. Few arrests are made, and the information it obtains is transmitted to field units for action. It has jurisdiction over some activities in addition to organized crime. For example, it maintains a close liaison with the Secret Service concerning persons who might be dangerous to the security of the President of the United States. Since it has no criminal investigation responsibility, no close, day-to-day liaison is maintained with the local district attorney's office. The prosecutor's office does not receive regular intelligence reports and does not participate in selection of targets for investigation. However, liaison is maintained with local, State, regional, national, and Federal agencies concerned with organized crime.

"The Los Angeles Police Department has 5,177 officers exclusive of civilian employees. The Intelligence Division has 51 full-time men assigned to it. These include one captain and four lieutenants. The division reports directly to the Chief of Police. Similar in part to Chicago, street-level vice activity is handled by commanders; area-wide activity by the Administrative Vice Division; and pure intelligence work by the Intelligence Division. The turnover of personnel is small, less than 10 percent a year. The average length of service for field investigators is about 15 years; for supervisors, about 22 years. Promotion and retirement are the primary factors leading to transfers into and out of the division.

"The division makes extensive use of physical surveillance, not only as a means of obtaining information, but also to prevent hoodlum contacts from being made or illegitimate activity from being carried on. Although expensive, this procedure has been effective. The division also maintains a seven-man detail at the International Airport which covers the movements of hoodlums on a 24-hour basis. Extensive use is made of public sources of information. Use of electronic equipment, however, has been severely limited by State law and is seldom employed. This is in sharp contrast with the practices of a few years ago, when the use of such equipment was considered legal and was widely and, in the opinion of the division, effectively employed.

"The Los Angeles Police Department was one of the first local police agencies to

At present, well-developed organized crime investigation units and effective intelligence programs exist within police and prosecutive agencies in only a handful of jurisdictions.[96]

.   .   .   .   .

---

become aware in detail of the cartel nature of the organization of modern organized crime. This was a major working premise in Los Angeles when it was denied or discounted elsewhere. The department believes that its ability to contain a serious and expanding organized crime problem was due in part to the use of electronic equipment. Today its personnel believe that the division's effectiveness is seriously undercut by its inability to use such equipment. Its present intelligence estimates, for example, reflect the lack of this source of information. In addition, the effectiveness of the department as a whole is believed to be undercut by the widespread use of the telephone by organized crime groups in both the gambling and narcotics fields. Little reliance is placed on the use of paid informants by the division although funds are available for the purchase of information.

"Competence and dedication of the department has thus accounted, in part, for the present law-enforcement control of organized crime in Los Angeles. The absence of serious political corruption has also played a major role. This is accounted for, in part, by the traditions of the State dating back to former Governor Earl Warren and the wide use of civil service.

"The files of the Intelligence Division are indexed as to persons, classes of crime, areas of crime, and businesses. An excellent cross-index exists to speed information retrieval. The division regularly collects information from national newspapers and congressional and other investigative hearings."

  —Blakey, "Local Law Enforcement Response to Organized Crime," January 1967, unpublished report to the President's Commission on Law Enforcement and Administration of Justice.

[96] Illustrative of such organizations is that of the office of the district attorney for New York County, which has as its function the prosecution of all criminal matters occurring in that jurisdiction. The volume is staggering. In excess of 30,000 matters come up for consideration each year. The combined total is roughly equal to the other four counties which make up the greater New York area. These duties include listening to complaints brought directly to the office by citizens, examining matters brought to it by the police, preparing informations, presenting matters to the grand jury, handling preliminary matters in court, prosecuting trials, and defending and taking appeals. In addition, the office conducts or supervises certain direct and collateral investigations of its own.

The office regularly employs approximately 260 people. There are about 100 lawyers, 10 accountants, and 10 investigators. The rest are clerks, stenographers, process servers, and specialized employees, including a psychiatrist and a photographer. The district attorney is elected, although since 1942 there have been no election contests. Staff personnel are covered by civil service. Legal personnel are selected without regard for politics, solely on the basis of merit. Salaries are lower than those offered for positions in private practice. Consequently, there is a relatively large turnover; most stay only from four to five years, although some have remained in career positions out of dedication. All members of the staff work full time. Outside or personal work is not permitted. Since 1938, the office has been singularly free of corruption or political influence.

The office itself is organized into 13 bureaus. The names of most indicate their functions. The major bureaus include a Complaint Bureau, an Indictment Bureau, a Supreme Court Bureau (handles felony trials), a Criminal Courts Bureau (handles misdemeanor trials), a Homicide Bureau, and an Appeals Bureau. In addition, the office has a Frauds Bureau, an Accounting Bureau, an Investigations Bureau, and in response to the challenge of organized crime—a Rackets Bureau.

Traditionally the function of the prosecutor has been to present to the court evidence of criminal activity developed by the police or brought to him by a citizen. The concept of the Rackets Bureau as developed in New York County, however, has been a radical departure from that traditional view. From 1935 through 1937 Thomas E. Dewey

Limitations on Control Efforts

Efforts to curb the growth of organized crime in America have not been successful. It is helpful in devising a program for the future to examine the problems encountered in attempting to combat organized crime.

DIFFICULTIES IN OBTAINING PROOF

As described above, criminal cartels have organized their groups and operations to insulate their higher echelon personnel from law enforcement and regulatory agencies. Every measure has been taken to insure that governmental investigation, no matter how intensive, will be unable to secure live witnesses the sine qua non of prosecution.

.   .   .   .   .

Documentary evidence is equally difficult to obtain. Bookmakers at the street level keep no detailed records. Main offices of gambling enterprises can be moved often enough to keep anyone from getting sufficient evidence for a search warrant for a particular location. Mechanical devices are used that prevent even the telephone company from knowing about telephone calls. And even if an enforcement agent has a search warrant, there are easy ways to destroy written material[97] while the agent fulfills the legal requirements of knocking on the door, announcing his identity and purpose, and waiting a reasonable time for a response before breaking into the room.

---

conducted a special rackets investigation in New York County at the direction of Governor Herbert H. Lehman. When Dewey became district attorney in 1938, he carried into the office the experience of that signal investigation. The Rackets Bureau, the Frauds Bureau, the Accounting Bureau, and the Investigations Bureau were set up based on that experience and were, at that time, unparalleled in the country.

Dewey found that evidence of organized criminal activity and corruption was not to be had merely for the asking. Victims of underworld terror or exploitation did not volunteer to testify. Documentary proof of extortion or graft was carefully concealed in doctored books and records. Dewey thus found that the traditional role of the district attorney—merely that of courtroom accuser—was inadequate if the challenge of organized crime and corruption was to be met.

The Rackets Bureau and the Frauds Bureau operate in a similar fashion. The Frauds Bureau deals with modern commercial fraud. The Rackets Bureau deals with modern organized crime and corruption. Both employ the expert assistance of the trained criminal accountants and investigators of the Accounting and Investigations Bureaus.

[97] "Flash paper" and "rice paper" are both frequently used in gambling operations if written notations are essential. Flash paper is a paper that is chemically treated to convert the cellulose contained in the paper to nitrocellulose by treatment with a mixture of concentrated sulfuric and nitric acids.

"This paper is highly flammable and will burst into flame if a cigarette is placed on it. In less time than it will take a law enforcement officer to cross the room, a bookmaker can turn his records into a pile of ashes of no use as evidence against him." Testimony of Attorney General Robert Kennedy, *Hearings Before Subcommittee No. 5 of the House Committee on the Judiciary,* 87th Congress, 1st Session, series 16 at p. 30. Rice paper is water soluble paper treated chemically to cause it to dissolve very quickly when submerged in water. For a more extensive description, see *Modern Plastics Encyclopedia for 1948,* at p. 201.

LACK OF RESOURCES

No State or local law enforcement agency is adequately staffed to deal successfully with the problems of breaking down criminal organizations. Just one major organized crime case may take 2 to 3 years to develop and then several more years to complete through prosecution and appeal. Cases may require several man-years of investigative resources. The percentage of investigations that result in arrests is quite low. Requests for increased budgets in government are usually granted only upon a showing of success; i.e., a high number of arrests. An effective organized crime investigative effort may not be able to produce such statistics without years of intelligence gathering, and the drive for statistics may divert investigative energy to meaningless low-level gambling arrests that have little effect on the criminal organizations. Even with these known problems, the organized crime units of all but a few city police departments are staffed by less than 10 men, and only 6 prosecutors' offices have assigned assistants to work exclusively or particularly in organized crime cases.

LACK OF COORDINATION

Local police are hampered by their limited geographical jurisdiction, and law enforcement has not responded by developing sufficient coordination among the agencies.[98]

*   *   *   *   *

FAILURE TO DEVELOP STRATEGIC INTELLIGENCE[99]

Intelligence deals with all of the things that should be known before initiating a course of action. In the context of organized crime there are two basic types of intelligence information: tactical and strategic. Tactical intelligence is the information obtained for specific organized crime prosecutions. Strategic intelligence is the information regarding the capabilities, intentions, and vulnerabilities of organized crime groups. For example, the body of knowledge built up by the FBI concerning the structure, membership, activities, and purposes of La Cosa Nostra represents significant strategic intelligence.

[98] In regard to the problem of lack of coordination among police agencies, see the *General Report* of the President's Commission on Law Enforcement and Administration of Justice, *The Challenge of Crime in a Free Society* (Washington: U.S. Government Printing Office, 1967), pp. 119–120; for a more detailed treatment, see *Report of the Police Task Force*, chapter 4.

[99] With regard to the concept of strategic intelligence, see generally Kent, *Strategic Intelligence* (1949); Platt, *Strategic Intelligence Production* (1957). For a discussion of organized crime intelligence, see Office of the New York Counsel to the Governor, *Combating Organized Crime—A Report of the 1965 Oyster Bay, New York, Conferences on Combating Organized Crime* (1966), pp. 31–34.

FAILURE TO USE AVAILABLE SANCTIONS

Gambling is the largest source of revenue for the criminal cartels, but the members of organized crime know they can operate free of significant punishment. Street workers have little reason to be deterred from joining the ranks of criminal organizations by fear of long jail sentences or large fines. Judges are reluctant to jail bookmakers and lottery operators. Even when offenders are convicted, the sentences are often very light. Fines are paid by the organization and considered a business expense.

LACK OF PUBLIC AND POLITICAL COMMITMENT

The public demands action only sporadically, as intermittent, sensational disclosures reveal intolerable violence and corruption caused by organized crime. Without sustained public pressure, political office seekers and office holders have little incentive to address themselves to combatting organized crime.

[*The President's Commission on Law Enforcement and Administration of Justice,* Task Force Report: Organized Crime (*Washington: U.S. Government Printing Office, 1967*), pp. 1–8, 10–15.]

9 Narcotics and drug abuse

In 1962 a White House Conference on Narcotic and Drug Abuse was convened in recognition of the fact that drug traffic and abuse were growing and critical national concerns. Large quantities of drugs were moving in illicit traffic despite the best efforts of law enforcement agencies. Addiction to the familiar opiates, especially in big-city ghettos, was widespread. New stimulant, depressant, and hallucinogenic drugs, many of them under loose legal controls, were coming into wide misuse, often by students. The informed public was becoming increasingly aware of the social and economic damage of illicit drug taking.

Organized criminals engaged in drug traffic were making high profits. Drug addicts, to support their habits, were stealing millions of dollars worth of property every year and contributing to the public's fear of robbery and burglary. The police, the courts, the jails and prisons, and social-service agencies of all kinds were devoting great amounts of time, money, and manpower to attempts to control drug abuse. Worst of all, thousands of human lives were being wasted.

Some methods of medical treatment, at least for opiate-dependent persons, were being tried, but the results were generally impermanent; relapse was more frequent than cure. The established cycle for such persons was arrest, confinement with or without treatment, release, and then arrest again. And the cause of all of this, the drug-prone personality and the drug-taking urge, lay hidden somewhere in the conditions of modern urban life and in the complexities of mental disorder.

Responsibility for the drug abuse problem was not at all clear. Was it a Federal or a State matter? Was it a police problem or a medical one? If, as seemed evident, it was a combination of all of these, which agencies or people should be doing what? The Conference did not answer these questions, but it did bring to them a sense of national importance and commitment.[1]

[1] *Proceedings, White House Conference on Narcotic and Drug Abuse* (Washington, September 27, 1962), pp. 27–28 (hereinafter cited as *Proceedings*).

The President's Advisory Commission on Narcotic and Drug Abuse was created in 1963 to translate this commitment into a program of action. The Commission's final report, issued in November of that year, set forth a strategy designed to improve the control of drug traffic and the treatment of drug users.[2] The 25 recommendations of that report have been the basis for most of the subsequent Federal activity in this field. Many of them, notably those pertaining to civil commitment for narcotic addicts and the need for Federal controls on the distribution of nonnarcotic drugs,[3] have been or are in the process of being implemented.

This Commission has not and could not have undertaken to duplicate the comprehensive study and report on drug abuse so recently completed by another Presidential Commission. Yet any study of law enforcement and the administration of criminal justice must of necessity include some reference to drug abuse and its associated problems.

. . . . .

The Drugs and Their Regulation

The drugs liable to abuse are usually put into the two classifications of "narcotics" and "dangerous drugs," and the people who abuse them are usually called "addicts" and "users." The terms have been used carelessly and have gathered around them many subjective associations. Some precision is necessary if they are to be used as instruments of analysis.

Addiction

There is no settled definition of addiction. Sociologists speak of "assimilation into a special life style of drug taking." Doctors speak of "physical dependence," an alteration in the central nervous system that results in painful sickness when use of the drug is abruptly discontinued; of "psychological or psychic dependence," an emotional desire, craving or compulsion to obtain and experience the drug; and of "tolerance," a physical adjustment to the drug that results in successive doses producing smaller effects and, therefore, in a tendency to increase doses. Statutes speak of habitual use; of loss of the power of self-control respecting the drug; and of effects detrimental to the individual or potentially harmful to the public morals, safety, health or welfare.[4]

Some drugs are addicting, and some persons are addicted, by one definition but not by another. The World Health Organization Expert Committee

[2] President's Advisory Commission on Narcotics and Drug Abuse, *Final Report,* 1963.
[3] *Id.* at pp. 70–73, 43–44.
[4] On the general problem of defining addiction, see Lindesmith, "Basic Problems in the Social Psychology of Addiction and a Theory," in O'Donnell & Hall, eds., *Narcotics Addiction* (1966), pp. 91, 92–95.

on Addiction-Producing Drugs has recommended that the term "drug dependence," with a modifying phrase linking it to a particular type of drug, be used in place of the term "addiction."[5] But "addiction" seems too deeply imbedded in the popular vocabulary to be expunged. Most frequently, it connotes physical dependence, resulting from excessive use of certain drugs. However, it should be noted that one can become physically dependent on substances, notably alcohol, that are not considered part of the drug abuse problem. It should be noted also that psychic or emotional dependence can develop to any substances, not only drugs, that affect consciousness and that people use for escape, adjustment or simple pleasure.

Narcotics

The dictionary defines a "narcotic" as a substance that induces sleep, dulls the senses, or relieves pain. In law, however, it has been given an artificial meaning. It does not refer, as might be expected, to one class of drugs, each having similar chemical properties or pharmacological effects. It is applied rather to a number of different classes of drugs that have been grouped together for purposes of legal control. Under the Federal laws, narcotics include the opiates and cocaine.[6] Under most state statutes, marihuana is also a narcotic.[7]

THE OPIATES

These drugs have a highly technical legal definition,[8] but for purposes of this chapter they may be taken to include opium, morphine, their derivatives and compounds and their synthetic equivalents. The opiates have great medical value. They differ widely in their uses, effects, and addiction potential. The most common are morphine and codeine.[9] The former is a principal drug in the relief of pain, the latter in the treatment of cough. Many opiates are prescribed for use in approved medical settings. While the misuse or illicit use (drug "abuse" includes both) of some of these drugs has presented serious problems for State and Federal enforcement agencies, public concern as to the opiates is focused primarily on heroin, a morphine derivative. This is the chief drug of addiction in the United States.[10]

[5] Eddy, Halbach, Isbell, and Seevers, "Drug Dependence: Its Significance and Characteristics," *Bulletin of World Health*, 1965, 32:721, 722.

[6] *Internal Revenue Code of 1954*, Sec. 4731(a).

[7] *Uniform Narcotic Drug Act*, Sec. 1(14).

[8] *Internal Revenue Code of 1954*, Sec. 4731(g)(1).

[9] See generally U.S. Treasury Department, *Traffic in Opium and Other Dangerous Drugs*, 1965, pp. 54–55; Permanent Central Narcotics Board, *Report to the Economic and Social Council* on the work of the Board, 1965, pp. 15–43.

[10] American Medical Association Council on Mental Health, "Report on Narcotics Addiction," in AMA *Narcotics Addiction—Official Actions of the American Medical Association*, 1963, p. 11. See also *Proceedings*, pp. 280–281 (Report of an Ad Hoc Panel on Drug Abuse).

The effect of any drug depends on many variables, not the least of which are the mood and expectation of the taker.[11] Drug effects are therefore best expressed in terms of probable outcomes. The discussion here is selective rather than exhaustive. With these provisos, it may be said that heroin is a depressant. It relieves anxiety and tension and diminishes the sex, hunger, and other primary drives. It may also produce drowsiness and cause inability to concentrate, apathy, and lessened physical activity. It can impair mental and physical performance. Repeated and prolonged administration will certainly lead to tolerance and physical dependence.

This process is set in motion by the first dose. An overdose may lead to respiratory failure, coma, and death. With dosages to which a person is tolerant, permanent organic damage does not occur. However, secondary effects, arising from the preoccupation of a person with the drug, may include personal neglect and malnutrition. The ritual of the American addict is to inject the drug intravenously with a needle, and infections and abscesses may be caused by the use of unsterile equipment. Euphoria is an effect often associated with heroin, often reflecting the relief a particular individual gets from chronic anxiety. Among the symptoms of the withdrawal sickness, which reaches peak intensity in 24 to 48 hours, are muscle aches, cramps, and nausea.[12]

The Bureau of Narcotics maintains a name file of active opiate addicts. As of December 31, 1965, there were 52,793 heroin addicts (out of a total of 57,199 opiate addicts) listed.[13] Most of the names in the file are of persons arrested by State and local police agencies and reported voluntarily to the Bureau on a form the Bureau provides for this purpose. Thus the inclusion of a person's name in the file depends in large measure on his coming to the attention of the police, being recognized and classified as an addict, and being reported. There is some uncertainty at each step. Moreover, some police agencies and many health and medical agencies do not participate in the voluntary reporting system. There is also no place in the system for persons who use opiates without becoming addicted. For these reasons many people feel that the Bureau's file does not present a complete statisti-

[11] *Id.* at p. 275. See also Blum, assisted by Funkhouser-Balkaby, *Mind-Altering Drugs and Dangerous Behavior: Dangerous Drugs* (hereinafter cited as Blum, *Dangerous Drugs*), published as appendix A-1, President's Commission on Law Enforcement and Administration of Justice, *Task Force Report: Crime and Its Impact—An Assessment* (Washington: U.S. Government Printing Office, 1967); also Blum, assisted by Lauraine Braunstein, *Mind-Altering Drugs and Dangerous Behavior: Narcotics* (hereinafter cited as Blum, *Narcotics*), published as appendix A-2 in President's Commission on Law Enforcement and Administration of Justice, *Task Force Report: Crime and Its Impact—An Assessment* (Washington: U.S. Government Printing Office, 1967).

[12] For a discussion of the effects of heroin, see *id.* at pp. 280–281; Eddy, Halbach, Isbell, and Seevers, *supra* note 5 at pp. 724–725; Isbell, "Medical Aspects of Opiate Addiction," in *Narcotic Addiction, op. cit. supra* note 4 at p. 62 (1966); Maurer and Vogel, *Narcotics and Narcotic Addiction* (2nd ed., 1962); AMA Council on Mental Health, *supra* note 10 at pp. 11–13.

[13] U.S. Treasury Department, *Traffic in Opium and Other Dangerous Drugs,* 1965, pp. 37–46.

cal picture of opiate use in this country.[14] Indeed the Bureau makes no claims of infallibility for the reporting system. It is intended as a device for arriving at a workable estimate of the extent and concentration of opiate addiction. The Commissioner of Narcotics has testified numerous times that the Bureau's figures are only approximations.[15] The State of California is another source for statistics on drug addiction; it maintains a file of addicts-users in the State.

It should also be noted that other estimates of the present addict population, some of which cite figures as high as 200,000, are without a solid statistical foundation.[16]

More than one-half the known heroin addicts are in New York. Most of the others are in California, Illinois, Michigan, New Jersey, Maryland, Pennsylvania, Texas, and the District of Columbia.[17] In the states where heroin addiction exists on a large scale, it is an urban problem. Within the cities it is largely found in areas with low average incomes, poor housing, and high delinquency. The addict himself is likely to be male, between the ages of 21 and 30, poorly educated and unskilled, and a member of a disadvantaged ethnic minority group.[18]

The cost of heroin to the addict fluctuates over time and from place to place. So does the quality of the drug. Five dollars is a commonly reported price for a single "bag" or packet of heroin. The substance purchased ranges in purity from 1 to about 30 percent, the remainder consisting of natural impurities, and adulterants such as lactose and mannitol.[19] Usually the addict does not know the strength of the doses he buys. Today, however, the drug available on the street is generally so far diluted that the typical addict does not develop profound physical dependence, and therefore does not suffer serious withdrawal symptoms.[20]

The basic Federal control law, the Harrison Narcotic Act of 1914, is a tax

[14] Eldridge, *Narcotics and the Law* (1962), pp. 68–78; Lindesmith, *The Addict and the Law* (1965), pp. 99–134; Winick, "Epidemiology of Narcotics Use," in Wilner and Kasselbau, eds., *Narcotics* (1965), pp. 3–6; Chein, "The Use of Narcotics as a Personal and Social Problem," *id.* at pp. 103–108.

[15] E.g., *Hearings on S. 2113, S. 2114, S. 2152 Before a Special Subcommittee of the Senate Judiciary Committee,* 89th Congress, 2nd Session, 1966, pp. 455–456; *Hearings on Organized Crime and Illicit Traffic in Narcotics Before the Permanent Subcommittee on Investigations of the Senate Governmental Operations Committee,* 88th Congress, 1st and 2nd Sessions, 1964, part 3 at p. 670.

[16] *Proceedings* (Report of Ad Hoc Panel on Drug Abuse), pp. 290–291.

[17] U.S. Treasury Department, *Traffic in Opium and Other Dangerous Drugs,* 1966, pp. 37, 43.

[18] *Id.* at p. 41; "Epidemiology of Narcotics Use," in *Narcotics, op. cit. supra* note 14; California Narcotics Rehabilitation Advisory Council, *Second Annual Report* (1966); Public Health Service, *Division of Hospitals Annual Statistical Summary for Fiscal Year 1965,* part 2, at pp. 207–223. See also Blum, *Narcotics.*

[19] See, e.g., testimony of Henry L. Giordano, Commissioner, Federal Bureau of Narcotics, in *Hearings on S. 2113, S. 2114, S. 2152, supra* note 15 at p. 453; testimony of Patrick J. McCormack, Deputy Chief Inspector and Commanding Officer, Narcotics Bureau, New York City Police Department, in *Hearings on Organized Crime and Illicit Traffic in Narcotics, supra* note 15, at p. 733.

[20] *Proceedings* (Report of an Ad Hoc Panel on Drug Abuse), p. 281.

statute.[21] It is administered by the Bureau of Narcotics, an agency of the Treasury Department. The statute imposes a tax upon the manufacture or importation of all narcotic drugs. Payment of the tax is evidenced by stamps affixed to the drug containers. The statute authorizes transfers of narcotics in the original containers by and to persons who have registered with the Treasury Department and paid certain occupational taxes ranging from $1 to $24 a year. Official order forms must be used in completing these transactions. There is an exception for the physician acting in the course of his professional practice. Unauthorized possession under the statute is a criminal offense, whether or not the drug is intended for personal use. Unauthorized sale or purchase is a criminal offense. Unauthorized importation is made punishable by a separate Federal statute.[22] Unauthorized possession and sale are also criminal acts under the Uniform Narcotic Drug Act, the control statute in effect in most States.[23]

Heroin occupies a special place in the narcotic laws. It is an illegal drug in the sense that it may not be lawfully imported or manufactured under any circumstances,[24] and it is not available for use in medical practice. All the heroin that reaches the American user is smuggled into the country from abroad, the Middle East being the reputed primary point of origin. All heroin transactions, and any possession of heroin, are therefore criminal. This is not because heroin has evil properties not shared by other opiates. Indeed, while it is more potent and somewhat more rapid in its action, heroin does not differ in any significant pharmacological effect from morphine.[25] It would appear that heroin is outlawed because of its special attractiveness to addicts and because it serves no known medical purpose not served as well or better by other drugs.

COCAINE

This drug is included as a narcotic under Federal and other laws but, unlike the opiates, it is a powerful stimulant and does not create tolerance or physical dependence. It is derived from the leaves of the coca plant cultivated extensively in parts of South America. At present it is not the major drug of abuse that it once was.[26]

MARIHUANA

This is a preparation made from the flowering tops of the female hemp plant. This plant often is found growing wild, or it can be cultivated, in any temperate or semitropical climate, including the United States. Most of the

[21] *Internal Revenue Code of 1954*, Secs. 4701–4736.
[22] U.S.C., 1964, Secs. 171–185.
[23] *Uniform Narcotic Drug Act*, Sec. 2.
[24] 21 U.S.C., 1964, Secs. 173, 502, 505.
[25] *Proceedings*, pp. 280–281 (Report of an Ad Hoc Panel on Drug Abuse); AMA Council on Mental Health, *supra* note 10 at p. 11.
[26] *Proceedings*, pp. 285–286.

marihuana that reaches American users comes from Mexico. There it is cut, dried, and pulverized and then smuggled across the border, either loose or compressed in brick form. It is commonly converted into cigarettes and consumed by smoking. Other derivatives of the hemp plant, such as hashish, which are more potent than marihuana, are rarely found in the United States.[27]

Marihuana has no established and certainly no indispensable medical use. Its effects are rather complicated, combining both stimulation and depression. Much of its effect depends on the personality of the user. The drug may induce exaltation, joyousness and hilarity, and disconnected ideas; or it may induce quietude or reveries. In the inexperienced taker it may induce panic. Or one state may follow the other. Confused perceptions of space and time and hallucinations in sharp color may occur; the person's complex intellectual and motor functions may be impaired. These effects may follow within minutes of the time the drug is taken. The influence usually wears off within a few hours but may last much longer in the case of a toxic dose. The immediate physiological effects may include nausea and vomiting, but there are no lasting physical effects, and fatalities have not been noted. Tolerance is very slight if it develops at all. Physical dependence does not develop.[28]

There is no reliable estimate of the prevalence of marihuana use. To the limited extent that police activity is an accurate measure, use appears to be increasing. Bulk seizures of marihuana by Federal enforcement authorities totaled 5,641 kilograms in 1965 as against 1,890 kilograms in 1960.[29] Bureau of Narcotics arrests for marihuana offenses about doubled over the same period of time.[30] So did the number of arrests by California authorities.[31]

Marihuana use apparently cuts across a larger segment of the general population than does opiate use, but again adequate studies are lacking. An impressionistic view, based on scattered reports, is that use is both frequent and increasing in depressed urban areas, academic and artistic communities, and among young professional persons. There are many reports of widespread use on campuses, but estimates that 20 percent or more of certain college populations have used the drug cannot be verified or refuted.[32]

[27] See generally Maurer and Vogel, *supra* note 12, at pp. 103–108; Winick, "Marihuana Use by Young People," in *Harms*, ed., *Drug Addiction in Youth* (1965).

[28] Eddy, Halbach, Isbell and Seever, *supra* note 5, at pp. 728–729; Winick, "Marihuana Use by Young People," in Harms, ed., *Drug Addiction in Youth* (1965); *Proceedings*, p. 286; Blum, *Dangerous Drugs*.

[29] Compare U.S. Treasury Department, *Traffic in Opium and Other Dangerous Drugs* (1965), p. 51, with U.S. Treasury Department, *Traffic in Opium and Other Dangerous Drugs* (1960), p. 72.

[30] Compare U.S. Treasury Department, *Traffic in Opium and Other Dangerous Drugs* (1965), p. 47, with U.S. Treasury Department, Traffic in Opium and Other Dangerous Drugs (1960), p. 69.

[31] California Department of Justice, "1965 Drug Arrests in California: A Preliminary Survey" (an unpublished draft), p. 4.

[32] *New York Medicine*, May 5, 1966, p. 3. See also Blum, *Dangerous Drugs*.

Marihuana is much cheaper than heroin. The director of the Vice Control Division, Chicago Police Department, testified in 1966 that the price of marihuana in Chicago was roughly 50 to 75 cents for a single cigarette, roughly $25 for a can the size of a tobacco tin, and from $85 to $125 a pound.[33] Prices tend to be lower nearer the Mexican source.

The Federal law controlling marihuana is a tax statute, enacted in 1937 and enforced by the Bureau of Narcotics.[34] On its face the statute authorizes marihuana transactions between persons, such as importers, wholesalers, physicians, and others, who have paid certain occupational and transfer taxes. But, in fact, since there is no accepted medical use of marihuana, only a handful of people are registered under the law, and for all practical purposes the drug is illegal. Unauthorized possession, which in this context means possession under almost any circumstance, is a criminal act under Federal tax law. Sale or purchase of marihuana are also criminal offenses under this statute. Importation is made punishable by a separate statute.[35] Possession and sale are also offenses under the Uniform Narcotic Drug Act, which controls marihuana in most States.

Dangerous Drugs

The term "dangerous drugs" commonly refers to three classes of nonnarcotic drugs that are habit-forming or have a potential for abuse because of their stimulant, depressant or hallucinogenic effect. Central nervous system stimulants and depressants are widely used in medical practice and are not considered dangerous when taken in ordinary therapeutic doses under medical direction. They are available on prescription. Drugs in the hallucinogenic class have not yet been proven safe for medical purposes and are not legally available in drugstores. Their sole legitimate use at present is by qualified researchers in connection with investigations reported to and authorized by the Food and Drug Administration.[36] There is an exception in the case of peyote, the use of which is authorized in connection with religious ceremonies of the Native American Church.[3]

The Stimulants

The most widely used and abused of the stimulants are the amphetamines, which are known generally as "pep pills." They bear chemical names such as amphetamine sulfate or dextroamphetamine sulfate and particular nicknames such as "bennies" or "dexies" (after trade names of the two

[33] *Hearings on S. 2113, S. 2114, S. 2152, supra* note 15, at p. 185 (testimony of John J. Neurater).

[34] *Internal Revenue Code of 1954*, Secs. 4741–4776.

[35] U.S.C., Sec. 176a, 1964.

[36] Goddard, "The Menace of Drug Abuse," *American Education*, May 1966.

[37] The controlling regulation may be found in 21 C.F.R. Sec. 166.3.

drugs.) There are dozens of amphetamine preparations in the market. They are prescribed and apparently are medically effective for relief of fatigue, for control of overweight, and in the treatment of mental disorder.

The amphetamines cause wakefulness and have the capacity to elevate mood and to induce a state of well-being and elation. This is probably the basis of their medical value. It is also the likely reason for their abuse.

Tolerance develops with the use of amphetamines. This permits gradual and progressive increases in dosage. Too large a dose or too sudden an increase in dose, however, may produce bizarre mental effects such as delusions or hallucinations. These effects are more likely if the drug is injected intravenously in diluted powder form than if it is taken orally in tablet form. Nervousness and insomnia are milder symptoms of abuse. Physical dependence does not develop.[38]

The Depressants

The most widely used and abused of the depressant drugs are the barbiturates. These are known generally as "goofballs." They have chemical names, such as pentobarbital sodium and secobarbital sodium, and particular nicknames, such as "nimbies" and "seccy" (after trade names of the two drugs). There are more than 25 barbiturates marketed for clinical use. They are apparently useful because of their sedative, hypnotic, or anesthetic actions and are most commonly prescribed to produce sleep and to relieve tension and anxiety.

A person can develop tolerance to barbiturates, enabling him to ingest increasing quantities of the drug up to a limit that varies with the individual. Chronic administration of amounts in excess of the ordinary daily dose will lead to physical dependence, resulting, upon withdrawal of the drug, in a sickness marked at peak intensity by convulsions and a delirium, resembling alcoholic delirium tremens or a major psychotic episode. Excessive doses may also result in impairment of judgment, loss of emotional control, staggering, slurred speech, tremor, and occasionally coma and death. Barbiturates are a major suicidal agent. They are also reported, like amphetamines, to be implicated in assaultive acts and automobile accidents.[39]

[38] For a discussion of the effects of amphetamine abuse, see Eddy, Halbach, Isbell, and Seevers, *supra* note 5, at pp. 729–730; AMA Committee on Alcoholism and Addiction and Council on Mental Health, "Dependence on Amphetamines and Other Stimulant Drugs," *Journal of American Medical Association*, 1966, 197:1023; *Proceedings*, pp. 286–288; Blum, *Dangerous Drugs*.

[39] For a discussion of the effects of barbiturate abuse, see Eddy, Halbach, Isbell, and Seevers, *supra* note 5, at pp. 725–727; AMA Committee on Alcoholism and Addiction and Council on Mental Health, "Dependence on Barbiturates and Other Sedative Drugs," Journal of American Medical Association, 1965, 193:673; *Proceedings*, pp. 283–285; Fort, "The Problem of Barbiturates in the United States of America," *Bulletin on Narcotics*, January–March 1964, 16:17, reprinted in *Hearings on H.R. 2 Before the House Interstate and Foreign Commerce Committee*, 89th Congress, 1st Session, 1965, p. 66; Blum, *Dangerous Drugs*.

Among the other depressants involved in the drug abuse problem are a number of sedative and tranquilizing drugs, introduced since 1950, that are chemically unrelated to the barbiturates, but similar in effect. The best known of these are meprobamate (Miltown, Equanil), glutethimide (Doriden), ethinamate (Valmid), etchlorvynol (Placidyl), methyprylon (Noludar), and chlordiazepoxide (Librium). There is strong evidence that abuse of these agents may lead to drug intoxication and physical dependence. Suicide by overdose, and deaths during withdrawal from some of the drugs, have also been reported.[40]

The Hallucinogens

Hallucinogenic, or psychedelic, drugs and the controversy that surrounds them have recently aroused the attention of the mass media and the public. This is certainly due in part to the increasing incidence of their use on college campuses. It may also be due to the emergence of new substances, such as LSD, many times more potent than such older hallucinogens as peyote and mescaline. All these drugs have the capacity to produce altered states of consciousness. Generally they are taken orally.

LSD, the most potent of the hallucinogens, is a synthetic drug made by a chemical process; lysergic acid is the main component in the chemical conversion. Minute amounts of the drug are capable of producing extreme effects. It is usually deposited on sugar cubes in liquid form, although recently it has been found frequently in pill form.[41] Swallowing such a cube or pill is called "taking a trip." A recent publication of the Medical Society of the County of New York . . . cited as dangers of LSD: (1) prolonged psychosis; (2) acting out of character disorders and homosexual impulses; (3) suicidal inclinations; (4) activation of previously latent psychosis; and (5) reappearance of the drug's effects weeks or even months after use. It was reported that between March and December of 1965 a total of 65 persons suffering from acute psychosis inducted by LSD were admitted to Bellevue Hospital in New York.[42]

The only legal producer of LSD ceased manufacture in April 1966, and turned over its entire supply of the drug to the Federal Government. A few closely monitored experimental projects involving LSD are still in progress.[43]

[40] For discussion of the effects of these drugs when abused, see AMA Committee on Alcoholism and Addiction and Council on Mental Health, "Dependence on Barbiturates and Other Sedative Drugs," *Journal of American Medical Association,* 1965, 193:673; Essig, "Addiction to Nonbarbiturate Sedative and Tranquilizing Drugs," *Clinical Pharmacology and Therapeutics,* May–June 1964, 5:334, reprinted in *Hearings on H.R. 2, supra* note 39 at p. 33. See also Blum, *Dangerous Drugs.*

[41] See generally the testimony of James L. Goddard, Commissioner, Food and Drug Administration, in *Hearings on S. 2113, S. 2114, S. 2152, supra* note 15, at p. 320.

[42] *New York Medicine,* May 5, 1966, pp. 5–7.

[43] *Hearings on S. 2113, S. 2114, S. 2152, supra* note 15, at p. 330 (testimony of Commissioner Goddard).

Peyote is the hallucinogenic substance obtained from the button-shaped growths of a cactus plant found growing wild in the arid regions of Mexico. Mescaline is a natural alkaloid, which occurs in the same plant. These drugs have appeared in capsule and liquid form and as a powder that can be dissolved in water.[44]

Psilocybin is a substance extracted from a mushroom fungus. It appears in liquid and powder form.[45]

Different degrees of tolerance to the hallucinogens are reported. Physical dependence apparently does not develop.[46]

There is no reliable statistical information on the prevalence of dangerous drug abuse. However, there are indications of widespread and increasing abuse. The former Commissioner of the Food and Drug Administration, for example, has testified that enough raw material was produced in 1962 to make over 9 billion doses of barbiturates and amphetamines combined, and he estimated that one-half of these ended up in the bootleg market.[47] There is no similar estimate of the proportion of the more than 1 million pounds of tranquilizer drugs produced each year that fall into the hands of drug abusers, but the figure certainly is high. A spreading use of the hallucinogens has undoubtedly been caused in part by the activities and advertising of groups formed for the very purpose of promoting experience in these drugs. These groups, or cults, have made broad and appealing claims in regard to the capacity of the hallucinogens to expand the power of the mind to understand self, love, God, and the universe.[48] They are likely to understate the dangers that line the route to such mystical experiences. Whatever the other causes, cases of dangerous drug abuse coming to the attention of school and medical authorities and police officials have been steadily increasing in number.[49] The prices of illicit dangerous drugs vary sharply in time and place. Some approximate ranges of reported price are from $0.10 to $1 for an amphetamine or barbiturate tablet, from $1 to $10 for a sugar cube saturated with LSD, and from $0.01 to $0.50 for a peyote button.[50] All of these prices represent significant profits to the seller.

A series of Federal enactments that proved inadequate to deal with the traffic in dangerous drugs has given way to the Drug Abuse Control

[44] See Ludwig and Levine, "Patterns of Hallucinogenic Drug Abuse," *Journal of American Medical Association,* 1965, 191:92.

[45] *Id.* at p. 93.

[46] *Id.* at pp. 95–96; Eddy, Halbach, Isbell, and Seevers, *supra* note 5, at p. 731.

[47] *Hearings on H.R. 2, supra* note 39 at p. 23 (statement of George Larrick). See also Goddard, *supra* note 36.

[48] See, e.g., the testimony of Arthur Kleps, Director, Neo-American Church, in *Hearings on S. 2113, S. 2114, S. 2152, supra* note 15 at p. 413. There are also books and magazines (such as *Psychedelic Review*) which describe and promote experiences with hallucinogenic drugs.

[49] E.g., statement of John J. Neurater, Director, Vice Control Division, Chicago Police Department, in *Hearings on S. 2113, S. 2114, S. 2152, supra* note 15 at pp. 181, 186–187.

[50] Ludwig and Levine, *supra* note 44 at p. 93; *New York Medicine,* May 5, 1966, pp. 1–5; Blum, *Dangerous Drugs.*

Amendments of 1965.[51] The statute became effective February 1, 1966, and is now the principal Federal law in the field. It limits manufacture, sale, and distribution of any controlled drug to certain designated classes of persons, such as registered wholesale druggists and licensed physicians. It requires that inventories be taken and records of receipts and dispositions be maintained. It places restrictions on the refilling of prescriptions. Criminal penalties are provided for violations, including manufacture, sale, or distribution by unauthorized persons. The first offense is a misdemeanor; the second, a felony. Possession of drugs for personal use is not an offense under this statute.

All of the amphetamines and the barbiturates are controlled by specific language in the statute. In addition, any other drug with potential for abuse because of its depressant, stimulant, or hallucinogenic effect may be placed under control by designation. Some 22 other drugs have been so designated, including all the hallucinogens and three of the tranquilizers discussed above. The statute is enforced by the Bureau of Drug Abuse Control, is a newly created agency within the Food and Drug Administration.

Almost all States have some statutory scheme for controlling at least some of the dangerous drugs, but there is complete lack of uniformity in this legislation.

It is obvious that the increasing use of drugs, including particularly those like LSD with great potential for harm, presents a serious challenge to the Nation.

.   .   .   .   .

Enforcement

Drug enforcement is a question of finding the drugs and the people in the illicit traffic. Both tasks are formidable.

The Drugs

Different enforcement considerations are presented by the opiates (meaning heroin for purposes of this section) and marihuana on the one hand, and the dangerous drugs on the other. To get the former into the country requires an illegal act of smuggling, and their possession and sale in virtually every circumstance are criminal offenses over which the State and Federal governments have concurrent jurisdiction. The dangerous drugs for the most part enter the illicit market by way of diversion from domestic supplies. Simple possession of these drugs is not an offense under any Federal statute. Under State law it may or may not be an offense, depending on the State and the drug involved. It should also be noted that not all

[51] Pub. L. No. 89-74 (July 15, 1965).

abuse of dangerous drugs stems from an illicit traffic. Abuse may occur, for example, if a dose of barbiturates greater than that called for in a legal prescription is taken. Not even perfect and total enforcement of the drug laws could prevent abuse of this kind.

By multiplying the number of known addicts by an average daily dose, the Federal enforcement agencies have arrived at the very rough estimate that 1,500 kilograms (1 kilo = 2.2 pounds) of heroin a year are smuggled into the United States. On the average, less than one-tenth of this amount is seized by all enforcement agencies combined.

. . . . .

The estimated 1,500 kilograms of heroin illegally entering the country each year represent less than one-half of 1 percent of the licit opium production in the world, and an even smaller fraction of the combined licit and illicit production. The problem is thus how to block a small flow from a vast supply. To do this, the Bureau of Narcotics maintains 12 posts of duty in three overseas districts. Nineteen agents were assigned to these posts at the end of fiscal 1966. They work with authorities in the host country in attempting to locate and seize illicit opium and heroin supplies destined for the United States. This effort has had considerable success. In 1965, for example, the agents assisted in 82 investigations, which resulted in the seizure of 888 kilograms of raw opium, 128 kilograms of morphine base, and 84 kilograms of heroin.[52] But the effort has obvious limitations. It is somewhat like trying to dam a river at its widest point with much too little material.

The Bureau of Customs maintains a force at ports and along land borders to protect the revenue and to detect and prevent smuggling of contraband, including illicit drugs. This is not solely an enforcement task. Many nonenforcement personnel such as examiners, verifiers, and appraisers of merchandise are involved. Also in the nonenforcement category, although they play a vital role in the suppression of smuggling, are the inspectors, some 2,600 of whom were on the customs rolls at the end of fiscal 1966. These men handle the inspection of persons, their vehicles, and their efforts arriving from abroad. In 1965 more than 180 million persons and 53 million vehicles and trains arrived in the United States.[53] Obviously nothing more than a cursory inspection of most of them was possible. Such inspections are not well designed to uncover illicit drugs, which are generally small in bulk and cleverly concealed, but they often do lead to significant seizures and probably deter countless smuggling violations.

The customs' enforcement arm is the Customs Agency Service. This is composed of: (1) Customs port investigators and customs enforcement officers. There were 492 such men on duty at the end of fiscal 1966. They

---

[52] U.S. Treasury Department, *Traffic in Opium and Other Dangerous Drugs*, 1965, p. 26.

[53] *Hearings on Treasury Appropriations for 1967 Before a Subcommittee of the House Appropriations Committee*, 89th Congress, 2nd Session, 1966, p. 413.

conduct vessel and aircraft searches (more than 99,000 vessels and 210,000 aircraft arrived in the United States in 1965[54] perform uniformed patrol in marked vehicles and carry out plainclothes assignments and surveillances at airports, piers, and border crossing points. (2) Customs agents. These men, 276 of whom were assigned at the end of fiscal 1966, are the top-echelon criminal investigators within the Bureau. They develop intelligence and evidence concerning violations of the criminal statutes within customs enforcement jurisdiction.

Some 65 kilograms of heroin and other illicit narcotics excluding marihuana were seized at ports and borders in fiscal 1966.[55] Approximately one-half of all 1966 customs seizures of illicit drugs resulted from prior information received from informants.[56]

Once heroin enters the country, unless it is seized quickly in the hands of the courier, the job of finding it in significant quantities becomes even more difficult. This is because it is broken up into smaller lots and diluted as it moves through the channels of distribution. Enforcement against the upper echelons of the traffic is the business of the Bureau of Narcotics, which at the end of fiscal 1966 had a force of 278 agents stationed in 13 districts in the country. Lower echelons of the traffic are targets for State and local narcotics enforcement. An accurate total of the personnel engaged in number would probably exceed a thousand. Frequently narcotics enforcement is part of the responsibility of local vice control squads. Federal agents seized 156 kilograms of illicit opiates and cocaine in the internal traffic in 1965, 95 kilos of heroin coming in a single seizure.[57] No accurate total is available for illicit narcotic seizures by all states and municipal agencies.

Many of the considerations noted above are applicable to the enforcement of the marihuana laws. More than 5,600 kilograms were seized by Federal authorities in 1965, the majority of it by the Bureau of Customs at points of entry along the Mexican border.[58]

Serious Federal enforcement of the drug abuse control amendments is just beginning. A Bureau of Drug Abuse Control has recently been established within the Food and Drug Administration. It now has 200 agents assigned to nine field offices. It hopes to have 500 agents assigned by 1970. State and local enforcement is handled by the narcotic units or vice control squads.

The illicit traffic in depressant and stimulant drugs is quite new, and how it operates is only partially understood. It appears to be fed mainly by

[54] *Ibid.*

[55] Customs Agency Service, *Annual Report to the Commissioner of Customs for Fiscal 1966*, p. 9.

[56] *Id.* at p. 20.

[57] U.S. Treasury Department, *Traffic in Opium and Other Dangerous Drugs*, 1965, p. 51.

[58] *Ibid.* See also Customs Agency Service, *Annual Report to the Commissioner of Customs for Fiscal 1966*, p. 9.

diversions from the chain of legitimate drug distribution. Diversions are known to have occurred at all points in the chain from the manufacture of the basic chemicals to delivery of the finished dosage forms of the drug to the consumer. Large quantities of the basic depressant and stimulant powders have been ordered from chemical brokers and dealers by persons using fictitious names, indicating firms engaged in research. In some cases, involving diversions of millions of capsules over periods of a few months, drugs have been sold directly to illegal peddlers by manufacturers of the dosage form. In other cases drugs have been diverted by salesmen of manufacturing or wholesale firms, sometimes through the medium of fictitious drugstores. Again millions of tablets have been involved. Unlawful sales by retail pharmacists and by physicians have occurred. So, of course, have larcenies from plants and thefts from interstate shipments. Apparently unregistered drug manufacturers (whose product duplicates the genuine article in substance) and drug counterfeiters (whose product duplicates the genuine article in appearance only) are also major sources of illicit drugs. Fraudulent means of obtaining drugs, such as forging prescriptions, are also practiced.[59]

The hallucinogens are not available for legitimate distribution. In some cases the drugs are smuggled across the Mexican border. In other cases the raw materials are present in large supply in this country, and supplies of peyote have reputedly been obtained by placing an order with a "cactus company" in Texas.[60] LSD, while it may be produced by a relatively simple chemical process (the raw materials are also under Federal controls[61]), is thought to come frequently from foreign sources, both legal and illegal.[62] The problems of detecting this drug are special ones. It is colorless, tasteless, odorless; one two-hundred and eighty thousandth of an ounce is enough to cause the characteristic effects.[63]

The People

Those involved in illicit drug traffic are either suppliers or consumers. They range from the organized crime boss who organizes 50-kilo heroin shipments, to the college student who smokes a single marihuana cigarette.

The opiate traffic on the east coast is in heroin of European origin and is hierarchical in structure. The importers, top members of the criminal cartels

[59] The best available account of the dangerous drug traffic may be found in *Hearings on H.R. 2, supra* note 47, at p. 336 (Food and Drug Administration *Staff Memorandum on H.R. 2 Concerning Methods of Diversion of Depressant and Stimulant Drugs with Specimen Cases and Comments on Questions Arising During the Hearing*).

[60] Ludwig and Levine, *supra* note 44 at p. 94.

[61] See *Hearings on S. 2113, S. 2114, S. 2152, supra* note 15, at pp. 330–331 (testimony of James L. Goddard). See 21 C.F.R. Sec. 166.3.

[62] Staff interview with John Finlator, Director, Bureau of Drug Abuse Control. See also *Hearings on S. 2113, S. 2114, S. 2152, supra* note 5 at pp. 330–331.

[63] Bureau of Drug Abuse Control, *Fact Sheet No. 5*, August 25, 1966.

. . . , do not handle and probably do not ever see a shipment of heroin. Their role is supervisory and financial. Fear of retribution, which can be swift and final, and a code of silence protect them from exposure. Through persons working under their direction the heroin is distributed to high-level wholesalers, who are also members of the cartels. Beyond this point the traffic breaks out of the hands of the organized crime element and becomes increasingly diffuse. Low-level wholesalers are at the next echelon; they are on the neighborhood level. Retailers, street peddlers (who are often them-selves addicts) and addicts round out the system.

On the west coast the traffic is in heroin of Mexican origin and is carried on largely by independent operators. The actual smuggling is often done by persons hired for this purpose by the operators.

The marihuana trade resembles the heroin traffic on the west coast. Occasionally the same people are involved, but they are not likely to be major racketeers or to have dominant positions in the underworld.

Not enough of the people in the dangerous drug traffic have been caught to form valid judgments about the traffic's personnel. It appears that unreg-istered manufacturers and wholesalers and bulk peddlers are key figures. It has been alleged, but not proved, that trafficking in these drugs has become an activity of organized crime. Certainly the profits are there in the case of the depressant and stimulant drugs. The hallucinogenic drug traffic appears to be less profit oriented than others.[64]

.   .   .   .   .

Drug Abuse and Crime

Drug addicts are crime-prone persons. This fact is not open to serious dispute, but to determine its meaning is another matter. Analysis is best restricted to heroin because of the applicable laws, because of the informa-tion available, and because drugs with addiction liability present the clear-est issues. In order to obtain an accurate idea of the drug-crime relationship, it is necessary to make a clear distinction between the drug offenses and the nondrug offenses committed by addicts.

Drug Offenses

Addiction itself is not a crime. It never has been under Federal law, and a State law making it one was struck down as unconstitutional by the 1962

[64] On the people involved in illicit drug traffic generally, see the *Hearings on Organized Crime and Illicit Traffic in Narcotics Before the Permanent Subcommittee on Investigations of the Senate Government Operations Committee on Investigations of the Senate Government Operations Committee,* 88th Congress, 1st and 2nd Sessions, 1964 part 3; *Hearings on S. 2113, S. 2114, S. 2152 Before A Special Subcommittee of the Senate Judiciary Committee,* 89th Congress, 2nd Session, 1966; *Hearings on H.R. 2, supra* note 39.

decision of the Supreme Court in *Robinson* v. *California*.[65] It does not follow, however, that a state of addiction can be maintained without running afoul of the criminal law. On the contrary, the involvement of an addict with the police is almost inevitable. By definition, an addict has a constant need for drugs, which obviously must be purchased and possessed before they can be consumed. Purchase and possession, with certain exceptions not relevant in the case of an addict, are criminal offenses under both Federal and State law. So is sale, to which many addicts turn to provide financial support for their habits. In many States, the nonmedical use of opiates is punishable, as is the possession of paraphernalia such as needles and syringes designed for such use. In other States, vagrancy statutes make it punishable for a known or convicted addict to consort with other known addicts to be present in a place where illicit drugs are found.[66]

Thus, the addict lives in almost perpetual violation of one or several criminal laws, and thus gives him a special status not shared by other criminal offenders. Together with the fact that he must have continuous contact with other people in order to obtain drugs, it also gives him a special exposure to police action and arrest, and, in areas where the addiction rate is high, a special place in police statistics and crime rate computations.

Nondrug Offenses

The nondrug offenses in which the heroin addict typically becomes involved are of the fund-raising variety. Assaultive or violent acts, contrary to popular belief, are the exception rather than the rule for the heroin addict, whose drug has a calming and depressant effect.

Illicit drugs, as already noted, are expensive. Records compiled by the New York City police are sufficient proof of this. In May 1965, a total of 991 admitted users of heroin were arrested in New York City. The average daily cost of heroin to these users was $14.34. In December of that year, the 1,271 heroin users arrested spent a daily average of $14.04.[67] The price of the drug is not uniform in time or place; it differs in New York and Los Angeles and fluctuates everywhere according to the supply available on the street. But it is never low enough to permit the typical addict to obtain it by lawful means. So he turns to crime, most commonly to the theft of property. Stolen property cannot be converted at full value, especially by an addict who needs to dispose of it quickly. It is said that between $3 and $5 in merchandise must be stolen to realize $1 in cash.[68]

[65] *370 U.S. 660*, 1962.

[66] Eldridge, *Narcotics and the Law* (1962), pp. 149–193 (app. B.).

[67] New York City Police Department Statistical and Records Bureau, *Statistical Report of Narcotic Arrests of Narcotic Users, 1964–1965*.

[68] See, e.g., testimony of Henry L. Giordano and Patrick J. McCormack, *Hearings on Organized Crime and Illicit Traffic in Narcotics, supra* note 66, at pp. 677, 739–740.

The mathematics of this are alarming. Assuming that each of the heroin addicts in New York City, whose names were on file with the Bureau of Narcotics at the end of 1965, spent $15 a day for his drug, and that in each case the $15 represented the net cash proceeds after conversion of stolen property worth $50, the addicts would be responsible each year for the theft of property valued at many millions of dollars in New York City alone. This amount would, of course, have to be adjusted to take into accounts the addicts who are in jail or hospitalized; those who obtain the price of heroin either through lawful means or by prostitution, selling of drugs, thefts of cash, or any other method which does not require the conversion of stolen property; and the addicts who are unknown to the authorities. The impact of these adjustments might be enormous but it cannot be accurately measured.

The projected totals are so impressive that they lead one into the easy assumption that addicts must be responsible for most crimes against property where addiction is widespread. But this assumption cannot so easily be verified.

Records compiled by the New York City Police Department indicate that 11.1 percent of those arrested in 1965 for those felonies against property most often committed by addicts were admitted drug (mostly heroin) users. The comparable figure for 1964 was 12.5 percent; for 1963 it was 11.7 percent. The involvement of admitted drug users in arrests for selected felonies against the person was much lower—on the order of 2 percent. The 1965 figure for the involvement of admitted drug users in arrests for petit larceny was 9.8 percent.[69] It is impossible to judge what any of these figures might have been if they had reflected involvement in nondrug offenses of actual instead of admitted drug users.

For the fiscal years 1956–65 inclusive, an average of 8 percent of all persons committed to Federal prisons and other penal institutions had an admitted drug (again mostly heroin) use history. On the other hand, the New York City Department of Corrections reports that surveys taken of its average 1966 population (about 10,000 persons) show that almost 40 percent had an admitted history of drug use.[70]

As of December 31, 1966, there were 4,385 persons identified as users of heroin in the FBI's "Careers in Crime Program"—a computerized record of criminal histories. This data is based on criminal fingerprint cards submitted by local and Federal agencies.

[69] The data for 1964 and 1965 were gleaned from the New York City Police Department *Statistical Report, supra* note 67. The 1963 data are from *Hearings on Organized Crime and Illicit Traffic in Narcotics, supra* note 66, at p. 735 (testimony of Patrick J. McCormack).

[70] The 8% figure is derived from Bureau of Prisons Research and Statistical Branch, *Court Commitments in Federal Institutions and Number With a History of Using Drugs, by Fiscal Year and Selected Offenses: Fiscal Years 1956–1965* (unpublished). The source of the 40% figure was a staff interview with an official of the New York Department of Corrections.

The 4,385 people who were identified as heroin users had an average criminal career (the span of years between the first and last arrest) of 12 years during which they averaged 10 arrests. Six of these arrests on an average were for offenses other than narcotics. Of the total arrests accumulated by heroin users in the property crime and violent crime categories, 26 percent were arrests for violent crimes and 74 percent were arrests for property crimes. On the other hand, all criminal offenders in the program (over 150,000) averaged 23 percent arrests for violent crimes and 77 percent for property crimes. Seventy-two percent of all heroin users had an arrest for some other criminal act prior to their first narcotic arrest.[71]

The simple truth is that the extent of the addict's or drug user's responsibility for all nondrug offenses is unknown. Obviously it is great, particularly in New York City, with its heavy concentration of users; but there is no reliable data to assess properly the common assertion that drug users or addicts are responsible for 50 percent of all crime.

More broadly, the Commission's examination of the evidence on the causal connection between drug use and crime has not enabled it to make definitive estimates on this important issue. Since there is much crime in cities where drug use is not thought to be a major problem, to commit resources against abuse solely in the expectation of producing a dramatic reduction in crime may be to invite disappointment. While crime reduction is one result to be hoped for in eliminating drug abuse, its elimination and the treatment of its victims are humane and worthy social objectives in themselves.

Penalties

Since early in the century we have built our drug control policies around the twin judgments that drug abuse was an evil to be suppressed and that this could most effectively be done by the application of criminal enforcement and penal sanctions. Since then, one traditional response to an increase in drug abuse has been to increase the penalties for drug offenses. The premise has been that the more certain and severe the punishment, the more it would serve as a deterrent. Typically this response has taken the form of mandatory minimum terms of imprisonment, increasing in severity with repeated offenses, and provisions making the drug offender ineligible for suspension of sentence, probation, and parole.

Federal law was changed twice during the last decade. In 1951, following the post-World War II upsurge in reported addiction, mandatory minimum sentences were introduced for all narcotic and marihuana offenses, 2 years for the first offense, 5 years for the second, and 10 years for third and

[71] Memorandum prepared by the Federal Bureau of Investigation for the President's Commission on Law Enforcement and Administration of Justice, dated December 21, 1966. A similar FBI memorandum appears in *Hearings on Organized Crime and Illicit Traffic in Narcotics, supra* note 64, at p. 678.

subsequent offenses. At the same time, suspension of sentence and probation were prohibited for second offenders.[72] In 1956 the mandatory minimum sentences were raised to 5 years for the first and 10 years for the second and subsequent offenses of unlawful sale or importation. They remained at 2, 5, and 10 years for the offense of unlawful possession. Suspension of sentence, probation, and parole were prohibited for all but the first offense of unlawful possession.[73] Many State criminal codes contain comparable, though not identical, penalty provisions.

In support of existing mandatory minimum sentences for narcotics violations, it has been suggested that the high price and low quality of the heroin available on the street and the fact that serious physical dependence on the drug has become a rarity are evidence that there are fewer people willing to face the risk of more severe penalties. On the other hand, with respect to heroin, these trends may have preceded the pattern of mandatory minimum sentence provisions, and enforcement officials have also credited direct enforcement efforts against the international flow of heroin for the changes.[74] And despite the application of such sanctions to marihuana, the use of and traffic in that drug appear to be increasing.[75]

Since the evidence as to the effects of mandatory minimum sentences is inconclusive, the Commission believes that the arguments against such provisions, which appear in chapter 5, are a firmer basis upon which to rest its judgment in this case.

Within any classification of offenses, differences exist in both the circumstances and nature of the illegal conduct and in the offenders. Mandatory provisions deprive judges and correctional authorities of the ability to base their judgments on the seriousness of the violations and the particular characteristics and potential for rehabilitation of the offender.

There is a broad consensus among judges and correctional authorities that discretion should be restored. A 1964 policy statement of the Advisory Council of Judges[76] and repeated testimony by officials of the Bureau of Prisons and Board of Parole are expressions of this consensus.[77]

[72] Act of November 2, 1951, known as the *Boggs Act.*

[73] The present penalty provisions are contained in *Internal Revenue Code of 1954*, Sec. 7237.

[74] See testimony of Harry J. Anslinger, former Commissioner of Narcotics, *Hearings on Illicit Narcotics Traffic Before the Subcommittee on Improvements in the Federal Criminal Code of the Senate Judiciary Committee*, 84th Congress, 1st Session, 1955, p. 42; cf. Lindesmith, *supra* note 14 at p. 57.

[75] See Blum, *Dangerous Drugs*. See also *Hearings on S. 2113, S. 2114, S. 2152, supra* note 66, at p. 185 (statement of John L. Neurater of Chicago Police Department) and p. 224 (exhibit 46). And see references cited in notes 29–31 *supra.*

[76] Advisory Council of Judges of the National Council on Crime and Delinquency, *Narcotics Law Violations: A Policy Statement*, 1964, pp. 15–16.

[77] *Hearings on Civil Commitment and Treatment of Narcotic Addicts Before Subcommittee No. 2 of the House Judiciary Committee*, 89th Congress, 1st and 2nd Sessions, 1966, pp. 370, 376 (testimony of Myrl E. Alexander); *Proceedings*, p. 255 (statement of James V. Bennett) and p. 264 (statement of Richard A. Chappell). See also *id.* at p. 228 (statement of Senator Thomas J. Dodd), discussing a joint project of the Senate

Application of the mandatory minimums has had some measurable results. The first of these has been a substantial increase in the percentage of the Federal prison population serving sentences for narcotic and marihuana offenses. At the close of fiscal 1965 there were 3,998 drug-law violators confined in all Federal institutions. This number represented 17.9 percent of all persons confined. The average sentence being served by the drug-law violators was 87.6 months, and 75.5 percent of them were ineligible for parole. These figures compare with the 2,017 drug-law violators confined at the close of fiscal 1950, comprising 11.2 percent of all persons confined at that time. The 1950 violators were all eligible for parole, and while average sentence data is not available for that year, it would be safe to estimate that sentences averaged much less than one-half of 87.6 months.[78]

Some differential handling of narcotic addicts after conviction is permitted by the civil commitment laws discussed below, which bypass the penalty provisions. Other devices in the present law also permit some distinctions to be made among drug offenders. First offenders charged with unlawful possession under Federal law are eligible for suspended sentence, probation, and parole.[79] Persons under the age of 22 are eligible for indeterminate sentencing under the Federal Youth Corrections Act.[80] Some State laws distinguish mere possession from possession with intent to sell and provide separate penalties for the two offenses.[81] Informal practices also are common, such as reduction of charge by the prosecutor (whose discretion is not circumscribed by the law) to avoid the mandatory minimum sentence provided for the greater offense.[82]

In its recommendations on mandatory minimums, the President's 1963 Advisory Commission sought to avoid the evils of treating all narcotics and marihuana offenders alike by dividing offenses into four groups:[83]

> ☐ the smuggling or sale of large quantities of narcotics or the possession of large quantities for sale. This would subject the

---

Subcommittee on Juvenile Delinquency and the Subcommittee on National Penitentiaries. In the course of that project, a questionnaire was sent to Federal district judges, Federal chief probation officers, Federal prison authorities, and U.S. Attorneys, inquiring about the effects of the mandatory minimum sentence provisions, and the elimination of probation and parole in the handling of narcotic offenders. Of the Federal prison wardens who responded, 92 percent were opposed to the mandatory minimum sentence provisions, and 97 percent were opposed to the prohibition of probation or parole. Of the responding probation officers, 83 percent were opposed to the first, and 86 percent were opposed to the second. Of the Federal judges who responded, 73 percent were opposed the first, and 86 percent were opposed to the second. *Ibid.*

[78] The information in this paragraph was derived from unpublished statistical reports prepared by the Research and Statistics Branch of the Bureau of Prisons in 1965 an 1966.

[79] *Internal Revenue Code of 1954*, Sec. 7237(d).

[80] 18 U.S.C. Secs. 5005–5026 (1964).

[81] *New York Penal Law* Sec. 220 (effective September 1967).

[82] Cf. Eldridge, *op. cit. supra* note 66, at pp. 88–89.

[83] President's Advisory Commission on Narcotic and Drug Abuse, *Final Report*, 1963, pp. 40–42.

offender to mandatory minimum sentences. Probation, suspension of sentence, and parole would be denied.

☐ The smuggling or sale of small quantities of narcotics, or the possession of small quantities for sale. This would subject the offender to some measure of imprisonment but not to any mandatory minimum terms. Suspension of sentence would not be available but parole would.

☐ The possession of narcotics without intent to sell. The sentencing judge would have full discretion as to these offenses.

☐ All marihuana offenses. The sentencing judge would have full discretion.

．　　．　　．　　．　　．

Marihuana

The basic Federal control statute, the Marihuana Tax Act, was enacted in 1937 with the stated objectives of making marihuana dealings visible to public scrutiny, raising revenue, and rendering difficult the acquisition of marihuana for nonmedical purposes (the drug has no recognized medical value) and noncommercial use (the plant from which the drug comes has some commercial value in the production of seed and hemp).[84] At the heart of the act are provisions requiring that all persons with a legitimate reason for handling marihuana register and pay an occupational tax, requiring that all marihuana transactions be recorded on official forms provided by the Treasury Department, subjecting transfers to a registered person to a tax of $1 an ounce, and subjecting transfers to an unregistered person to a prohibitive tax of $100 an ounce.[85] Under the Uniform Narcotic Drug Act in force in most States, marihuana is defined and controlled as a narcotic drug.[86]

The act raises an insignificant amount of revenue[87] and exposes an insignificant number of marihuana transactions to public view, since only a handful of people are registered under the act. It has become, in effect, solely a criminal law imposing sanctions upon persons who sell, acquire, or possess marihuana.

Marihuana was placed under a prohibition scheme of control because of its harmful effects and its claimed association with violent behavior and crime.[88] Another reason now advanced in support of the marihuana regula-

---

[84] *Senate Report No. 900,* 75th Congress, 1st Session, 1937; *House of Representatives Report No. 792,* 75th Congress, 1st Session, 1937, p. 1.

[85] *Internal Revenue Code of 1954,* Secs. 4741, 4744, 4751, 4753.

[86] *Uniform Narcotic Drug Act,* Sec. 1(14).

[87] The revenues attributable to Federal marihuana taxes (occupational tax, transfer tax, and charges for order forms) for the 5 fiscal years 1962–1966 total $418,000. By contrast, the revenues attributable to the Federal narcotic taxes (occupational tax, commodity tax, and charges for order forms) for the same period total $5,813,000. Staff interview with officials in the Reports Division, Internal Revenue Service.

[88] *Senate Report No. 900, supra* note 84 at p. 3; *House of Representatives Report No. 792, supra* note 84, at pp. 1–2.

tions is that the drug is a steppingstone or forerunner to the use of addicting drugs, particularly heroin.[89]

The law has come under attack on all counts, and the points made against it deserve a hearing.

The Effects

Marihuana is equated in law with the opiates, but the abuse characteristics of the two have almost nothing in common. The opiates produce physical dependence. Marihuana does not. A withdrawal sickness appears when use of the opiates is discontinued. No such symptoms are associated with marihuana. The desired dose of opiates tend to increase over time, but this is not true of marihuana. Both can lead to psychic dependence, but so can almost any substance that alters the state of consciousness.[90]

The Medical Society of the County of New York has classified marihuana as a mild hallucinogen[91] and this is probably as good a description as any, although hallucinations are only one of many effects the drug can produce. It can impair judgment and memory; it can cause anxiety, confusion, or disorientation; and it can induce temporary psychotic episodes in predisposed people. Any hallucinogenic drug, and many of the other dangerous drugs, can do the same. Marihuana is probably less likely to produce these effects than such moderately potent hallucinogens as peyote, mescaline, and hashish (another derivative of the plant from which marihuana comes), and much less likely to do so than the potent hallucinogen LSD.[92]

Marihuana, Crime, and Violence

Here differences of opinion are absolute and the claims are beyond reconciliation. One view is that marihuana is a major cause of crime and violence. Another is that marihuana has no association with crime and only a marginal relation to violence.

Proponents of the first view rely in part on reports connecting marihuana users with crime. One such report by the district attorney of New Orleans was referred to in the hearings on the 1937 act.[93] It found that 125 of 450 men convicted of major crimes in 1930 were regular marihuana users.

[89] See references cited in note 28, *supra.* See also Bromberg, "Marihuana: A Psychiatric Study," *Journal of American Medical Association*, 1939, 113:4 Reichard, "Some Myths About Marihuana," *Federal Probation*, October–December 1946, 10:15; Murphy, "The Cannabis Habit: A Review of Recent Psychiatric Literature," *Bulletin on Narcotics,* January–March 1943, 15:15. And see *Hearings on S. 2113, S. 2114, S. 2152, supra* note 64, at p. 449 (testimony of Henry L. Giordano); Blum, *Dangerous Drugs.*

[90] See references cited in note 89 *supra.*

[91] *New York Medicine,* May 5, 1966, pp. 3–4.

[92] See references cited in note 89 *supra.*

[93] *Hearings on Taxation of Marihuana Before the House Ways and Means Committee,* 75th Congress, 1st Session, 1937.

Approximately one-half the murderers (an unstated number) and a fifth of those tried for larceny, robbery, and assault (again an unstated number) were regular users.[94] However, the main reliance is on case files of enforcement agencies. Excerpts from these files have been used to demonstrate a marihuana-crime causal relation.[95] The validity of such a demonstration involves three assumptions which are questioned by opponents of the present law: (1) The defendant was a Marihuana user. Usually this can be determined only by the defendant's own statement or by his possession of the drug at the time of arrest. (2) He was under the influence of marihuana when he committed the criminal act. Again a statement, perhaps a self-serving one, is most often the source of the information. Chemical tests of blood, urine, and the like will not detect marihuana.[96] (3) The influence of the marihuana caused the crime in the sense that it would not have been committed otherwise.

Those who hold the opposite view cannot prove their case, either. They can only point to the prevailing lack of evidence. Many have done so. The Medical Society of the County of New York has stated flatly that there is no evidence that marihuana use is associated with crimes of violence in this country.[97] There are many similar statements by other responsible authorities. The 1962 report of the President's Ad Hoc Panel on Drug Abuse found the evidence inadequate to substantiate the reputation of marihuana for inciting people to antisocial acts.[98] The famous Mayor's Committee on Marihuana, appointed by Mayor La Guardia to study the marihuana situation in New York City, did not observe any aggression in subjects to whom marihuana was given.[99] In addition there are several studies of persons who were both confessed marihuana users and convicted criminals, and these reach the conclusion that a positive relation between use and crime cannot be established.[100]

One likely hypothesis is that, given the accepted tendency of marihuana to release inhibitions, the effect of the drug will depend on the individual

[94] The New Orleans report has also been mentioned in Bromberg, "Marihuana: A Psychiatric Study," *Journal of American Medical Association,* 1939, 113:4; and Winick, "Marihuana Use by Young People," in Harms, ed., *Drug Addiction in Youth* (1965).

[95] See, e.g., Anslinger and Tompkins, *The Traffic in Narcotics* (1953), pp. 20–25; Munch, "Marihuana and Crime," *Bulletin on Narcotics,* April–June, 1966, 18:15.

[96] Murphy, *supra* note 89, at p. 15.

[97] *New York Medicine,* May 5, 1966, p. 3.

[98] *Proceedings,* p. 286.

[99] Mayor's Committee on Marihuana, *The Marihuana Problem in the City of New York: Sociological, Medical, Psychological and Pharmacological Studies* (1944).

[100] See, e.g., Anrade, "The Criminogenic Action of Cannabis (Marihuana) and Narcotics," *Bulletin on Narcotics,* October–December, 1964, 16:23; Bromberg, "Marihuana: A Psychiatric Study," *Journal of American Medical Association,* 1939, 113:4; Bromberg, "Marihuana Intoxication," *American Journal of Psychiatry,* 1934, 91:302; Bromberg and Rogers, "Marihuana and Aggressive Crime," *American Journal of Psychiatry,* 1946, 102:825; Reichard, "Some Myths about Marihuana," *supra* note 89 at pp. 17–18; Blum, *Dangerous Drugs.*

and the circumstances. It might, but certainly will not necessarily or inevitably, lead to aggressive behavior or crime. The response will depend more on the individual than the drug. This hypothesis is consistent with the evidence that marihuana does not alter the basic personality structure.[101]

Marihuana as a Prelude to Addicting Drugs

The charge that marihuana "leads" to the use of addicting drugs needs to be critically examined. There is evidence that a majority of the heroin users who come to the attention of public authorities have, in fact, had some prior experience with marihuana.[102] But this does not mean that one leads to the other in the sense that marihuana has an intrinsic quality that creates a heroin liability. There are too many marihuana users who do not graduate to heroin, and too many heroin addicts with no known prior marihuana use, to support such a theory. Moreover there is no scientific basis for such a theory. The basic text on pharmacology, Goodman and Gilman, *The Pharmacological Basis of Therapeutics* (Macmillan 1960) states quite explicitly that marihuana habituation does not lead to the use of heroin.[103]

The most reasonable hypothesis here is that some people who are predisposed to marihuana are also predisposed to heroin use. It may also be the case that through the use of marihuana a person forms the personal associations that later expose him to heroin.[104]

The amount of literature on marihuana is massive. It runs to several thousand articles in medical journals and other publications. Many of these are in foreign languages and reflect the experience of other countries with the use of the drug and with other substances derived from the hemp plant. The relevance of this material to our own problem has never been determined. Indeed, with the possible exception of the 1944 LaGuardia report, no careful and detailed analysis of the American experience seems to have been attempted. Basic research has been almost nonexistent, probably because the principal active ingredient in marihuana has only recently been isolated and synthesized.[105] Yet the Commission believes that enough information exists to warrant careful study of our present marihuana laws and the propositions on which they are based.

.   .   .   .   .

[101] Blum, *Dangerous Drugs.*

[102] *New York Medicine,* May 5, 1966, p. 4. California Narcotics Rehabilitation Advisory Council, *Second Annual Report,* 1966, p. 9.

[103] Pp. 173–174.

[104] Eddy, Halbach, Isbell, and Seevers, "Drug Dependence: Its Significance and Characteristics," *Bulletin of World Health Organization,* 1966, 32:721, 729.

[105] Goodman and Gilman, *The Pharmacological Basis of Therapeutics* (1960), p. 171; staff interview with Dr. Roger E. Mayer, Research Psychiatrist, Center for Studies of Narcotics and Drug Abuse, NIMH.

Treatment

Until quite recently treatment opportunities for opiate addicts were largely restricted to the two Federal narcotic hospitals at Lexington, Ky., and Fort Worth, Tex. Within the past decade, numerous new programs for the treatment of addiction have been developed. However, there are virtually no programs for the treatment of users of the other dangerous drugs.

Lexington and Fort Worth

The Public Health Service hospitals were established, in 1935 and 1938 respectively, for the primary purpose of providing treatment to Federal prisoners who were addicted to narcotic drugs. Voluntary patients, who make up almost one-half the hospital population at any given time, are admitted on a space-available basis after Federal prisoners have been accommodated. Since 1935 there have been more than 80,000 admissions of addict-patients to the two hospitals. The constructed capacity of Lexington is 1,042 beds and of Fort Worth 777 beds.[106]

After withdrawal of the drug and psychiatric evaluation, a wide range of services is available to the patient. These are mainly designed to develop and improve functional skills and to accustom the patient to a stable environment. The recommended length of stay for a voluntary patient is 5 months, but most check out much sooner against medical advice. The hospital authorities are powerless to prevent this.[107]

There is no effective aftercare or supervision in the community, except in the case of a prisoner-patient who is granted parole.[108] The relapse rate is high, but there is growing evidence that it is not as high as the 94-percent rate found in one short-term followup study.[109] Much depends on whether relapse is taken to mean return to drugs once during a period of time or to refer to the drug status of the patient at the end of a period of time.[110] One recent long-term (12-year) followup, using the second method of classification, found that, although 90 of the 100 heroin addicts studied had returned

[106] A good account of the operations of the Lexington and Fort Worth hospitals may be found in Maddux, "Hospital Management of the Narcotic Addict," in Wilner and Kassebaum, eds., *Narcotics* (1965), p. 159. Dr. Maddux is the former Medical Officer in Charge at Fort Worth. See also *Hearings on S. 2113, S. 2114, S. 2152 Before a Special Subcommittee of the Senate Judiciary Committee,* 89th Congress, 2nd Session, p. 259 (statement of William H. Stewart, U.S. Surgeon General) and p. 531 (statement of Robert W. Rasor, Medical Officer in Charge at Lexington (1966). And see the testimony of Luther Terry, former U.S. Surgeon General, *Hearings on Civil Commitment and Treatment of Narcotic Addicts, supra* note 90, at p. 118.

[107] See the references cited in *supra* note 106.

[108] See the references cited in *supra* note 106.

[109] Duvall, Locke and Brill, "Follow-up Study of Narcotic Drug Addicts Five Years After Hospitalization," *Public Health Report,* 1963, 78:185; Hunt and Odoroff, "Follow-up Study of Narcotic Drug Addicts After Hospitalization," *id.,* 1962, 77:41.

[110] O'Donnell, "The Relapse Rate in Narcotic Addiction: A Critique of Follow-up Studies," in *Narcotics, op. cit. supra* note 106 at p. 226.

in drug use at some time, 46 of them were drug-free in the community at the time of death or last contact. Among the 30 who were considered to have made the best adjustment, the average length of abstinence was 7 years. Significantly, the best outcomes were found among those who had undergone some form of compulsory supervision after discharge.[111]

The California Rehabilitation Center

This facility, operated by the California Youth and Adult Corrections Agency, was established in 1961. Most admissions are of addicted misdemeanants and felons convicted in California courts and committed by order of the court.

The program involves a combination of inpatient and outpatient treatment. The addicts are required to remain on inpatient status for at least 6 months, although the average is close to 15 months. During this period they are divided into 60-patient units for purpose of treatment. Work therapy, vocational courses, and a full academic course through high school also are offered.

Upon release to outpatient status, the patients are supervised by caseworkers with special training and small caseloads. Patients are chemically tested for the presence of drug five times a month, both on a regular and a surprise basis, for at least the first 6 months. Failure of the test or other indications of relapse to drug results in return to the institution. A halfway house, the Parkway Center, provides guidance for those making a marginal adjustment in the community. The patient becomes eligible for final discharge after 3 drug-free years as an outpatient.[112]

The capacity of the Rehabilitation Center is 2,300 patients. Between September 15, 1961, and December 31, 1965, there were 5,300 admissions. During this period 3,243 persons were transferred to outpatient status. Although many were returned to the center, 1,700 persons remained on such status as of December 31, 1965; 27 persons had been finally discharged.[113]

[111] See Vaillant, "A Twelve-Year Follow-up of New York Narcotic Addicts: In the Relation of Treatment to Outcome," *American Journal of Psychiatry*, 1966, 122:727; Vaillant, "A Twelve-Year Follow-up of New York Narcotic Addicts; IV. Some Characteristics and Determinants of Abstinence," *American Journal of Psychiatry*, 1966, 123:573 Vaillant and Rasor, "The Role of Compulsory Supervision in the Treatment of Addiction," *Federal Probation*, June 1966, 30:53.

[112] The information about the California Rehabilitation Center was drawn from the following sources: *Proceedings*, p. 101 (statement of Roland W. Wood, Superintendent, California Rehabilitation Center); McGee, "New Approaches to the Control and Treatment of Drug Abusers in California," in *Narcotics, op. cit. supra* note 120, at p. 263 (Mr. McGee is Administrator of the California Youth and Adult Correction Agency); *Hearings on S. 2113, S. 2114, S. 2152, supra* note 106, at p. 111 (statement and testimony of Roland W. Wood); *Hearings on Civil Commitment and Treatment of Narcotic Addicts, supra* note 77, at p. 355 (statement of Richard A. McGee) and p. 358 (statement of Roland W. Wood).

[113] See the reference cited in note 112 *supra,* and California Narcotics Rehabilitation Advisory Council, *Second Annual Report*, 1966.

New York State Program

Between the effective date of the Metcalf-Volker Act, January 1, 1963, and June 30, 1966, there were 6,799 admissions of addicts to treatment units maintained by the State Department of Mental Hygiene. The majority of these were persons who chose treatment in lieu of prosecution for a crime. The treatment units were located in six State hospitals having a total of 555 beds for addict-patients; they could handle over 2,200 addicts a year. Both inpatient and outpatient phases of treatment were provided.[114]

A new and more comprehensive program for the treatment and prevention of addiction is now planned in New York under legislation passed in 1966 and administered by a new agency, the State Narcotic Control Commission. Facilities will be greatly expanded, as indicated by a $75 million appropriation for capital construction. The Commission is authorized, among other things, to conduct basic, clinical, and statistical research; to operate rehabilitation and aftercare centers; and to establish a unified program of education, prevention, care, and community referral.[115]

Synanon

This is a private antiaddiction society founded in 1958. The central location is in Santa Monica, but there are other installations inside and outside California. The organization is made up and managed entirely by ex-addicts, aided by a volunteer medical staff. Membership is voluntary and not always available. The addict who seeks admission must first be screened by a committee. Once admitted, his compulsion to take drugs is countered by "attack" therapy and group pressure. If he does not respond, he can be expelled. If he does, he can move upward to levels of responsibility within the society, perhaps to an executive position. Some members return to the community; others become permanent Synanon residents. As of March 1964, according to its officers, there were 400 drug-free persons affiliated with Synanon.[116]

Daytop Lodge

This is a voluntary program serving addicts placed on probation by the local courts in Brooklyn, N.Y. It resembles Synanon in approach, but is

[114] Meiselas, "The Narcotic Addiction Program of the New York State Department of Mental Hygiene," in *Narcotics,* op. cit. *supra* note 109, at p. 249; Temporary Commission on Narcotics Addiction, *Report to the Mayor of the City of New York,* November 1965; *Hearings on S. 2113, S. 2114, S. 2152, supra* note 109, at p. 154 (statement of Dr. Donald B. Louris, representing New York Governor Rockefeller).

[115] *New York Mental Hygiene Law* Sections 200–216 (as amended by chapter 192 of the Laws of 1966).

[116] See Yablonsky and Dederich, "Synanon: An Analysis of Some Dimensions of the Social Structure of an Antiaddiction Society," in *Narcotics, op. cit. supra* note 109, at p. 193; Yablonsky, *Synanon: The Tunnel Back* (1965).

supported by a Federal grant and is under court sponsorship. Its capacity, presently 25 addicts, is being expanded.[117]

Methadone Maintenance

This is an experimental method of treatment for heroin addiction. Its principal sponsors are Drs. Vincent P. Dole and Marie Nyswander. They began their program of research in January 1964, at the Rockefeller University Hospital in New York City. Subsequently treatment units were established at Manhattan General and other New York hospitals. Patients are admitted on a voluntary but selective basis. Motivation and a past record of treatment failures are among the important selection criteria. The patients are free to leave the program at any time. Of the 108 heroin addicts admitted prior to February 1, 1966, 101 were still in the program on that date. The other seven had been dismissed from the program.

The first phase of the treatment involves hospitalization and withdrawal from heroin. The patient is then started on daily doses of methadone, a synthetic opiate that is itself addicting. The daily doses are gradually increased and finally become stable. The median stable dose is 100 milligrams per day. This phase of the program lasts about 5 weeks. It is followed by release to the outpatient phases of the treatment. These involve supportive contacts with the hospital staff and hopefully lead the patient to a secure and responsible position in society. Many of the outpatients are, in fact, employed or in school. No attempt has yet been made to withdraw any outpatient from methadone.

As used in the maintenance program, the methadone is dissolved in fruit juice and taken orally under supervision. It is always dispensed from a hospital pharmacy, and the outpatients are required to return each day for their doses. No prescriptions have been given to patients for the purchase of methadone at drug stores. The patients must also give daily urine samples for analysis.

According to the sponsors of the maintenance program, methadone given in adequate doses blocks the euphoric effects of heroin and does not itself produce euphoria, sedation, or distortion of behavior. The patients allegedly remain alert and functionally normal.

The question being tested here is whether an opiate drug, regularly administered as part of a medical program, can contribute to the rehabilitation of a heroin addict. The emphasis is on drawing the patient out of the addict community and away from a career of crime and into new social attitudes and relationships. The social rehabilitation of the addict is seen as a more important treatment goal than the medical cure of addiction itself.

---

[117] See Cole, *Report on the Treatment of Drug Addiction,* published as appendix C in *supra* note 11 (hereinafter cited as *Cole*). This paper is also a general reference for most points in the treatment of this chapter.

The results of the methadone maintenance research are fragmentary. No final judgments about its suitability as treatment or as a public health approach are yet possible.[118]

Cyclazocine Treatment

This method involves daily administration of a new drug, cyclazocine, which is a long-acting opiate antagonist and blocks the effects of heroin. The drug is not itself a narcotic. This treatment has been tried, with urinalysis to detect heroin use, on a pilot basis in New York.[119]

Parole

Parole is of course not a medical technique, but it may fairly be classified as a form of treatment insofar as it is used to overcome a person's dependence on drugs. Several parole projects, with specially trained staffs carrying small caseloads, are in operation.[120] The theory is that a parole agency, with its authority over the addict, is ideally situated to arrange and coordinate his adjustments in the community. Frequent contact and intensive supervision are necessary. The outpatient phase of the California rehabilitation program mentioned above is a special parole project in method, if not in name. The prototype of such a project, however, was developed in New York.

The 1960 final report of the Special Narcotic Project of the New York State Division of Parole described the results of a study of 344 addict parolees supervised between 1956 and 1959. Of the total number supervised, 119 offenders had never been declared delinquent, and another 36 had been declared delinquent for reasons not related to drug use. Thus 155, or 45 percent, were found to be abstinent. A followup study of the same project parolees reported that, by the end of 1962, the abstinence rate had fallen to 32 percent. The median length of supervision of the 344 addict-parolees was 15 months in 1962, as against 8 months in 1959.[121] The New York project now operates as the Narcotic Treatment Bureau. As of December

[118] See generally *Cole:* Dole and Nyswander, "A Medical Treatment for Diacetylmorphine (Heroin) Addiction," *Journal of American Medical Association,* 1965, 193:646; Dole, Nyswander, et al., "Methadone Maintenance, A Report of Two Years' Experience," presented to the Committee on Problems of Drug Dependence, National Academy of Sciences, National Research Council, February 11, 1966 (cited with the permission of Dr. Dole).

[119] See *Cole.*

[120] See *Cole.*

[121] See Diskind, "New Horizons in the Treatment of Narcotic Addiction," *Federal Probation,* December 1960, 24:56; Diskind and Klonsky, "A Second Look at the New York State Parole Drug Experiment," *Federal Probation,* December 1964, 28:34.

1966, there were 22 parole officers in the Bureau with an average caseload of 30 parolees.[122]

Treatment of narcotic addiction is by no means a certain or perfected medical art. The most remarkable feature of the treatment programs mentioned above, and these represent only a sample, is their diversity of method. Careful and continuing evaluation of these programs, which has often been absent in the past, is imperative. There is great need for better standards for measuring the outcome of treatment. To think only in terms of "cure" is not very meaningful in the case of a chronic illness such as addiction. There is little knowledge about why a good outcome is achieved for one addict but not another, by one method but not another. More trained personnel are desperately needed.[123] Methods of treatment for abusers of nonopiate drugs must be developed, and there is a general need for research effort in the whole area of personality disorder, of which drug abuse is usually a symptom.[124] New facilities will certainly be needed. The $15 million authorized by the Narcotic Addict Rehabilitation Act of 1966 for fiscal 1967 and for fiscal 1968 for grants to State and local governments is a bare minimum.[125] States with drug-abuse problems but without specialized treatment programs must initiate such programs. Hospitals and medical schools must devote more attention to drug abuse. This is the beginning of what needs to be done.

. . . . .

[*The President's Commission Report on Law Enforcement and Administration of Justice,* Task Force Report: Narcotics and Drug Abuse (*Washington: U.S. Government Printing Office, 1967*), *pp. 1–7, 10–16.*]

[122] Letter from Meyer H. Diskind, Director, Narcotic Treatment Bureau, December 12, 1966.

[123] See *Cole.*

[124] Kolb, *Drug Addiction: A Medical Problem* (1962).

[125] Pub. L. No. 89–793, Sec. 402(a), November 8, 1966.

10 *Drunkenness offenses*

Two million arrests in 1965—one of every three arrests in America—were for the offense of public drunkenness.[1] The great volume of these arrests places an extremely heavy load on the operations of the criminal justice system. It burdens police, clogs lower criminal courts, and crowds penal institutions throughout the United States.

Because of the sheer size of the problem and because of doubts that have recently been raised about the efficacy of handling drunkenness within the system of criminal justice, the Commission sought to reexamine present methods of treating drunkenness offenders and to explore promising alternatives. It was not in a position to undertake a comprehensive study of the complex medical, social, and public health problems of drunkenness.

The Existing System

Drunkenness Laws

Drunkenness is punishable under a variety of laws, generally describing the offense as being "drunk in a public place," often without providing a precise definition of drunkenness itself.[2] Some laws include as a condition that the offender is "unable to care for his own safety."[3]

[1] 1965 FBI *Uniform Crime Reports,* p. 117 (table 25). In 1965, 1,516,548 drunkenness arrests were reported by 4,043 agencies, embracing a total population of 125,139,000. Projections based upon these figures indicate that there were over 2 million arrests in the entire country during 1965. An undetermined number of additional arrests for drunkenness are made under disorderly conduct, vagrancy, loitering, and related statutes. See, e.g., Foote, "Vagrancy-Type Law and Its Administration," *University of Pennsylvania Law Review,* 1956, 104:603 (discussion of interchanging of statutes for like purposes); Murtagh, "Arrests for Public Intoxication," *Fordham Law Review,* 1966, 35:1–7 (description of the prior New York City practice of using a disorderly conduct statute to arrest nondisorderly inebriates.

[2] E.g., *D. C. Code Annotated* Secs. 25–128 (1961). The D. C. statute also prohibits drinking an alcoholic beverage in public.

[3] E.g., *Wisconsin Statutes* Sec. 947.03 (1955).

In some jurisdictions there are no laws prohibiting drunkenness, but any drunkenness that causes a breach of the peace is punishable. In Georgia and Alabama, for example, drunkenness that is manifested by boisterous or indecent conduct, or loud and profane discourse, is a crime.[4] Other jurisdictions apply disorderly conduct statutes to those who are drunk in public. In Chicago, for example, the police, having no drunkenness law to enforce, use a disorderly conduct statute to arrest nondisorderly inebriates.[5] Some jurisdictions permit police to make public drunkenness arrests under both State laws and local ordinances.[6]

The laws provide maximum jail sentences ranging from 5 days to 6 months; the most common maximum sentence is 30 days. In some States an offender convicted of "habitual drunkenness" may be punished by a 2-year sentence of imprisonment.[7]

The Offenders

The 2 million arrests for drunkenness each year involve both sporadic and regular drinkers. Among the number are a wide variety of offenders—the rowdy college boy; the weekend inebriate; the homeless, often unemployed single man. How many offenders fall into these and other categories is not known. Neither is it known how many of the offenders are alcoholics in the medical sense of being dependent on alcohol. There is strong evidence, however, that a large number of those who are arrested have a lengthy history of prior drunkenness arrests, and that a disproportionate number involve poor persons who live in slums. In 1964 in the city of Los Angeles about one-fifth of all persons arrested for drunkenness accounted for two-thirds of the total number of arrests for that offense. Some of the repeaters were arrested as many as 18 times in that year.[8]

A review of chronic offender cases reveals that a large number of persons have, in short installments, spent many years of their lives in jail. In 1957 the Committee on Prisons, Probation and Parole in the District of Columbia studied six chronic offenders and found that they had been arrested for

[4] *Alabama Criminal Code* Secs. 14–120 (1958); *Georgia Code Ann.* Secs. 58–608 (1965).

[5] See note, "The Law on Skid Row," *Chicago-Kent Law Review*, CR:22,42 (1964) ("they are detained, whether or not their actions fit the legal criteria of 'disorderly conduct.'") *Chicago Police Department Bulletin No. 9*, March 4, 1963.

[6] *New York Penal Law* Sec. 1221 (McKinney 1944); Syracuse, New York, *Review of Ordinances*, chapter 16, sec. 5, 1961.

[7] *North Carolina General Statutes*, Secs. 14–335 (1953). See *Driver v. Hinnant*, 356 F. 2d 761 (4th Circuit, 1966) for reversal of conviction and 2-year sentence under the North Carolina statute.

[8] Statistics gathered by the Los Angeles Police Department. During 1964 there were 71,494 drunkenness arrests—47,401, of which involved 13,048 offenders. In 1955, 45,748 of the drunkenness arrests in Los Angeles involved 6,665 offenders. In 1961, 12,000 individuals accounted for approximately 30,000 of the 49,000 arrests in Atlanta, Georgia. Department of Psychiatry, Emory University School of Medicine, Alcohol Study Project 5 (unpublished 1963 (hereinafter cited as *Emory Department of Psychiatry*).

drunkenness a total of 1,409 times and had served a total of 125 years in penal institutions.[9]

The great majority of repeaters live on "skid row"—a dilapidated area found in most large and medium-size cities in the United States. On skid row substandard hotels and rooming houses are intermingled with numerous taverns, pawn shops, cheap cafeterias, employment agencies that specialize in jobs for the unskilled, and religious missions that provide free meals after a service. Many of the residents—including the chronic drunkenness offenders—are homeless, penniless, and beset with acute personal problems.[10]

The Arrest of the Drunkenness Offender

The police do not arrest everyone who is under the influence of alcohol.[11] Sometimes they will help an inebriate home. It is when he appears to have no home or family ties that he is most likely to be arrested and taken to the local jail.[12] . . .

Drunkenness arrest practices vary from place to place. Some police departments strictly enforce drunkenness statutes, while other departments are known to be more tolerant. In fact, the number of arrests in a city may be related less to the amount of public drunkenness than to police policy. . . .

In some large and medium-size cities, police departments have "bum squads" that cruise skid rows and border areas to apprehend inebriates who appear unable to care for their own safety, or who are likely to annoy others.[13] Such wholesale arrests sometimes include homeless people who are not intoxicated.[14]

[9] *D.C. Commission on Prisons, Probation, and Parole Report* (1957), pp. 114–119.

[10] Bogue, *Skid Row in American Cities* (1963), pp. 1–4.

[11] It is often the express policy of a police department to refrain from arresting a person for drunkenness in cases in which he may be placed in a taxicab or he is with friends who are able to escort him home. See, e.g., Columbus, Ohio, *Police Department Training Bulletin*, rev. August 1958, unit 6, 1:2; President's Commission on Crime in the District of Columbia, *Report 475*, 1966, citing letter from District of Columbia Police Chief John B. Layton to President's Commission on Crime in the District of Columbia, April 1, 1966.

[12] The police make this determination by observing, *inter alia*, the apparent affluence of the inebriate. Moreover, the lack of funds for transporting will influence the determination to arrest. The result is that the poor are more likely to be arrested than the well-to-do. See President's Commission on Crime in the District of Columbia, *Report 475*, 1966. See also *Washington Daily News*, December 21, 1965, p. 5 at p. 35 (interview with precinct commanding officer: "We do tend to enforce the laws more rigidly on 14th Street than in, say, Crestwood, a better part of the precinct.")

[13] Lafave, *Arrest: The Decision to Take a Suspect into Custody* (1965), p. 441 note 13.

[14] The Atlanta Alcohol Study Project found that there are a "significant number of individuals who are arrested for public intoxication and who are not drunk at the time of arrest." *Emory Department of Psychiatry*, p. 18. Similar findings were reported in other cities: see, for example, reports by Klein, "The Criminal Law Process vs. the Public

Operation of the Criminal System
After Arrest

Following arrest, the drunk is usually placed in a barren cell called a "tank," where he is detained for at least a few hours. The tanks in some cities can hold as many as 200 people, while others hold only 1 or 2. One report described the conditions found in a tank in this way:

> Although he may have been picked up for his own protection, the offender is placed in a cell, which may frequently hold as many as 40–50 men where there is no room to sit or lie down, where sanitary facilities and ventilation are inadequate and a stench of vomit and urine is prevalent.
>
> The drunken behavior of some of the inmates is an added hazard. It is questionable whether greater safety is achieved for the individual who is arrested for his safekeeping.[15]

The chronic alcoholic offender generally suffers from a variety of ailments and is often in danger of serious medical complications,[16] but medical care is rarely provided in the tank; and it is difficult to detect or to diagnose serious illness since it often resembles intoxication.[17] Occasionally, chronic

---

Drunkenness Offender in San Francisco," 1964 (unpublished, on file at Stanford University Institute for the Study of Human Problems), and by Nash, "Habitats of Homeless Men in Manhattan," November 1964 (unpublished, on file at Columbia University Bureau of Applied Social Research).

[15] Committee on Alcoholism Community Welfare Council of the Greater Sacramento Area, Inc., "The Alcoholic Law Offender," p. 4 (unpublished 1965). Another tank was described in a 1966 newspaper article:
  "There are at least two men in each 4 x 8 cell and three in some. . . . The stench of cheap alcohol, dried blood, urine and excrement covers the cell blocks. . . . There are no lights in the cells. . . . There are no mattresses. Mattresses wouldn't last the night, a policeman explains. And with prisoners urinating all over them, they wouldn't be any good if they did last. . . ."
Hoagland, "Cell Blocks' Common Denominator: A Stench of Alcohol and Dried Blood," *Washington Post*, March 29, 1966, p. A–1, col. 3.

[16] University of Minnesota and Minneapolis Housing and Redevelopment Authority, "A General Report on the Problem of Relocating the Population of the Lower Loop Redevelopment Area," p. 170 (unpublished 1958) ("health conditions in this area are catastrophically bad"). The report provided a detailed description of illnesses which exist in skid row areas and states that the "tuberculosis rate in the lower loop is 320 times as high as the rate for the rest of the city." *Id.* at p. 170. See also Department of Psychiatry, Temple University School of Medicine, "The Men of Skid Row: A Study of Philadelphia's Homeless Man Population," p. 88 (unpublished 1960) (57% of the men reported one or more serious conditions). Bogue's study, *op. cit. supra* note 10, at pp. 222–223, depicted the great need for medical care and observed that "among the heavy drinkers, alcoholism is complicated by chronic sickness in a substantial portion of cases."

[17] One of the biggest obstacles in handling a case of drunkenness is that it is often difficult to distinguish between effects produced by alcohol or drugs and those produced by injury or illness. For instance, a person may smell of alcohol, and he may stagger and seem drunk . . . or lie unconscious in an apparent drunken stupor. Yet he may have had only a drink or two—or none at all! . . . Correctional Association of New York and International Association of Chiefs of Police, *Alcohol and Alcoholism, A Police Handbook* (1965), p. 22.

offenders become ill during pretrial detention and die without having received adequate medical attention.[18]. . .

If the offender can afford bail, he usually obtains release after he sobers up.[19] In many jurisdictions an offender is permitted to forfeit bail routinely by not appearing in court.[20] Thus, if the arrested person has the few dollars required, he can avoid prosecution;[21] if he has no money, as is usually the case, he must appear in court.

Drunkenness offenders are generally brought before a judge the morning after their arrest, sometimes appearing in groups of 15 or 20. Rarely are the normal procedural or due process safeguards applied to these cases.[22]

[18] "Man, 52, Dies in Court Lockup," *Washington Post*, September 5, 1965, p. A–3; "Man Detained as Drunk Dies from Pneumonia," *id.*, December 15, 1965, p. D–21, cols. 1–2; "Man, 63, Found Dead in Alexandria Jail Cell," *id.*, November 22, 1966, p. B–4, cols. 1–2. In the President's Commission on Crime in the District of Columbia, *Report 476* (1966), it was reported that "16 persons arrested for intoxication died while in police custody in 1964–1965."

[19] Stationhouse bail permits the release of defendants pending a subsequent court appearance. See generally Freed and Wald, *Bail in the United States* (1964). Outright release—with no obligation to return to court—is sometimes permitted by the police. See Lafave, *op. cit. supra* note 16, at pp. 440–442, for a variety of release systems ranging from outright police discretion to a payment to the city of $4.35. In Detroit the police have a "golden rule" procedure which resulted in 1965 in the release of 2,383 offenders out of a total of 8,715 drunkenness arrests. In Omaha, Nebraska, the majority of offenders are released after a few hours of detention. The Omaha system includes referral to community agencies following release, in appropriate cases. The police bring some offenders to the agencies where shelter and food are provided.

[20] Bail or collateral forfeiture is common in some jurisdictions. The defendant pays $10 to $20, depending upon the stipulated amount in the jurisdiction, and he is not penalized for failing to return to court. See President's Commission on Crime in the District of Columbia, *Report 477* (1966); *Emory Department of Psychiatry*, p. 11.

[21] In Washington, D.C., for example, approximately 20,000 of the 44,218 people arrested during 1965 obtained release by forfeiting $10 collateral. President's Commission on Crime in the District of Columbia, *Report 475* (1966). In Atlanta, Georgia, approximately 20,000 of 49,805 arrests during 1961 resulted in ($15) collateral forfeitures. *Emory Department of Psychiatry*, p. 11. Those who post and forfeit collateral avoid the risk of a jail sentence.

[22] See generally Foote, *supra* note 1; Labovitz, "Some Legal Problems of Skid Row Residents," draft of report to be issued by the Diagnostic and Relocation Center, Philadelphia, Pennsylvania. These conclusions are supported by observations made in court during the early part of 1966 by Commission staff attorneys. The right of cross-examination, confrontation of the accuser, and the privilege against self-incrimination were repeatedly disregarded. In the absence of counsel the courts and prosecutors sometimes act sua sponte to assure that all defenses are asserted on behalf of the defendant. Chief Judge Green of the District of Columbia Court of General Sessions has concluded that "the court has the obligation to inject this issue [alcoholism] on its own motion when it appears likely from the evidence that the defense may be available." *District of Columbia v. Walters, Congressional Record*, 112:22716 (daily ed., September 22, 1966). See also *Whalem v. United States*, U.S. App. D.C. 331, 346 F.2d 812 (D.C. Cir. 1965) (en banc); *Overholser v. Lynch*, 109 U.S. App. D.C. 404, 288 F.2d 388 (D.C. 1961), *rev'd in part on other grounds*, 369 U.S. 705 (1962); *Pate v. Robinson*, 383 U.S. 375 (1966). With respect to the importance of prosecutors bringing potential defenses to the attention of the court, see Canon 5 of the *Canons of Professional Ethics of the American Bar Association, United States v. Ragen*, 86 F. Supp. 382, 387 (N.D., Ill., 1949) (holding the "suppression of vital evidence [to be] . . . a denial of due process"); Jackson, "The Federal Prosecutor," *Journal of American Judicial Society*,

Usually defendants are processed through the court system with haste and either released or sentenced to several days or weeks in jail.[23] In some cities only those offenders who request it are jailed.[24] In others chronic offenders, who are likely to be alcoholics, are generally sent to jail.[25] . . .

After serving a brief sentence, the chronic offender is released, more likely than not to return to his former haunts on skid row, with no money, no job, and no plans.[26] Often he is arrested within a matter of hours or days.

In a memorandum of law submitted in a recent case of a homeless alcoholic, defense counsel noted that his client had been arrested 31 times in a period of 4 months and 6 days. Counsel maintained that "it is fair to conclude [in view of three commitments during that period of time] that he must have been arrested once out of every 2 days that he appeared on the public streets of the District of Columbia."[27]

Evaluation of the Existing System

Effect on the Offender

The criminal justice system appears ineffective to deter drunkenness or to meet the problems of the chronic alcoholic offender. What the system usually does accomplish is to remove the drunk from public view, detoxify him, and provide him with food, shelter, emergency medical service, and a brief period of forced sobriety. As presently constituted, the system is not in a position to meet his underlying medical and social problems.

1940, 24:18. See generally address by Peter Barton Hutt, attorney, *The Recent Court Decisions on Alcoholism: A Challenge to the North American Judges Association and Its Members*, NAJA annual meeting, Colorado Springs, Colorado, November 3, 1966, published as appendix H of President's Commission on Law Enforcement and Administration of Justice, *Task Force Report: Drunkenness* (Washington: U.S. Government Printing Office, 1967).

[23] In Portland, Oregon, for example, the first offense receives a suspended sentence, the second offense brings a 2-day jail sentence, and the fifth offense within a 12-month period brings a 6-month sentence. *The Sunday Oregonian*, April 17, 1966, p. F-4, col. 4; Oregon Mental Health Division, *Proceedings: the Alcoholic and the Court* (1963), p. 39. In Atlanta, Georgia, the fourth conviction within a 12-month period brings a fine, and the fifth conviction results in a 30-day jail sentence. *Emory Department of Psychiatry*, p. 28. A 1957 study showed that 13,146 sentences out of 15,111 in Washington, D.C., were for 30 days or less. D.C. Commission on Prisons, Probation, and Parole, *Report 106* 1957.

[24] Labovitz, *supra* note 22. This procedure was observed by the Commission staff.

[25] See Pittman and Gordon, *Revolving Door: A Study of the Chronic Police Case Inebriate* (1958), pp. 30, 125; *supra* note 11.

[26] "He is merely transported from the workhouse to the city of Washington, dumped on the streets at 14th and Independence Avenue S.W., with only the clothes on his back. He has no place to stay, no food to eat, and no job. It is ridiculous, under such circumstances, to expect any improvement in the problem of the 'skid row' alcoholic." D.C. Commission on Prisons, Probation, and Parole, *Report 110* (1957).

[27] *District of Columbia v. Strother*, Motion to Reopen Proceedings, No. 25861–66, D.C. Court of General Sessions, September 14, 1966.

Effect on the System of Criminal Justice

Including drunkenness within the system of criminal justice seriously burdens and distorts its operations. Because the police often do not arrest the intoxicated person who has a home, there is in arrest practices an inherent discrimination against the homeless and the poor. Due process safeguards are often considered unnecessary or futile. The defendant may not be warned of his rights or permitted to make a telephone call.[28] And although coordination, breath, or blood tests to determine intoxication are common practice in "driving-while-intoxicated" cases, they are virtually nonexistent in common drunk cases. Yet, without the use of such chemical tests, it is often difficult to determine whether the individual is intoxicated or suffering from a serious illness that has symptoms similar to intoxication.[29]

> Authorities in this field recognize that the most skilled physician would have difficulty in arriving at an accurate diagnosis of alcoholic influence or intoxication simply by observing outward indications—clinical or objective symptoms. Ordinarily, a lengthy and detailed clinical examination is required to rule out absolutely many of the pathological conditions which are known to produce the same symptoms.

The handling of drunkenness cases in court hardly reflects the standards of fairness that are the basis of our system of criminal justice.[30] One major

[28] Some police officials told staff members of the President's Commission on Law Enforcement and Administration of Justice that the defendant charged with drunkenness is not permitted to place a telephone call upon request until a 4-hour "sobering-up" period following arrest has elapsed. Such policy would deny the use of the telephone to some innocent people and to others who would be physically able to confer with counsel. A Commission staff attorney observed the right denied to a person charged with drunkenness who was physically able to call counsel. In another case a 17-year-old youth with no prior criminal record was arrested at 10 P.M. and denied the right to telephone his parents until the end of the "sobering-up" period. Since the call had to be placed to a neighbor's home (his parents were unable to afford a telephone), he chose not to exercise his right at what he considered an unreasonable hour. He appeared in court the following morning without counsel, pleaded guilty to public intoxication, and was sentenced to 3 months in jail. His parents were not notified of his whereabouts until he arrived in the county penitentiary. They contacted an attorney who secured the youth's release pending appeal of the conviction. Transcript of proceedings, *People v. Jones,* Syracuse, New York, Police Court, September 13, 1965.

[29] See *People v. Butts,* 21 Misc. 2d 799, 804–05, 201 New York S. 2d 926, 932–33 (1960); Donigan, *Chemical Tests and the Law* (Northeastern University Traffic Institute, 1957), p. 4:

[30] See generally Foote, *supra* note 1. Observations made in court by Commission staff attorneys support this thesis. One case observed in the early part of 1966 involved an obviously indigent defendant charged with "drinking in public." The police officer testified that a bottle containing an alcoholic beverage was in the defendant's pocket. The trial judge asked the officer whether the defendant was drinking from the bottle. The officer replied that "he must have been" since the bottle was "half empty." The defendant was found guilty and fined $30. He lacked the funds to pay the fine and was compelled to serve 30 days in jail.

reason is that counsel is rarely present.[31] Drunkenness cases often involve complex factual and medical issues. Cross-examination could be conducted on "observations" of the arresting officer such as "bloodshot" and "glassy" eyes, "staggering gait," "odor" of alcohol on the defendant's breath. The testimony of an expert medical witness on behalf of the defendant could be elicited.[32]

The extent of police time allotted to handling drunkenness offenders varies from city to city and from precinct to precinct. In most cities a great deal of time is spent.[33] The inebriate must be taken into custody, transported to jail, booked, detained, clothed, fed, sheltered, and transported to court. In some jurisdictions, police officers must wait, often for hours, to testify in court.

There is a commensurate burden on the urban courts. Notwithstanding the fact that an overwhelming caseload often leads judges to dispose of scores of drunkenness cases in minutes, they represent a significant drain on court time which is needed for felony and serious misdemeanor cases. More subtly, drunkenness cases impair the dignity of the criminal process in lower courts, which are forced to handle defendants so casually and to apply criminal sanctions with so little apparent effect.

In correctional systems, too, resources are diverted from serious offenders. After court appearance, some offenders are sent to short-term penal institu-

[31] The assignment of counsel to skid row inebriates had a profound effect on the handling of such cases in New York City. More than 95% of the defendants were acquitted after trial on disorderly conduct charges. See Murtagh, "Comments," *Inventory* 16:13,14 (North Carolina Rehabilitation Program, July-September 1966), for a discussion of the background and reasons for the program. In March 1966 there were 1,326 defendants arraigned in Social Court in New York City, of whom 1,280 were acquitted. In March 1965, in the absence of defense counsel, there were 1,590 arraignments, 1,259 guilty pleas and only 325 acquittals." Address by Hon. Bernard Botein, Presiding Justice, Appeals Division, 1st Department Superior Court, April 22, 1966, in Governor Rockefeller's Conference on Crime (1966), p. 149; *New York Times,* April 23, 1966, p. 14, col. 4. Court records show that in April and May 1966, 1,838 of 2,103 defendants in New York City's Social Court were acquitted. As a result of the high acquittal rate Chief Judge John M. Murtagh directed court clerks not to draw complaints on nondisorderly drunkenness. From June 1, 1966, through September 30, 1966, a total of 189 cases was brought to Social Court, of which 161 resulted in convictions.

The effect of the assignment of counsel was to reduce the number of arrests in New York City's skid row. The appearance of many more inebriated people on skid row seemed to make the underlying public health problem more visible, and the establishment of alternate facilities became more urgent. See "Derelicts Dislike Non-Arrest Policy," *New York Times,* July 29, 1966, p. 27, col. 8.

[32] See President's Commission on Crime in the District of Columbia, *Report 500* (1966), in which the following recommendation was made: "As long as drunkenness offenders remain subject to penal sanctions, the Commission believes that they should be provided with counsel."

[33] The extent to which drunkenness offenses interfere with other police activity is illustrated in Washington, D.C., where the uniformed tactical police force, a special unit used "to combat serious crime," devotes a substantial amount of time to the handling of drunks. *The Washington Daily News,* December 1, 1965, p. 5. During one 9-month sample period, the tactical force made 14,542 arrests, of which 6,363 were for drunkenness. Statistics supplied by Washington, D.C., Police Department to President's Commission on Crime in the District of Columbia.

tions, many of which are already overcrowded. Correctional authorities estimate that one-half the entire misdemeanant population is comprised of drunkenness offenders.[34] In one city it was reported that 95 percent of short-term prisoners were drunkenness offenders.[35]

[34] One study showed that in August 1962, 63% of all inmates in the Monroe County Penitentiary (Rochester, New York) were committed for drunkenness. Rochester Bureau of Municipal Research, *Man on the Periphery, Report on the Monroe County Penitentiary,* 1964, p. 29.
[35] See *Emory Department of Psychiatry,* p. 51.

[*The President's Commission on Law Enforcement and Administration of Justice,* Task Force Report: Drunkenness (*Washington: U.S. Government Printing Office, 1967*), *pp. 1–5.*]

11 *The police*

The police—some 420,000 people working for approximately 40,000 separate agencies that spend more than $2½ billion a year —are the part of the criminal justice system that is in direct daily contact both with crime and with the public. The entire system—courts and corrections as well as the police—is charged with enforcing the law and maintaining order. What is distinctive about the responsibility of the police is that they are charged with performing these functions where all eyes are upon them and where the going is roughest, on the street. Since this is a time of increasing crime, increasing social unrest, and increasing public sensitivity to both, it is a time when police work is peculiarly important, complicated, conspicuous, and delicate.

· · · · ·

The rate of apprehension of offenders in property crimes is extremely low—approximately 22 percent of those reported. The police have greater success with violent crimes—approximately 59 percent of those reported. In large part this is because more victims of violent crimes know or can identify their assailants. The ability of a victim or witness to identify the criminal is the factor responsible for solving a large percentage of the crimes that are solved.

To say that the police have a limited ability to prevent crime is not to criticize the police. The police, more than anybody, are frustrated by the wide gap between the task they are expected to perform and the methods at their disposal to perform it.

· · · · ·

As America has grown and policing has become correspondingly complex, the existing law enforcement system has not always been altered to meet the needs of a mechanized and metropolitan society.

Over the years, the proliferation of independent and, for the most part, local policing units has led to an overlapping of responsibilities and a duplication of effort, causing problems in police administration and in the coordination of efforts to apprehend criminals. America is a nation of small, decentralized police forces.

· · · · ·

Serious study of police reform in America began in 1919. The problems exposed then and those faced by police agencies today are similar in many respects. For example, in 1931 the Wickersham Commission noted that the average police chief's term of office was too short, and that his responsibility to political officials made his position insecure. The Commission also felt that there was a lack of competent, efficient, and honest patrolmen. It said that no intensive effort was being made to educate, train, and discipline prospective officers, or to eliminate those shown to be incompetent. The Wickersham Commission found that with perhaps two exceptions, police forces in cities above 300,000 population had neither an adequate communications system nor the equipment necessary to enforce the law effectively. It said that the police task was made much more difficult by the excessively rapid growth of our cities in the past half century, and by the tendency of different ethnic groups to retain their language and customs in large cities. Finally, the Commission said, there were too many duties cast upon each officer and patrolman.[1]

.   .   .   .   .

There are today in the United States 40,000 separate agencies responsible for enforcing laws on the Federal, State, and local levels of government. But law enforcement agencies are not evenly distributed among these three levels, for the function is primarily a concern of local government. There are only 50 law enforcement agencies on the Federal level of government and 200 departments on the State level. The remaining 39,750 agencies are dispersed throughout the many counties, cities, towns, and villages that form our local governments.[2]

.   .   .   .   .

Because the concept of local autonomy in enforcing laws has prevailed throughout our history and because the many local policing agencies have held firmly to their traditional jurisdictional authority, responsibility for maintaining public order is today extremely decentralized. . . . The problems caused by decentralization are many, particularly where a number of police agencies exist within a radius of a few miles. Jurisdictional barriers are often erected between these agencies; maintaining adequate communication is difficult, and obtaining assistance from several adjacent agencies when needed becomes a complex operation.

.   .   .   .   .

Due to the great difficulties of attracting capable personnel, almost all large police departments in the United States are substantially below their authorized strength. . . .

The difficulties in filling quotas are increased by a low rate of eligibility among police applicants. . . .

Manpower problems are also caused by turnover in personnel. . . .

[1] National Commission on Law Observance and Enforcement, *Report on the Police* (Washington: U.S. Government Printing Office, 1931), pp. 5–7.

[2] A. C. Germann, Frank D. Day, and Robert R. J. Gallati, *Introduction to Law Enforcement* (Springfield: Charles C. Thomas, 1966), p. 153.

The present need for manpower and the anticipated rate of turnover both indicate that over 50,000 new police officers will be required in 1967 alone.

.   .   .   .   .

Police personnel are predominately Caucasian. The 1960 census showed that only 3.5 percent of law enforcement employees throughout the Nation were nonCaucasian. A study by the Civil Rights Commission in 1962 revealed that only one-fifth of 1 percent of State police officers were Negro. Of the 36 Negroes serving as State police officers in the Nation, 24 were employed in Illinois.[3] The same Civil Rights Commission survey polled 271 sheriffs' offices and found that in 1962 there was a Negro-white employment ratio of 1 to 20 on the county level of government.

.   .   .   .   .

More than 70 percent of the Nation's police departments have set the high school diploma level as an educational requirement for employment. About one-fourth of the agencies require no more than some degree of elementary education.[4] . . .

Physical requirements for police employment are rigid. The minimum standards usually require that a recruit be between the ages of 21 and 35, have nearly perfect vision, weigh between 150 and 250 pounds, and be at least 5 feet 8 or 9 inches tall.

.   .   .   .   .

Almost all local police departments require that an applicant take written intelligence tests. . . . In 1961 a survey showed that only about 15 percent of the local agencies screened their candidates for emotional fitness as a routine procedure.[5]

Law Enforcement Policy: The Police Role

. . . [T]he term "police" is used to refer to all persons having law enforcement responsibility, but major emphasis is upon the men who have the responsibility in the large urban areas for dealing with the wide range of social and behavioral problems that are of primary concern today.

.   .   .   .   .

It is obviously difficult and often impossible for police officers to respond in an appropriate manner to the numerous incidents called to their attention.

.   .   .   .   .

While neither articulated nor officially recognized, common responses obviously tend to develop in frequently recurring situations.

.   .   .   .   .

[3] U.S. Commission on Civil Rights, *Administration of Justice, 1963* (staff report, draft submitted 1963), pp. 13–16.

[4] George W. O'Connor, *Survey of Selection Methods* (Washington: International Association of Chiefs of Police, 1962), table 15.

[5] *Id.* at table 19.

Unique situations do arise, usually where the frequency of a given kind of incident is small, for which there is no routine response. Under such circumstances, the decision of the individual officer will reflect his own personal values and opinions about people and about group behavior.

Improvement in the capacity of law enforcement agencies to perform the essential and highly sensitive functions that comprise the total police task requires a willingness on the part of the public and the police to take several bold steps.

There must, in the first place, be a more widespread recognition on the part of the citizenry and the police of both the range and the complexity of the problems which the police confront. Secondly, there must be a willingness on the part of the police to respond to these problems by the careful development and articulation of policies and practices which are subject to continuing reevaluation in the light of changing social conditions.

.   .   .   .   .

Direct confrontation of policy issues would inevitably require the police administrator to face the fact that some police practices, although considered effective, do not conform to constitutional, legislative, or judicial standards. By adopting a "let sleeping dogs lie" approach, the administrator avoids a direct confrontation and thus is able to support "effective" practices without having to decide whether they meet the requirements of the law.

.   .   .   .   .

As a result, individual officers continue to depend primarily upon routine responses and upon their individual judgment when functioning in these areas. And critical problems which the police confront do not receive the kind of attention they require.

.   .   .   .   .

Most practices currently used by police to deal with crime or potential crime situations give rise to important and sensitive policy questions of a kind that can and should be dealt with carefully and systematically by a law enforcement agency. Illustrative of these are the decision as to whether or not to make an arrest; the decision to use or not use certain methods of detection or investigation such as surveillance, field interrogation, or search; the decision to release rather than prosecute some guilty persons who have been arrested; the effort to keep public order by breaking up crowds and ordering people to keep moving; the settlement of minor disputes by the use of various formal or informal devices; and the effort to protect the right of free expression for individuals or groups who wish to express views unpopular to the majority of people in the community.

.   .   .   .   .

For police officials who have not previously been called upon to fulfill the function, the task [of policy formulation] requires the development of a systematic process by which important issues are identified, studied, and resolved. The police are, of course, in a position to benefit in this effort from the experiences of other administrative agencies and are, in varying degrees, committed to developing guidelines covering their respective operations.

. . . . .

It is in the nature of an administrative organization that the establishment of policies to guide the exercise of discretion by individuals is not enough. There is need also for the development of methods for assuring compliance. This requires a system of administrative controls to be applied within an agency.

. . . . .

The operations of the police, like the operations of any other administrative agency that exercises governmental authority, must be subject to effective legislative, executive, and judicial review and control. This is important when the police are called upon to carry out specific legislative, executive, or judicial mandates. It is doubly important in areas in which the police are left with discretion to develop their own policies within broad legislatively or judicially fixed limits.

. . . . .

Ultimate control, in local government, is normally exerted through the ballot box. But efforts to protect the police from partisan political influence have, in many jurisdictions, made the police immune from the local election processes. Early efforts to assure popular control of the police did include provisions in some cities for the chief of police to be elected. In others, the police were made responsible to the local legislative body. It became quickly apparent, however, that such direct control led to a pattern of incompetence, lax enforcement, and the improper use of police authority.

. . . . .

Fear of being accused of political interference and an awareness of the sensitive nature of the police task have often resulted in the mayor abdicating all responsibility for police operations by granting complete autonomy to his police department.

. . . . .

The prosecutor, State's attorney, or district attorney is designated as the chief law enforcement officer under the statutes of some States. However, despite this designation he is not generally conceived of in this country as having overall responsibility for the supervision of the police.

. . . . .

. . . [N]either the police nor the prosecutor assumes that the prosecutor has the responsibility either to stimulate or to participate in the development of administrative policies to control the wide range of police practices.

. . . . .

In many jurisdictions, the trial judge has acted as a sort of chief administrative officer of the criminal justice system, using his power to dismiss cases as a method of controlling the use of the criminal process. But except in those cases in which his action relates to the admissibility of evidence, this has been done largely on an informal basis and has tended to be haphazard, often reflecting primarily the personal values of the individual trial judge.

.   .   .   .   .

The primary need is for the development of methods of external control which will serve as inducements for police to articulate important law enforcement policies and to be willing to have them known, discussed, and changed, if change is desirable. There is obviously no single way of accomplishing this.

.   .   .   .   .

The creation of an institutional framework to encourage the development and implementation of law enforcement policies which are effective and also consistent with democratic values is obviously difficult. To achieve this requires a basic rethinking of the relationship between the police and legislatures, courts, prosecutors, local government officials, and the community as a whole.

Police Organization, Management and Operations

.   .   .   .   .

Since traditional police practices have at best been only modestly successful in deterring criminal behavior and in apprehending offenders, it is obvious that blind adherence to tradition will not do. Also, traditional organizational structures and operational procedures have detracted from the attractiveness of police work. This is one reason for the rising resignation rates in our Nation's police departments, and for the increasing difficulty many departments have had in recruiting adequate numbers of personnel. Other than such factors as low pay and financial insecurity, these problems are caused by procedures which stifle initiative and, in some departments, by poor direction and control, by confused responsibility, and by improper grouping of duties. Even though these conditions are apparent, there is only slight evidence that the departments most in need of reorganization are taking steps in that direction.

To assist in evaluating the present state of U.S. police organization, management, and operations, the Commission staff:

> (1) Conferred with expert advisory panels;
> (2) Sought guidance from 250 police leaders and representatives from professional bodies;
> (3) Reviewed police literature and textbooks;
> (4) Reviewed police consultant surveys of 75 police departments;
> (5) Reviewed a comprehensive study of police organization and management which was prepared by California State College at Los Angeles for the U.S. Department of Justice; and
> (6) Reviewed responses to a letter sent to 2100 police agencies by the Attorney General requesting information on effective procedures.

.   .   .   .   .

Findings and Recommendations

The Commission's studies enabled it to identify a number of generally prevalent deficiencies in police organization, management, and operations, and suggested to it the means for correcting these deficiencies. . . . [I]n summary, the Commission has found:

(1) Many departments lack qualified leadership. . . .

(2) Many departments are not organized in accordance with well-established principles of modern business management. . . .

(3) Many departments resist change, fail to determine shortcomings of existing practice and procedures through research and analysis, and are reluctant to experiment with alternative methods of solving problems. . . .

(4) Many departments lack trained personnel in such fields as research and planning, law, business administration and computer analysis. . . .

(5) Many departments fail to deploy and utilize personnel efficiently. . . .

(6) Many departments have not adequately applied technological advances that would be beneficial to law enforcement. . . .

(7) Finally, States, through their commissions on police standards or other appropriate agencies, should provide financial and technical assistance to departments to conduct surveys and make recommendations to improve police organization, management, and operations.

.   .   .   .   .

Coordination and Consolidation of Police Services

.   .   .   .   .

A fundamental problem confronting law enforcement today is that of fragmented crime repression efforts resulting from the large number of uncoordinated local governments and law enforcement agencies. It is not uncommon to find police units working at cross purposes in trying to solve the same or similar crimes.

.   .   .   .   .

In the context of this report, consolidation is the merging, in whole or in part, of one governmental jurisdiction, or function thereof, with another governmental jurisdiction, or function thereof.

Cooperation or cordination presupposes a formal agreement between two or more governmental jurisdictions each with defined responsibilities to jointly provide a common service.

.   .   .   .   .

Several techniques were utilized in the preparation of this report. A detailed review was made of available literature, ranging from general metropolitan studies to studies of specialized police activities. . . . The project staff also reviewed selected State constitutions, pertinent legislation, opinions of attorneys general, court decisions, and other sources to determine legal authorizations, prohibitions, or restrictions relating to the coordination or consolidation of law enforcement activities.

Members of the project staff made several field visits to a number of governmental jurisdictions and agencies to obtain firsthand impressions and factual data relating to the coordination and consolidation of law enforcement activities.

General Findings and Conclusions

The ensuing discussion summarizes the general findings and conclusions of a detailed study of the problems and potential of coordination and consolidation for the achievement of better police services. . . .

1. . . . [M]any [police agencies] lack the necessary resources for recruiting and selecting qualified personnel and for providing the training needed at all levels of service. . . . These endeavors lend themselves to an areawide approach through coordination or consolidation of the efforts of a number of jurisdictions.

. . . . .

2. Staff activities associated with public information, inspection, and internal investigation are appropriately the tools of the individual police administrator and only rarely, or in limited degree, lend themselves to performance on an areawide basis.

3. Organized intelligence is a staff service that does not fall precisely into either of the two general groups. In one sense, it is a tool of the individual administrator; however, in order to be fully effective, the organized crime intelligence activities of one department must be coordinated with the activities of other departments engaged in similar and related work.

. . . . .

4. The auxiliary services of records and communications, crime laboratory services, and detention are the police responsibilities best suited to coordination and consolidation on an areawide basis; and with the possible exception of training, these are the services most often performed jointly.

. . . . .

5. Selected field services, among them criminal investigation, vice and delinquency control, and special task force operations, require specialized training and manpower beyond the capacity of most jurisdictions to supply adequately. These selected field services lend themselves to performance through coordinated or consolidated programs covering wide areas.

. . . . .

6. Many local jurisdictions cannot provide adequate police protection unless they receive assistance from other jurisdictions; and many jurisdictions for one reason or another cannot provide even basic patrol services.

These situations call for the coordination or consolidation of effort and services.

A number of approaches have been used successfully in consolidating police responsibilities. They include: comprehensive reorganization under metropolitan-type governments; the use of subordinate service taxing districts under a strong county government; intergovernmental agreements; and annexation by municipalities of fringe areas. One additional approach, the use of single-purpose special districts, has been utilized occasionally.

. . . . .

7. Generally, the political and social pressures inherent in the desire for local self-government, rather than legal restrictions, militate against the coordination and consolidation of police services. . . . Moves for the coordination and consolidation of local police services must take into account the strength of the political and social pressures for local self-government.

Police Personnel

. . . . .

There is impressive evidence that in many cities there are too few policemen. The current police-population ratio of 1.7 policeman per thousand is misleading, for in San Diego there are 1.07 policemen per thousand and in Boston 4.04.

. . . [M]ere addition of manpower without accompanying efforts to make the best use of existing personnel strength might serve only to aggravate the problem of inefficiency.

. . . . .

Under traditional police organization, the initial responsibility for confronting the entire range of police problems rests with the patrolman. Along with responding to criminal behavior, the patrolman is responsible for such matters as enforcing traffic regulations and for performing a myriad of services for the public.[6]

. . . . .

A survey of the Kansas City Police Department in 1966, for example, revealed that patrol officers devoted only 32 percent of their time to criminal matters.[7]

. . . . .

The existing wide range of patrol responsibility hampers efforts to attract more highly qualified personnel into police service. Present police departments are monolithic in structure. All sworn police personnel, regardless of

---

[6] In 1933, a job analysis of the police service in California determined that police work required over 3,000 types of skills and applications of knowledge. *Analysis of Police Service* (Sacramento: California State Department of Education, 1933).

[7] Survey conducted by Public Administration Service for the President's Commission on Law Enforcement and Administration of Justice.

individual qualifications or experience, normally begin their careers as patrolmen, assigned to patrol or traffic duties. . . . Police work, therefore, tends to attract persons who are willing to perform its mechanical aspects and to accept its status and compensation. For example, in a survey conducted of the Metropolitan Police Department of Washington, D.C., in 1966, it was revealed that over 60 percent of the applicants for positions in that department were holding clerical, sales, manufacturing, or transportation jobs at the time of application and that the majority of the remaining applicants were in the military service.[8]

.   .   .   .   .

It seems evident that a more rational division of assignments, particularly in the larger departments, would greatly alleviate some of these deficiencies.

.   .   .   .   .

At present, a patrolman is equally responsible for the most complex and the most menial of police tasks. The wide range of skills required in performing all these tasks seems possible of attainment for only limited numbers of personnel.[9] This being so, these tasks should be divided according to the skills required to perform them. . . .

To implement this recommendation, police departments in large and medium-sized cities should establish three classes of officers, which for purposes of this report will be referred to as the police agent, the police officer, and the community service officer (CSO). Tasks would be assigned to these officers on the basis of the skills, intelligence, and education necessary to perform those tasks well.

.   .   .   .   .

The Police Agent

. . . [P]olice departments should establish a distinct classification of officers, designated herein as police agents, who would be assigned to the most complicated, sensitive, and demanding police tasks.

.   .   .   .   .

. . . [A] police agent should have considerable educational attainment: at least 2 years of college and preferably a baccalaureate degree in the liberal arts or social sciences. . . . Agents would replace, but have a much wider responsibility than, the existing detective.

.   .   .   .   .

[8] Century Research Crop., *Recruitment and Retention Factors in the Metropolitan Police Department,* prepared for the President's Commission on Crime in the District of Columbia and the Office of Law Enforcement Assistance (Arlington: Va., 1966), table 11, p. 23.

[9] August Vollmer, *The Police and Modern Society* (Berkeley: University of California Press, 1936), pp. 221–223.

An obvious advantage of the police agent position is that it could make police work an attractive career for highly qualified young men.

The Police Officer

The police officer would perform the police duties of enforcing laws and investigating those crimes that can be solved by immediate followup investigations or are most likely to have suspects close to the crime scene. He would respond to selected calls for services, perform routine patrol, render emergency services, and enforce traffic regulations and investigate traffic accidents.

Since a substantial portion of police time is currently devoted to these tasks, police departments would undoubtedly need a greater number of police officers than agents.

.   .   .   .   .

The Community Service Officer

The Commission visualizes the CSO as a young man, typically between the ages of 17 and 21, with the aptitude, integrity and stability necessary to perform police work. A CSO would be, in effect, an apprentice policeman—replacing the present police cadet. He would work on the street under close supervision, and in close cooperation with the police officer and police agent. He would not have full law enforcement powers or carry arms, neither would he perform only clerical duties, as many police cadets do today. He would be a uniformed member of the working police who performs certain service and investigate duties on the street. He would maintain close contact with the juveniles in neighborhoods where he works. He might be available at a neighborhood storefront office or community service center and might use a radio-dispatched scooter to move around the community.

.   .   .   .   .

The purposes of creating the position of community service officer are many: (1) to improve police service in high crime rate areas; (2) to enable police to hire persons who can provide a greater understanding of minority groups problems; (3) to relieve police agents and officers of lesser police duties; (4) to increase the opportunity for minority group members to serve in law enforcement; and (5) to tap a new reservoir of manpower by helping talented young men who have not been able as yet to complete their education to qualify for police work.

.   .   .   .   .

A young man might be accepted as a CSO despite a minor offense record; otherwise it might be difficult to recruit members of minority groups for this position since Commission studies show that . . . it is more likely than not that a Negro youth who grows up in a slum will have such a record.

.   .   .   .   .

Team Policing

In almost all large police departments there is a considerable amount of organizational fragmentation. Traditionally and almost universally, patrol and investigative forces have separate lines of command and tend to be isolated from one another; often they keep separate sets of records; frequently they work different shifts or are based in different places so that there is a minimum of contact between patrolmen and detectives. . . . At both the staff and the field levels, this overseparation of functions, or overspecialization, can have undesirable results. . . .

The concept, which might be called "team policing," is that all police work, both patrol and criminal investigation, in a given number of city blocks should be under unified command. A "field supervisor" would have under his command a team of agents, officers, and community service officers. The team would meet at the beginning of a tour of duty and receive a briefing on the current situation in the neighborhood. . . . On this basis, the members would be assigned to specific areas or duties.

The Commission believes that team policing would result in both increased crime solution and the most advantageous use of the time and talents of all policemen. It wishes to stress, furthermore, that experiments with team policing are not dependent on the agent-officer-CSO division of functions. They could easily be conducted with existing personnel. . . .

The Police and the Community

The need for strengthening police relationships with the communities they serve is critical today in the Nation's large cities and in many small cities and towns as well. The Negro, Puerto Rican, Mexican-American, and other minority groups are taking action to acquire rights and services which have been historically denied them.

.   .   .   .   .

Hostility, or even lack of confidence of a significant portion of the public, has extremely serious implications for the police. These attitudes interfere with recruiting, since able young men generally seek occupations which are not inordinately dangerous and which have the respect and support of their relatives and friends.

Public hostility affects morale and makes police officers less enthusiastic about doing their job well. It may lead some officers to leave the force, to accept more prestigious or less demanding employment.

Many police officers now view their relations with the public as poor.

This attitude is reflected in surveys of patrolmen as well as in frequent statements by police officials.

Recently a survey of policemen in a western municipal department disclosed that 70 percent thought that the prestige of police work was fair or poor while only 29 percent said good and 2 percent excellent. Twenty-six percent of the officers believed that "relations with public" was the principal problem faced by police.[10] Another survey of officers in a big-city department found that over 70 percent had an acute sense of citizen hostility or contempt.[11] A Commission survey of police officers conducted in eight precincts in three large cities found that the officers considered "prestige and respect one gets from a job" next to last among the factors they liked about police work; when asked what was least liked about police work when they entered the force, 22 percent cited public lack of respect; only the hours worked were rated lower.[12]

. . . . .

Poor police-community relations adversely affect the ability of the police to prevent crime and apprehend criminals. People hostile to the police are not so likely to report violations of law, even when they are the victims. They are even less likely to report suspicious persons or incidents, to testify as witnesses voluntarily, or to come forward to provide information. For example, a study in St. Louis found that 43 percent of Negroes and 36 percent of whites believed that "most of the city residents seem to be afraid to contact their police."[13]

. . . . .

Statistics compiled by the FBI reveal that 20,523 officers were assaulted, 6,836 injured, and 53 killed during 1965.[14] . . . [M]any of the minor assaults (and some of the more serious ones as well) resulted, as least partially, from general hostility toward the police. Consequently, poor community relations can increase the danger of police work. . . .

In addition, poor police-community relations has contributed to the disturbances and riots which have increasingly afflicted our cities. . . . [M]ore often than not, riots were set off by some quite ordinary and proper action

[10] Jerome H. Skolnick, *Justice Without Trial: Law Enforcement in a Democratic Society* (New York: John Wiley & Sons, Inc., 1966), p. 50.

[11] James Q. Wilson, "Police Attitudes and Citizen Hostility," quoted in *supra* note 11 at p. 62.

[12] Albert J. Reiss, Jr., *Police Officer Attitudes Toward Their Work and Job* (Ann Arbor: University of Michigan, 1966), table 7, report prepared for President's Commission on Law Enforcement and Administration of Justice. This report is a preliminary draft which is being included with the Commission's records in the National Archives. It is presently being revised and supplemented by the University of Michigan and will be embodied in research studies to be published by the Commission.

[13] Edmund Joseph Casey, "Citizen Attitudes Toward the Police and Law Enforcement" (unpublished Ph.D. thesis, St. Louis University, 1966), p. 100.

[14] U.S. Department of Justice, Federal Bureau of Investigation, *Uniform Crime Reports—1965* (Washington: U.S. Government Printing Office, 1966), pp. 33, 152–153.

by a policeman. Some riots, however, started after improper or at least unwise police conduct. . . .

Public Attitudes Toward the Police

THE GENERAL PUBLIC

Contrary to the belief of many policemen, the overwhelming majority of the public has a high opinion of the work of the police. A national survey conducted by the National Opinion Research Center (NORC) for the Commission produced these answers to the following questions:[15]

Do you think that the police here do an excellent, good, fair, or a poor job of enforcing the laws?

	Percent
Excellent	22
Good	45
Fair	24
Poor	8

How good a job do the police do on giving protection to people in the neighborhood?

	Percent
Very good	42
Pretty good	35
Not so good	9
No opinion	14

.   .   .   .   .

The public generally believes that the police do not engage in serious misconduct. A Gallup poll in 1965 showed that only 9 percent of the public believed that "there is any police brutality in this area."[16] The 1966 NORC survey found, in answer to the question, "How good a job do the police do on being respectful to people like yourself?", that the public answered:[17]

	Percent
Very good	59
Pretty good	26
Not so good	4
No opinion	10

.   .   .   .   .

[15] National Opinion Research Center, "A National Sample Survey Approach to the Study of the Victims of Crimes and Attitudes Toward Law Enforcement and Justice" (Chicago: unpublished, 1966) chapter 8, p. 1.

[16] Gallup poll, "Tabulation Request Survey AIPO No. 709" (prepared for the President's Commission on Law Enforcement and Administration of Justice, 1966), p. 2.

[17] *Supra* note 15 at chapter 8, p. 1.

The University of California surveys for the Commission in San Diego and Philadelphia found that the large majority of white community leaders thought that police-community relations were good, although there was some dissent.[18] The general findings of the Michigan State University survey of 16 jurisdictions were similar.[19]

These studies might seem to suggest that there is no widespread police-community relations problem. And, if the persons showing greatest skepticism toward the police were evenly distributed through all kinds of communities and neighborhoods, this would be true. In fact, however, this is not so.

THE NEGRO COMMUNITY

The NORC survey shows that nonwhites, particularly Negroes, are significantly more negative than whites in evaluating police effectiveness in law enforcement. In describing whether police give protection to citizens, nonwhites give a rating of "very good" only half as often as whites and give a "not so good" rating twice as often. These differences are not merely a function of greater poverty among nonwhites; they exist at all income levels and for both men and women.[20]

. . . . .

. . . Negroes show even greater attitude differences from whites with regard to police discourtesy. The NORC national survey found, as to respectfulness to "people like yourselves," the following differences between the attitudes of Negroes and whites:[21]

[18] Joseph D. Lohman and Gordon E. Misner, *The Police and the Community* (Berkeley: University of California School of Criminology, 1966), vol. I, p. 50; vol. II, p. 78. Report prepared for the President's Commission on Law Enforcement and Administration of Justice by the School of Criminology at the University of California. The study consisted of intensive analysis of police-community relations problems and programs in San Diego and Philadelphia, with six-man teams visiting the two cities for 6 weeks each. During the time, they accompanied the police in their daily work and interviewed hundreds of police officials and officers, judges, lawyers, minority group leaders, civic leaders, juveniles, and average citizens.

[19] Raymond Galvin and Louis Radelet, *A National Survey of Police and Community Relations* (East Lansing: Michigan State University, 1967), p. 12. Report prepared for the President's Commission on Law Enforcement and Administration of Justice by the National Center on Police and Community Relations at the School of Police Administration and Public Safety of Michigan State University. Questionnaires were sent to the police departments in all cities with populations of over 100,000; a 10-percent sample of cities between 25,000 and 100,000 population; the 30 most populous counties; and all State police agencies. Separate questionnaires were sent to approximately a half-dozen civic and minority group leaders knowledgeable in police-community relations in the same cities; visitations of 1 or 2 weeks at a time were made by teams with 1 to 3 men to 12 medium and large cities, 2 rural counties, and 2 State agencies. In addition, there was a review of the police-community relations literature and a reliance on the Institute's extensive experience concerning other localities throughout the country.

[20] *Supra* note 15, at table 8—2.

[21] *Supra* note 15, at table 8—3.

	White annual income		Nonwhite annual income	
	$0 to $2,999	$6,000 to $9,000	$0 to $2,999	$6,000 to $9,000
Males:	Percent	Percent	Percent	Percent
Police very good	56	67	34	31
Police not so good	4	4	22	6
Females:				
Police very good	62	66	28	41
Police not so good	3	1	12	45

.   .   .   .   .

The Commission's studies of police-community relations in 11 localities throughout the country showed serious problems of Negro hostility to the police in virtually all medium and large cities. In short, as the Philadelphia Urban League's 1965 report states, "many Negroes see the police as their enemies; and they see them as protectors of white people, not as protectors of Negroes as well."[22]

. . . The NORC survey disclosed that sharp differences exist as to how citizens view police honesty. About two-thirds of whites but only one-third of Negroes thought the police to be "almost all honest;" less than 2 percent of whites thought that they were "almost all corrupt" in comparison to 10 percent of nonwhites.[23] A Louis Harris poll in 1966 found that approximately 15 percent of Negroes (almost four times as many as whites) believed that many police officers in their communities took bribes.[24] A survey in St. Louis found that 46 percent of Negroes in contrast to 24 percent of whites believed that "dishonesty is one of the characteristics of many of our city police."[25]

. . . Although surveys disclose that Negroes are substantially more hostile to the police than whites, Negroes also feel strongly about the need for police protection. This is not surprising since a much greater proportion of Negroes than whites are the victims, as well as perpetrators, of crime. For example, in Watts, of the 41 percent of Negroes who believed that the police are doing a "not so good" or "poor" job (47 percent thought that the police were doing an "excellent or pretty good job"), many cited lack of adequate protection as the basis of their opinion rather than brutality, discourtesy, or discrimination.[26] The Cincinnati survey of junior high school students showed that 83 percent of the Negro boys agreed that "without police there would be crime everywhere."[27] . . .

[22] Philadelphia Urban League, *Year-End Report; 1965* cited in *supra* note 19, at p. 16.
[23] *Supra* note 15, at table 8—4.
[24] Louis Harris, "Eye-for-an-Eye Rule Rejected," *The Washington Post,* July 3, 1966, sec. E, p. 3–3, col. 5.
[25] *Supra* note 13, at p. 101.
[26] John F. Kraft, Inc., *Attitudes of Negroes in Various Cities* (New York: John F. Kraft, Inc., 1966), pp. 25–26. Report prepared for the Senate Subcommittee on Executive Reorganization.
[27] Robert G. Portune, *Attitudes of Junior High School Pupils Toward Police Officers* (University of Cincinnati, 1966), p. 2.

OTHER MINORITY GROUPS

The American Negro is not the only minority group which expresses hostility toward the police. The Michigan State University survey found that Latin Americans also tend to "look upon the police as enemies who protect only the white power structure."[28] The University of California survey in Philadelphia found that some Puerto Rican leaders felt even more alienated from the police department than did Negroes.[29] Such findings are consistent with the evidence provided by the 1966 riots among Puerto Ricans in Chicago and Perth Amboy, N.J., disturbances which were started by conflicts with the police and were followed by expression of community problems relating to the police.

Both the University of California and Michigan State University surveys revealed that relations between Mexican-Americans and the police in San Diego and other western cities could be improved.[30] A survey in Los Angeles found that Mexican-Americans were generally less negative toward the police than Negroes but considerably more so than whites, as the following figures show:[31]

	One of the very best police departments in the country	Definitely below standard in comparison with other police departments
	Percent	Percent
Whites	30	8.5
Mexican-Americans	22.8	14.5
Negroes	14.4	20.3
	Police always respect constitutional rights of suspected criminals	Police often conscienceless and brutal in performing duties
	Percent	Percent
Whites	34.8	11.1
Mexican-Americans	21.2	44.4
Negroes	12.1	38.2

YOUTH

Tension also exists between the police and youth generally. For example, responses to the following question in a 1965 Gallup poll showed significant differences based on age:[32]

> How much respect do you have for the police in your area—a great deal, some, or hardly any?

[28] *Supra* note 19, at p. 30.
[29] *Supra* note 18, at vol. II, p. 106.
[30] *Supra* note 18, at vol. I, p. 92; and *supra* note 19, at pp. 12, 30.
[31] G. Douglas Gourley, *Public Relations and the Police* (Springfield: Charles C. Thomas, 1953), pp. 75–76.
[32] *Supra* note 16, at p. 13.

Age	A great deal	Some	Hardly any	Don't know
	Percent	Percent	Percent	Percent
20–29	57	31	8	4
60–69	76	19	2	3

A recent survey among junior high school students in Cincinnati showed that only 44 percent of white boys disagreed with the statement that the "police accuse you of things you didn't do"; only 54 percent disagreed that the "police try to act big shot" and that the "police try to get smart with you when you ask a question." The favorable answers by white girls were approximately 12 to 16 percent greater.[33]

THE POOR

Two recent polls show that the poor have generally less favorable attitudes toward the police than more affluent citizens. The NORC survey showed, as to the effectiveness of the police in enforcing the laws, the following attitudes of white males broken down by income levels:[34]

Annual income	$0 to $2,999	$3,000 to $5,999	$6,000 to $9,999	Above $10,000
	Percent	Percent	Percent	Percent
Excellent	17	25	24	32
Good	49	43	47	41
Fair	24	25	22	23
Poor	10	7	7	4

A 1965 Gallup poll obtained the following responses to this question:[35]

> How much respect do you have for the police in your area—a great deal, some, or hardly any?

	A great deal	Hardly any
	Percent	Percent
Under $3,000 a year	65	6
Above $10,000 a year	75	2

Sixteen percent of those earning under $3,000 thought that there was police brutality in their area, while only 8 percent of those earning more than $10,000 believed so.[36]

[33] *Supra* note 27, at p. 2.
[34] *Supra* note 15, at table 8–1.
[35] *Supra* note 16, at p. 15.
[36] *Id.* at p. 22.

Police Programs Directly Related to
Community Relations

. . . In this section three main techniques at present employed by police departments to work with the community are analyzed: (1) police-community relations unites, (2) citizen advisory committees, and (3) special programs which bring the police into continuing contact with the community. . . .

POLICE-COMMUNITY RELATIONS UNITS

Although the Commission's surveys clearly indicate that most police departments are keenly aware of serious community relations problems, they have been slow to institute programs to confront them. A 1964 survey conducted by the International Association of Chiefs of Police and the United States Conference of Mayors found that only 46 of 165 cities either with populations over 100,000, or with more than 30,000 population and 5 percent nonwhite population, had extensive community relations programs; of these only 37 had a community relations unit within the department.[37] . . .

In the last few years there has been some progress. In several major departments community relations units have been established.[38] The need for such a unit or its expansion has often been recognized after a major disorder, as in Watts, or after an inflammatory racial incident, as in Seattle.[39] Nevertheless, the 1966 Michigan State University survey showed that only 38 percent of the cities over 100,000 population had a community relations unit.[40]

.   .   .   .   .

. . . [B]oth the Michigan State University and the University of California studies found that community relations units have not generally won the confidence of minority groups. Individual community relations officers have often been liked and respected by minority leaders. But the units have usually been known only to a small proportion of the minority community and then generally only to the middle class. Those who respect the officers of the unit have generally seen them as distinct from the department and as having little support from it. This belief is often confirmed by the unit's lack of influence and prestige within the department itself.[41]

.   .   .   .   .

[37] International Association of Chiefs of Police and United States Conference of Mayors, *Police-Community Relations Policies and Practices* (Washington: IACP, 1965), p. 9.

[38] *Supra* note 19, at p. 6.

[39] Los Angeles Police Department, Memorandum No. 27, Sept. 28, 1965; *New York Times,* July 24, 1966, p. 45, col. 6.

[40] *Supra* note 19, at p. 60.

[41] *Supra* note 19, at pp. 62–63, 67–68; *supra* note 18, at vol. I, pp. 56–59, and vol. II, pp. 65, 286.

A commonly accepted function of community relations units is working with citizen groups—sending speakers to such groups, participating in their programs, and listening to their grievances. Over 95 percent of the units responding to the Michigan State survey were involved in such efforts. In addition, in more than 62 percent of the units, the community relations staff ran school programs in order to develop friendly relationships with and give a positive police image to the children in the community.[42] Units also run or conduct a variety of other programs including neighborhood advisory committees, police-community relations institutes, and tours of police stations.

.   .   .   .   .

One of the fundamental purposes of a community relations unit is to prevent, if possible, situations of high tension between the police and community residents, and to help deal with such situations when they occur.

.   .   .   .   .

The Michigan State survey found that community relations officers are generally not picked on the basis of the best man for community relations; instead, they are often selected on the same criteria as line officers.[43]

CITIZEN ADVISORY COMMITTEES

Police departments must become increasingly aware that isolation from the neighborhoods they protect can interfere with good policing, as well as with good police-community relations. . . . Perhaps the most promising mechanism that has evolved for this purpose is the police advisory committee. Yet a 1964 survey by the International Association of Chiefs of Police and United States Conference of Mayors found that of the 165 reporting cities with over 100,000 population, or between 30,000 and 100,000 population with more than 5 percent nonwhite population, only 8 had organized precinct committees and only 19 a citywide committee.[44] Since that time, however, a number of other cities have initiated such committees.

The advisory committees take different forms in different places. Basically they consist of groups of citizens, usually formed, under police auspices, to discuss policing problems. They have no formal authority, but act as advisers to the department leaders.

.   .   .   .   .

According to the Michigan State survey, most neighborhood advisory committees consist mainly of businessmen, civic organization leaders, clergymen, and other people whose "stake in the community" is readily apparent.[45] Generally, membership includes only those persons who agree with the police or otherwise do not cause trouble.[46] It is doubtful that such

[42] *Supra* note 19, at p. 90b.
[43] *Supra* note 19, at pp. 74–75.
[44] *Supra* note 37, at p. 9.
[45] *Supra* note 19, at p. 70.
[46] *Id.* at p. 72.

persons are representative of those who are hostile to the police or that they are even cognizant or sympathetic to citizen grievances. The study found that "all current programs (surveyed) have failed to reach the very segments which are in conflict" with the police or other "grassroots" people.[47]

. . . . .

At present, the meetings of most citizens committees include little frank and open discussion of controversial police policies; more typically they feature explanatory talks concerning crime conditions in the area and other noncontroversial subjects. The introduction of controversial topics by citizens was generally discouraged in meetings which were attended during the Michigan State survey. In one city, when such issues as stop-and-frisk were raised, the questions were met with the adamant refusal of the police to discuss them.[48] In another meeting, the commander became defensive whenever police practices were questioned and changed the subject. The citizens did not express their true feelings because, as one later said, it "is useless for the police become hostile, and [they are] not really interested in listening."[49] The study concluded that while the program looked good on paper and was widely so regarded, it did not really open communication with persons hostile to the police.[50]

. . . . .

SPECIAL POLICE-COMMUNITY RELATIONS PROGRAMS

Besides citizen advisory committees, existing community relations activities normally are of three types: programs to educate the public concerning some aspects of police work, programs to prevent crimes, and programs to provide services other than law enforcement to the community. These programs may be run by community relations units, advisory committees, public information officers, juvenile squads, or line officers.

. . . . .

Most police departments (95 percent in the Michigan State survey) readily accept speaking invitations to appear before civic organizations.[51] Many run a speaker's bureau with a list of officers who can speak on specialized subjects such as narcotics, the canine corps, or traffic control. . . .

The Michigan State survey found, however, that the speakers are not always chosen to fit the level of sophistication of the group.[52] Too often the topics offered are noncontroversial, and, if important, constitute merely a recitation of a department's outstanding programs. The survey found that

---

[47] *Supra* note 19, at p. 91.
[48] *Id*. at p. 72.
[49] *Id*. at p. 71.
[50] *Id*. at p. 72.
[51] *Id*. at p. 88.
[52] *Id*. at p. 89.

many of the speakers were hesitant to engage in debate on police policies or to acknowledge possible departmental error.[53]

.   .   .   .   .

Personnel

The characteristics of personnel within a police department have a direct bearing upon police-community relations. If, for example, police departments hire officers who are prejudiced against minority groups or who do not understand minority group problems, serious conflicts will develop. And if police departments, through their hiring or promotion policies, indicate that they have little interest in hiring minority group officers, the minority community is not likely to be sympathetic toward the police.

.   .   .   .   .

If educational standards are raised . . . [they] should have a significant, positive long-term effect on community relations. Police personnel with two to four years of college education should have a better appreciation of people with different racial, economic, and cultural backgrounds or, at the least, should have the innate ability to acquire such understanding. Studies support the proposition that well-educated persons are less prejudiced toward minority groups than the poorly educated.[54]

.   .   .   .   .

Few police departments have yet devised systematic methods for screening out biased officers. In one Commission study of police practices in several large northern cities, it was found that a large proportion of officers expressed strong racial prejudice to neutral observers; and the Michigan state survey similarly found that officers often show prejudice in private references to minority groups.[55] Further, a study of juvenile officers in a western police force of particularly high standards found that 18 of 27 officers openly admitted a dislike of Negroes, attributing their attitude to experience as police officers, and another study of officers generally in that city found that "hostile feelings toward the Negro are characteristic of policemen in general. . . ."[56] And a survey of Philadelphia policemen, made in the 1950's, found that over 59 percent of white patrolmen said they would object to riding with Negro officers in a patrol car, and over one-third said

[53] *Id.* at p. 89; *supra* note 18, at vol. I, pp. 41–46.

[54] See Robin M. Williams, Jr., *Strangers Next Door: Ethnic Relations in American Communities* (Englewood Cliffs: Prentice-Hall, Inc., 1964), p. 54.

[55] *Supra* note 19, at p. 341; Donald J. Black and Albert J. Riess, Jr., *Patterns of Behavior in Police and Citizen Transactions* (Ann Arbor: University of Michigan, 1967), table 25, report prepared for the President's Commission on Law Enforcement and the Administration of Justice.

[56] Irving Piliavin and Scott Briar, "Police Encounters with Juveniles," *American Journal of Sociology*, 70: 206–214, 212; *supra* note 10, on p. 82.

that they would object to taking orders from a Negro sergeant or captain.[57] The same survey found that some Negro officers were extremely hostile to Negro offenders and have emotions of shame, indignation, and disgrace concerning Negro crime.[58]

Whatever bias an officer has when he joins the force, without adequate training it will often get worse. Officers see the worst side of life and, in view of the higher crime rate, especially the worst side of the ghetto. As a result, their stereotypes of Negroes, as well as of other minority groups, may be strengthened. And such prejudices are likely to become increased by virtue of the large number of other officers who express prejudice.[59]

. . . . .

The study of a western police department found that racial prejudice did not have any apparent effect as to some assignments. In other assignments, however, including patrol, it had an effect such as in treatment of Negroes as suspects on the basis of a vague description.[60] A study of patrolmen in one city also found that these patrolmen stopped and interrogated Negroes more frequently than other youths, often even in the absence of evidence that an offense had been committed, and Negroes usually received more severe dispositions by the officer for the same violations. One reason for this difference in treatment was long-held prejudice on the part of the individual officer.[61] The Commission's studies in several northern cities, however, found no discriminatory treatment against Negroes in comparison to whites of the same economic level; indeed, if anything, low-income whites received slightly more severe treatment.[62]

. . . . .

The Commission's study of police procedures in several large cities found that often men who were acknowledged as among a department's worst were assigned to police minority group neighborhoods. In fact, such assignments have sometimes been given as punishment, a kind of exile.[63]

. . . . .

[The community service officer] could make a major contribution to police-community relations. . . . Since many community service officers

---

[57] William M. Kephart, *Racial Factors and Urban Law Enforcement* (Philadelphia: University of Pennsylvania Press, 1957), pp. 185, 187. The University of California, while making no detailed survey, surmised that prejudice among Philadelphia's police officers had somewhat declined in recent years. *Supra* note 18, at vol. II, pp. 192–193.

[58] *Ibid.* at p. 118.

[59] *Supra* note 54, at pp. 96, 345–348.

[60] *Supra* note 10, at pp. 83–87.

[61] *Supra* note 56, at p. 212.

[62] Donald J. Black and Albert J. Reiss, Jr., *Police and Citizen Behavior in Field Encounters: Some Comparisons According to the Race and Social Class Status of Citizens* (Ann Arbor: University of Michigan, 1966), p. 10, report prepared for the President's Commission on Law Enforcement and Administration of Justice. This report is a preliminary draft which is being included with the Commission's records in the National Archives. It is presently being revised by the University of Michigan and will be embodied in research studies to be published by the Commission.

[63] *Supra* note 18, at vol. II, pp. 162, 191.

would be drawn from minority groups, this would make a substantial contribution to increasing the percentage of minority employees on the force.

· · · · ·

The very presence of a predominantly white police force in a Negro community can serve as a dangerous irritant. . . . In neighborhoods filled with people suffering from a sense of social injustice and exclusion, many residents will reach the conclusion that the neighborhood is being policed not for the purpose of maintaining law and order but for the purpose of maintaining the status quo.

· · · · ·

Police officers have testified to the special competence of Negro officers in Negro neighborhoods. For example, while a study in Philadelphia found that commanding officers were divided as to whether Negro policemen are more effective in Negro neighborhoods than white policemen, more than three-fourths of the patrolmen thought that Negro policemen did better jobs. The reasons given include: they get along better with, and receive more respect from, the Negro residents; they can get more information; and they understand Negro citizens better.[64]

· · · · ·

Police forces generally rely heavily upon referrals from their own members as a source for qualified recruits. . . . Since relatively few police officers are from minority groups, referrals are an inadequate source of minority group candidates. Consequently, new recruiting techniques must be developed.

· · · · ·

In addition, no recruiting drive can succeed as long as police departments discriminate against their own minority officers. In some police departments the legal powers vested in an officer depend on whether he is white or Negro. For example, a 1961 survey found that 28 police departments (31 percent of those surveyed) restricted the right of Negroes to make felony arrests. In 18 of the departments, the officer could hold a white suspect until a white policeman appeared; if none was available, the Negro officer could make the felony arrest. In 10 others, the Negro officer could not arrest a white suspect at all, although 3 required the Negro policeman to keep the suspect under surveillance. The power of Negro officers to arrest for misdemeanors was even more limited.[65]

· · · · ·

Certain selection standards may have the unintended effect of arbitrarily barring large numbers of minority group applicants who could adequately perform police work. For example, minimum height restrictions prevent many Puerto Ricans, Mexican-Americans, and Orientals from joining police

[64] *Supra* note 57, at pp. 44–45, 59–61, 83–85.
[65] U.S. Civil Rights Commission, *Administration of Justice Staff Report* (Washington: U.S. Government Printing Office, 1963), chapter 11, p. 26.

forces. The minimum height requirement was recently changed in Chicago from 5 feet 8 inches to 5 feet 7 inches, in part because of the need to recruit Puerto Ricans. Similarly, restrictions on flat feet and other physical defects have barred many Negroes; eyesight problems, many Oriental-Americans.[66] . . .

Careful consideration should also be given to the evaluation of applicants' criminal records. Young men who have grown up in poor and particularly minority group neighborhoods run a very great risk of acquiring a police record.[67] In such circumstances, arrest records or conviction of a minor offense does not necessarily mean that the applicant is irresponsible or of poor character.

.   .   .   .   .

Increasing the number of ranking officers from minority groups is as important as, and closely related to, recruiting new officers of minority group background.

.   .   .   .   .

The 1962 survey of the Civil Rights Commission of localities with a Negro population of over 5,000 showed that Negroes were still seriously underrepresented at command and supervisory levels.[68]

.   .   .   .   .

. . . [D]iscrimination is practiced against minority group officers, perhaps more in promotion than in recruitment. The promotion in some police departments of one or two Negroes to relatively high rank is often only a token show of nondiscrimination.[69] The Michigan State survey found, in a number of police departments, that Negro officers are discouraged from taking promotion examinations.[70]

.   .   .   .   .

While it is not clear how much of this discrimination still exists, Negro officers have been discriminated against in the South by being assigned to separate precincts and divisions[71] and throughout the country in assignments to foot patrols rather than to cars and to desk jobs. . . . The Civil Rights Commission survey in 1962 showed that of the 68 non-Southern counties with Negro deputies, in 18 all field patrols were white, and Negro deputies were given other jobs to do.[72]

.   .   .   .   .

Segregation presently exists in patrol assignments in many departments. A recent survey showed that, of 165 cities either with populations over

---

[66] *Supra* note 19, at pp. 277–279.

[67] For example, a study of Baltimore in 1939 to 1942 found that in almost all Negro areas, more than 20 percent of the boys between 10 and 15 had been before a juvenile court and in many areas the percentage was over 70 percent. Forty percent of Negro boys aged 14 and 15 came before the court. Bernard Lander, *Toward an Understanding of Juvenile Delinquency* (New York: Columbia University Press, 1954), pp. 20, 32.

[68] *Supra* note 65, at chapter 11, p. 17.

[69] *Supra* note 19, at p. 270.

[70] *Supra* note 65, at chapter 11, pp. 18–19.

[71] See, e.g., *supra* note 65, at chapter 11, pp. 29–30.

[72] *Supra* note 65, at chapter 12, p. 11.

100,000 or with populations of between 30,000 and 100,000 but with 5 percent nonwhites, 4 never assigned Negro and white officers together, 40 did so only for special details, 54 did so occasionally, and 74 did so "generally."[73] The Michigan State survey found that of the eight departments in the South responding, three used integrated patrols. In contrast, outside the South, 19 of 26 departments used at least some integrated patrols.[74]

These figures, however, overstate the amount of real integration. Where, for instance, the composition of patrols or teams has been left to the voluntary choices of the individuals involved, the result has usually been mostly all-white and all-Negro teams.[75]

. . . . .

The mere lack of contact between white and minority group officers on the force will make other measures to end prejudice and discrimination less effective. Studies of prejudice show that stereotypes tend to be modified and prejudices reduced when whites have contacts with Negroes on an equal footing.[76] As a white police officer told the Philadelphia study, "When somebody's shooting at you, it doesn't matter what color you are."[77] The same study found that the more white officers worked with Negro policemen, the less they were prejudiced against them.[78]

. . . . .

On the other hand, the significantly disproportionate assignment of most minority officers to minority neighborhoods raises the appearance of segregation which would be as harmful as segregated patrols, teams, or units.

POLICE FIELD PRACTICES

. . . Although many allegations of police misconduct or discriminatory treatment are unwarranted, Commission surveys reveal that police practices exist which cannot be justified. For example, the Commission found that abusive treatment of minority groups and the poor continues to occur. Many established police policies—such as the use of arrests for investigative purposes—alienate the community and have no legal basis. Departments may utilize procedures, such as the use of dogs to control crowds, without balancing the potential harm to police-community relations. And some valuable law enforcement techniques, like field interrogation, are frequently abused to the detriment of community relations. Too few departments give necessary guidance to assist their personnel in resolving potentially explosive social and criminal problems.

. . . . .

[73] *Supra* note 37, at p. 9.
[74] *Supra* note 19, at p. 284.
[75] *Id.* at p. 261.
[76] *Supra* note 54, at pp. 156–159, 167–168, 185, 191, 217, 220.
[77] *Supra* note 57, at pp. 71–72.
[78] *Ibid.* at pp. 98–99, 188–189.

Commission studies reveal that there are abuses in some cities which range from simple discourtesy to clearly unwarranted excessive use of force against persons of all ages. . . .

No matter is more important to police-community relations than the manner in which police officers talk to people on the street. The Michigan State survey found that while allegations of excessive physical force receive the most attention, verbal abuse and discourtesy were probably greater irritants to community relations.[79] . . .

Commission surveys revealed that a number of officers treat citizens in a demeaning manner. In one Commission study, observations were made in several cities of several hundred routine contacts between police and citizens, usually in a home or on the street. Most of the persons interviewed were witnesses, bystanders, and victims, rather than suspects. The study showed 9 percent of the persons received a polite request from the officers; 5 percent received an impersonal summons which was neither polite nor nasty; 66 percent were interrogated without introduction; and 15 percent of the interrogations began with a brusque or nasty command like "Come 'ere, punk" or "Get your * * * over here, pork chop."[80]

Discriminatory statements, in particular, produce both anger and strong counterprejudice among minority groups.[81] The use of racial epithets, such as "nigger," "coon," "boy," and "Panch" appears to be widespread, even though their use is condemned by responsible police administrators. The President's Commission on Crime in the District of Columbia found that "offensive terms such as 'boy' or 'nigger' are too often used by officers of the Department" and that "in most cases, the language is chosen deliberately to demean the citizen and demonstrate the superiority of the officer."[82] . . . It is precisely this type of language which solidifies the conflict between minority groups and the police.

. . . [P]olice officers should be encouraged to talk to citizens about nonpolice matters while on duty, as they are in New York, rather than prohibited from conducting such conversations with citizens.[83] The BSSR survey of three Washington, D.C., precincts shows that hostility in Negro males declines as informal contacts with the police increase.[84]

. . . . .

The Commission believes that physical abuse is not as serious a problem as it was in the past. The few statistics which do exist suggest small

---

[79] *Supra* note 19, at p. 17.
[80] *Supra* note 62, at table 14.
[81] *Supra* note 54, at pp. 46–48, 253, 257–258, 283, 301.
[82] President's Commission on Crime in the District of Columbia, *Report of the Metropolitan Police Department* (Washington: U.S. Government Printing Office, 1966), pp. 66–67. The report of this Commission resulted in a reorganization of the department.
[83] Thomas A. Johnson, "New Police Plan Used on Crowds," *New York Times*, July 25, 1966, p. 16, col. 1.
[84] For a similar result, see Donald Lowell Johns, "A Study of Some Factors Related to the Formation of Attitudes Toward the Police" (unpublished master's thesis, University of California at Berkeley, School of Criminology, 1966), pp. 122, 144.

numbers of cases involving excessive use of force.[85] . . . It is clear, however, that excessive force remains a serious problem in parts of the South. . . . Moreover, one study undertaken by the Commission also determined that excessive use of force still remains as a significant problem outside the South as well. During this study, Commission observers systematically accompanied police officers on regular patrol in a number of major cities—primarily in high crime and slum precincts—for periods ranging from 5 to 8 weeks. During the survey, observers witnessed, during 850 8-hour patrols, 5,339 police-citizen encounters—encounters which included police contacts with suspects, witnesses, victims, and bystanders. While watching these encounters, Commission observers reported that there were 20 instances where officers used force where none was clearly required or where its use was plainly excessive. Of the incidents observed, most did not appear to be based upon racial prejudice. More than half of those subjected to excessive force were white. Almost all of the victims appeared to be poor. They included drunks, sexual deviates, or juveniles who were regarded by the police as hoodlums, and most appeared to contest verbally the police officer's authority.[86]

. . . . .

A survey of policemen in one midwestern city in 1951 also indicated that many officers had misconceptions about when they are justified in using force. Officers were asked to respond to this question: "When do you think a policeman is justified in roughing a man up?" They gave the following responses:[87]

Reason	Percentage
Disrespect for police	37
To obtain information	19
For the hardened criminal	7
When you know the man is guilty	3
For sex criminals	3
When impossible to avoid	23
To make an arrest	8

[85] In the fiscal year 1965, FBI statistics show that there were only 9 convictions out of 1,787 cases of excessive force investigated and in fiscal 1966 there were 1,671 excessive force complaints investigated and only 3 resulted in convictions. These data were provided by Jerome Daunt, Chief, Uniform Crime Reporting Section, FBI, Mar. 7, 1967.

[86] Albert J. Reiss, Jr., *The Use of Physical Force in Police Work* (Ann Arbor: University of Michigan, 1966), pp. 16–17, report prepared for the President's Commission on Law Enforcement and Administration of Justice.

[87] William A. Westley, "Violence and the Police," *American Journal of Sociology,* 59: 34–41, 38, as quoted in Carl Werthman and Irving Piliavin, "Gang Members and the Police," in David Bordua, ed., *The Police* (New York: John Wiley & Sons, Inc., 1967). Only one reason was counted—either that first mentioned or that given most heatedly or at greatest length—for each officer. Dr. Westley believed that the officers were cautious with him because of recent criticisms by the Chief of Police and the community about the use of violence.

The interviews provided considerable detail concerning the officers' rationale. They believed that the use of force to obtain evidence which would justify an arrest in a felony case was acceptable—"to rough him up a little, up to a point * * * You feel that the end justifies the means."[88] Force was seen to be permissible with sex criminals when the officer knew that a person was guilty, did not have enough evidence, and considered it necessary to ensure that the criminal was punished. The officers said that force was justified in cases involving disrespect such as:[89]

> I was on the beat, and I was taking [a man] down to the station. There were people following us. He kept saying that I wasn't in the army. Well, he kept going on like that, and I finally had to bust him one. I had to do it. The people would have thought I was afraid otherwise.

The officers believed that the only way to treat certain groups of people, including Negroes and the poor, is to treat them roughly.[90] On the other hand, this study did conclude that illegal force was not used as frequently and with as little provocation as the officers' statements would suggest.

The University of California study found that members of minority groups in Philadelphia and San Diego generally believed that discrimination is practiced against both middle class and poor persons from minority groups.[91] Polls of minority groups show similar results.[92] It is extremely difficult to establish the extent to which such allegations are accurate since discrimination is likely to be only one of several factors which affect an officer's decision in any particular situation. Negroes, other minority groups, and the poor are arrested and probably stopped in disproportion to their numbers. However, these groups frequently live in high-crime areas. Consequently, normal, completely fair police work would doubtless produce the arrest or stopping of larger numbers of these groups.

Two studies of referrals to juvenile courts in several cities found that the police referred significantly more Negro than white juveniles for the same types of offenses, particularly for minor offenses.[93] Another study of police handling of juveniles in two large cities found that the eastern, nonprofessional police force referred three times as many Negro juveniles to court as

---

[88] *Id.* at p. 36.
[89] *Id.* at p. 39.
[90] *Id.* at p. 40.
[91] *Supra* note 18, at vol. I, 78, 107; vol. II, 105, 153.
[92] Bureau of Social Science Research, "Salient Findings on Crime and Attitudes Toward Law Enforcement in the District of Columbia" (a preliminary technical report submitted to the U.S. Department of Justice, Office of Law Enforcement Assistance, 1966), p. 13B.
[93] Nathan Goldman, *The Differential Selection of Juvenile Offenders for Court Appearances* (Washington: National Council on Crime and Delinquency, 1963), pp. 42–44, 57–58, 65–67, 73–75, 88–89; *supra* note 56 at p. 212.

whites. On the other hand, the western, more professional police force tended to treat similar types of offenders alike.[94] And the Commission's study, based on observation of routine police work in several northern cities, found that the police did not discriminate between whites and Negroes of the same economic class; instead, police conduct seemed to depend on economic status and on whether the person was a drunk, a homosexual, or otherwise an outcast.[95]

. . . . .

RECEPTION OF COMPLAINTS

Since citizen complaints are extremely important to police departments, efforts should be made to encourage citizens with grievances to file them. Unfortunately, police officers and departments often regard a citizen complaint as an attack on the police as a whole rather than a complaint against an individual officer.[96] The discouraging of citizen complaints not only deprives a department of valuable information but also convinces the public that the kinds of practices complained about are condoned or even expected.

. . . . .

Complaint Investigations

Although 90 percent of police departments surveyed by Michigan State and the National League of Cities now require an investigation of all citizen complaints, many forces do not have a designated special unit for dealing with complaints. Those forces lacking such units in the survey group tended to be state police organizations, departments in cities below 75,000 population, and Southern departments. But there were some larger cities as well. The following tabulation shows the means available in departments for processing citizen complaints:[97]

	Michigan State Survey N=57		National League of Cities Survey N=395	
	Number	Percent	Number	Percent
No special unit	27	47.3	114	28.8
Special unit	29	50.8	191	48.3
No answer or other	1	1.7	90	22.8

. . . . .

[94] James Q. Wilson, "The Police and the Delinquent in Two Cities" (unpublished report), pp. 9–10, 29–30.

[95] Werthman and Piliavin, *supra* note 87; *supra* note 62, at pp. 9–10, 14–17.

[96] *Supra* note 18, vol. I, 153–154; vol. II, 100, 187.

[97] *Supra* note 19, at p. 194. The National League of Cities data are from its Department of Urban Studies.

The Michigan State survey concluded that "probably the strongest criticism that can be offered is that seldom is meaningful disciplinary action taken against officers guilty of one or more of the forms of brutality."[98]

Police Integrity

The violations in which police are involved vary widely in character. The most common are improper political influence; acceptance of gratuities or bribes in exchange for nonenforcement of laws, particularly those relating to gambling, prostitution, and liquor offenses, which are often extensively interconnected with organized crime; the "fixing" of traffic tickets; minor thefts; and occasional burglaries. The Commission's work also revealed some instances of police officers in high-crime neighborhoods engaging in such practices as rolling drunks and shake-downs of money and merchandise in the very places where respect for law is so badly needed.

. . . . .

It is the police themselves, in the vast majority of cases, who are ridding their profession of the unethical and the corrupt.

. . . . .

There are a number of specific directions in which action to ensure integrity should be taken.

. . . . .

Political accountability of the police should be resolved solely at the executive level. The police chief should be responsible to only one executive, and not to minor officials.

. . . . .

Police departments should establish policies that outline in detail proper and improper police practices.

. . . . .

Internal investigation units should be established in all medium-sized and large police departments. These should serve in the dual role of general intelligence and investigation of specific reported cases of police misconduct.

. . . . .

Officers should be taught the importance of ethics in law enforcement.

Implementation Through State Commissions on Police Standards

A state Commission on Police Standards can do much to improve local law enforcement. Without removing control of law enforcement from local agencies, a Commission can help to establish adequate personnel selection

[98] *Supra* note 19, at p. 186.

standards, to strengthen training procedures, to coordinate recruitment, and to improve the organization and operation of local departments.

> [*The President's Commission on Law Enforcement and Administration of Justice,* Task Force Report: The Police (*Washington:* U.S. Government Printing Office, 1967), pp. 1, 3, 7, 11, 13–14, 16–19, 21–33, 42–45, 48, 68, 70–73, 95–96, 120–133, 144–198, 208, 221.]

12 *The courts*

The courts are the pivot on which the criminal justice system turns. Two decisions the courts make are crucial to the criminal process: whether a person is to be convicted of a crime, and what is to be done with him if he is. The courts have great power over the lives of the people brought before them. At the same time the limits of this power are carefully laid out by the Constitution, by statute, and by elaborate procedural rules, for the courts are charged not only with convicting the guilty but with protecting the innocent. Maintaining a proper balance between effectiveness and fairness has always been a challenge to the courts. In a time of increasing crime, increasing social unrest, and increasing public sensitivity to both, it is a particularly difficult challenge. An inquiry into the performance of America's criminal courts, therefore, must of necessity examine both their effectiveness and their fairness, and proposals for improving their operations must aim at maintaining or redressing the essential equilibrium between those two qualities.

This report does not purport to be a comprehensive survey of American criminal courts or of the activities of the men and women who work in and around them: judges, prosecutors, defense counsel, probation officers, and other court officials. On the contrary, it confines itself to those parts of the court system and those aspects of the criminal process that the Commission has found to be the most in need of reform. It dwells at length on urban courts and their problems and particularly on urban lower courts. It is in the cities that crime rates are highest. It is in the cities that poor and ignorant defendants who most need protection are concentrated. It is in the cities that courts have so enormous a volume of cases that they are able neither to mete out prompt and certain justice nor to give defendants the full protection that they should have.

The report considers in detail two important nontrial aspects of the criminal process: the prosecutor's charge decision and the negotiated plea of guilty. These administrative and largely invisible procedures now determine the disposition of a majority of criminal cases in many courts, particularly in the cities. The report analyzes the sentencing decision, the laws under which it is made, the procedures by which it is made, and the training of the men who make it. It discusses the problems relating to pretrial release of persons accused of crime. It explores such subjects as structural reorganization of the courts, methods for scheduling cases and ensuring that they proceed expeditiously, and the treatment of jurors and witnesses. It recognizes the importance of reform of the substantive criminal law and the inherent limits of effective law enforcement.

Finally, the report reflects the Commission's finding that a major need of many courts is more manpower, and a major need of all courts is better qualified, better trained personnel. It examines, therefore, the selection and training of judges and prosecutors. And since there is no doubt that during the next few years the most pressing manpower need by far will be for defense counsel, it considers with special care what defense counsel will be doing in years to come and how they should be recruited and trained.

Disposition Without Trial

Much of the basic legal structure of the criminal process rests on the assumption that criminal cases initiated by the police will be decided in a trial by court or by jury. Limited statistical data and a number of studies, including those recently conducted by the American Bar Foundation,[1] by the Commission staff, and by others,[2] indicate that this assumption is not justified.

Most cases are disposed of outside the traditional trial process, either by a decision not to charge a suspect with a criminal offense or by a plea of guilty. In many communities between one-third and one-half of the cases begun by arrest are disposed of by some form of dismissal by police, prosecutor, or judge.[3] When a decision is made to prosecute, it is estimated that in many courts as many as 90 percent of all convictions are obtained by guilty pleas.[4]

.   .   .   .   .

[1] The history of the American Bar Foundation Project, which commenced in 1953, is recounted in LaFave, *Arrest—The Decision to Take a Suspect into Custody* ix (1965). The discussion that follows draws heavily on the work of the American Bar Foundation Project, including Professor LaFave's book and another volume in the series, Newman, *Conviction—The Determination of Guilt or Innocence Without Trial* (1966), as well as manuscripts of several other volumes now in preparation.

[2] Staff Studies, *Administration of Justice in the Municipal Court of Baltimore* and *Administration of Justice in the Recorders' Court of Detroit,* printed in appendix B of President's Commission on Law Enforcement and Administration of Justice, *Task Force Report: The Courts* (Washington: U.S. Government Printing Office, 1967); Rubin, *Criminal Justice in a Metropolitan Court* (1966); President's Commission on Crime in the District of Columbia, *Report,* 1966, pp. 239–240.

[3] See, e.g., 1965 FBI *Uniform Crime Reports,* p. 103, table 12; California Department of Justice, *Crime and Delinquency in California* (1965), p. 53; 1964 *Illinois Superior Court Ann. Report,* p. 63; 1964–1965 *Administrative Director of the New Jersey Courts Ann. Report,* p. 13, table B–8.

[4] See p. 9 *infra.*

The Decision Whether to Bring Charges

Before a formal information or indictment is lodged in court, the prosecution has an opportunity to consider not only which charges to press but also whether to press toward conviction at all. The decision whether to file formal charges is a vitally important stage in the criminal process. It provides an opportunity to screen out cases in which the accused is apparently innocent, and it is at this stage that the prosecutor must decide in cases of apparent guilt whether criminal sanctions are appropriate.

.   .   .   .   .

The police have a similar decision to make earlier in the process, and they adopt varying responses to criminal conduct.[5] When serious criminal conduct is involved, the police objective will be arrest and full invocation of the criminal process. When less serious violations are involved, the police may ignore the situation (as in some instances of intoxication), or they may attempt on-the-scene conciliation (as in some instances of family disputes). Sometimes offenders are arrested and released (as may be true in the case of fights and brawls), and often referrals to social agencies are deemed appropriate (as in the case of some mentally disordered offenders).

But the police decision whether to arrest must usually be made hastily, without relevant background information, and often under pressure of a pending disturbance. There is ordinarily no opportunity for considered judgment until the time when formal charges must be filed, usually the next stage of the proceedings.

In some places particularly when less serious offenses are involved, the decision to press charges is made by the police or a magistrate rather than by the prosecutor. The better practice is for the prosecutor to make this decision, for the choice involves such factors as the sentencing alternatives available under the various possible charges, the substantiality of the case for prosecution, and limitations on prosecution resources—factors that the policeman often cannot consider and the magistrate cannot deal with fully while maintaining a judicial role.[6]

The legitimacy and necessity of the prosecutor's discretion in pressing charges have been long recognized.[7]

.   .   .   .   .

[5] See, e.g., LaFave, *op. cit supra* note 1; Skolnick, *Justice Without Trial—Law Enforcement in Democratic Society* (1966); Goldstein, "Police Discretion Not to Invoke the Criminal Process—Low-Visibility Decisions in the Administration of Justice," *Yale Law Journal*, 1960, 69:543. See also *Report of the Police Task Force* of the President's Commission on Law Enforcement and Administration of Justice, chapter 2.

[6] Cf. Ali, *Model Code of Pre-Arraignment Procedure*, Sec. 6.02 (Tentative Draft No. 1, 1966).

[7] "He [the prosecutor] must appraise the evidence on which an indictment may be demanded and the accused defendant tried, if he be indicted, and in that service must judge of its availability, competency, and probative significance. He must on occasion consider the public impact of criminal proceedings, or, again, balance the admonitory

When there is sufficient evidence of guilt, tactical considerations and law enforcement needs may make it inadvisable to press charges. Prosecutors may, for example, drop charges in exchange for a potential defendant's cooperation in giving information or testimony against a more serious offender. They may need to conserve their resources for more serious cases.

In some cases invocation of the criminal process against marginal offenders seems to do more harm than good. Labeling a person a criminal may set in motion a course of events which will increase the probability of his becoming or remaining one. The attachment of criminal status itself may be so prejudicial and irreversible as to ruin the future of a person who previously had successfuly made his way in the community, and it may foreclose legitimate opportunities for offenders already suffering from social, vocational, and educational disadvantages.[8] Yet a criminal code has no way of describing the difference between a petty thief who is on his way to becoming an armed robber and a petty thief who succumbs once to a momentary impulse. The same criminal conduct may be the deliberate act of a professional criminal or an isolated aberration in the behavior of a normally law-abiding person. The criminal conduct describes the existence of a problem, but not its nature or source. The system depends on prosecutors to recognize these distinctions when bringing charges.[9]

Among the types of cases in which thoughtful prosecutors commonly appear disinclined to seek criminal penalties are domestic disturbances; assaults and petty thefts in which victim and offender are in a family or social relationship; statutory rape when both boy and girl are young; first offense car thefts that involve teenagers taking a car for a short joyride; checks that are drawn upon insufficient funds; shoplifting by first offenders, particularly when restitution is made; and criminal acts that involve offenders suffering from emotional disorders short of legal insanity.

In addition, a large proportion of the cases in the criminal courts involve annoying or offensive behavior rather than dangerous crime.[10] Almost half of all arrests are on charges of drunkenness, disorderly conduct, minor assault, petty theft, and vagrancy. Many such offenders are burdened by economic, physical, mental, and educational disadvantages. In many of these cases effective law enforcement does not require prosecution.

---

value of invariable and inflexible punishment against the greater impulse of 'the quality of mercy.' He must determine what offenses, and whom, to prosecute. . . . Into these and many others of the problems committed to his informed discretion it would be sheer impertinence for a court to intrude. And such intrusion is contrary to the settled judicial tradition." *Howell v. Brown*, 85 F. Supp. 537, 540 (D. Nebraska 1949). See also *Pugach v. Klein*, 193 F. Supp. 630, 635 (S.D.N.Y. 1961); Kaplan, "The Prosecutorial Discretion—A Comment," *Northwestern University Law Review*, 1965, 60:174.

[8] See Goldstein, *supra* note 5, at p. 590 (appendix).

[9] Remington and Rosenblum, "The Criminal Law and the Legislative Process," *University of Illinois Law Review*, 1960, p. 481.

[10] 1965 FBI *Uniform Crime Reports*, pp. 110–111, table 19; General Report, President's Commission on Law Enforcement and Administration of Justice (Washington: U.S. Government Printing Office, 1967), chapter 2.

THE EXISTING SYSTEM

A major difficulty in the present system of nontrial dispositions is that when an offender is dropped out of the criminal process by dismissal of charges, he usually does not receive the help or treatment needed to prevent recurrence. A first offender discharged without prosecution in the expectation that his conduct will not be repeated typically is not sent to another agency; in fact, in most communities there are few agencies designed to deal with his problems. Whether mental illness, youth, or alcoholism is the mitigating factor, there rarely is any followup. In the struggle to reduce the number of cases that compete for attention, there is little time to consider the needs of those who are dropped out of the process.

.   .   .   .   .

In most places there is little liaison between the prosecutor and community agencies which could assist an offender. The prosecutor, frequently overworked, has difficulty searching out noncriminal dispositions, and it is open to question whether he is the appropriate official to perform this searching function. He may have few professional qualifications to decide what treatment alternatives are appropriate for particular offenders. Consultative services to analyze the offender's medical, psychiatric, and social situation; to consider that situation in light of available community resources; and to make appropriate recommendations are at best limited and in many places are not available. But the basic problem is that in many communities the resources for dealing with offenders and their problems are totally inadequate. The development of such resources is clearly essential.

.   .   .   .   .

The Negotiated Plea of Guilty

The question of guilt or innocence is not contested in the overwhelming majority of criminal cases. A recent estimate is that guilty pleas account for 90 percent of all convictions; and perhaps as high as 95 percent of misdemeanor convictions.[11] But the Commission has found it difficult to calculate with any degree of certainty the percentage of cases disposed of by guilty plea, since reliable statistical information is limited. Clearly it is very high. The following statistics [Table 1] indicate the number and percentage of guilty plea convictions in trial courts of general jurisdiction in States in which such information was available.

A substantial percentage of guilty pleas are the product of negotiations between the prosecutor and defense counsel or the accused, although again

[11] American Bar Association *Project on Minimum Standards for Criminal Justice, Pleas of Guilty* (Tentative Draft 1967), p. 1; Newman, *op. cit. supra* note 1, at p. 3, note 1.

Table 1

State (1964 statistics unless otherwise indicated)	Total convictions	Guilty pleas	
		Number	Percent of total
California (1965)_____	30,840	22,817	74.0
Connecticut_____	1,596	1,494	93.9
District of Columbia (year ending June 30, 1964)_	1,115	817	73.3
Hawaii____ _____	393	360	91.5
Illinois_____	5,591	4,768	85.2
Kansas_____	3,025	2,727	90.2
Massachusetts (1963)_____	7,790	6,642	85.2
Minnesota (1965)__ _____	1,567	1,437	91.7
New York_____	17,249	16,464	95.5
Pennsylvania (1960)_____	25,632	17,108	66.8
U.S. District Courts_____	29,170	26,273	90.2
Average [excluding Pennsylvania] [1]_____	------------	------------	87.0

[1] The Pennsylvania figures have been excluded from the average because they were from an earlier year, and the types of cases included did not appear fully comparable with the others.

precise data are unavailable.[12] Commonly known as "plea bargaining," this is a process very much like the pretrial settlement of civil cases. It involves discussions looking toward an agreement under which the accused will enter a plea of guilty in exchange for a reduced charge or a favorable sentence recommendation by the prosecutor. Even when there have been no explicit negotiations, defendants relying on prevailing practices often act on the justifiable assumption that those who plead guilty will be sentenced more leniently.

.   .   .   .   .

The system usually operates in an informal, invisible manner. There is ordinarily no formal recognition that the defendant has been offered an inducement to plead guilty. Although the participants and frequently the judge know that negotiation has taken place, the prosecutor and defendant must ordinarily go through a courtroom ritual in which they deny that the guilty plea is the result of any threat or promise.[13] As a result there is no judicial review of the propriety of the bargain—no check on the amount of pressure put on the defendant to plead guilty. The judge, the public, and

[12] *The University of Pennsylvania Law Review* surveyed 205 prosecutors' offices in the most populous counties of 43 States. Roughly 80 responses were received. More than half of the offices in this group reported that 70 percent or more of the defendants pleaded guilty, and of these guilty pleas between 30 and 40 percent resulted from negotiations. Approximately 11 percent of the offices responding indicated that 70 percent or more of guilty pleas were negotiated, while 28 percent indicated that 10 percent or less were negotiated. See Note, "Guilty Plea Bargaining—Compromises by Prosecutors to Secure Guilty Pleas," *University of Pennsylvania Law Review*, 1964, 112:865, 896–899; cf. Comment, "The Influence of the Defendant's Plea on Judicial Determination of Sentence," *Yale Law Journal*, 1956, 66:204.

[13] Cf. *Shelton v. United States*, 242 F.2d 101 (5th Cir.), rev'd 246 F.2d 571 (5th Cir. 1957) (en banc), rev'd per curiam on confession of error, 356 U.S. 26 (1958).

sometimes the defendant himself cannot know for certain who got what from whom in exchange for what. The process comes to look less rational, more subject to chance factors, to undue pressures, and sometimes to the hint of corruption. Moreover, the defendant may not get the benefit he bargained for. There is no guarantee that the judge will follow the prosecutor's recommendations for lenient sentence. In most instances the defendant does not know what sentence he will receive until he has pleaded guilty and sentence has been imposed. If the defendant is disappointed, he may move to withdraw his plea, but there is no assurance that the motion will be granted, particularly since at the time he tendered his guilty plea, he probably denied the very negotiations he now alleges.[14]

.   .   .   .   .

PROBLEMS IN CURRENT PLEA BARGAINING PRACTICES

There are many serious problems with the way that the plea bargaining system is administered. In the first place bargaining takes place at a stage when the parties' knowledge of their own and each other's cases is likely to be fragmentary. Presentence reports and other investigations into the background of the offender usually are made after conviction and are unavailable at the plea-bargain stage. Thus the prosecutor's decision is usually made without the benefit of information regarding the circumstances of the offense, the background and character of the defendant, and other factors necessary for sound dispositional decisions. In too many places the acceptance of pleas to lesser offenses, which began as a device to individualize treatment, becomes routine, with a standard reduction for certain charges.

The informality and wide variation in practice among prosecutors and trial judges regarding plea bargains often cause bewilderment and a sense of injustice among defendants. Some may be denied the opportunity to participate in the bargaining process and the benefits which may accrue because they or their counsel are unaware of the customary practices of plea negotiation. Others may come away from a system which invites judge shopping with justifiable feelings that they have been treated improperly.

Too often the result may be excessive leniency for professional and habitual criminals who generally have expert legal advice and are best able to take full advantage of the bargaining opportunity. Marginal offenders, on the other hand, may be dealt with harshly, and left with a deep sense of injustice, having learned too late of the possibilities of manipulation offered by the system.

The most troublesome problem is the possibility that an innocent defendant may plead guilty because of the fear that he will be sentenced more

---

[14] See, e.g., *United States v. Hughes*, 325 F.2d 789 (2d Cir. 1964), cert. denied, 377 U.S. 907 (1965); *United States v. Lester*, 247 F.2d 496 (2d Cir. 1957); cf. *Georgia Code Ann.* Secs. 27–404, allowing withdrawal of guilty plea as a matter of right at any time before judgment.

harshly if he is convicted after trial or that he will be subjected to damaging publicity because of a repugnant charge. The danger of convicting the innocent obviously must be reduced to the lowest possible level, but the fact is that neither trial nor plea bargain is a perfectly accurate procedure. In both, the innocent face the risk of conviction. The real question is whether the risks are sufficiently greater in the bargaining process to warrant either abandoning it entirely or modifying it drastically. Such improper practices as deliberate and unwarranted overcharging by the prosecutor to improve his bargaining position, threats of very heavy sentences if the defendant insists on a trial, or threats to prosecute relatives and friends of the defendant unless he pleads guilty may, on occasion, create pressures that can prove too great for even the innocent to resist. The existence of mandatory minimum sentences aggravates this problem since they exert a particularly heavy pressure on defendants to relinquish their chance of an acquittal.[15] Inadequate discovery procedures often impair counsel's ability to appraise the risks of trial. Clearly those courts that continue to use a negotiated-plea system must take vigorous steps to reduce these potential abuses.

$$\cdot \quad \cdot \quad \cdot \quad \cdot \quad \cdot$$

Sentencing

The imposition of sanctions on convicted offenders is a principal vehicle for accomplishing the goals of the criminal law. The difficulty of the sentencing decision is due in part to the fact that criminal law enforcement has a number of varied and often conflicting goals: The rehabilitation of offenders, the isolation of offenders who pose a threat to community safety, the discouragement of potential offenders, the expression of the community's condemnation of the offender's conduct, and the reinforcement of the values of law abiding citizens.

Although in some cases these various goals may lead to the same result, in many other cases the judge must choose to enforce one goal while subordinating the others. Thus a person who violates the income tax or selective service laws may be sentenced to prison as an example to potential violators despite the fact that he presents no threat to the community's safety and is not apparently in need of correctional treatment. In another case a judge may properly impose a lenient sentence on a youthful offender who has committed a serious crime in order to maximize his chances for successful rehabilitation.

The burden of accommodating these values in each case falls primarily on the trial judge. Although his authority is limited by the statutory provi-

---

[15] Studies show a far greater incidence of bargaining in Michigan, where sentences for certain crimes are legislatively mandated, than in Wisconsin, where judges have greater discretion in sentencing. See Newman, *op. cit, supra* note 1, at pp. 53–56, 177–84.

sions which establish the range of sentencing alternatives, these statutes rarely provide any standards to guide the exercise of his discretion. Furthermore, his ability to impose an appropriate sentence is limited because knowledge about the deterrent or rehabilitative effect of any particular sentence is limited. And in many jurisdictions information about the offender's background, which is needed to predict the offender's potential for rehabilitation, is not furnished to the sentencing judge.

Statutory Sentencing Framework

Over half the States are now engaged in penal law revision, including reconsideration of their sentencing codes, and in October 1966 Congress, at the request of President Johnson, established a special commission to study and propose revisions of Federal penal laws and sentencing statutes. These revision efforts emphasize the importance of considering the problems in existing sentencing codes.

Statutory provisions affect sentencing decisions in individual cases in two primary ways. The statutes distribute sentencing authority among the legislature, the court, and the correctional agencies. They also determine the criteria used by the courts and correctional agencies to make the decisions delegated to them and place limits on their authority.[16]

The influence of the statutory sentencing framework may be illustrated by the case of a hypothetical adult offender who stands convicted of armed robbery and who previously has been imprisoned for a felony. Under typical American penal codes, at the time of sentence the court might impose imprisonment, probation, or a fine. In a few jurisdictions the death penalty is available for armed robbery, but it is rarely imposed.

If the offender is sentenced to prison, the two most important decisions are how long he may be kept there and when he will first become eligible for release on parole. In all jurisdictions the legislature fixes the maximum length of imprisonment for an offense, but in most States the courts are permitted to select a sentence for each offender within a range provided by the statute, such as "any term up to 20 years" or "any term between 10 and 20 years." In a few States, however, the judge is limited to the imposition of a fixed statutory maximum term, with all other aspects of the actual length of imprisonment later set administratively by correctional authorities.

The laws of many States would impose further limitations on the judge's authority. A number of states provide a mandatory minimum sentence of imprisonment, sometimes 10 years or more, for particularly dangerous crimes, such as armed robery. In addition a majority of States require heavier punishment for repeated offenders by a mandatory provision applicable to all recidivists. In most of the remaining States heavier punishment is permitted at the judge's discretion.

[16] Note, "Statutory Structures for Sentencing Felons to Prison," *Columbia Law Review,* 1960, 60:1134.

Few prisoners serve their maximum terms of imprisonment. After serving a fraction of their maximum sentences most are released on parole or on conditional release earned because of good time credit. In many States prisoners are eligible for parole when they serve a fixed part, typically one-third or one-half, of their maximum sentences. In most, the courts have authority to impose a specific minimum sentence that an offender must serve in prison before he becomes eligible for parole. The date of parole eligibility is determined solely by the correctional authorities in a few States.

In all States the court may sentence an offender to serve a period of probation up to a maximum fixed by statute. But statutes in a number of States would prohibit probation for an armed robber with a prior felony conviction because of the seriousness of the offense or because of his criminal record.

The maximum amount of the fine which the court may impose is also fixed by statute. It is unlikely that the court would sentence an armed robber to pay a fine, since few judges would consider a fine adequate punishment for a violent offense and, in any event, few felons have the money to pay a substantial fine.

.   .   .   .   .

Information for Sentencing

It is essential that there be systematic procedures for providing relevant information about the offense and the offender to the sentencing judge. This section discusses several procedures to satisfy the information needs for sentencing, including the presentence investigation and report, the sentencing hearing, and the diagnostic commitment. It also suggests the need for scientific evaluation of the usefulness of the information contained in presentence reports.

THE PRESENTENCE INVESTIGATION AND REPORT

The statutes or rules of court in about one-quarter of the States make a presentence report mandatory for certain classes of offenses, generally those punishable by imprisonment in excess of one year.[17] In the great majority of States and in the Federal system a request for a presentence report is discretionary with the trial judge,[18] although in some of these States probation may not be granted unless a presentence report has been prepared.[19]

.   .   .   .   .

[17] See, e.g., *California Penal Code* Sec. 1203; *Indiana Ann. Stat.* Sec. 9–2252 (Supp. 1965); *Michigan Stat. Ann.* Sec. 28.1144 (1954).
[18] See, e.g., *Minnesota Stat. Ann.* Sec. 699.115(1) (1964); *Federal R. Criminal P.*, p. 32(c)(1).
[19] See, e.g., *Ohio Rev. Code Ann.* Sec. 2951.03 (Page Supp. 1964).

The importance of adequate presentence investigation has long been recognized. The National Commission on Law Observance and Enforcement and many of the State crime commissions chartered in the 1920's recommended increased use of presentence reports.[20] More recently the drafters of the Model Penal Code stated that the use and full development of the presentence investigation and report offer the "greatest hope for the improvement of judicial sentencing."[21]

.   .   .   .   .

Procedures should be developed to furnish basic sentencing information to the courts in cases where full presentence reports are not prepared, particularly in less serious misdemeanor cases where the limited range of sentencing alternatives makes an extensive background report of little value. Among the facts which appear to be most important are the defendant's prior criminal record, his family status, his educational and employment history, and his financial and physical conditions, These basic facts could be obtained and verified quickly, with the cooperation of the police, prosecutor, defense counsel, and the defendant himself, by a person who need not possess the qualifications of a probation officer.

The method might resemble the factual investigation of the Manhattan Bail Project.[22] Prior to the bail hearing probation department employees or defender agency representatives interview defendants to obtain information on their personal history and roots in the community. This is verified by telephone calls, and a brief factual summary is provided to defense counsel for use in arguing motions for release on recognizance.

Use of a short form presentence report is at best a temporary step, although it may be dictated by existing manpower and financial problems. By providing a modicum of information the form represents an improvement over existing practice in many courts, but it is only an incremental step toward the goal of full presentence investigation. Its usefulness may be increased by experimentation and development of techniques for identifying facts particularly relevant to the sentencing decision.

DUTIES OF DEFENSE COUNSEL

. . . This role of defense counsel extends to the gathering and evaluation of facts relevant to sentencing and, most important, to their presentation in court at the time of sentencing. Certainly in view of the shortage of competent lawyers to perform all the legal tasks in the criminal process, it would be unwise to rely exclusively on defense counsel to gather and evaluate sentencing facts. However, the ultimate responsibility for ensuring

[20] See National Commission on Law Observance and Enforcement, *Report on Prosecution,* 1931, pp. 135–138.
[21] *Model Penal Code* Sec. 7.07, comment (Tentative Draft No. 2, 1954), p. 1.
[22] See Botein, "The Manhattan Bail Project," *Texas Law Review,* 1965, 43:319. See also pp. 38–39 *infra.*

that facts are gathered and evaluated and for persuasively presenting them to the court rests with counsel.[23]

.   .   .   .   .

A project of the Legal Aid Agency of the District of Columbia shows one way to meet the lawyer's limitations in gathering sentencing facts. A staff, resembling that of the court probation office,[24] conducts investigations, sometimes beginning before conviction, with a view toward presenting a positive program for rehabilitation to the court through defense counsel. These services are made available to Legal Aid Agency attorneys and to appointed counsel in certain cases. The adoption of similar programs by other jurisdictions would do much to provide defense counsel with the facts and evaluation necessary for an intelligent presentation of the sentencing alternatives to the court.

Defense counsel's primary duty is to ensure that the court and his client are aware of the available sentencing alternatives and that the sentencing decision is based on complete and accurate information. Counsel must familiarize himself with possible dispositions and with the sentencing practices of the court so that he can make an intelligent and helpful presentation. In jurisdictions where the presentence report is disclosed to the defense, counsel should attempt to verify the important information in the report. He should be prepared to supplement it when it is incomplete and to challenge it when it is inaccurate. When the presentence report is not disclosed, the only way in which counsel can ensure that the sentencing decision is based on adequate facts is to gather and present information to the court himself, although this may involve wasteful duplication of effort if a presentence report has been prepared for the court.

When counsel believes that probation would be an appropriate disposition for his client, he should be prepared to suggest a positive program of rehabilitation. He should explore possibilities for employment, family services, educational improvement, and perhaps mental health services and attempt to make specific and realistic arrangements for the defendant's return to the community.

Finally, defense counsel should explain to his client the consequences of the various types of sentences which he may receive. Most defendants are unaware of the effects of imprisonment or probation on their families or their own future. A defendant who understands the adjustments which his sentence demands is morely likely to respond favorably.

DISCLOSURE OF PRESENTENCE REPORTS

A serious obstacle to the full participation by defense counsel in the sentencing process is that in many jurisdictions he does not have access to the presentence report. The question whether the presentence report should

[23] See generally Kadish, "The Advocate and the Expert—Counsel in the Peno-Correctional Process," *Minnesota Law Review*, 1961, 45:803.

[24] See Nye, "The Administration of Criminal Justice," *Columbia Law Review*, 1966, 66:286, 296–299.

be disclosed to the defendant or his counsel has engendered extensive debate among lawyers, judges, and correctional authorities.[25] At the present time disclosure is generally a matter of judicial discretion. In almost all States and in the Federal system statutes or rules either expressly give the trial judge the power to disclose the presentence report or their silence is interpreted as permitting disclosure.[26] In a few states disclosure is mandatory, and nowhere is it expressly forbidden.[27] The actual practice of disclosure varies from jurisdiction to jurisdiction and among the various judges of a single court.[28]

. . . . .

Experience in several jurisdictions indicates that a general rule favoring disclosure can operate fairly and without undesirable consequences. In the U.S. District Court for the District of Maryland, for example, presentence reports are prepared in two parts: The bulk of the information is set forth in a document which is made available by the judge to defense counsel in chambers; at the same time a cover sheet containing the probation officer's recommendation, any confidential information, and any data which might injure the defendant's relationships with others is submitted separately. The latter document is not shown to defense counsel, although the judge discusses it with him. This disclosure policy has not resulted in any loss of sources of confidential information or in any instances of unfavorable reactions by defendants against sources of information or probation officers.[29]

As a first step toward fuller disclosure, jurisdictions should experiment with an expanding policy of partial disclosure to test the arguments against disclosure and to devise suitable procedures to protect information which should be withheld. This process might begin with the disclosure of information such as the defendant's prior criminal record, his marital status, his educational and employment record, his financial resources, and any other information obtained from the defendant himself. Disclosure of these data presents minimal risks, and if the practice is successful, it should be expanded to include more subjective information.

THE SENTENCING HEARING

Fuller participation by the defense counsel and disclosure of presentence reports do not mean that there must be a full trial on the question of

[25] See, e.g. Roche, "The Position for Confidentiality of the Presentence Investigation Report," *Albany Law Review*, 1965, 29:206; Higgins, "In Reply to Roche," *id.*, at p. 225; Parsons, "The Presentence Report Must Be Preserved as a Confidential Document," *Federal Probation*, March 1964, p. 3. See generally Rubin, *op. cit. supra* note 12, at pp. 90–101; Tappan, *op. cit. supra* note 2, at p. 558.

[26] See Rubin, *op. cit. supra* note 12, at pp. 90–91.

[27] See, e.g., *California Penal Code* Sec. 1203; *Minnesota Stat. Ann.* Sec. 690.115(4) (1964).

[28] See "Symposium—Discovery in Federal Criminal Cases," *F.R.D.*, 1963, 33:47, 125–127.

[29] See Thomsen, "Confidentiality of the Presentence Report—A Middle Position," *Federal Probation*, March 1964, p. 8.

sentence. The right to challenge material presented to the court can be afforded without encumbering the sentencing proceeding with rigid evidentiary rules and formal procedures. The scope of the presentation should properly be left to the discretion of the court.[30]

The interests both of fairness to the defendant and of imposing an appropriate sentence indicate that the prosecution and defense should be given a reasonable opportunity to contest the accuracy of important factual statements in the presentence report.[31] A sentence based on inaccurate information may be too lenient for the protection of society or unduly severe, in either case detracting from efforts to reintegrate the offender into the community.

.   .   .   .   .

DIAGNOSTIC COMMITMENTS

Even when there is a full presentence investigation, there is only a limited opportunity to observe a defendant prior to the time of sentencing. Such factors as a serious emotional disturbance or physical disease may be present, indicating a need for further study. To provide more information to the sentencing judge, several jurisdictions have established diagnostic facilities which administer psychological and physical examinations to prisoners during brief periods of confinement and report their findings and recommendations to the judge before a final sentence is imposed.[32]

Under the procedure employed in the Federal system, which is similar to that used in most of the States having diagnostic commitments, the judge imposes the maximum term authorized for the offense, and the offender is sent to a diagnostic facility maintained by the Bureau of Prisons.[33] Within three months the diagnostic facility prepares a report on the offender containing the results of its examinations and of tests to determine the offender's aptitude and vocational skills. The report also suggests a correctional program for the offender keyed to the facilities available at a particular institution. After reviewing these findings and recommendations, the court may affirm the original sentence, reduce it, or grant probation.

[30] See generally Parsons, "Aids in Sentencing," *F.R.D.*, 1964, 35:423, 425–428.

[31] See generally Rubin, *op. cit. supra* note 12, at pp. 101–107. Under the Model Sentencing Act a defendant is entitled, subject to the direction of the court, to cross-examine those who have prepared presentence or diagnostic reports. *Model Sentencing Act,* Sec. 4 (1963). The *Model Penal Code* provides that a defendant shall have a "fair opportunity . . . to controvert" the facts or conclusions in the presentence report. *Model Penal Code* Sec. 7.07(5) (Proposed Official Draft 1962). Before an extended term may be imposed, however, the court must hold a hearing to establish the grounds for an extended term, at which the defendant "shall have the right to hear and controvert the evidence against him and to offer evidence upon the issue." *Id.* at Sec. 7.07(6). Under the amended Federal Rule 32, when disclosure of the presentence report is made to the defendant, the court must "afford the defendant or his counsel an opportunity to comment thereon." *Fed. R. Crim.*, p. 32.

[32] See, e.g., *Cal. Pen. Code* Sec. 1203.03 (Supp. 1966); *N.J. Rev. Stat.* Sec. 30:4A-1–17 (1964).

[33] 18 U.S.C. Sec. 4208 (b), (c) (1964). See generally Carter, "Use of Section 4208 (b) and (c), Commitment for Study," 27 *F.R.D.* 307–15 (1961).

Experience in the Federal system indicates that most diagnostic commitments are requested in cases in which the court feels a need for a psychiatric evaluation of the defendant. In 1965, for example, only 442 diagnostic commitments were ordered, which was less than one percent of the total number of commitments.[34] In Kansas, on the other hand, the diagnostic facility is a part of the State center for reception and classification of prisoners, and about one-third of all felony offenders committed each year are given diagnostic studies.[35] The most extensive use of the diagnostic commitment is found in Hawaii, where diagnostic study is required by statute for every offender committed to a State penal institution.[36]

Most authorities agree that the diagnostic commitment is a valuable aid to the sentencing judge. It provides him with more comprehensive information on the personality of the offender and enables him to consider the recommendation of correctional experts in determining sentence.

．　　．　　．　　．　　．

The Exercise of Court Sentencing Authority

IMPROVEMENT OF JUDICIAL SENTENCING PROFICIENCY

The sentencing demands considerable expertise on the part of the trial judge. He must have a thorough knowledge of the whole range of sentencing alternatives and of their usefulness in dealing with the many types of offenders appearing before him. And he must develop sophisticated skills for interpreting presentence and psychiatric evaluations.

A number of programs have been developed to improve judicial sentencing proficiency. During the last five years the Joint Committee for the Effective Administration of Justice assisted in the organization of over 40 regional seminars which were available to almost every trial judge sitting in a State court of general jurisdiction.[37] Most of these seminars included discussion of sentencing theories and alternatives and the development of uniform sentencing criteria.

The National College of State Trial Judges, founded in 1964, annually conducts a four-week program of intensive study, primarily for judges who have recently assumed the bench.[38] In its first two years, 200 judges from 49 States attended classes at the College. A case method of instruction is used in the course on sentencing. The judges are given a set of presentence reports, and the sentence which each judge selects is discussed and evaluated by the other judges in the class.

[34] 1965 *Federal Bureau of Prisons Statistical Tables* 35 (table B-12-C).

[35] See Cape, "A New Look at a State's Penal System," *Police*, Mar.–Apr. 1966, p. 47.

[36] *Hawaii Rev. Laws* Sec. 252–58 (1955).

[37] Institute of Judicial Administration, *Judicial Education in the United States* (1965), pp. 89–111.

[38] *Id.* at pp. 111–118.

Another technique for improving the sentencing skills of judges is through institutes devoted entirely to sentencing, which are at present conducted in the Federal system and in California, New York, and Pennsylvania. Since the Federal sentencing institute program was inaugurated in 1959,[39] 16 institutes have been held, and the judges of all circuits have had an opportunity to participate in at least one institute.[40]

The content of the programs of the Federal institutes has varied. For example, at the most recent institute, held in July 1966 for the judges of the 8th and 10th Circuits, papers were delivered on the identification and treatment of dangerous offenders and on the Model Sentencing Act's provisions for sentencing dangerous and nondangerous offenders. After each topic was introduced, the judges were divided into panels to discuss particular problems in sentencing and treatment for the two classes of offenders. Other institutes have used the same format to consider the problems presented by the mentally disordered offender and to develop standards for sentencing in certain types of cases, such as income tax evasion and interstate transportation of stolen automobiles.[41]

At the Federal Institute on Disparity of Sentences each judge selected a sentence on the basis of a presentence report, and a discussion of relevant sentencing principles followed.[42] This method, which revealed widely disparate sentencing philosophies among the judges, has been used in subsequent institutes where the problem of disparity was considered.

One important feature of the Federal sentencing institutes is that several have been held in the vicinity of Federal correctional institutions. This provides an opportunity for the judges to visit these facilities and to observe the type of rehabilitative programs which are available.

The California sentencing institutes have followed the procedures used in the Federal system.[43] The first California institute, held in 1964, explored standards for commitment to local correctional facilities and to State penal institutions, and the judges were informed of the adult authority's policies on term setting and parole eligibility.

It would be highly desirable for all jurisdictions to conduct sentencing institutes on a regular basis.[44] They provide a forum for judges to discuss the causes of disparity within their courts and to formulate uniform policies to be applied in individual cases. They open valuable channels of communication between the courts and correctional authorities on the most effective

---

[39] See 28 U.S.C. Sec. 334 (1964).

[40] See 37 *F.R.D.*, 1965, pp. 115–116.

[41] See, e.g., 37 *F.R.D.*, 1965, p. 111; 35 *F.R.D.* 1961, p. 381.

[42] 30 *F.R.D.*, 1961, p. 401.

[43] See Institute of Judicial Administration, *op. cit. supra* note 37, at pp. 225–226.

[44] See generally Bennett, "Countdown for Judicial Sentencing," *Federal Probation,* September 1961, pp. 22, 26; Youngdahl, "Remarks Opening the Sentencing Institute Program," *F.R.D.*, 1964, 35:387, 390–391; Van Dusen, "Trends in Sentencing Since 1957 and Areas of Substantial Agreement and Disagreement in Sentencing Principles," *id.* at p. 395.

use of sentencing alternatives and on the content of correctional programs. And judges are given expert guidance on the characteristics and problems of certain types of defendants, such as the dangerous or mentally disordered offender.

In addition, the development of new opportunities for judges to meet and discuss the problems of sentencing should be studied. One type of program might be a summer session at a university, at which judges, correctional authorities, social scientists, law professors, and other interested specialists could meet in seminars to discuss the theories and practical problems of sentencing and treatment of offenders. Through such a program judges could enlarge their own knowledge while providing perspectives from which to evaluate the sentencing process.

THE PROBLEM OF DISPARITY

Within certain limits a lack of uniformity in sentences is justifiable. Indeed the reason for giving judges discretion in sentencing is to permit variations based on relevant differences in offenders. Unequal sentences for the same offense may also result from the fact that statutory definitions of crimes encompass a fairly broad range of conduct having varying degrees of seriousness. Finally, lack of uniformity may reflect geographic factors, such as differences in public apprehension of crime among communities in the same jurisdiction, or institutional considerations, such as the need to offer more lenient sentences to defendants who furnish information or testimony for the prosecution.

The problem of disparity arises from the imposition of unequal sentences for the same offense, or offenses of comparable seriousness, without any reasonable basis. The existence of unjustified disparity has been amply demonstrated by many studies.[45] It is a pervasive problem in almost all jurisdictions. In the Federal system, for example, the average length of prison sentences for narcotics violations in 1965 was 83 months in the 10th Circuit, but only 44 months in the 3d Circuit.[46] During 1962 the average sentence for forgery ranged from a high of 68 months in the Northern District of Mississippi to a low of 7 months in the Southern District of Mississippi; the highest average sentence for auto theft was 47 months in the Southern District of Iowa, and the lowest was 14 months in the Northern District of New York.[47]

[45] See, e.g., Gaudet, Harris, and St. John, "Individual Differences in the Sentencing Tendencies of Judges," *Journal of Criminal Law, Criminology, and Police Science*, 1933, 23:811; McGuire and Holzoff, "The Problem of Sentence in the Criminal Law," *Boston University Law Review*, 1940, 20:423. See generally Rubin, *op. cit. supra* note 12, at pp. 116–119; Tappan, *Crime, Justice and Correction* (1960), pp. 441–446.

[46] See 1965 Federal Bureau of Prisons *Statistical Tables* 26–27 (table B-7).

[47] See Youngdahl, *supra* note 44, at pp. 387, 389–390 (1964). Substantial disparity among the district courts also exists in the use of probation. In 1964 probation was granted to 29 percent of all convicted defendants in the Eastern District of Kentucky, 38 percent in the Southern District of New York, 54 percent in the Southern District of

Disparity among judges sitting in the same court is illustrated by the findings of a recent study of the Detroit Recorder's Court.[48] Over a 20-month period in which the sample cases were about equally distributed among the 10 judges, one judge imposed prison terms upon 75 to 90 percent of the defendants whom he sentenced, while another judge imposed prison sentences in about 35 percent of the cases. One judge consistently imposed prison sentences twice as long as those of the most lenient judge. The study also showed that judges who imposed the most severe sentences for certain crimes also exhibited the most liberal sentencing policy for other offenses.

Other illustrations of disparity may be found in the results of the workshop sessions at the Federal Institute on Disparity of Sentences.[49] The judges were given sets of facts for several offenses and offenders and were asked what sentences they would have imposed. One case involved a 51-year-old man with no criminal record who pleaded guilty to evading $4,945 in taxes. At the time of his conviction he had a net worth in excess of $200,000 and had paid the full principal and interest on the taxes owed to the Government. Of the 54 judges who responded, 3 judges voted for a fine only; 23 judges voted for probation (some with a fine); 28 judges voted for prison terms ranging from less than 1 year to 5 years (some with a fine). In a bank robbery case the sentences ranged from probation to prison terms of from 5 to 20 years.

.   .   .   .   .

Unjustified disparity cannot be eliminated completely, if for no other reason than because reasonable men applying the same standards will not always reach precisely the same result. There are several steps, however, that may reduce the range in which individual differences among judges can affect the length and type of sentences. Enactment of criteria for sentencing, together with educational programs to improve judicial sentencing proficiency, would aid in the development of uniform sentencing policies. Furthermore, the removal of inconsistencies in severity of punishment among offenses and the elimination of severe mandatory sentences would tend to reduce the wide disparities caused by prosecutorial and judicial nullification.

The following sections consider two procedures, sentencing councils and appellate review of sentences, which are particularly helpful in reducing disparity.

SENTENCING COUNCILS

The sentencing council is a procedure by which several judges of a multijudge court meet periodically to consider what sentences should be

---

California, 71 percent in the Eastern District of Pennsylvania, and 78 percent in the Southern District of West Virginia. Administrative Office of the U.S. Courts, *Federal Offenders in the District Courts, 1964,* at pp. 78–79 (app. table 2).

[48] Saul R. Levin Foundation, *Report of Study of Recorder's Court* (mimeo 1966).

[49] See "Seminar and Institute on Disparity of Sentences," *F.R.D.,* 1961, 30:401, 429–431.

imposed in pending cases. Sentencing councils have been instituted on a regular basis in three U.S. district courts;[50] no evidence of their systematic use in state courts has been found.

. . . . .

Foremost among the advantages of the sentencing council is that it reveals to the participating judges their differences in sentencing philosophies, and it provides a forum in which these differences may be debated in the context of particular cases and from which a consensus on sentencing standards may emerge. It also promotes fuller consideration of the sentencing alternatives available to the court. Finally, where the sentencing council procedure is accompanied by the collection of data on the initial recommendations and final sentencing decisions, as in Michigan and Illinois, it provides a mechanism for periodic evaluation of the sentencing practices of the court.

One troublesome aspect of existing sentencing council procedures is that the judges meet prior to the sentencing hearing. The sentencing judge thus presides over the hearing after having heard the views of his colleagues about the case and after having taken a position himself within the sentencing council. This may impair the judge's ability to give openminded consideration to the arguments and information presented at the sentencing hearing. At the same time the judges participating in the council do not have the benefit of the facts and insights presented by the prosecutor, defense counsel, or the defendant himself. Particularly where there is disclosure of the presentence report, the hearing may reveal that the deliberations in the sentencing council were based on inaccurate or incomplete information.

Some of these difficulties might be avoided by permitting defense counsel and the prosecutor to make a presentation at the sentencing council. However, this would greatly encumber the procedure and perhaps make it impractical for busy urban courts. A preferable solution would be to hold the sentencing council after the hearing, at which time the sentencing judge could inform his colleagues of the arguments and information presented at the hearing and of his resolution of disputed factual questions. Although this would require a separate proceeding for the imposition of sentence, it is likely that the additional burden on the courts could be minimized by careful scheduling.

. . . . .

APPELLATE REVIEW OF SENTENCES

In all Western countries except the United States, grossly excessive sentences are subject to routine review and correction by appellate tribunals.[51]

---

[50] See generally Smith, "The Sentencing Council and the Problem of Disproportionate Sentences," *Federal Probation,* June 1963, p. 5; Doyle, "A Sentencing Council in Operation," *Federal Probation,* September 1961, p. 27.

[51] *Hearings on S. 2722 Before the Subcommittee on Improvements in Judicial Machinery of the Senate Committee on the Judiciary,* 89th Congress, 2nd Session, 1966, pp. 83–102 (hereinafter cited as *Senate Hearings*).

The great majority of jurisdictions in the United States, however, vest sentencing power solely within the discretion of the trial judge, with appellate review available only to correct sentences which do not conform to the statutory limits. Authority for appellate review of the merits of sentences has been expressly granted by the legislatures of about one-quarter of the states and by Congress for military courts.[52] In addition, the appellate courts of a few States have construed general review statutes as including such authority.[53]

. . . . .

The most important contribution of appellate review is the opportunity it provides for the correction of grossly excessive sentences. Although appellate review will not totally eliminate the problem of disparity of sentences, by reducing the peaks of disparity, it would narrow the range in which individual differences among judges can affect the length and type of sentences.

Moreover, appellate review aids the development of a uniform sentencing policy within a jurisdiction. It tends to cause both trial and appellate courts to give sustained consideration to the justification for particular sentences. And the opinions of appellate courts in modifying excessive sentences can provide a body of law to guide trial courts in all cases.

Finally, appellate review would tend to reduce the number of anomalous decisions on procedural and substantive law which appellate courts have made in order to reverse cases involving unusually harsh sentences.

. . . . .

The primary objection to appellate review is that it might greatly increase litigation because review would become available for all those defendants who plead guilty—between 70 and 90 percent of all convicted offenders—and who are generally unable to obtain direct review of their convictions.[54]

. . . . .

A second objection to appellate review is that sentencing is a discretionary matter involving questions of judgment and not of law such as appellate courts are used to handling.[55]

. . . . .

A third objection is that appellate judges are less able to assess an appropriate sentence because of their inability to observe the defendant.[56]

. . . . .

[52] See, e.g., *Connecticut General Stat. Ann.* Secs. 51–195 to 196 (1964); *Illinois Ann. Stat.*, chapter 38, Secs. 121–129 (1964).

[53] See, e.g., *State v. Johnson*, 67 N.J. Super. 414, 170 A.2d 296 (1961); *Hudson v. State*, 399 P.2d 296 (Oklahoma Criminal Appeals 1965). See generally Note, *Columbia Law Review* 1960, 60:1134, 1162–1164 and notes 199–206.

[54] See, e.g., Brewster, "Appellate Review of Sentences," *F.R.D.*, 1966, 40:79, 80–81.

[55] See, e.g., *Symposium*, pp. 281–285.

[56] See Parsons, "Aids in Sentencing," *F.R.D.*, 1964, 35:423, 425–426.

JURY SENTENCING

Although a majority of States permit the jury to recommend or fix punishment at life imprisonment in capital cases, in about one-quarter of the States the jury determines the type and length of punishment for some or all offenses.[57] The jury's sentencing power in most of these states is limited to cases in which it has determined the guilt of the defendant,[58] but in a few States jury sentencing is available at the option of a defendant who pleads guilty,[59] and in Tennessee the jury is required to fix the sentence in all cases.[60] Where the sentence is imposed by a jury, the judge's role usually is confined to modifying a legal but excessive sentence or to conforming an illegal sentence to the statutory limits.

The origin of jury sentencing in this country has been assigned to the colonials' reaction to harsh penalties imposed by judges appointed and controlled by the Crown and to the early distrust of governmental power.[61] At the present time the principal arguments for its retention are that jurors will not become calloused to the fate of defendants, that jury sentences are less likely to be the result of individual prejudices or political considerations, and that jurors may be better able than judges to express the community sentiment with regard to the offense.[62]

There are serious disadvantages of jury sentencing which argue strongly for its abolition in noncapital cases.[63] The principal objection to sentencing by juries is that the transitory nature of jury service virtually precludes rational sentencing. Sentencing is a job for experts, and juries do not have the opportunity to develop expertise in this extremely complex area. The extent of the failings of jury sentencing was revealed by a recent study in Atlanta which showed that for some offenses first offenders received on the average more severe sentences than recidivists.[64]

Jury sentencing may result in confusion between conviction and punishment. Juries may compromise their doubts as to guilt with a light sentence, and unless the law provides for separate hearings on guilt and sentence, defense counsel may be put in the awkward position of arguing that his client is not guilty but, if he is, he should receive a light sentence.

Finally, jury sentencing makes it difficult to obtain a sentencing decision

[57] See Note, *Columbia Law Review,* 1960, pp. 1134, 1154–1155.
[58] E.g., *Missouri Revised Stat.,* Sec. 546.410 (1959).
[59] E.g., *Texas Code of Criminal Proceedings,* article 37.07 (1965).
[60] *Tennessee Code Ann.* Secs. 40–2310 (1955).
[61] National Commission on Law Observance and Enforcement, *Report on Criminal Procedure,* 1931, p. 27.
[62] See, e.g., Betts, "Jury Sentencing," *N.P.A.J.,* 1956, 2:369, 370.
[63] See, e.g., rubin, *Criminal Correction* (1963), pp. 107–108, 124–128; Betts, *supra* note 62; Jones, "On Modernizing Missouri's Criminal Punishment Procedure," *Kansas City Law Review,* 1932, 20:299, 304; Note, "Consideration of Punishment by Juries," *University of Chicago Law Review,* 1950, 17:400.
[64] Atlanta Commission on Crime and Juvenile Delinquency, *Opportunity for Urban Excellence* (1966), p. 72, appendix D-6.

based on adequate background information about the defendant. Much of this information is properly inadmissible on the question of guilt, and its admission on the question of sentence when the jury considers both issues simultaneously may be highly prejudicial to the defendant. In order to provide the jury with a presentence report, the jury would have to be reassembled after the report was prepared or a new jury would have to be impaneled. The only alternative, which is used in some jurisdictions, is to have a separate hearing at which background information is presented to the jury after the verdict. This procedure increases the time and cost of jury trials, however, and it does not compensate for the jury's lack of expertise.

Capital Punishment

Whether capital punishment should be retained is the subject of legislative consideration, popular referendum, and public debate in many states. This question is not an easy one, for the use of the death penalty touches upon fundamental moral beliefs as well as utilitarian values. Whether capital punishment is an appropriate sanction is a decision properly left to each state. But it is appropriate here to point out several aspects of the administration of capital punishment which merit careful consideration.

The most salient characteristic of capital punishment is that it is infrequently used. During 1966 only one person was executed in the United States; the trend over the last 36 years shows a substantial decline in the number of executions, from a high of 200 in 1935 to last year's low of one [65] All available data indicate that judges, juries, and governors are becoming increasingly reluctant to impose or authorize the carrying out of a death sentence. Only 67 persons were sentenced to death by the courts in 1965, half the number of death sentences imposed in 1961; and 62 prisoners were relieved of their death sentences by commutation, reversals of judgment, or other means. In some States in which the penalty exists on the statute books, there has not been an execution in decades.[66]

This decline in the application of the death penalty parallels a substantial decline in public and legislative support for capital punishment. According to the most recent Gallup Poll, conducted in 1966, 47 percent of those interviewed were opposed to the death penalty for murder, while 42 percent were in favor of it; a poll conducted in 1960 on the same question reported a majority in favor of the death penalty. Since 1964 five states effectively abolished capital punishment. There are now eight States in which the death penalty is completely unavailable and five States in which it may be imposed only for exceptional crimes such as murder of a prison guard or

[65] See Federal Bureau of Prisons, *Executions* (1930–1965), at p. 8, chart 1.

[66] In Delaware, Massachusetts, and North Dakota the last execution was held prior to 1950, in Montana prior to 1945, and in New Hampshire prior to 1940. *Id.* at p. 11, table 2.

inmate by a prisoner serving a life sentence, murder of a police officer, or treason. In 1965 Great Britain experimentally suspended use of the death penalty for five years.

There has not been a uniform trend toward repeal of capital punishment laws, however. In 1961 the Delaware legislature reenacted the death penalty after having repealed it in 1958. Last year the voters in Colorado rejected a proposed constitutional amendment which would have abolished capital punishment. In Indiana an abolition bill passed by both houses of the legislature was vetoed by the Governor. And in a number of States bills providing for repeal of the penalty have been defeated in the legislature.

One of the principal arguments for the retention of capital punishment is that it is an effective and necessary deterrent against the commission of heinous crimes. While it is presently impossible to prove or disprove the validity of this argument, the most extensive study on the question, made by Prof. Thorsten Sellin, raises doubts as to the unique deterrent effect of the death penalty.[67] Professor Sellin charted the 1930–1937 homicide rates of several groups of neighboring and otherwise similar States; within each group one or more States had abolished capital punishment. He found that the trends in homicide rates were similar for comparable capital and noncapital punishment States, and "within each group of States having similar social and economic conditions and populations, it is impossible to distinguish the abolition State from the others."[68] He examined the experience of States which had experimented with the abolition of the death penalty and then restored it, and the data did not reveal any significant increase in homicide rates when it was abolished nor any significant decrease in the rates when it was restored. He also made a survey of the number of metropolitan policemen killed in the line of duty in States which abolished capital punishment and in States which retained it. His data revealed that there was no significant difference between the two types of States in the safety of policemen.

It is also argued that prisoners convicted of capital crimes, if not executed, pose an undue risk of danger to prison guards and other inmates and are likely to commit crimes of violence against the public if they are ever paroled. The available data on these questions are far from conclusive, but several prison wardens have expressed their belief that prisoners serving prison sentences for capital crimes pose no greater risk to the safety of other inmates or guards and often are model prisoners capable of assuming positions of responsibility. One study revealed that of 121 assaults with intent to kill committed in the penal institutions of 27 states during a 10-year period, none was committed by a prisoner whose death sentence for murder had been commuted to life imprisonment, 10 (or 8 percent) were committed by prisoners originally sentenced to life imprisonment for mur-

---

[67] See Sellin, "The Death Penalty, in *Model Penal Code* (Tent. Draft No. 9, 1950).
[68] *Id.* at p. 34.

der, and the remainder were committed by prisoners sentenced for other offenses. Although there have been instances where paroled murderers have committed another homicide, available data indicate that they have a substantially lower recidivism rate than other classes of offenders.[69]

Whatever views one may have about the efficacy of the death penalty as a deterrent, it clearly has an undesirable impact on the administration of justice. The trial of a capital case is a stirring drama, but that is perhaps its most dangerous attribute. Selecting a jury often requires several days; each objection or point of law requires excessive deliberation because of the irreversible consequences of error. The jury's concern with the death penalty may result in unwarranted acquittals and there is increased danger that public sympathy will be aroused for the defendant, regardless of his guilt of the crime charged.[70]

. . . . .

The imposition of a death sentence is but the first stage of a protracted process of appeals, collateral attacks, and petitions for executive clemency. The decline in the number of executions has caused a sharp increase in the number of prisoners on death row: At the beginning of 1960 there were 189 prisoners under sentence of death in the United States, by the end of 1965 there were 331, and there undoubtedly was a substantial increase during 1966.[71] The prisoners awaiting execution at the end of 1965 had been under sentence for an average of almost 31 months; 61 of these prisoners had been on death row for 5 years or more. The 7 persons who were executed in 1965 had been under sentence for nearly 4 years. The spectacle of men living on death row for years while their lawyers pursue appellate and collateral remedies contradicts our image of humane and expeditious punishment of offenders. But no one would seriously propose to limit the right of a condemned man to have errors at his trial corrected or to obtain the mercy of the executive. Finally, there is evidence that the imposition of the death sentence and the exercise of dispensing power by the courts and the executive follow discriminatory patterns. The death sentence is most frequently imposed and carried out on the poor, the Negro, and the members of unpopular groups.

The Lower Courts

No findings of this Commission are more disquieting than those relating to the condition of the lower criminal courts. These courts are lower only in the sense that they are the courts before which millions of arrested persons are first brought, either for trial of misdemeanors or petty offenses or for

[69] See Bedau, *The Death Penalty in America* (1964), pp. 397–399, 400, 495.

[70] See New York Temporary Commission on Revision of the Penal Law and Criminal Code, *Fourth Interim Report*, 1965, p. 69.

[71] In August 1966 the State of California was forced to open a "Death Row Annex" at San Quentin Penitentiary to hold 32 additional prisoners because the existing death row, which has space for 60 prisoners, was filled to capacity.

preliminary hearing on felony charges. Although the offenses that are the business of the lower courts may be "petty" in respect to the amount of damage that they do and the fear that they inspire, the work of the lower courts has great implications. Insofar as the citizen experiences contact with the criminal court, the lower criminal court is usually the court of last resort. While public attention focuses on sensational felony cases and on the conduct of trials in the prestigious felony courts, 90 percent of the Nation's criminal cases are heard in the lower courts.

. . . . .

The significance of these courts to the administration of criminal justice lies not only in sheer numbers of defendants who pass through them but also in their jurisdiction over many of the offenses that are most visible to the public. Most convicted felons have prior misdemeanor convictions, and although the likelihood of diverting an offender from a career of crime is greatest at the time of his first brush with the law, the lower courts do not deal effectively with those who have come before them.

. . . . .

. . . The National Commission on Law Observance and Enforcement (the Wickersham Commission) concluded that the lower courts were the most important in the criminal justice system and yet were the most neglected. In the following years numerous studies have echoed these findings.[72]

It is distressing to report that these warnings have gone largely unheeded. The Commission has gathered available studies and statistical data, and the staff has made brief field studies of the lower courts in several large cities. The inescapable conclusion is that the conditions of inequity, indignity, and ineffectiveness previously deplored continue to be widespread.

. . . . .

The Urban Courts

PRACTICES AND PROCEDURES OF THE LOWER COURTS

Every day in the courthouses of metropolitan areas the inadequacies of the lower criminal courts may be observed. There is little in the process

[72] See, e.g., Sheridan, *Urban Justice* (1964); Rubin, *Criminal Justice in a Metropolitan Court* (1966); American Bar Foundation, *The Administration of Criminal Justice in the United States Pilot Project Report* (mimeo 1957), pp. 1–7; *Pennsylvania Attorney General, Report on the Investigation of the Magisterial System* (1965); Dash, "Cracks in the Foundation of Justice," *Illinois Law Review*, 1951, 46:385; Foote, "Vagrancy-Type Law and Its Administration," *University of Pennsylvania Law Review*, 1956, 104:603; Note, "Metropolitan Criminal Courts of First Instance," *Harvard Law Review*, 1956, 70:320.

Even before the turn of the century a Philadelphia judge remarked that "complaints of the rapacity of local magistrates have come down to us, continuously, from the earliest periods." *Commonwealth v. Alderman Hogan, Philadelphia Report*, 1872, 9:574, in *Pennsylvania Attorney General, supra* at p. 1.

which is likely to instill respect for the system of criminal justice in defendants, witnesses, or observers. Some representative observations are set forth below.

Initial Presentment

Following arrest, the defendant is initially presented in court, often after many hours and sometimes several days of detention. In theory the judge's duty is to advise the defendant of the charges against him and of his rights to remain silent, to be admitted to bail, to retain counsel or to have counsel appointed, and to have a preliminary hearing. But in some cities the defendant may not be advised of his right to remain silent or to have counsel assigned. In others he may be one of a large group herded before the bench as a judge or clerk rushes through a ritualistic recitation of phrases, making little or no effort to ascertain whether the defendants understand their rights or the nature of the proceedings. In many jurisdictions counsel are not assigned in misdemeanor cases; even where lawyers are appointed, it may not be made clear to the defendant that if he is without funds he may have free representation. One Commission staff report notes:

> In the cases observed no defendant was told that he had a right to remain silent or that the court would appoint a lawyer to represent him if he were indigent, notwithstanding the court rule that counsel will be assigned whenever a defendant may be sentenced to more than six months or fined more than $500. We were told that at least one judge takes great care to advise defendants fully, but the three judges we observed did not.[73]

The judges have little time to give detailed consideration to the question of bail. Little is known about the defendant other than the charge and his prior criminal record. The result is that bail is based on the charge instead of on the circumstances of each case; high money bonds are almost invariably set by established patterns, and large numbers of defendants are detained.

Disposition

The initial appearance is also the final appearance for most defendants charged with misdemeanors or petty offenses. While those who can afford to retain counsel are released on bond to prepare for trial at a later date or to negotiate a disposition, a majority of defendants plead guilty immediately, many without advice of counsel. Pleas are entered so rapidly that they cannot be well considered. The defendant is often made aware that if

[73] *Staff Study, Administration of Justice in the Municipal Court of Baltimore,* appendix B, *supra* note 96.

he seeks more time, his case will be adjourned for a week or two and he will be returned to jail.

> Most of the defendants . . . pleaded guilty and were sentenced immediately, without any opportunity for allocution. When they tried to say something in their own behalf, they were silenced by the judge and led off by the bailiff. . . .[74]

Trial

An observer in the lower criminal courts ordinarily sees a trial bearing little resemblance to those carried out under traditional notions of due process. There is usually no court reporter unless the defendant can afford to pay one. One result is an informality in the proceedings which would not be tolerated in a felony trial. Rules of evidence are largely ignored. Speed is the watchword. Trials in misdemeanor cases may be over in a matter of 5, 10, or 15 minutes; they rarely last an hour even in relatively complicated cases. Traditional safeguards honored in felony cases lose their meaning in such proceedings; yet there is still the possibility of lengthy imprisonment or heavy fine.

In some cities trials are conducted without counsel for either side; the case is prosecuted by a police officer and defended by the accused himself. Staff observations in one city were summed up as follows:

> A few defendants went to trial, but the great majority of them did so without counsel. In these cases the judge made no effort to explain the proceedings to the defendants or to tell them of their right to cross-examine the prosecution's witnesses or of their right to remain silent. After the policeman delivered his testimony, the judge did not appear to make any evaluation of the sufficiency of the evidence but turned immediately to the defendant and asked, "What do you have to say for yourself?" Where counsel appeared at a trial, the procedure was slightly more formal, but the judge conducted most of the questioning himself.[57]

Sentence

Most defendants convicted in the lower criminal courts are sentenced promptly. Usually there are no probation services or presentence investigations. Unless the defendant has an attorney who has taken time to inquire into his background, little will be known about him. Sentence may be based on the charge, the defendant's appearance, and the defendant's response to such questions as the judge may put to him in the few moments allotted to sentencing. In the lower courts of one State the availability of violator's

[74] *Staff Study, Administration of Justice in the Recorder's Court of Detroit, Ibid.*
[75] *Ibid.*

records is the exception rather than the rule. Even in the larger cities when the judge wishes to see the record of individual defendants he must send for the record and then delay the trial until it arrives. Delay and inconvenience so caused often lead to a situation where the judge merely asks the defendant what his record is and relies upon his word for its accuracy. . . .[76]

Short jail sentences of one, two, or three months are commonly imposed on an assembly-line basis. A defendant's situation can hardly be considered individually. When a defendant is fined but is unable to pay, he may be required to work the penalty off at the rate of $1 to $5 for each day spent in jail.[77]

Petty Offenses

The conditions described above are found in more aggravated form in lower courts which handle petty offenses. Each day in large cities hundreds of persons arrested for drunkenness or disorderly conduct, for vagrancy or petty gambling, or for prostitution are led before a judge. Among the defendants are slum dwellers who drink in public and young men who "loiter" on street corners or "fail to move on" when ordered to do so. Typically, they have no private place to go, no money to spend, and no family or lawyer to lend them support.

Judges sometimes seem annoyed at being required to preside in these courts. Defendants are treated with contempt, berated, laughed at, embarrassed, and sentenced to serve their time or work off their fines.[78] Observers have sometimes reported difficulty in determining what offense is being tried in a given case,[79] and instances have come to light in which the disposition bears little relationship to the original charge. A trial of a defendant charged by police with drunkenness consisted of this exchange:

> MAGISTRATE: "Where do you live?"
> DEFENDANT: "Norfolk."
> MAGISTRATE: "What are you doing in Philadelphia?"
> DEFENDANT: "Well, I didn't have any work down there, so I came up here to see if I could find. . . ."
> MAGISTRATE (who had been shaking his head): "That story's not good enough for me. I'm going to have you investigated. You're a vagrant. Three months in the House of Correction."[80]

The offender subjected to this process emerges punished but unchanged. He returns to the streets, and it is likely that the cycle soon will be repeated in all its futility.

.   .   .   .   .

---

[76] Sheridan, *op. cit., supra* note 72, at p. 41.
[77] See chapter 2 *supra*.
[78] See, e.g., Sheridan, *op. cit. supra* note 72, at pp. 72–78.
[79] Foote, *supra* note 72, at pp. 72–78.
[80] *Id.* at p. 611.

Justice of the Peace Courts

Justice of the peace courts are the rural counterparts of the urban lower criminal courts. These courts developed in an era of slow transportation and communication to provide isolated small communities with a quick means of hearing minor criminal cases and exercising committing authority locally. But the conditions which gave rise to the development of justices' courts largely disappeared with the advent of modern means of travel and almost instantaneous communication. As a result, the laymanned, fee-paid court is an anachronism.

Legal authorities, reform groups, and laymen long have drawn attention to deficiencies in justice of the peace courts. While some improvements have been made, there is pervasive evidence that substantial problems still must be solved in the operation of these courts and in the quality of justice they dispense.

As of 1965, in 32 of the 35 States in which the justice of the peace heard criminal cases or exercised committing authority, he was remunerated for his services by a fee or assessment against the parties depending upon the outcome or volume of litigation.[81] In three States the justice still receives payment only when he convicts and collects his fee from the defendant, despite a Supreme Court decision 40 years ago holding such a practice unconstitutional.[82]

Use of the fee system in justice courts has been condemned for years.[83] Most authorities have agreed that it distorts the administration of justice.

.   .   .   .   .

[81] Alabama, Arkansas, Delaware, Florida, Georgia, Indiana, Iowa, Kansas, Kentucky, Louisiana, Michigan, Minnesota, Mississippi, Montana, Nebraska, Nevada, New Mexico, North Carolina, Oklahoma, Oregon, Pennsylvania, South Carolina, South Dakota, Tennessee, Texas, Utah, Vermont, Virginia, Washington, West Virginia, Wisconsin, and Wyoming. Institute of Judicial Administration, *The Justice of the Peace Today* (1965), tables 1 and 2.

[82] See *Tumey v. Ohio*, 273 U.S. 510 (1927). See also *Hulett v. Julian*, 250 F. Supp. 208 (M.D. Alabama 1966). In Delaware, Kansas, Nebraska, Mississippi, New Mexico, South Dakota, and Washington justices are paid by the defendant if he is convicted or by the State or county if he is acquitted. Vanlandingham, "The Decline of the Justice of the Peace," *Kansas Law Review,* 1964, 12:389, 393. Other less direct forms of nonsalaried payment to justices exist, but all are based on the volume or outcome of cases before the justice. See Reynolds, "The Fee System Courts—Denial of Due Process," *Oklahoma Law Review,* 1964, 17:373.

[83] See, e.g., American Bar Association Section of Judicial Administration, *The Improvement of the Administration of Justice* (4th ed., 1961), p. 96; Coe, *A Study of the Justice of the Peace in Onondaga County* (1931); Lummus, *The Trial Judge* (1937), pp. 77, 80; Maitland, *The Constitutional History of England* (1908), p. 135; Warren, *Traffic Courts* (1942); Morris, "The 'J.P.'—Should He Be Abolished?" *Saturday Evening Post,* October 11, 1958, p. 19; Kennedy, "The Poor Man's Court of Justice," *Journal of American Judicature Society,* 1940, 23:221; Reynolds, *supra* note 82, at p. 385; Smith, "The Justice of the Peace System in the United States, *California Law Review,* 1927, 15:118; Sunderland, "A Study of the Justices of the Peace and Other Minor Courts," *Connecticut Bar Journal,* 1947, 21:300; Vanlandingham, *supra* note 82 at p. 392; Vanlandingham, "Pecuniary Interest of the Justices of the Peace in Kentucky—The Aftermath of *Tumey v. Ohio*," *Kentucky Law Journal,* 1957, 45:607. See also *State ex. rel. Osborne v. Chinn,* 146 West Virginia 610, 121 S.E. 2d t10 (1961).

Reports from States in which justices are paid on an annual basis by the county or State for cases resulting in acquittal indicate that justices tend to convict to avoid having to wait for the county to pay.[84] No matter what form of fee system is used, the public is unlikely to go beyond the fact that fees are collected and can draw only adverse conclusions from the fact.

Other widespread criticisms of the justice of the peace are that he lacks legal training and is ignorant of proper judicial procedure. Recent research indicates that the justice is not required to be a lawyer in all or some part of 34 States.[85] In addition, there are indications that justices occasionally fail to carry out the requirements of due process and keep abreast of current developments in the law and that they sometimes have disregarded or failed to understand jurisdictional limitations.[86]

Other defects in the justice-of-the-peace courts arise from the lack of supervision and control of their activities. Questionable practices may often go unchecked.

. . . . .

Because most of these courts are independent entities dependent on local financial resources, they are often unable to afford courtrooms, office facilities, or clerical assistance necessary for effective operation.[87] In Montana one justice reportedly tried a case while repairing an automobile; another justice disposed of a case while sitting on a tractor during a pause from plowing his field.[88] Where courtrooms are available, undignified and inconvenient physical conditions are the rule rather than the exception.

The unhealthy tendency to view these courts as local revenue-producing devices as well as the justice's political responsibility to a small area colors the quality of justice dispensed in these courts. It has often been noted that

[84] Vanlandingham, "The Decline of the Justice of the Peace," *Kansas Law Review,* 1964, 12:389, 394.

[85] Alabama, Arizona, Arkansas, Delaware, Florida (admission to practice required in two counties), Georgia, Idaho, Indiana, Kansas, Kentucky, Louisiana, Maryland (legal training required in some counties), Michigan (legal training required in larger cities), Minnesota, Mississippi (training course required of nonlawyer JP's beginning 1968), Montana, Nebraska, Nevada, New Mexico (justices must attend one justice of the peace conference a year), New York (completion of training course required of nonlawyers), Oklahoma, Oregon, Pennsylvania, South Carolina, South Dakota, Tennessee, Texas, Utah, Vermont, Virginia, Washington (must be admitted to practice in cities over 5,000 population), West Virginia, Wisconsin, Wyoming. Institute of Judicial Administration, *op. cit. supra* note 81, tables 1 and 2. In Oregon during 1966 only 9 of 70 justices of the peace had law degrees. *1966 Oregon Judicial Council Ann. Report 24.* In Nevada during 1963 only one lawyer served as justice of the peace in the entire state. Vanlandingham, *supra* note 84, at p. 391.

[86] Moreland, *Modern Criminal Procedure* (1959), pp. 165–166; *Virginia Judicial Conference Report,* pp. 23, 25; Sunderland, *supra* note 83, at p. 316; Vanlandingham, *supra* note 84, at p. 392.

[87] Mason and Kimball, "Montana Justices' Courts—According to the Law," *Montana Law Review,* 1961, 23:62,65. Twenty-four States make no provision for clerical aid to justices of the peace. Twelve States provide clerks for justices in larger governmental units or leave the matter for local determination. Institute of Judicial Administration, *op. cit. supra* note 81, tables 1 and 2.

[88] Montana Legislative Council, *Report on Justice of the Peace Courts* (1960), p. 3.

local offenders may have cases, usually traffic offenses, fixed in advance, while out-of-State defendants must pay the full fine or penalty.[89]

. . . . .

Court Proceedings

Specific aspects of court proceedings not dealt with elsewhere in this volume have great impact on the administration of justice. Methods of changing initial proceedings, through bail reform and summons procedures, are discussed in this chapter, as is the development of early factfinding techniques and mutual discovery between prosecution and defense. The possibility of appeal by the prosecution is considered, and ways to improve the present cumbersome habeas corpus process are proposed. Finally, the chapter discusses the problem of poverty and discrimination in the criminal process and also reviews current proposals that seek to balance the need for freedom of activity by news media and the requirements for a fair trial.

Bail

Bail is a procedure for releasing arrested persons on financial or other condition to ensure their return for trial. Money bail is a prime example of a traditional practice in the criminal law that has not proven adequate to meet the needs of an evolving concept of criminal justice. Recent bail reform has shown that careful fact gathering for pretrial release decisions, experimentation with standards for release without bail, and the mobilization of broad public and professional interest can change long-established practices. The directions in which changes should be encouraged have become clear as a result of the work of the Vera Institute of Justice, bail and summons projects throughout the country, and the enlightened approach of the Federal Bail Reform Act of 1966.

THE BAIL SYSTEM IN OPERATION

The shortcomings of the traditional bail system are now widely known and well documented. The National Conference on Bail and Criminal Justice, held in 1964, focused attention on the wastefulness and unfairness of the system.[90] Numerous studies all over the country also have documented its deficiencies.[91] The system's major fault is exclusive reliance on

[89] See, e.g., Vanlandingham, *supra* note 84, at p. 391; American Bar Association Section of Judicial Administration, *op. cit. supra* note 83, at p. 98.
[90] See National Conference on Bail and Criminal Justice, *Proceedings and Interim Report* (1965).
[91] See *Attorney General's Commission on Poverty and the Administration of Federal Criminal Justice, Report* (1963), pp. 58–59 (hereinafter cited as *Attorney General's Report*); Ares, Rankin, and Sturz, "The Manhattan Bail Project—An Interim Report on the Use of Pre-Trial Parole," *New York University Law Review*, 1963, 38:67; Rankin, "The Effects of Pretrial Detention," *New York University Law Review*, 1964, 39:641;

the posting of money to ensure the defendant's return. Typically an arrested person is brought by the police before a committing magistrade or judge who fixes an amount of money as security for his appearance at trial. In some courts bail schedules set an amount for each offense, and if the defendant can post that amount, the judge seldom considers the case individually. Under either method if the defendant can post the required amount or can pay a bondsman to post it for him, he is released until trial. If he cannot, he remains in jail. If the defendant fails to appear for trial, the bond may be forfeited.

The standard rate of premiums paid to bondsmen is about 10 percent of the face amount of the bond, although rates as high as 20 percent have been reported.[92] When bail is set at more than $500, premiums become more than many defendants can afford. A study of New York bail practices indicates that 25 percent of all defendants failed to make bail at $500, 45 percent failed at $1,500, and 63 percent at $2,500.[93] Although the proportion of persons failing to make bail varies widely from place to place, a recent study of large and small counties shows that it often is substantial.[94]

.   .   .   .   .

A central fault of the existing system is that it detains too many people, with serious consequences for defendants, the criminal process, and the community. The aim of reform, therefore, must be to reduce pretrial detention to the lowest level without allowing the indiscriminate release of persons who pose substantial risks of flight or of criminal conduct.

Another serious fault of the present bail system is that it fails to promote decisions founded on facts about the accused. Money bail is traditionally set on the basis of the alleged offense rather than on the background of the particular defendant, principally because little information about him is ordinarily available except his prior criminal record. As a result, prohibitively high bail may be set where there is in fact little risk of flight, while at the same time unreliable defendants are released with inadequate assurance that they will appear for trial.

.   .   .   .   .

Discrimination and Poverty

Justice is most seriously threatened when prejudice distorts its capacity to operate fairly and equally, whether the prejudice that blinds judgment operates purposefully, as in discrimination in jury selection or sentencing

---

Foote, "A Study of the Administration of Bail In New York City," *University of Pennsylvania Law Review*, 1958, 106:693; Note, "Compelling Appearance in Court—Administration of Bail in Philadelphia," *University of Pennsylvania Law Review*, 1954, 102:1031.

[92] Freed and Wald, *Bail in the United States: 1964* (1964), pp. 23–24.

[93] Foote, *supra* note 72.

[94] Silverstein, "Bail in the State Courts—A Field Study and Report," *Minnesota Law Review*, 1966, 50:621, 627, 630–631.

based on racial factors, or unintentionally, through substantially disadvantaging the poor.[95]

These threats to justice may be seen in disparate settings. While important progress has been made in all sections of the country, in some rural southern courts practices persist that are the product of a system in which Negroes long have been excluded from juries and from the electorate which selects judges and prosecutors, a system which operates in blatant violation of Federal constitutional amendments and statutes almost a century old. Discrimination in dispensing justice is accompanied by less glaring but equally vicious practices, courtroom segregation and continuing displays of disrespect for Negro defendants, witnesses, and attorneys. There is evidence that the same segregated system often results in enforcement of a dual standard of justice: Charges and sentences habitually are more severe in cases where Negro defendants are asserted to have committed crimes against the person of white victims than in other cases involving identical crimes.

But discrimination, racial or otherwise, certainly is not an exclusively Southern phenomenon. In many places throughout the nation court personnel, judges, lawyers, prosecutors, and clerks are disproportionately drawn from the white members of the community, reflecting at least in part the limited educational and political opportunities that have been open to the Negro. Even the fairest of men find their judgment distorted by stereotypes and prejudice.

The problems of the Nation's cities which are not directly racial in character contribute to the problems of the courts. The populations of many cities are collections of groups that have little understanding of each other's ways. The law and court procedures are not understood by and seem threatening to many defendants, and many defendants are not understood by and seem threatening to the court and its officers. Even such simple matters as dress, speech, and manners may be misinterpreted. Most city prosecutors and judges have middleclass backgrounds and a high degree of education. When they are confronted with a poor, uneducated defendant, they may have difficulty judging how he fits into his own society or culture. They can easily mistake a certain manner of dress or speech, alien or repugnant to them but ordinary enough in the defendant's world, as an index of moral worthlessness. They can mistake ignorance or fear of the law as indifference to it. They can mistake the defendant's resentment against the social evils with which he lives as evidence of criminality. Or conversely, they may be led by neat dress, a polite and cheerful manner, and a show of humility to believe that a dangerous criminal is merely an oppressed and misunderstood man.

It also is evident that the treatment of the poor is often disproportionately

[95] See generally Wald, *Poverty and Criminal Justice*, printed as appendix C, President's Commission on Law Enforcement and Administration of Justice, *Task Force Report: The Courts* (Washington: U.S. Government Printing Office, 1967).

harsh in the courts, principally because of the litigation disadvantages which they suffer. They lack resources demanded by an adversary procedure, and there is a relatively restricted range of dispositional possibilities available for poor defendants. These problems mirror the disadvantages to which the poor are subject in almost every aspect of social and economic life. Clearly a major effort must be made to make poverty as irrelevant as possible in criminal justice as well as other vital areas.

The unfairness of the disadvantages which poor persons accused of crime often suffer because they are poor is a discrete and obvious major flaw. The most serious of those disadvantages, inadequate defense representation, inadequate access to investigative resources and expert assistance needed to prepare and conduct a defense, commitment to jail pending trial for inability to make bail, commitment to jail after conviction for inability to pay fines, disproportionate susceptibility to sentences of imprisonment for want of community relationships which facilitate programs of supervised release, are dealt with in detail elsewhere in this report. It deserves emphasis here that these disabilities are cumulative; they often combine to deny equal justice to the impoverished defendant, regardless of his innocence or guilt, at every step in the proceeding.

Held in default of bail in an amount that he cannot afford, the defendant without funds may be shut up in jail for weeks or months prior to the trial at which he may be found not guilty or, if found guilty, found also to be a fit subject for probation. While in jail he may lose his job, and his family ties may be shaken. An acquittal will not repair these harms, and in the event of a conviction his joblessness and any lack of sympathy of members of his family will weigh strongly against a nonprison disposition. Appointed counsel is likely to be overburdened and undercompensated; he is unlikely to be an effective investigator himself in the portion of the city where the defendant's witnesses live and in which a stranger wearing business clothes is unwelcome. Counsel feels that it is inconvenient enough that he is required to go across town to the jail and undergo the lengthy visiting procedures merely to visit the defendant in a nonremunerative case. He may find it difficult to understand or believe his client, who is inarticulate and inattentive in a jail interview and whom he is likely to view as an irresponsible type. Certainly a jury is less likely to regard the defendant favorably, particularly as they see him come escorted into the courtroom through the lockup door. Every relevant indication, therefore, is that the defendant's case is weak. The prosecutor knows this and may be unwilling to make concessions that he would make in a stronger case. The Attorney General's Committee on Poverty and the Administration of Federal Criminal Justice emphasized that "one of the prime objectives of the civilized administration of justice is to render the poverty of the litigant an irrelevancy."[96]

That committee wrote:

[96] *Attorney General's Commission on Poverty and the Administration of Federal Criminal Justice, Report* (1963).

When government chooses to exert its powers in the criminal area, its obligation is surely no less than that of taking reasonable measures to eliminate those factors that are irrelevant to just administration of the law but which, nevertheless, may occasionally affect determinations of the accused's liability or penalty. While government may not be required to relieve the accused of his poverty, it may properly be required to minimize the influence of poverty on its administration of justice.

The Committee, therefore, conceives the obligation of government less as an undertaking to eliminate "discrimination" against a class of accused persons and more as a broad commitment by government to rid its processes of all influences that tend to defeat the ends a system of justice is intended to serve. Such a concept of "equal justice" does not confuse equality of treatment with identity of treatment. We assume that government must be conceded flexibility in devising its measures and that reasonable classifications are permitted. The crucial question is, has government done all that can reasonably be required of it to eliminate those factors that inhibit the proper and effective assertion of grounds relevant to the criminal liability of the accused or to the imposition of sanctions and disabilities on the accused at all stages of criminal process?[97]

[*The President's Commission on Law Enforcement and Administration of Justice,* Task Force Report: The Courts (*Washington: U.S. Government Printing Office, 1967*), pp. 1, 4–7, 9–12, 14–15, 18–31, 34–35, 37, 50–51.]

[97] *Id.* at p. 10.

13 *Corrections*

The American correctional system is an extremely diverse amalgam of facilities, theories, techniques, and programs. It handles nearly 1.3 million offenders on an average day; it has 2.5 million admissions in the course of a year; and its annual operating budget is over a billion dollars.[1] Correctional operations are administered by Federal, State, county, and municipal governments. Some jurisdictions have developed strong programs for the control and rehabilitation of offenders. But most lack capacity to cope with the problems of preventing recidivism —the commission of further offenses. Some fail even to meet standards of humane treatment recognized for decades.

Corrections Today

Corrections remains a world almost unknown to law-abiding citizens, and even those within it often know only their own particular corner. This report therefore begins with an outline of the system as it operates today, and a brief account of its development, as background for the presentation of the directions it must take in the future.

.   .   .   .   .

About three-quarters of those under custody or community treatment on an average day in 1965 were adults, the great bulk of them felons. One-third of all offenders (426,000) were in institutions; the remaining two-thirds (857,000) under supervision in the community.

Individual offenders differ strikingly. Some seem irrevocably committed to criminal careers; others subscribe to quite conventional values or are aimless and uncommitted to goals of any kind. Many are disturbed and frustrated boys and young men. Still others are alcoholics, narcotic addicts, victims of senility, or sex deviants. This diversity poses immense problems to correctional officials, for in most institutions or community treatment

---

[1] Unless otherwise indicated, data in this chapter are drawn from the National Survey of Corrections and special tabulations provided by the Federal Bureau of Prisons and the Administrative Office of the U.S. Courts.

caseloads a wide range of offender types must be handled together. Several broad special offender groups are, however, generally recognized and accorded distinct treatment.

For some serious crimes in certain States, juveniles (usually persons under 18, but ranging from under 16 in some jurisdictions to under 21 in a few others) are held responsible as adults and are handled together with them. But, by and large, juveniles are processed in special courts under special procedures and referred to special correctional programs. Five States and the Federal Government make special provisions for young people who cannot reasonably be classified as juveniles but who, it is thought, should be dealt with differently from the fully responsible adult. The various statutes differ in the age limits set for these "youth offenders"; the lowest age is 16 and the highest is 23.

Correctional systems everywhere must provide at least to some degree for special handling of mentally ill offenders. Many of the smaller states have set up segregated quarters for them within their prisons and training schools and a few larger jurisdictions have provided special institutions. Probation and parole agencies also confront the need to provide clinical services for these persons. In recent years there has been some contention that several other classes of offenders would be more appropriately handled as psychologically disturbed persons than as criminals. Among these are alcoholics and narcotic addicts.

But beneath such diversities, certain characteristics predominate. About 95 percent of all offenders are male. Most of them are young, in the age range between 15 and 30. Juveniles alone comprise nearly a third of all offenders under correctional treatment, 63,000 in institutions and 285,000 under community supervision on an average day in 1965.

Many come from urban slums. Members of minority groups that suffer economic and social discrimination are present in disproportionate numbers. In fact, the life histories of most offenders are case studies in the ways in which social and economic factors contribute to crime and delinquency. Education, for example, is as good a barometer as any of the likelihood of success in modern America. Census data show . . . that over half of adult felony inmates in 1960 had no high school education.

Offenders also tend to lack vocational skills. Census data . . . show a higher proportion of unskilled laborers among prisoners than in the civilian labor force.

Many too have had failures in relationships with family and friends. This pattern of cumulative failure has prevented many offenders from developing a sense of self-respect, thus creating another obstacle to rehabilitation.

Theories and Methods of Corrections

Corrections today displays evidences of a number of evolutions in thought and practice, each seeking to cope with the difficult problems of punishing, deterring, and rehabilitating offenders. None has resolved these problems, and change from one to another has probably been more a product of humanitarian impulse than of rational or scientific process.

Until about the middle of the 18th century, European corrections was motivated principally by punishment and retribution, the state taking upon itself the tasks of vengeance that had earlier fallen to a victim's neighbors or kinsmen. Most crimes were dealt with by corporal punishment, and a great many by execution. The death penalty was freely prescribed by statute as deterrence; transportation and banishment to other lands were also used to accomplish the purpose of incapacitation. Those familiar with such incidents as the Salem witch trials in the late 17th century will also recall that corporal punishment and execution were used to exorcise the evil spirits that were seen as the cause of a person's crimes, and to prevent harm and contamination of the innocent.

Notions of punishment still underlie much of corrections today, particularly in popular views of what ought to be done with those who commit criminal acts. The criminal too in many cases accepts the idea of retribution—"paying the price" by undergoing punishment. However, the extent to which, and the situations in which, various sorts of punishment act as deterrents is wholly unestablished by objective research or study.

In the late 18th and early 19th centuries, with the rise of the rationalism of the Enlightenment, criminals came to be seen not as possessed by evil, but as persons who had deliberately chosen to violate the law because it gave them pleasure or profit. As developed notably by Jeremy Bentham, the rational response to crime was to penalize lawbreakers in the measure deemed necessary to offset the pleasures of illicit gain and to effect deterrence. The prison, previously used chiefly for debtors, political prisoners, and criminals awaiting other dispositions, was developed as the major correctional tool.

Not only did imprisonment suit the deterrent theories of the time, since its length could be varied with the crime, but it also served two other ends that were beginning to be emphasized in contemporary thought. One of these was humanitarianism; for incarceration seemed generally less severe than former punishments. This movement was in line with the rise of ideas associated with the Quakers and various evangelical sects that also brought reforms in the treatment of the poor, slaves, and the mentally ill. The other was reformation, for the prison was intended to serve as a place for reflection in solitude leading to repentance and redemption.

This concept gave rise to such establishments as the Eastern State Penitentiary in Pennsylvania, with cells arranged so that the inmate lived, worked, and was exercised and fed without seeing or talking to his fellow prisoners. This kind of prison was eventually abandoned in the United States because it was so inconvenient to manage, but it was copied abroad perhaps more than any other American correctional invention.

A more widespread architectural survival in this country is the kind of prison originally built at Auburn, N.Y., where inmates were housed in single cells but fed and employed together. Forbidden to speak with each other, prisoners were marched in mute lockstep from cell to factory to mess hall. Discipline was maintained by the lash. Labor of prisoners under this system was profitable to the State. Economies of constructing and maintaining such an institution appealed to legislators, and fortress prisons served effectively to incapacitate and punish even when the finer points of the philosophies that fostered them were forgotten.[2]

The idea of restraint as a necessary ingredient in corrections remains as a philosophic legacy of this era. And, to an extent that no outsider can appreciate, corrections today is shaped also by the tangible remnants of the outmoded but durable structures in which it is housed. The barriers to communication, which are literally built into prisons designed for the old "silent system" of managing prisoners, have remained as barriers to attempts to promote normal human relationships long after the rule of silence has been abandoned.

It is difficult to hold group counseling sessions when there are no rooms of a size between a cell and a mess hall. It is difficult to have modern work release when available jobs are miles away in the nearest town. It is difficult to instill self-discipline and responsible independence in an institution dedicated by its architecture to constant authoritarian control.

In practice, the operations of many such fortress prisons fell far short of the ideals which prompted the originators of the restraint model. Offenders and social misfits of all kinds were confined in immense institutions, unsegregated by sex, age, or health status. Epidemics decimated the populations of many prisons as the result of filthy surroundings, bad food, and callous administration.

Such abuses gave rise, shortly after the Civil War, to a reform government that continues to this day. At its establishment in 1870,[3] the American Prison Association adopted an almost visionary declaration of principles and established a goal that American correctional leaders have struggled ever since to achieve: "Reformation, not vindictive suffering, should be the purpose of penal treatment." The reform movement was heavily influenced by the rise of the psychological sciences, which helped to shape its emphasis on treatment of the individual, and its view of the offender as a person with social, intellectual, or emotional deficiencies that should be corrected to a point that would permit him to resume his place in the community.

On the reform model was built a far more complex approach to corrections than had existed before. Specialized institutions for various categories of offenders were developed. A wide range of services were to be provided: education, vocational training, religious guidance, and eventually psycho-

---

[2] For a contemporary account of the Auburn system, see Gustave de Beaumont and Alexis de Tocqueville, *On the Penitentiary in the United States and Its Application in France*, ed. H. R. Lantz (Carbondale, Ill.: Southern Illinois University Press, 1964), pp. 54–60, 161–165.

[3] For a fuller treatment of the reform movement than is possible here, see Harry Elmer Barnes and Negley K. Teeters. *New Horizons in Criminology* (3rd ed., Englewood Cliffs, N.J.: Prentice-Hall, Inc., 1959), pp. 322–347.

therapy in its various forms. It was assumed that prison schools and work-shops would cure some and prison factories accustom others to the satisfactions of regular employment as against the irregular gains of crime.

Perhaps the most important product of this movement was the initiation of community treatment programs—probation and parole—beginning with the pioneering work of John Augustus in 1841. These services provided an alternative to confinement and opportunity to confront an individual's problems in the environment where eventually almost all offenders must succeed or fail. Such approaches, and the development of innovative institutions that attempt to incorporate some community programs, have been most widely developed with juvenile offenders.

The reform model introduced into corrections some of its most valuable concepts and methods—the idea of rehabilitation, diagnosis and classification, probation and parole. But these and similar measures have never been tested definitively. And the reform movement has seldom managed more than uneasy coexistence with earlier methods and purposes.

Correctional Institutions

There are today about 400 institutions for adult felons in this country, ranging from some of the oldest and largest prisons in the world to forestry camps for 30 or 40 trusted inmates. Some are grossly understaffed and underequipped—conspicuous products of public indifference. Overcrowding and idleness are the salient features of some, brutality and corruption of a few others. Far too few are well organized and adequately funded. Juvenile institutions tend to be better, but also vary greatly. The local jails and workhouses that handle most misdemeanants are generally the most inadequate in every way.

Although most inmates of American correctional institutions come from metropolitan areas, the institutions themselves often are located away from urban areas and even primary transportation routes. The original reasons for such locations were diverse and, to a large extent, now outdated: interest in banishing dangerous persons to a remote locale; belief that a rural setting is salutary for slum-reared delinquents; the desire of rural legislators to create public employment among their constituents. Remoteness interferes with efforts to reintegrate inmates into their communities and makes it hard to recruit correctional staff, particularly professionals.

Prisons designed for secure custody typically have been built of stone, steel, and concrete. They are noteworthy for their endurance. Sixty-one prisons opened before 1900 are still in use. In the juvenile field, 16 percent of the living units in State training schools are at least 50 years old.

There are still many large maximum-security prisons operating in the United States today. The directory of the American Correctional Association showed a 1965 average population of over 2,000 inmates in 21 prisons.

Four of these had well over 4,000 inmates each: San Quentin in California; the Illinois State Prison complex at Joliet and Stateville; the Michigan State Prison at Jackson; and the Ohio State Penitentiary at Columbus.

Rehabilitative services for the adult offender are most likely to be available in correctional facilities for felons. Very few jails, where misdemeanants are confined, have advanced beyond the level of minimum sanitation and safety standards for inmates and guards. The net result is that only a small fraction of the adult offenders who were incarcerated in jails in 1965 were receiving any correctional services except restraint.

. . . . .

Community Treatment

While most offenders now under correctional control—some two-thirds, including those on parole after institutionalization—are in the community, the "treatment" afforded them is more illusion than reality. Impressive probation and parole operations do exist here and there around the country. Some experimental projects have built up evidence for particular techniques and documented their superiority to penal confinement for reducing recidivism. But the United States spends only 20 percent of its corrections budget and allocates only 15 percent of its total staff to service the 67 percent of offenders in the corrections workload who are under community supervision.

Probation and parole officers have too much to do and too little time in which to do it. Over 76 percent of all misdemeanants and 67 percent of all felons on probation are in caseloads of 100 or over, though experience and available research data indicate an average of 35 is about the highest likely to permit effective supervision and assistance. At best, they receive cursory treatment from overworked probation officers who must also spend typically half of their time preparing presentence investigations for the court. In addition, their efforts often are held suspect by employers, police, school officials, and other community figures whose help is essential if the offender is to be fitted into legitimate activities.

The statistics from the National Survey of Corrections make clear the enormity of the community treatment task and the smallness of the resources available to accomplish it. They do not, however, convey the everyday problems and frustrations which result from that disparity.

. . . . .

Presentence Investigation and Diagnosis

. . . . .

At present, many jurisdictions fall far short of achieving optimum dispositions of offenders at sentencing. Sentencing patterns even in terms of the grossest alternative, between probation and institutionalization, vary radically among jurisdictions and even judges. A study in one State of county-to-county variations in commitments to State institutions as opposed to placement on probation, for example, revealed differences as great as 10 to 1 between counties. Even when those counties with similar ethnic, social, and economic compositions were compared, they showed differences of from 50 to 100 percent in commitment rates to institutions as opposed to probation.[4]

. . . . .

The lack of adequate dispositional information of the sort corrections could provide is, however, without a doubt a major cause for irrational sentencing. In the vast majority of cases, particularly less serious ones, the judge's exposure to a defendant is far too cursory to give an adequate impression of his character and background for determination of the best correctional treatment for him. Moreover, a courtroom setting is unsuited to discovering many of the sorts of information relevant to sentencing, and many judges lack the training and experience to evaluate such information as they can elicit.

Presentence Investigation

At present, the main tool for providing background information for sentencing is the presentence report. This report is prepared in most cases by the probation staff of a court on the basis of investigation and interviews. It seeks to assess the offender's background and present circumstances and to suggest a correctional disposition.

A fully developed presentence investigation usually includes, among other items, an analysis of the offender's motivations, his identification with delinquent values, and his residential, educational, employment, and emotional history. It relates these factors to alternative plans of treatment and explores the resources available to carry out the suggested treatment.

. . . . .

Clinical Diagnosis

Presentence investigations are supplemented by clinical diagnosis by psychologists and psychiatrists in some cases where severe emotional problems, mental illness, or retardation appear to have played a distinct role in an offender's conduct, particularly where it may form the basis for his defense or where he may be committed to a mental institution in lieu of normal correctional treatment.

. . . . .

[4] California Department of the Youth Authority, *Annual Statistical Report, 1965* (Sacramento: The Department, 1966), p. 17.

Reception and Classification Centers

Reception and classification centers operated by correctional agencies represent another resource now being developed to improve intake decision-making. Such centers provide a chance for more extended testing and screening to secure data to be used in choosing the best correctional program for offenders. Such information can be gathered over the course of several weeks, during which interviews, observation, and testing can explore the past behavior and present attitudes of an offender, his educational level and vocational skills and aptitudes, his family and social background, and other factors relevant to development of a plan of disposition and treatment.

. . . . .

Classification of Offenders

. . . . .

Classification systems have had quite different purposes. Some are of immediate relevance to corrections, either in determining treatment or enabling more efficient and effective management of offenders in institutions. Some have less immediate implications, seeking out causes or explanations for criminal behavior that may bear on correctional treatment ultimately but are not framed in these terms directly.

. . . . .

It has been pointed out more recently that the development of relatively uniform groupings and methods of classification would aid immeasurably in the comparative evaluation of different programs and might form the basis for more accurate predictions of the performance of a given offender under different correctional alternatives. The intake process would thus become one in which correctional screening produced dispositional recommendations based on previous empirical experience with like offenders under a variety of treatment alternatives. The establishment of typologies would open the way to a science of correctional intervention.

A Preliminary Typology

With these advantages in mind, several efforts have been made to work toward a common basis for groupings. At a conference on delinquent typologies sponsored by the National Institute of Mental Health in 1966, a cross-tabulation of a number of classification systems was attempted. There are many areas of present agreement and overlap among the different typologies, and there seems to be considerable agreement about the validity as a preliminary grouping of the following major types of offender.

THE PROSOCIAL OFFENDER

Most offenders of this type are viewed as "normal" individuals, identifying with legitimate values and rejecting the norms of delinquent subcultures. Their offenses usually grow out of extraordinary pressures. They are most frequently convicted of crimes of violence, such as homicide or assault, or naively executed property offenses, such as forgery.

Some prosocial offenders, while attached to the legitimate system, may exhibit various neurotic manifestations. They are referred to in the descriptive typologies as "intimidated," "disturbed," "overinhibited," "anxious," "depressed," or "withdrawn."

Many of these offenders, it seems agreed, really need no rehabilitative treatment at all. The problem with some of them is to get them out of the correctional cycle before they are harmed by contact with other offenders. For example, one study of prosocial offenders in a reformatory setting found that the lowest recidivism rates occurred among the members of this type who served the briefest possible sentences and who were isolated and not involved in therapy programs. By contrast, those who stayed longer and took part in treatment programs—that is, participated actively with other inmates—did less well.[5]

Those prosocial offenders who exhibit neurotic symptoms of various kinds need treatment aimed primarily at resolving the anxiety and conflicts exhibited. Ordinarily, these offenders need greater insight into the reasons for their delinquent behavior and need to learn how to manage conflicts and anxieties more effectively. Thus, individual and group counseling, psychotherapy, and family services are most frequently recommended.

THE ANTISOCIAL OFFENDER

This type of offender identifies with a delinquent subculture, if he resides in an area which has such a subculture, or exhibits a generally delinquent orientation by rejecting conventional norms and values. He is usually described as "primitive," "underinhibited," "impulsive," "hostile," "negativistic," or "alienated." It is generally agreed that he does not see himself as delinquent or criminal but rather as a victim of an unreasonable and hostile world. His history often includes patterns of family helplessness, indifference, or inability to meet needs of children, absence of adequate adult role models, truancy in school, and inadequate performance in most social spheres.

The antisocial offender, it is agreed in many of the typologies, should be provided an environment with clear, consistent social demands but one in

[5] Duane Strinden, "Parole Prediction Using Criminological Theory and Manifold Classification Techniques" (unpublished master's thesis, University of Washington, 1959). See also Donald L. Garrity, "The Prison as a Rehabilitation Agency," in D. R. Cressey, ed., *The Prison* (New York: Holt, Rinehart, and Winston, 1961).

which concern for his welfare and interests is regularly communicated to him. Methods of group treatment are recommended in order to increase the offender's social insight and skill.

In the last analysis, however, the offender's value system must be changed. The attempt to get him to identify with a strong and adequate adult role model is an important part of most treatment programs designed for this group. Treatment also aims at enlarging the cultural horizon of the antisocial offender, redefining his contacts with peers, and broadening and revising his self-conception.

THE PSEUDOSOCIAL MANIPULATOR

This type of offender is described as not having adopted conventional standards, as being guilt-free, self-satisfied, and power-oriented, nontrusting, emotionally insulated, and cynical. Personal histories reveal distrustful and angry families in which members are involved in competitive and mutually exploitative patterns of interaction, parents who feel deprived and who expect the children to meet their dependency needs, parental overindulgence alternating with frustration, and inconsistent patterns of affection and rejection.

Many and diverse recommendations are made for handling this type. Some investigators recommended long-term psychotherapy. Others encourage the offender to redirect his manipulative skills in a socially acceptable manner. Still others call for the establishment of a group setting in which the offender's capacity for playing contradictory roles is immediately discovered; he is confronted with evidence of his inconsistent conduct and is forced to choose among the alternatives. In general, the investigators give a rather discouraging picture of prospects for successful treatment.

THE ASOCIAL OFFENDER

Another type of offender is one who acts out his primitive impulses, is extremely hostile, insecure, and negativistic, and demands immediate gratification. An important characteristic is his incapacity to identify with others. This distinguishes the asocial from the antisocial type who, although committed to delinquent values, is often described as being loyal to peers, proud, and capable of identifying with others.

The asocial offender requires elementary training in human relations. The most striking characteristic of this group is an inability to relate to a therapist or to the social world around them. Most investigators recommend a simple social setting offering support, patience, and acceptance of the offender, with only minimal demands on his extremely limited skills and adaptability.

Before pressures toward conformity can be exerted, the asocial offender needs to learn that human interaction is always a two-way process. Methods need to be used which reduce the offender's fear of rejection and abandonment. When these fundamentals have been learned, he is probably ready for more conventional therapy in both group and individual settings.

Uses and Difficulties of Classification

. . . . .

While a standardized typology for all correctional purposes and the quantified science of corrections that it would make possible remain, for the present at least, merely theoretical possibilities, the value of classifications formed for specific management and treatment of purposes seems much clearer.

A study by Beck, for example, suggests that socialized delinquents should be placed in open and relaxed institutions where their energies can be channeled into nondelinquent activities, but that unsocialized aggressive delinquents should not be placed in a permissive institutional environment since that would only make them more difficult to handle.[6] Another typologist, Gibbons, suggests that predatory gang delinquents be segregated from other boys and that casual, nongang delinquents be kept as far as possible entirely out of the correctional system.[7] These are obviously only very general examples, and most typologists would identify a variety of subgroups within such classifications for whom treatment should vary.

Work along these lines has, however, been confined to relatively small and highly staffed experimental programs, and methods of classification are still in almost all cases far too cumbersome for routine administration. In many cases it has been found that treatment typologies are effective in predicting success almost in the degree to which they become complex and elaborate. The Community Treatment Project in California, for example, began with a fairly elaborate classification system developed by Warren on the basis of the maturity levels of delinquents and has been developed into an extremely detailed classification system with increasingly specific treatment strategies.[8]

. . . . .

Diversion Prior to Adjudication

The correctional function in sentencing decisions has been outlined above. But there remain the substantial number of persons who come into the system of criminal justice, particularly at the juvenile and petty offender

[6] B. M. Beck, "What We Can Do About Juvenile Delinquency," *Child Welfare* 1954 pp. 33–37.

[7] D. C. Gibbons, *Changing the Lawbreaker* (Englewood, N.J.: Prentice-Hall, 1965).

[8] M. Q. Warren et. al., "Interpersonal Maturity Level Classification (Juvenile): Diagnosis and Treatment of Low, Middle, and High Maturity Delinquents" *Community Treatment Project Report* (Sacramento: California Youth Authority, 1966).

levels, who are or could be diverted well before the sentencing point to alternative treatment programs or simply released with a warning.

There is increasing evidence . . . that, for many lesser and first offenders, full exposure to criminal justice processes and formal correctional treatment may only contribute to the possibility of recidivism. Labeled as delinquents or criminals, cast among hardened offenders in jails and prisons, separated in many cases for weeks or months from jobs, school, and other important institutions in the normal community, persons may be confirmed in crime who would otherwise have returned to law-abiding ways.

The reintegrative services necessary to rehabilitate many of these minor offenders are much easier to provide in a noncorrectional setting, preferably through normal noncriminal institutions in the community. It is simpler and more effective, for example, to provide remedial education and job training, necessary to secure for a delinquent a responsible place in society, in regular schools, than it is in a reformatory.

There are also a large variety of offender groups for whom specialized treatment of a noncriminal nature holds in many cases greater promise than traditional correctional approaches. Drunkenness offenders, vagrants, non-support and domestic relations cases, the mentally ill and retarded are among such groups. Civil detoxification and residential aftercare facilities for drunks, welfare and conciliation services, mental hospitals and sheltered workshops are all in many of these cases more rational and effective dispositions than the regular criminal justice process.

．　．　．　．　．

Disposition Pending Trial

Corrections also has an important role in the nondecisional aspect of intake: the handling of persons pending adjudication. At present this role is almost entirely confined to detention of those not released on bail or on their own recognizance. For adults, local jail facilities used for detention are in fact . . . generally operated by law enforcement officials and limited to merely custodial functions. Both for those who are held in custody and for those released in the community pending adjudication, however, there are much wider possibilities for correctional service.

．　．　．　．　．

While the situation for juveniles in detention is deplorable in many jurisdictions, conditions for adult detainees can only be described as worse. Local jails are commonly used not only for prisoners serving sentences but for detention of suspects awaiting trial and not released on bail or other-wise. The lengthy delays often attendant upon pretrial processes give rise to frequent situations of persons serving weeks or months while legally inno-cent only to be released or given a shorter term upon conviction.

. . . [O]ther prosecutorial reforms . . . Bail would go far to alleviate this situation by eliminating unnecessary delays and obtaining release pending trial for a greater number of individuals for whom detention is not necessary for community security. Corrections has an important role to play in providing information for the decisions which must be made in these programs. Indeed, over one-third of the 42 bail projects operating in 1965 utilized correctional personnel for screening.[9]

Largely because of the historical development of bail procedures and the shortage of probation staff, there has been very little use of correctional resources to supervise persons released in the community pending trial. It is quite common for persons released on recognizance to be placed under the responsibility of their families, their lawyers, or other private citizens interested in them. In some jurisdictions, such as St. Louis, persons released on recognizance are required to check in periodically with a probation officer. Such supervision is also authorized by the Federal Bail Reform Act of 1965. With adequate resources, it might be employed to advantage in many cases, at least to ascertain a suspect's presence in the jurisdiction.

.   .   .   .   .

It is probably true that persons who have not yet been convicted of a crime are subjected to the worst aspects of the American correctional system. Unconvicted persons, as yet legally innocent, are almost inevitably subjected to the tightest security and receive the least attention of any group in jails.

.   .   .   .   .

This primary concern for security imposes regimentation, repeated searches, and close surveillance on detainees. Most jails also have poor facilities for visiting, thus hampering a detainee's efforts to arrange for his defense and maintain contacts with the community. A detainee's lawyer, family, and friends have little opportunity for privacy. Where extreme security measures are the rule, visiting takes place in rooms where visitors are separated from the prisoner by heavy screens and conversation is carried on by telephone. . . .

Pretrial detention involves substantial numbers of persons each year, although incomplete reporting makes it difficult to estimate precisely the number of persons detained. Some data from various jurisdictions give an indication that the numbers are quite large. A one-day census in California revealed that about 25,000 persons were confined in local jails and camps. Of this number 9,000 were unsentenced prisoners.[10] In Multnomah County, Oregon, more than 1,700 were confined awaiting trial during fiscal year 1966.[11] The District of Columbia held 10,520 during a comparable period.[12]

[9] "Bail and Summons: 1965," *Institute on the Operation of Pretrial Release Projects,* New York, October 14–15, and *Justice Conference on Bail and Remands in Custody, London, November 27, 1965* (Washington: U.S. Department of Justice and Vera Foundation, Inc., 1966), foldout sheet.

[10] *Crime and Delinquency in California, 1965* (Sacramento: California Department of Justice, 1966), p. 131.

[11] Data supplied by the Sheriff's Office, Multnomah County, Oregon.

[12] Data supplied by the District of Columbia Department of Corrections.

According to several surveys, the percentage of persons charged who were subsequently detained awaiting trial ranged from 31 percent in a New Jersey County to 75 percent in Baltimore. Average time served in detention ranged from 6 weeks to 8 months in some jurisdictions.[13]

Probation

Slightly more than half of the offenders sentenced to correctional treatment in 1965 were placed on probation—supervision in the community subject to the authority of the court. Table 1 sets forth data from the

Table 1—Number of Offenders on Probation, and on Parole or in Institutions, 1965; Projections for 1975

Location of offender	1965		1975	
	Number	Percent	Number	Percent
Probation_____	684,088	53	1,071,000	58
Parole or institution_____	598,298	47	770,000	42
Total_____	1,282,386	100	1,841,000	100

SOURCES: 1965 data from National Survey of Corrections and special tabulations provded by the Federal Bureau of Prisons and the Administrative Office of the U.S. Courts; 1975 projections by R. Christensen, of the Commission's Task Force on Science and Technology, as described in Appendix B of this report.

National Survey of Corrections and the Federal corrections system on the number of persons under probation on an average day in 1965 and the number in institutions or on parole. Also shown are estimates of what these populations are likely to be in 1975. . . . As the table indicates, probation is the correctional treatment used for most offenders today and is likely to be used increasingly in the future.[14]

The estimates for probation shown in the above table project a growth in the number of adults on probation almost 2½ times greater than the growth in institutional and parole populations. The projected growth in juvenile probation is also substantial. . . . [T]here are rapidly developing very

[13] Freed and Wald, *op. cit.*, pp. 40–41.
[14] These projections are drawn from the special study completed by R. Christensen, of the *Commission's Task Force on Science and Technology*, which is described in appendix B of this report. The projections, together with the 1965 data supplied by the National Survey of Corrections and special tabulations provided by the Federal Bureau of Prisons and the Administrative Office of the U.S. Courts, indicate the following: the number of adults in jails and prisons and on parole in 1965 was 475,042; for 1975 it is projected as 560,000. There were 459,140 adults on probation in 1965; for 1975 the number is projected as 693,000. The population of juvenile training schools and parole programs in 1965 was 123,256; for 1975 it is projected as 210,000. The number of juveniles on probation in 1965 was 224,948, and for 1975 the number is projected as 378,000.

promising intensive community supervision and residential programs, which could further shift the number of juveniles destined for institutions to community-based treatment. Thus, the projections for juvenile probation might actually be low.

The best data available indicate that probation offers one of the most significant prospects for effective programs in corrections. It is also clear that at least two components are needed to make it operate well. The first is a system that facilitates effective decision-making as to who should receive probation; the second is the existence of good community programs to which offenders can be assigned. Probation services now available in most jurisdictions fall far short of meeting either of these needs.

Present Services and Needs

Current probation practices have their origin in the quasi-probationary measures of an earlier day. The beginnings of probation are usually traced to Boston, where in 1841 a bootmaker bailed a number of defendants in the lower court on a volunteer basis. In 1897, Missouri passed legislation that made it possible to suspend execution of sentence for young and for petty offenders. This statute did not make provision for the supervision of probationers. However, Vermont established such a plan on a county basis in 1898, and Rhode Island established a state-administered system in 1899.[15]

After the turn of the century, the spread of probation was accelerated by the juvenile court movement. Thirty-seven States and the District of Columbia had a children's court act by 1910. Forty of them had also introduced probation for juveniles. By 1925, probation for juveniles was available in every State, but this did not happen in the case of adult probation until 1956.

Within States, probation coverage is still often spotty. Services for juveniles, for example, are available in every county in only 31 States. In one State, a National Survey staff observer noted, only two counties have probation services. A child placed on probation in the other counties is presumed to be adjusting satisfactorily until he is brought back to court with a new charge.

Table 2 shows the number of delinquents and adult felons on probation at the end of 1965 and the annual costs of these services. It is quickly apparent in terms of the number of persons served and of total operating costs that the juvenile system has relatively greater resources than the adult. Cost comparisons, however, require qualification. The juvenile total includes the cost of many foster homes and some private and public institutional costs. Furthermore, juvenile probation in some jurisdictions has a

[15] Paul W. Tappan, *Crime, Justice, and Correction* (New York: McGraw-Hill Book Co., 1960), pp. 546–549.

Table 2—Number of Felons and Juveniles on Probation, 1965, and Annual Costs of Services for Each Group

Type of probation	Number on probation	Annual costs
Felony	257,755	$37,937,808
Juvenile	224,948	75,019,441
Total	482,703	112,957,249

SOURCES: National Survey of Corrections and special tabulations provided by the Federal Bureau of Prisons and the Administrative Office of the U.S. Courts.

substantial responsibility for orphaned or other nondelinquent dependent children.

Probation in the United States is administered by hundreds of independent agencies operating under a different law in each State and under widely varying philosophies, often within the same State. They serve juvenile, misdemeanant, and felony offenders. In one city, a single State or local agency might be responsible for handling all three kinds of probation cases; in another, three separate agencies may be operating, each responsible for a different type of probationer. All of these probation programs must contend with similar issues.

Advantages of Probation

There are many offenders for whom incarceration is the appropriate sanction—either because of their dangerousness or the seriousness of their offense, or both. But in the vast majority of cases where such a sanction is not obviously essential, there has been growing disenchantment with relying heavily on institutions to achieve correctional goals. The growing emphasis on community treatment is supported by several kinds of considerations.

One has already been discussed in some detail. . . . [T]he correctional strategy that presently seems to hold the greatest promise, based on social theory and limited research, is that of reintegrating the offender into the community. A key element in this strategy is to deal with problems in their social context, which means in the interaction of the offender and the community. It also means avoiding as much as possible the isolating and labeling effects of commitment to an institution. There is little doubt that the goals of reintegration are furthered much more readily by working with an offender in the community than by incarcerating him.

These justifications seems to be borne out by the record of probation services themselves. Probation services have been characteristically poorly staffed and often poorly administered. Despite that, the success of those placed on probation, as measured by not having probation revoked, has been surprisingly high. One summary analysis of outcomes observed in 11

probation studies indicates a success rate of from 60 to 90 percent.[16] A
survey of probation effectiveness in such States as Massachusetts and New
York and a variety of foreign countries provides similar results with a
success rate at about 75 percent.[17] An exhaustive study was undertaken in
California when 11,638 adult probationers granted probation during the
period 1956–58 were followed up after 7 years. Of this group, almost 72
percent were successful in terms of not having their probation revoked.[18]

These findings were not obtained under controlled conditions, nor were
they supported by data that distinguished among the types of offenders who
succeeded or the types of services that were rendered. Nevertheless, all of
the success rates are relatively high. They are the product of a variety of
kinds of probation administered at different times and places. Even when
interpreted skeptically, they are powerful evidence that a substantial number of persons can be placed on probation and have a relatively high rate of
success.

. . . . .

Perhaps the best known effort to determine the extent to which probation
services could be used was a demonstration project conducted in Saginaw,
Mich., over a 3-year period.[19] Here, trained probation officers with relatively
low caseloads were assigned to an adult criminal court that had used
probation a little more than the 50 percent average for the state. With full
services available, including complete social histories for the use of the
court at the time of sentencing, judges imposed prison sentences for only
about 20 percent of all of the defendants who appeared before them. There
is some evidence that the revocation rate for those granted probation was
lower than in the prior 3-year period. Although these findings require more
rigorous testing, they lend weight to the view that a high percentage of
offenders can be supervised in the community and succeed.

Offenders can be kept under probation supervision at much less cost than
in institutions. The National Survey found, for example, that the average
State spends about $3,400 a year (excluding capital costs) to keep a youth
in a state training school, while it costs only about one tenth that amount to
keep him on probation.

Objections might be raised as to the validity of such comparisons, since
expenditures for probation services are now much too meager. However,
with the 1-to-10 cost ratios prevailing, probation expenditures can clearly be

[16] Ralph W. England, Jr., "What is Responsible for Satisfactory Probation and
Post-Probation Outcome?" *Journal of Criminal Law, Criminology, and Police Science,*
March-April 1957, 47:667–676.

[17] Max Crunhut, *Penal Reform* (New York, The Clarendon Press, 1948), pp. 60–82.

[18] George F. Davis, "A Study of Adult Probation Violation Rates by Means of the
Cohort Approach," *Journal of Criminal Law, Criminology, and Police Science,* March
1964, 55:70–85.

[19] "The Saginaw Probation Demonstration Project," *Michigan Crime and Delinquency
Council of the National Council on Crime and Delinquency* (New York: The Council,
1963).

increased several fold and still remain less expensive than institutional programs. This is especially true when construction costs, which now run up to and beyond $20,000 per bed in a correctional institution, are included. The differential becomes even greater if the cost of welfare assistance for the families of the incarcerated and the loss in taxable income are considered.

. . . . .

Probation and Reintegration

. . . . .

The reintegration procedures through which the offender is geared into the school or the job are not clearly defined or established. The problems are much easier to describe than the solutions. However, an approach can be defined and some specific correctional strategies discussed for dealing with the major social institutions—the family, the school, and employment.

THE FAMILY

Two major approaches shape the methods of family therapy. One is the use of the family as a field for corrective intervention on behalf of one or more of its members. Personality difficulties of these members are addressed with the family as the milieu from which the individuals emerge, but the focus is on the individual rather than the family as a whole.

The other approach sees the whole family as the target for treatment. This is the essentially reintegrative type of family therapy. Its objectives are the rehabilitation of the entire family as a healthy functioning unit. There is heavy concentration on instilling healthy child-rearing practices in cases where the children are young, on developing in adolescents the ability to cope with their present situation and those [situations] in which they may eventually find themselves, and on making complementary the dual roles of husband-and-wife and father-and-mother. An effort is made to strengthen family ties generally, and to help the family (including the delinquent or predelinquent) become effective in the community.

The Youth Development Project, conducted as a psychiatric outpatient clinic connected with the University of Texas Medical Branch, involves a team of therapists who engage in an extensive diagnostic-treatment effort lasting 2 or 3 days, during which the entire family of a delinquent are patients at the clinic. Described as multiple impact therapy, the treatment seeks to give insight and direction to the family that is motivated to seek help with its problems. Probation officers participate in these programs and later maintain contacts with the family in an effort to encourage and renew the self-reformation effort. The technique is particularly appropriate to those sparsely populated regions where treatment resources are scarce.

Other forms of family therapy have been used with the families of delinquents in large cities, often from lower socio-economic groups. Nathaniel Ackerman, of New York City, a pioneer in family therapy, has worked with families of delinquents using an approach which combines analysis, group therapy, and family education. Virginia Satir, of a group in Palo Alto, California, which has developed "conjoint family therapy," has coached a variety of workers in correctional institutions and community-based programs in methods of family therapy.

At Wyltwick School for delinquent boys in New York, an experiment has been carried on for some time with families of delinquents from slum areas. At first, the family is interviewed together, using joint therapists. Then the parents talk with one therapist and the children with another. Often in these second sessions "the lid comes off," and the parents and children express their true feelings about each other and what is wrong with the family situation. Delinquent acts may be revealed as rooted in complete misunderstanding by the children or the parents. Reassembled once more, the family may be able to clear up some of these misunderstandings and jointly find a way to deal with the roots of delinquency.

The experiment is now being evaluated. Charles H. King, superintendent of the school, believes that the vast majority of families of delinquents can profit from family therapy, although some families will gain more from it than others and retain their gains better.

THE SCHOOL

Educational programs for offenders in the community are of several kinds. The first group is directed toward increasing the competence of offenders to participate more effectively in school programs through special classes for the educationally retarded and the use of programmed learning techniques.

Other programs directed toward offenders include those which simultaneously affect their motivations, behavior, and education skills. A particularly interesting attempt in this direction in the Collegefield project carried on in conjunction with the Newark State Teachers College, New Jersey. Delinquents assigned by a juvenile court participate in group counseling sessions for half of the day and then are taught by teachers experienced in the public school system. In this setting, youngsters are enabled not only to upgrade their academic skills but also to learn the kind of behavior required to participate in school. Moreover, the group experience increases motivation as peers define success in school as important to status in the group. When youths complete this program, they are moved into regular classroom situations.

Another major category of programs for offenders are those which direct their effort toward the school system itself. Some juvenile courts, for example, make a probation officer responsible for encouraging a specific school to develop intensive programs to attract and hold youths with deficiencies and to develop a greater tolerance on the part of administrators and teachers toward them.

A program which focuses on the school and the offender at the same time is carried out as part of the California Community Treatment project described in the next chapter. Experienced and certificated tutors assist marginal students to meet the demands of the educational system. In addition to educational coaching, the tutor counsels the youth concerning his personal behavior in school. He invests considerable time in communication with school counselors and other officials in order to interpret the youngster's needs and problems, to secure development of specialized, low-stress school programs—in short, to increasing the tolerance level of the school system. Program supervisors credit this special program with maintaining a substantially larger proportion of the delinquent population in school and with assuring some educational achievement for the youth who has been suspended or expelled.

EMPLOYMENT

The kind of job a person holds determines, to a large extent, the kind of life he leads. This is true not merely because work and income are directly related, but also because employment is a major factor in an individual's position in the eyes of others and indeed of himself. Work is therefore directly related to the goals of corrections. Glaser concludes in his extensive study, "The Effectiveness of a Prison and Parole System," that "unemployment may be among the principal causal factors in recidivism of adult male offenders."[20] It is difficult for probationers, and often to a greater extent for parolees, to find jobs. They are frequently poor, uneducated, and members of a minority group. They may have personal disabilities—behavior disorders, mental retardation, poor physical health, overwhelming family problems. And they have in any case the stigma of a criminal record to overcome.

A recent study of Federal releasees shows that, during the first month after release, only about 1 out of every 4 releasees was employed at least 80 percent of the time, and 3 out of 10 were unable to secure jobs. After 3 months, only about 4 out of 10 had worked at least 80 percent of the time, and nearly 2 out of 10 still had not been able to find work of any kind.[21]

·   ·   ·   ·   ·

Halfway Programs: The Prerelease Guidance Center

In corrections as in related fields, the "halfway house" is an increasingly familiar program. Initially, such programs were conceived for offenders

[20] Daniel Glaser, *The Effectiveness of a Prison and Parole System* (Indianapolis: Bobbs-Merrill, 1964), p. 329.
[21] *Ibid.,* p. 328.

"halfway out" of institutions, as a means of easing the stresses involved in transition from rigid control to freedom in the community. The prerelease guidance centers of the Federal Bureau of Prisons are the best-known halfway-out programs in the United States. Recently the halfway house has come to be viewed as a potential alternative to institutionalization, and thus a program for those "halfway in" between probation and institutional control.

Federal Prerelease Guidance Centers

The first prelease guidance centers of the Federal Bureau of Prisons were opened in 1961 in New York, Chicago, and Los Angeles, and others were established subsequently in Detroit, Washington, and Kansas City. Each center accommodates about 20 Federal prisoners who are transferred to it several months before their expected parole date. Thus they complete their terms in the community but under careful control.

Some of the centers are located in what were large, single-family houses; some occupy a small section or scattered rooms in a YMCA hotel; and one is located in a building once operated as a small home for needy boys. All are in neighborhoods with mixed land usage, racial integration, and nearby transportation.

Offenders transferred to these centers wear civilian clothes. They generally move from prison to the centers by public transportation without escort. For a day or two they are restricted to the building, although they may receive visitors there. In the YMCA's they eat in a public cafeteria in the building and use the public recreation areas, taking out YMCA memberships. Following a day or two of orientation and counseling, they go out to look for jobs. After they are on a job, they are gradually given more extensive leaves for recreational purposes and for visits with their families. As their parole date approaches, some may even be permitted to move out of the center, although they are still required to return to the center for conferences several times a week.

These centers are staffed in large part by persons rotated from regular institution staff who are highly oriented to counseling. One full-time employee is an employment counseling specialist. Several others, such as college students in the behavioral sciences, are employed on a part-time basis and provide the only staff coverage during the late night hours and part of the weekend. In addition to individual counseling, there are several group sessions a week. Federal probation officers, who will supervise the offenders when they go on parole, participate in the center's counseling activities. By the time a resident is ready to begin his parole, almost all of his individual counseling has been assumed by his parole supervision officer.

A major function of these temporary release programs has been to aug-

ment the information available to correctional staff. This information includes both diagnostic data on the individuals temporarily released and
information on the assets and deficiencies of correctional programs and
personnel. In addition, they provide optimum circumstances for counseling,
since the counseling can deal with immediate realities as they are encountered, rather than with the abstract and hypothetical visions of the past and
the future or the purely institutional problems to which counseling in
institutions is largely restricted.

Inmate misbehavior while on work release or in prerelease guidance centers is not a rare thing, particularly for youthful offenders. Although a majority adjust quite satisfactorily, some get drunk, some get involved in fights
and auto accidents when out with old or new friends, and some are late in
returning to the center. An appreciable number of the youth have difficulty
in holding jobs, some fail to go to work or to school when they are supposed
to be there, a few abscond, and a few get involved in further crime. The
important point is that they would be doing these things in any case, and
probably more extensively, if they had been released more completely on
their own through parole or discharge. Under the latter circumstances,
however, correctional staff would know of the releasee's difficulties, if at all,
not nearly so promptly as is possible with temporary release measures.

When an individual returns from a temporary release to home, work, or
school, his experience can be discussed with him by staff, to try to assess his
probable adjustment and to note incipient problems. Many difficulties can
be anticipated in this way. The inmate's anxieties can be relieved by
discussion, and discussion may also help him develop realistic plans for
coping with prospective problems. When persistent or serious misbehavior
occurs, sanctions are available to staff, ranging from restriction of further
leaves or temporary incarceration to renewed institutionalization, with a
recommendation to the parole board that the date of parole be deferred.

A number of offenders on work release live in prerelease guidance centers. Some of them attend school part- or full-time, in addition to or instead
of working; this sometimes is called "study release." It is particularly appropriate for juvenile and youthful offenders and is highly developed at
several State establishments resembling the Federal prerelease guidance
centers.

State Prerelease Centers

The Kentucky Department of Corrections, under a grant from the Office
of Economic Opportunity, has a series of vocational training courses in its
State reformatory which are identical with courses established at several
centers in the State under the Department of Labor. Prerelease guidance
centers were established near these centers in three cities, so that reformatory inmates could continue their institution courses in the community,

where as trainees they receive a small stipend, in addition to highly developed job placement services.

The Federal Bureau of Prisons assisted in establishing these centers and sends Federal inmates from these cities to the centers. Conversely, State correctional agencies share in the operation of the Federal prelease guidance centers in Detroit and Kansas City, assigning some state inmates there, and the District of Columbia Department of Corrections plays a major role in the operation of the center in Washington. This State-Federal collaboration could well serve as a model for many types of correctional undertaking.

Correctional Institutions

. . . . .

Just as probation and parole fail to recognize their potential, so do prisons, training schools, and other institutions. Incarceration can serve not only as a means of incapacitating offenders for whom considerations of community safety permit no other alternative, and as a deterrent and sanction in a wider range of cases, but also as an aid to treatment and rehabilitation. A period of institutionalization can in some cases help an offender by removing him from the pressures and undesirable influences of his outside life, so that he may be subjected to intensive treatment which will provide a basis for reconstruction of noncriminal community ties.

The present use of institutionalization, however, almost universally falls short of this optimum. Deficiencies in resources, inadequate knowledge, and lack of community support handicap institutions as they do community treatment. Institutional corrections suffers also from long and indiscriminate use simply for punishment and banishment, purposes which inspire in the system little imagination, hope, or effort to improve.

The average daily population handled by all correctional services in the United States in 1965 was about 1.3 million. Of this total, about 5 percent were in juvenile institutions and 28 percent were in prisons or jails. . . .

The number of inmates in State and Federal prisons for adults has decreased about 1 percent per year in the past few years, despite increases in the total population of the country and in serious crime.[22] Apparently the courts are making increased use of alternatives to commitment at the adult level. The population projection for the prison system shows the smallest aggregate increase of any of the correctional activities. By 1975 an estimated increment of some 7 percent is expected to bring the State and Federal prison load to a total of 237,000 inmates.

. . . . .

According to the National Survey of Corrections, there were 398 State facilities for adults in 1965 and 220 for juveniles. These included a variety of special facilities such as forestry camps, reception centers, minimum-secu-

[22] U.S. Department of Justice, Bureau of Prisons, *National Prisoner Statistics: Prisoners in State and Federal Institutions for Adult Felons, 1965* (Washington: The Bureau, 1966), table 1.

rity prisons, institutions with specialized functions such as trade training, and maximum-custody institutions. Most of the special facilities were found in a relatively few States. The majority of States typically had only a training school for boys, a training school for girls, a penitentiary, and usually a separate facility, such as a reformatory, for younger felons.

. . . . .

The Traditional Institution

To appreciate the problems and potentials of correctional institutions, one must have an understanding of the kind of regime that developed in the authoritarian, fortress-style prisons . . . and that still persists to a greater or lesser degree in many institutions today.

PREMISES OF THE AUTHORITARIAN REGIME

A major premise of traditional institutions is that, in order to minimize the danger to both the institutional staff and the community, security should be regarded as the dominant goal. Mechanical security measures are instituted, including the building of high walls or fences around prisons, construction of gun-towers, the searching of inmates as they pass through certain check-points, pass systems to account for inmate movement, and counts at regular intervals. The objective of custody is met quite effectively, since few prisoners escape and those who do usually are quickly apprehended.

These measures also serve the idea that deterrence requires extremes of deprivation, strict discipline, and punishment, all of which, together with considerations of administrative efficiency, make institutions impersonal, quasi-military places. Mail is censored, visiting is limited and closely supervised, privacy is virtually nonexistent, inmates march in groups and are identified by number.

Rules stressing custodial control result in special forms of "etiquette" for maintaining distance between staff and inmates. Staff are discouraged from, or even suspended or dismissed for, calling inmates "mister"; they must address prisoners only by first name, last name, or nickname. But prisoners are required to address staff members as "mister," "officer," "lieutenant" or some other title, together with their surname. Staff are not to "fraternize" with prisoners; they must deal with them in an authoritative and impersonal manner, while inmates may not "act familiar" with staff. If differences of opinion occur, particularly as to how an inmate behaved, the staff version is always to be regarded as correct.

Social distance between staff and inmates is reinforced by the mass handling of prisoners. If inmates are almost always marched in groups—to work, to eat, to play, to the barbershop, to the commissary, to their sleeping quarters—there is little chance for staff to treat them on a personal basis, especially when the groups are large. If staff see most inmates only for brief specialized functions, such as checking them through a gate or issuing them prison clothing, there also is likely to be little opportunity for them to be viewed as individuals.

Actually, in a traditional institution, these differences frequently break down, particularly when the assignment of inmates places them in contact with staff over an extended period of time. The differences also tend to break down where the staff and inmates cooperate in a common job which they share an interest in completing satisfactorily. But they still give to life in traditional institutions its basic character.

The authoritarian institution often seems to proceed, too, on the premise that it, and it alone, should be responsible for changing the offender. This assumption justifies the isolation of inmates from community contact and results in similar isolation for staffs. Not only are such institutions generally located away from large cities and frequently even from main transportation lines, but they are also generally expected to operate without any disturbance or incident that would attract public attention: escapes resulting from failures of security, crimes committed by parolees, even the appearance of inmates in the community.

An exaggerated concern for security and the belief in autonomous institutional responsibility for handling offenders combine to limit innovation and the development of community ties. Isolated, punitive, and regimented, the traditional prison and many juvenile training schools develop a monolithic society, caste-like and resistive to change.

Inmate Subcultures

Distance between staff and inmates is accentuated by forces that operate unofficially through inmates. Because staff have nearly absolute authority to punish or reward, inmates are especially concerned with keeping many of their activities covert. Accordingly, whenever an inmate communicates with staff, he runs the risk of being accused by his fellows of informing on them and thus of suffering violent reprisals.

In a situation where inmates have minimal recourse to staff, they are also more vulnerable to abuse and exploitation by other inmates. As a consequence, inmates tend to become progressively more wary of each other as well as of staff. "Do your own time" becomes the inmate slogan, signifying aloofness from and indifference to the interests of both staff and other inmates. This selfcenteredness is, in turn, encouraged by staff as a device to inhibit solidarity among inmates.

As a result of this situation, a peculiar social structure develops among both inmates and staff.[23] The elite inmate group, the "politicians" or "big

---

[23] See chapter 8 by Clarence Schrag and chapters 4 and 7 by Richard H. McCleery in Donald R. Cressey, ed., *The Prison: Studies in Institutional Organization and Change* (New York: Holt, Rinehart and Winston, 1961). See also John Irwin and Donald R. Cressey, "Thieves, Convicts and the Inmate Culture" in Howard S. Becker, ed., *The Other Side: Perspective on Deviance* (New York: Free Press, 1964), pp. 225–245.

shots," are those inmates who have not only earned respect among their fellows but also have developed rapport with staff. These tend to be persons with extensive institutional experience, who have been tested in interactions with other inmates sufficiently that they are neither readily "pushed around" by their fellows nor distrusted as "stool pigeons."

They have also been tested sufficiently by staff to be assigned jobs in offices or other locations where they can communicate readily with staff and often have access to institutional records. Because of their possession of "inside" information and their access to staff, they can command considerable deference from other inmates. However, they can also convince inmates that they generally work for their interest through manipulating the staff. They are thus the leadership in the inmate caste and the middlemen between the staff and inmates.

Beneath the "politicians" in status are the great mass of inmates, often called "right guys" or "straights." Among them a few may ultimately move to politician status. Most of them, however, are not routinely thrown into very personal contact with staff. Should they have an opportunity for private communication with staff, they are likely to be suspected by inmates.

The lowest stratum of inmate society is occupied by the sex offenders, the physically weak and immature, the mentally disordered and retarded. Aggressive inmates are distrusted by both staff and inmates and do not necessarily occupy a high position in the inmate society. They are feared by inmates and sometimes by the staff. Their tendency toward violence rather than manipulation imperils the stability of the institution and the maintenance of reciprocal relationships between staff and inmates.

In all institutions, but especially in those for juveniles, the achievement or preservation of a reputation for toughness, smartness, and independence from authority can be a primary inmate concern—even an obsession. Such a reputation may be nurtured by conspicuous challenge to staff authority or by evasion of institution rules. In institutions for juveniles and youth, these pursuits are often collective endeavors by cliques or gangs, organized at least partially in groups reflecting lines of affiliation in the large cities from which the inmates come.

In a stable repressive institution, the staff controls inmates largely through other key inmates. A few State prisons still use selected inmates to guard others. In many other prisons there is less blatant but still serious exploitation of inmates by those who are in strategic assignments and on good terms with staff. The resulting system permits extensive rackets, coerced homosexuality, and much violence to occur unknown to the staff.

A prisoner's prime concern in such an institution is to cope with the most aggressive inmates. He comes to have extreme distrust of all persons, but especially of all officials. He sees violence or threat of violence as a practical necessity for preserving self-integrity in even relatively minor conflict situations.

In this kind of institution, custodial staff clearly dominate, and such treatment staff as may be employed—chaplains, teachers, caseworkers, physicians—either share the repressive orientation of custodial staff or are relatively isolated and uninfluential. The treatment emphasis of the past century has promoted a very gradual expansion in the number and influence of treatment staff of all types in traditional institutions. They usually affect decisions on institutional programs through such relatively mechanical methods as participating with senior custody staff in a prison's classification committee.

However, in most prisons such a committee's recommendations tend to be advisory only and affect primarily the work and living assignment plans for new inmates. Because custody has traditionally been considered the first function of prison management and because custodial staff are more numerous and have more firsthand knowledge of inmates than do treatment staff, they make most of the day-to-day decisions in innate management.

It is easy to see why deterring offenders from further crime is almost impossible in such a climate. Despite its avowed purpose, the authoritarian regime is deficient in instilling discipline and respect for authority. The maintenance of distance between staff and inmates reinforces the idea of many criminals and delinquents that law and authority are ranged against them; the emphasis on a myriad of rules, unexplained to inmates and often unreasoned in their operation, hardly educates a prisoner in the values of order of society. The existence of an illegitimate subculture of inmate relationships, often founded on violence and corruption, intensifies the criminal's commitment to these values.

The Collaborative Institution

In the past few decades, and increasingly in recent years, the traditional institutional regime has been undergoing modifications along the "collaborative" lines. . . . The collaborative institution is structured around the partnership of all inmates and staff members in the process of rehabilitation. It tries to oppose the tendency for an institution to become isolated from the community physically and in terms of values, and instead seeks to assimulate inmates in normal noncriminal ways of life, partly through close identification with staff and partly through increased communication with the outside community.

. . . . .

Parole and Aftercare

The text of the success of institutional corrections programs comes when offenders are released to the community. Whatever rehabilitation they have received, whatever deterrent effect their experience with incarceration has had, must upon release withstand the difficulties of readjustment to life in society and reintegration into employment, family, school, and the rest of community life. This is the time when most of the problems from which offenders were temporarily removed must be faced again and new problems arising from their status as ex-offenders must be confronted.

Many offenders are released outright into the community upon completion of their sentences, but a growing number—now more than 60 percent of adult felons for the Nation as a whole—are released on parole prior to the expiration of the maximum term of their sentences. Parole supervision, which is general resembles probation in methods and purposes, is the basic way—and one of the oldest—of trying to continue in the community the correctional program begun in the institution and help offenders make the difficult adjustment to release without jeopardy to the community. Furloughs, halfway houses, and similar programs . . . are important supplements to effective parole programs, as are prerelease guidance and other social services discussed later in this chapter.

Parole is generally granted by an administrative board or agency on the basis of such factors as an offender's prior history, his readiness for release, and his need for supervision and assistance in the community prior to the expiration of his sentence. The Federal system and those of a few states have a mandatory supervision procedure for offenders not released on parole. Under such a procedure, when an inmate is released for good behavior before serving his maximum term, he is supervised in the community for a period equivalent to his "good time credit."

.   .   .   .   .

History and Present Extent of Parole

Parole has had a long history. Its early traces appeared in the United States in the 19th century. The first official recognition came in 1876 at New York's Elmira Reformatory. Parole for juveniles, sometimes referred to as "aftercare," can be traced back to the houses of refuge for children established in the latter half of the 19th century. Juvenile parole developed for many years as part of the general child welfare field, but recently, while still retaining a close involvement with child welfare programs, has assumed a more distinct status.

The growth of parole services has been continuous, though uneven, the adult field expanding more rapidly than the juvenile. There remain, however, significant gaps in its use. The one of probably most general importance is its infrequent use for misdemeanants sentenced to jail. The National Survey of Corrections found that most misdemeanants are released from local institutions and jails without parole. Information available from a sample of 212 local jails indicates that 131 of them (62 percent) have no parole procedure; in the 81 jails that nominally have parole, only 8 percent of the inmates are released through this procedure. Thus, 92 percent are simply turned loose at the expiration of their sentence.

.   .   .   .   .

Theory and Purpose

While parole has on occasion been attacked as "leniency," it is basically a means of public protection, or at least has a potential to serve this purpose if properly used. Actually prisoners serve as much time in confinement in jurisdictions where parole is widely used as in those where it is not. No consistent or significant relationship exists between the proportion of prisoners who are released on parole in a state and the average time served for felonies before release. The most recent tabulation of median time served for felonies before first release, which was made in 1960, showed that the five States with the longest median time served were Hawaii, Pennsylvania, Illinois, New York, and Indiana. The percentages released by parole in these States in the same year were 99, 89, 47, 87, and 88 respectively. The five States with the shortest median time served for felonies before first release were New Hampshire, Maine, South Dakota, Montana, and Vermont, with percentages of release by parole of 98, 92, 49, 90, and 5 respectively.[24]

Arguments couched in terms of "leniency" deflect attention from a more important problem. The fact is that large numbers of offenders do return to the community from confinement each year. The task is to improve parole programs so that they may contribute to the reintegration of these offenders. The best current estimates indicate that, among adult offenders, 35 to 45 percent of those released on parole are subsequently returned to prison.[25] The large majority of this group are returned for violations of parole regulations; only about one-third of those returned have been convicted of new felonies. Violation rates are higher for juveniles. However, because additional kinds of violations are applicable to them, such as truancy and incorrigibility, precise comparison with adult rates is difficult.

Ideally, the parole process should begin when an offender is first received in an institution. Information should be gathered on his entire background, and skilled staff should plan an institutional program of training and treatment. A continuous evaluation should be made of the offender's progress on the program. At the same time, trained staff should be working in

[24] U.S. Department of Justice, Federal Bureau of Prisons, *National Prisoner Statistics: Characteristics of State Prisoners, 1960* (Washington: The Bureau, n.d.), table R-1, p. 67.

[25] Daniel Glaser and Vincent O'Leary, *Personal Characteristics and Parole Outcome* National Parole Institutes, Office of Juvenile Delinquency and Youth Development, U.S. Department of Health, Education, and Welfare (Washington: U.S. Government Printing Office, 1966).

the community with the offender's family and employer to develop a release plan.

Information about the offender, his progress in the institution, and community readiness to receive him would, under such ideal conditions, be brought together periodically and analyzed by expert staff for presentation to a releasing authority whose members were qualified by training and experience. After thoughtful review, including a hearing with the offender present, the releasing authority would decide when and where to release him. On release, he would be under the supervision of a trained parole officer able to work closely with him and the community institutions around him. If there were a violation of parole, a careful investigation would be made and the reasons behind the violation evaluated. A report would be submitted to the releasing authority which, on the basis of careful review of all the evidence and a hearing with the offender, would decide whether to revoke his parole.

Unfortunately, there are wide discrepancies between this description of what parole purports to be and the actual situation in most jurisdictions.

. . . . .

 ### *Directions for the Future*

In several senses corrections today may stand at the threshold of a new era, promising resolution of a significant number of the problems that have vexed it throughout its development. At the very least, it is developing the theory and practical groundwork for a new approach to rehabilitation of the most important group of offenders—those, predominantly young and lower-class, who are not committed to crime as a way of life and do not pose serious dangers to the community.

It is beginning to accumulate evidence from carefully controlled experimentation that may help guide its efforts more scientifically. Its increasing focus on rehabilitation has, according to recent opinion polls, found widespread acceptance among members of the general public. And, sitting as it were at the crossroads of a dozen disciplines—among them law, sociology, social work, psychology, and psychiatry—dealing with problems of poverty, unemployment, education, and morality, corrections has also attracted the interest of increasing numbers of talented people.

Estimates indicate that corrections will have to cope with very substantial increases in offender populations over the next decade.

. . . . .

Data with respect to the use of probation, as opposed to incarceration, are not available on a nationwide basis. Most correctional officials believe that probation is being used increasingly across the Nation. To take this into account, data from California were used. It is the largest State; it has a variety of probation agencies; it has had a definite increase in the use of probation; and its records in this regard are quite complete.

Because probation terms are longer on the average than jail terms, projections assuming a growth in its use yield a larger total population under correctional control at any given time than would have been the case if sentencing trends had been held constant. Thus the estimates of the total correctional population in 1975 . . . would be about 7 percent lower if no allowance were made for an increased use of probation. . . .

However calculated, all evidence indicates that there will be increasing pressure on adult and juvenile probation and on the juvenile system generally in the coming years. Changes in correctional practice must deal simultaneously with these pressures as well as old practices.

. . . . .

Reintegration of the Offender into the Community

The general underlying premise for the new directions in corrections is that crime and delinquency are symptoms of failures and disorganization of the community as well as of individual offenders. In particular, these failures are seen as depriving offenders of contact with the institutions that are basically responsible for assuring development of law-abiding conduct: sound family life, good schools, employment, recreational opportunities, and desirable companions, to name only some of the more direct influences. The substitution of deleterious habits, standards, and associates for these strengthening influences contributes to crime and delinquency.

The task of corrections therefore includes building or rebuilding solid ties between offender and community, integrating or reintegrating the offender into community life—restoring family ties, obtaining employment and education, securing in the larger sense a place for the offender in the routine functioning of society. This requires not only efforts directed toward changing the individual offender, which has been almost the exclusive focus of rehabilitation, but also mobilization and change of the community and its institutions. And these efforts must be undertaken without giving up the important control and deterrent role of corrections, particularly as applied to dangerous offenders.

. . . . .

The connection between social factors and crime was first systematically revealed in a series of studies carried on by Shaw and McKay at the University of Chicago during the 1920's.[26] These showed consistently high rates of delinquency in deteriorated areas within large cities, areas characterized by poverty and unemployment, residential mobility, broken homes, and evidence of disrupted social relationships such as mental illness, sui-

---

[26] See, for example, Clifford R. Shaw, Henry D. McKay, and others, *Delinquency Areas, a Study of the Distribution of School Truants, Juvenile Delinquents, and Adult Offenders in Chicago* (Chicago: University of Chicago Press, 1929).

cide, alcoholism, and narcotic addiction. Crime became in this perspective one of a wide array of symptoms of urban disorganization.

Other researchers undertook to explain the connection. One key to understanding delinquency in such deteriorated areas is the fact that people acquire the beliefs, values, attitudes, and habits of the groups with whom they are most closely associated. This idea is elaborated in Edwin Sutherland's theory of differential association,[27] which hypothesized that people become delinquent to the extent that they participate in groups and neighborhoods where delinquent ideas and techniques are viewed favorably. The earlier, the longer, the more frequently, and the more intensely people participate in such social settings, the greater is the probability of their becoming delinquent.

An important corollary of this theory is that a person's attitude toward himself is determined by the evidence of support or opposition he sees in the responses of others toward him. If he receives praise, he comes to think of himself in the same light. When praise is associated with violations of society's codes and laws, the individual may accept nonconformity as a pathway of the favorable appraisals of others. The reverse, of course, is also true.

Other modern theories place emphasis on the concepts of "cultural disorganization" and "delinquent subcultures." Culture in this context refers to the system of goals and values that guide the conduct of a society's members. Cultural disorganization occurs when goals are contradictory and values conflicting. The term subculture describes a group that strongly endorses values and goals at odds with those of the dominant culture; a delinquent subculture is a system of values, beliefs, and practices that encourages participation in law violation and awards status on the basis of such participation.

Perhaps the development of these concepts most pertinent to reintegration as a mode of correctional treatment is that of Cloward and Ohlin[28] which built on work by Cohen[29] and others. It asserts that much delinquency is the result of inability to gain access to legitimate opportunities in our society, coupled with availability of illegitimate opportunities that are seized as alternatives by frustrated persons. Corrective action therefore should seek to increase the opportunities of the offender to succeed in law-abiding activities, while reducing his contacts with the criminal world.

Such theories have been formulated mainly in the context of crime by slum dwellers, particularly the young. The experiments and data on which they are based have most concerned this group, and their concentration on

[27] Edwin H. Sutherland and Donald R. Cressey, *Principles of Criminology* (7th ed., Philadelphia: J. B. Lippincott Co., 1966), pp. 77–100.
[28] Richard A. Cloward and Lloyd E. Ohlin, *Delinquency and Opportunity* (Glencoe, Ill.: Free Press, 1960).
[29] See Albert K. Cohen, *Delinquent Boys: The Culture of the Gang* (Glencoe, Ill.: Free Press, 1955).

economic and social deprivation as the causative background of crime and delinquency reflects this perspective. But in fact these theories are not so exclusive in their implications. They can, for example, be applied to the many instances of middle-class and suburban delinquency in which school failure, family problems, and even the lack of exciting and challenging legitimate opportunities for use of leisure time are precipitating factors.

Nor do they deny that psychological causes operate in many criminal cases, particularly because the social and family disturbances on which they concentrate are also recognized today as important in psychological disturbance. Admittedly, however, further research and experimentation are necessary to develop these theories of social effect to the point where they can be of specific help in correctional treatment of particular offender types.

.   .   .   .   .

Blurring Lines Between Institution and Community

Closely allied in premise and method to new concepts in community treatment are a variety of attempts to remove some of the isolating effects of institutionalization and to ease the difficult transition back into the community for those who have been confined to prison or training school. Historically, parole itself began in part as such an attempt, and such other means as halfway houses and work-release programs have also been used in a few States for years.

But this report envisions such basic changes as construction of a wholly new kind of correctional institution for general use. This would be architecturally and methodologically the antithesis of the traditional fortress-like prison, physically and psychologically isolated from the larger society and serving primarily as a place of banishment. It would be small and fairly informal in structure. Located in or near the population center from which its inmates came, it would permit flexible use of community resources, both in the institution and for inmates released to work or study or spend short periods of time at home. Its closest existing models are some of the residential centers developed in the special juvenile treatment programs mentioned above, and the halfway houses that have been developed in a number of communities for released prisoners.

This type of institution would perform many functions. It would receive newly committed inmates and carry out extensive screening and classification with them. For those who are not returned quickly to community treatment, the new institutions would provide short-term, intensive treatment before placing them in the community under appropriate supervision. Still other offenders, after careful diagnosis, would be sent to the higher custody facilities required for long-term confinement of more difficult and dangerous inmates. But they might be eventually returned to the small facility as a port of reentry to the community.

The "partial release" programs that such a community-based institution would facilitate can also in many instances be employed in traditional facilities. In recent years the most dramatic increase in programs of graduated release from prisons has been in the area of work release. A work-release program was first introduced in Wisconsin institutions for misdemeanants in 1913 under that State's Huber Act, but for over four decades its use spread slowly. Large-scale extension to adult felons began with North Carolina legislation in 1959. Favorable experience there led to work release for felons in the early 1960's in South Carolina, Maryland, and other States in rapid succession. Work release for Federal prisoners was authorized by the Prisoner Rehabilitation Act of 1965. The record with work release has been predominantly favorable, despite some difficulties inherent in the lack of experience in administering it.

A variant of this program, sometimes called study release, is particularly appropriate for juvenile and youthful offenders. It is highly developed at several State establishments and at the Federal prerelease guidance centers. Prerelease guidance centers and halfway houses are themselves central to the concept of reintegrating offenders into the community and should be developed as complete alternatives to traditional institutionalization for some offenders. The New York State Youth Board, for example, has several centers consisting of a few apartments within large apartment buildings that serve primarily as an alternative to traditional training school commitment but are also used as prerelease centers.

Such programs permit offenders to cope with release problems in manageable pieces, rather than trying to develop satisfactory home relationships, employment, and leisure-time activity all at once. They also permit staff to carry out early and continuing assessment of individuals' progress under actual stresses.

Maximizing Participation in Treatment

Traditional prisons, jails, and juvenile institutions are highly impersonal and authoritarian. Mass handling, countless ways of humiliating the inmate in order to make him subservient to rules and orders, special rules of behavior designed to maintain social distance between keepers and inmates, frisking of inmates, regimented movement to work, eat, and play, drab prison clothing, and similar aspects of daily life—all tend to depersonalize the inmate and reinforce his belief that authority is to be opposed, not cooperated with. The phrase much heard in inmate circles—"do your own time"—is a slogan which expresses alienation and indifference to the interests of both staff and other inmates. Such an attitude is, of course, antithetical to successful reintegration.

In contrast with this traditional system, a new concept of relationships in correctional institutions, the "collaborative regime," has been evolving during the past few decades. An outstanding feature of this trend is increased communication between custodial staff, inmates, and treatment staff. Custodial staff, by virtue of their number and their close contact with all aspects of an inmate's life, have a great potential for counseling functions, both with individual inmates and in organized group discussions. Instructors, administrators, and business staff also have been brought into the role of counselors and have been assigned rehabilitative functions in some programs.

Another important dimension of this collaborative concept of institutional life is the involvement of inmates themselves in important treatment functions. Group counseling sessions, particularly, have become settings in some institutions for inmates to help each other, often through hard and insistent demands for honesty in self-examination, demands that cannot be provided with equal force and validity by staff who have not as individuals shared experience in the manipulative world of criminal activity. Group counseling has also been extended with success to community treatment.

Differential Handling

More individualized and systematically differentiated treatment and control of offenders is another major requisite of more rational and effective corrections. Mass handling remains the predominant practice today. It is true that there is some attempt in the more progressive institutions to fit programs to each inmate's needs. And a small proportion of probationers and parolees receive handling determined by staff evaluations of their individual requirements. But most offenders under correctional control are given quite standardized attention.

A number of research projects have indicated the importance of differential handling of various types of offenders from the standpoint of rehabilitative treatment. One attempt at early release of a sample of all types of offenders with intensive supervision in special small caseloads found, for example, that first offenders so treated had markedly fewer violations on parole than their counterparts given longer institutionalization, while those with prior records had more,[30] suggesting that shorter institutional terms followed by intensive supervision may be appropriate for first offenders but ineffective for some of those with prior records.

Another study of three treatment methods—parole, forestry camp, and training school—found that the effectiveness of each of these treatments varied with different kinds of offenders. Conforming and overinhibited boys had higher success rates when assigned to parole or to forestry camps.

[30] Don M. Gottfredson, "A Strategy for Study of Correctional Effectiveness" (paper presented at the Fifth International Correctional Congress, Montreal, Canada, 1965).

Emotionally disturbed offenders, with no evidence of progressive involvement in criminality, did best on parole and poorest under training school assignment. Aggressive and antisocial delinquents had a uniformly high violation rate under all of the alternatives investigated.[31]

The relationship between the characteristics of offenders and the characteristics of those supervising them has also been explored. The Camp Elliott study by Grant and Grant, for example, investigated the response of military offenders to an experimental living group program. Among the conditions controlled were the level of maturity of the offenders and the social and psychological characteristics of the team of supervisors who were in charge of the group. The treatment methods of some supervisory teams did more to increase the success rates of some kinds of offenders, but they were markedly detrimental to the chances for success of other kinds of offenders. The study showed that, if the characteristics of both the offenders and their supervisors are considered, there are wide variations in the success rate among the different combinations. It also showed that when all offenders are lumped together the effects of variations in treatment are negligible.[32] Similar results were reported by Adams in the Pilot Intensive Counseling Study, a program of individual therapy with training school wards.[33]

.   .   .   .   .   .

A great deal of further research and demonstration is needed to confirm and refine these conclusions. But at least such studies demonstrate the importance of differential treatment and help explain the fact that, while evaluation has shown a few treatment efforts to yield some subsequent improvement on the part of offenders, a few have shown negative effects and the great majority no appreciable difference in the conduct of offenders to whom they have been applied. Bailey, for example, reviewed the outcome of correctional programs in 100 studies conducted between 1940 and 1959 and noted that those studies in which the greatest care had been taken in the experimental design reported either harmful effects of treatment or, more frequently, no change at all.[34] In most cases, the subjects who received treatment improved according to some measure of change, but they showed no improvement or changed for the worse by other measures.

Differential treatment would involve identifying dangerous offenders who require rigorous control and surveillance as well as selecting appropriate methods of rehabilitation. It would also lead to economies, since offend-

[31] Paul F. Mueller, "An Objective Approach to a Behavior Classification of Juvenile Delinquents" (unpublished Ph.D. dissertation, University of Washington, 1959).

[32] J. D. Grant and M. Q. Grant, "A Group Dynamics Approach to the Treatment of Nonconformists in the Navy," Annals of the American Academy of Political and Social Science, 1959, 322: 126–135.

[33] Stuart A. Adams, "Interaction Between Individual Interview Therapy and Treatment Amenability in Older Youth Authority Wards," in *Inquiries Concerning Kinds of Treatment for Kinds of Delinquents*, Monograph No. 2 (Sacramento: California Department of Corrections, 1961), pp. 27–41.

[34] Walter C. Bailey, "Correctional Outcome: An Evaluation of 100 Reports," *Journal of Criminal Law, Criminology, and Police Science*, June 1966, 57:153–160.

ers who need minimal supervision could be handled expeditiously, while those who require intensive treatment and control could be handled accordingly.

Concern for Fairness

It is perhaps ironic that trends in modern corrections toward more humane treatment and greater emphasis on rehabilitation and community supervision have increasingly raised issues of fair process and the rights of offenders. At one time an offender's correctional course was largely determined at trial. If he was sentenced to prison, he went and served the term appointed for him by the judge or statute, and by and large he was treated in prison just like everybody else. But today correctional decisions are far more numerous and complex, and many of them are made administratively by correctional staff rather than by a judge or statute.

What sort of program or treatment an offender should receive at various points in his correctional career; whether and when he should be moved into or out of halfway houses, work-release programs, minimum-security facilities; whether he should have his probation or parole revoked or suspended—these and other questions are now becoming routine in corrections. They would become even more important and more frequent under the sort of regimen this chapter envisions for the future.

At the same time, there is today growing concern for the rights of persons subject to administrative process in the criminal justice system. Courts have already, of course, probed deeply into questions of police handling of suspects, and the U.S. Supreme Court has recently accepted two cases involving right to counsel in probation revocation.[35] Changes in correctional philosophy have encouraged this concern for the rights of offenders. As long as the dominant purpose of corrections was punishment, the treatment of offenders could be and was regarded in law as a matter of grace in which offenders had few rights. But when decisions are made with the object of helping offenders, and when moreover they purport to have some rational or even scientific basis, it becomes anomalous to regard them as unreviewable matters of grace.

[*The President's Commission on Law Enforcement and Administration of Justice,* Task Force Report: Corrections (*Washington: U.S. Government Printing Office, 1967*), *pp. 1–5, 18–25, 27–28, 30–32, 40–41, 45–47, 60, 62, 6–7, 9–12, 16.*]

[35] *Memphis v. Rhay, Walkling v. Rhay,* Nos. 424, 734, 1966 term.

14 *A national strategy*

America can control crime. This report has tried to say how. It has shown that crime flourishes where the conditions of life are the worst, and that therefore the foundation of a national strategy against crime is an unremitting national effort for social justice. Reducing poverty, discrimination, ignorance, disease and urban blight, and the anger, cynicism or despair those conditions can inspire, is one great step toward reducing crime. It is not the task, indeed it is not within the competence, of a Commission on Law Enforcement and Administration of Justice to make detailed proposals about housing or education or civil rights, unemployment or welfare or health. However, it is the Commission's clear and urgent duty to stress that forceful action in these fields is essential to crime prevention, and to adjure the officials of every agency of criminal justice—policemen, prosecutors, judges, correctional authorities—to associate themselves with and labor for the success of programs that will improve the quality of American life.

This report has shown that most criminal careers begin in youth, and that therefore programs that will reduce juvenile delinquency and keep delinquents and youthful offenders from settling into lives of crime are indispensable parts of a national strategy. It has shown that the formal criminal process, arrest to trial to punishment, seldom protects the community from offenders of certain kinds and that, therefore, the criminal justice system and the community must jointly seek alternative ways of treating them. It has shown that treatment in the community might also return to constructive life many offenders who quite appropriately have been subjected to formal process.

This report has pointed out that legislatures and, by extension, the public, despite their well-founded alarm about crime, have not provided the wherewithal for the criminal justice system to do what it could and should do. It has identified the system's major needs as better qualified, better trained manpower; more modern equipment and management; closer cooperation among its functional parts and among its many and varied jurisdictions; and, of course, the money without which far-reaching and enduring improvements are impossible.

Finally, this report has emphasized again and again that improved law enforcement and criminal administration is more than a matter of giving additional resources to police departments, courts, and correctional systems. Resources are not ends. They are means, the means through which the agencies of criminal justice can seek solutions to the problems of preventing and controlling crime. Many of those solutions have not yet been found. We need to know much more about crime. A national strategy against crime must be in large part a strategy of search.

What State and Local Governments Can Do

Almost every recommendation in this report is a recommendation to State or local governments, the governments that by and large administer criminal justice in America. A special difficulty of writing the report has been finding terms general enough to describe criminal administration in 50 States and thousands of local communities, and at the same time specific enough to be helpful. The Commission is acutely aware that the report does not discuss many distinctive local conditions and problems, that its descriptions often are quite broad, that no one of its recommendations applies with equal force to every locality, that, indeed, some of its recommendations do not apply at all to some localities.

On the whole the report concentrates on cities, for that is where crime is most prevalent, most feared, and most difficult to control. On the whole the report dwells on the criminal justice system's deficiencies and failures, since prescribing remedies was what the Commission was organized to do. Some States and cities are doing much to improve criminal administration; their work is the basis for many of the report's recommendations. Finally, because the report is a national report, it is not and cannot be a detailed manual of instructions that police departments, courts, and correctional systems need only to follow step by step in order to solve their problems. It is of necessity a general guide that suggests lines along which local agencies can act.

Planning—The First Step

A State or local government that undertakes to improve its criminal administration should begin by constructing, if it has not already done so, formal machinery for planning. Significant reform is not to be achieved overnight by a stroke of a pen; it is the product of thought and preparation. No experienced and responsible State or city official needs to be told that. The Commission's point is not the elementary one that each individual action against crime should be planned, but that all of a State's or a city's actions against crime should be planned together, by a single body. The police, the courts, the correctional system and the noncriminal agencies of the community must plan their actions against crime jointly if they are to make real headway.

The relationships among the parts of the criminal justice system and between the system and the community's other institutions, governmental and nongovernmental, are so intimate and intricate that a change anywhere may be felt everywhere. Putting into effect the Commission's recommendation for three entry "tracks" in police departments could involve the rewriting of civil service regulations, the revision of standard police field procedures, the adjustment of city budgets, possibly the passage of enabling legislation. A reform like organizing a Youth Services Bureau to which the police and the juvenile courts, and parents and school officials as well, could refer young people will require an enormous amount of planning. Such a bureau will have to work closely with the community's other youth-serving agencies. It will affect the caseloads of juvenile courts, probation services and detention facilities. It will raise legal issues of protecting the rights of the young people referred to it. It could be attached to a local or State government in a variety of ways. It could offer many different kinds of service. It could be staffed by many different kinds of people. It could be financed in many different ways.

Most of the recommendations in this report raise similar problems. Later in this chapter a large-scale program of Federal support for State and local agencies is proposed. If this program is adopted, States and cities will need plans in order to secure their share of Federal funds.

Furthermore, concerted and systematic planning is not only a necessary prelude to action. It is a spur to action. The best way to interest the community in the problems of crime is to engage members of it in planning. The best way to mobilize the community against crime is to lay before it a set of practical and coherent plans. This report often has had occasion to use the word "isolation" to describe certain aspects of the relationship between the criminal justice system and the community. State and city planning agencies could do much to end that isolation.

The Commission recommends:

In every State and every city, an agency, or one or more officials, should be specifically responsible for planning improvements in crime prevention and control and encouraging their implementation.

It is impossible, of course, to prescribe in a national report the precise forms that State or city planning agencies should take. No two States have identical constitutions or penal codes or crime problems. State-city relationships vary from State to State, and often within States according to the size of cities. County governments have more or less power, depending on the State. Municipal government takes many forms. However, there are certain principles that are universally applicable.

First, much of the planning for action against crime will have to be done at the State level. Every State operates a court system and a corrections system, and has responsibility for certain aspects of law enforcement. State legislatures, as a rule, control local finances. The States are in the best position to encourage or require the coordination or pooling of activities that is so vitally necessary in metropolitan areas and among rural counties. Many States have units, some independent and some a part of the Governor's office, that are actively engaged in planning in the field of juvenile delinquency.

In addition, a number of Governors have responded to the President's suggestion in March 1966 that they establish State planning committees to maintain contact with this Commission during its life and with other interested Federal agencies, to appraise the needs of their State criminal systems, and to put into effect those proposals of the Commission that they find to be worthwhile. The Commission urges all Governors to establish similar committees.

Second, much of the planning will have to be done at the municipal level. The problems of the police and, to a certain extent, of the jails and the lower courts are typically city problems. Welfare, education, housing, fire prevention, recreation, sanitation, urban renewal, and a multitude of other functions that are closely connected with crime and criminal justice are also the responsibility of cities. In some cities members of the mayor's or the city manager's staff, or advisory or interdepartmental committees, coordinate the city's anticrime activities; in most cities there is as yet little planning or coordination.

Third, close collaboration between State and city planning units is obviously essential. Representatives of a State's major cities should serve on the State body, and staff members of the State body should be available to the city bodies for information and advice. Money, manpower, and expertise are in too short supply to be squandered in activities that duplicate or overlap each other and, conversely, when there is no collaboration there is always a risk that some important field of action will be overlooked.

Fourth, however much the structure and composition of planning units vary from place to place, all units should include both officials of the criminal justice system and citizens from other professions. Plans to improve criminal administration will be impossible to put into effect if those responsible for criminal administration do not help to make them. On the other hand, as this report has repeatedly stressed, crime prevention is the task of the community as a whole and, as it has also stressed, all parts of the criminal justice system can benefit from the special knowledge and points of view of those outside it. Business and civic leaders, lawyers, school and welfare officials, persons familiar with the problems of slum dwellers, and members of the academic community are among those who might be members of planning boards, or who might work with such boards as advisers or consultants.

Fifth and finally, planning boards must have sufficient authority and prestige, and staffs large enough and able enough, to permit them to furnish strong and imaginative leadership in making plans and seeing them through.

The first thing any planning unit will have to do is to gather and analyze facts: statistics about crime and the costs and caseloads of the criminal justice system; knowledge about the programs and procedures being used in its own jurisdiction, and about those that have proved successful elsewhere; data about the social conditions that appear to be linked with crime; information about potentially helpful individuals and organizations in the community.

In few States or cities has information of these kinds been compiled systematically. Gathering facts will be an invaluable process for any planning body, not only because of the importance of the facts themselves, but also because they will have to be gathered from people and organizations experienced in crime prevention and criminal administration: judges, correctional officials, police officials, prosecutors, defense counsel, youth workers, universities, foundations, civic organizations, service clubs, neighborhood groups.

These people and organizations can be combined into a network of support for the changes the planning body will propose. Such a network will be able to do much to overcome resistance to change, or fear of it, inside and outside the criminal justice system, by showing how changes can be made carefully and practically.

On the basis of the facts it gathers, the planning body will be able to appraise objectively and frankly the needs of its State or city and the resources that are available for meeting those needs. It would ask, for example, whether in its jurisdiction police training is adequate; whether the lower and juvenile courts are failing in any of the ways cited by the Commission; whether the correctional system is beginning to make fundamental improvements of the sort the Commission has found are widely needed.

It will discover needs that can be met rapidly by putting into effect programs that have succeeded in other places; for example, bail reform projects, systems for the assignment of defense counsel to indigents, police standards commissions, rehabilitation programs in jails, sentencing institutes for judges. An excellent model of how much a planning body can do is the work of the President's Commission on Crime in the District of Columbia, which undertook a comprehensive study of the criminal justice system and other agencies concerned with crime and delinquency in the District, and made detailed recommendations for change.

The one caution about planning bodies the Commission feels it must make is that they not serve as an excuse for postponing changes that can be made immediately. For example, most police departments could immediately add legal advisers to their staffs, or launch police-community relations programs. In many cities there is no question about whether more prosecutors and probation officers are needed in the lower courts; they clearly are, and they should be provided at once. Sentencing councils could be organized with no more effort than it would take for a number of judges to arrange to meet regularly. Other recommendations that one jurisdiction or another could put into effect at once, without elaborate planning, will be found in the pages of this report. Simple changes that can be made immediately should be, not only because justice demands it but because making them will contribute to creating a climate in which complicated, long-range reform will be feasible.

Major Lines for State and Local Action

Money

The most urgent need of the agencies of criminal justice in the States and cities is money with which to finance the multitude of improvements they must make. As is set forth in the next section of this chapter, the Commission believes that Federal financial support of improved criminal administration in the states and cities is necessary and appropriate. But even more essential is an increase in State support. Plans for change must include realistic estimates of financial requirements and persuasive showings of the gains that can be achieved by spending more on criminal administration.

A central task of planning bodies and the network of agencies and individuals working with them will be to mobilize support, within legislatures and by the public, for spending money on innovation and reform. The collaboration of police, prosecutors, correctional officials, and others involved in the agencies of justice is crucial in this, for they know best how vital the need for greater resources is, and how little is accomplished by identifying scapegoats or resorting to simplistic answers as solutions to the complicated problems of crime and criminal justice.

Personnel

The Commission has found that many of the agencies of justice are understaffed. Giving them the added manpower they need is a matter of high priority for protection of public safety and of the rights of individuals accused of crime. But even more essential is a dramatic improvement in the quality of personnel throughout the system. Establishment of standard-setting bodies, such as police standards commissions that exist in several States, is one approach to this problem. Better and more numerous training programs are another. State and city planning groups must consider to what extent each operating agency can and should provide its own training and to what extent metropolitan, statewide, or regional programs should be developed instead.

If the agencies of justice are to recruit and retain the able, well-educated people they badly need, they will have to offer them higher pay and challenging and satisfying work. For example, it is clear to the Commission that until the single recruitment and promotion "track" that now prevails in all police forces is abandoned, upgrading of the police will be extremely difficult. Thus, one of the first and most difficult tasks of planning bodies will be to consider major changes in the personnel structures of the agencies of justice.

Programs to Meet New Needs

This report has described how modern urban life has burdened the criminal justice system with a range of almost entirely new problems. It has attempted to suggest promising ways of dealing with them. For example, it outlines a model for future development in corrections that predicates treatment on a new kind of facility: a small institution, located in the community it serves, that can be used flexibly for short-term incarceration and as a base for intensive community treatment. It has proposed police communications centers that take advantage of modern technology. It has described how necessary it is, in the interest of preventing delinquency, for the community to reassess the current practices of schools, welfare departments, and housing officials, particularly in poor neighborhoods. It has proposed, as a new alternative to criminal disposition for less serious juvenile offenders, Youth Services Bureaus that would provide them with a variety of treatment services and keep them from being grouped with serious criminals. It has proposed greatly strengthened community relations programs to improve respect for law and increase police effectiveness in the highest crime neighborhoods of America's cities. In addition, broader methods of meeting problems presented by the increasing complexity and anonymity of life in large urban areas are obviously important. Thus, some cities may wish to consider developing procedures or agencies . . . to assist citizens in understanding and dealing with the many official agencies that affect their lives. These are only a few important examples of the many new services the Commission recommends that State and local planning bodies develop.

In many instances establishing new programs will be costly. The Commission is therefore recommending that the emphasis of proposed Federal financial aid be placed on innovation. The Commission further recommends that State and local governments carefully consider the feasibility and desirability of devoting to new programs increasing proportions of the funds allocated to crime control.

Organization and Procedures of
Agencies of Justice

An important matter for planning units and operating agencies to consider is how the police, the courts, and corrections can improve their organization and their operations. Since there are throughout the Nation many examples to draw on, and since legislative action often will not be required, early and substantial improvements can be made. Such of the Commission's proposals as those for regularizing the procedures in pretrial disposition of cases and in sentencing; for providing clearer guidance by police chiefs to field officers on such matters as the making of arrests in domestic disputes, drunkenness, and civil disturbance situations; and for developing a "collaborative" regime within prisons, can be considered almost at once and acted upon without legislative action and, in many instances, without significant increases in spending.

The success of such changes in the States or cities where they have been made should greatly help the agencies in States and cities where they have not been made to act promptly. Planning bodies and other State and local groups may find themselves chiefly providing support, encouragement, and continuing pressure for change. In some cases it may be desirable for State or local agencies to obtain suggestions from recognized professional or governmental groups such as the International Association of Chiefs of Police or the Bureau of Prisons as one means of identifying specific needs and possible ways of meeting them.

Law Reform

While many improvements in the system of criminal justice do not require legislative action other than the appropriation of funds, others do require new laws or changes in existing laws. Proposals for court reorganization may even require constitutional change. Therefore, at an early stage in their work, planning bodies should appraise the needs for legislative change. Legislative changes could include such diverse actions as enacting new gun control laws; amending existing laws to aid in organized crime prosecutions; changing legal disabilities of former prisoners; and enacting controls over dangerous drugs that are uniform with Federal law.

More general and fundamental reevaluation is also called for. A number of State legislatures, including those in Illinois, California, and New York, have recently completed or are now engaged in major revisions of their criminal codes. For States that have not yet addressed this problem, the carefully formulated provisions of the American Law Institute's Model Penal Code serve as a valuable starting point. In many places there are bar associations and other groups with continuing interest in law revision; clearly such groups should be involved in the planning process. Governors and State legislatures should also give strong consideration to appointing law revision commissions comparable to that established by the Congress for review of all Federal criminal statutes.

What the Federal Government Can Do

Although day-by-day criminal administration is primarily a State and local responsibility, the Federal Government's contribution to the national effort against crime is crucial. The Federal Government carries much of the load of financing and administering the great social programs that are America's best hope of preventing crime and delinquency, and various of its branches concern themselves actively with such specific criminal problems as preventing juvenile delinquency and treating drug addiction and alcoholism.

Thé Federal Government has the direct responsibility for enforcing major criminal statutes against, among other things, kidnapping, bank robbery, racketeering, smuggling, counterfeiting, drug abuse, and tax evasion. It has a number of law enforcement agencies, a system of criminal courts and a large correctional establishment. Some of the Commission's recommendations, notably those concerning organized crime, drug abuse, firearms control, and the pooling of correctional facilities and of police radio frequencies, are addressed in part to the Federal Government.

The Federal Government has for many years provided information, advice and training to State and local law enforcement agencies. These services have been extremely important. In many towns and counties, for example, the Federal Bureau of Investigation's on-site training programs for police officers and sheriffs are the only systematic training programs available. The Department of Justice, under the Law Enforcement Assistance Act of 1965, has begun to give State and city agencies financial grants for research, for planning, and for demonstration projects.

The Commission wants not only to endorse warmly Federal participation in the effort to reduce delinquency and crime, but to urge that it be intensified and accelerated. It believes further that the Federal Government can make a dramatic new contribution to the national effort against crime by greatly expanding its support of the agencies of justice in the States and in the cities.

Federal Prevention Programs

The Federal Government is already doing much in the field of delinquency prevention. An Office of Juvenile Delinquency and Youth Development, which funds research and demonstration projects by both governmental and nongovernmental State and local agencies, is an important part of the Department of Health, Education, and Welfare. The office is supporting projects, to give only a few examples, aimed at providing job training and opportunities to delinquents; enabling school dropouts to continue their education; controlling the behavior of youthful gangs; involving young people in community action; devising alternatives to juvenile court referral and finding ways to give delinquents the support and counseling they do not get from their families. The same Department's Children's Bureau has for years given technical aid to police and juvenile court personnel. The Vocational Rehabilitation Administration in the Department has recently developed job training programs specifically designed for delinquent young people. The Commission is convinced that efforts like these are of great immediate, and even greater potential, value, and urges that they be strengthened.

Other Federal programs of greater scope work against delinquency and crime by improving education and employment prospects for the poor and attacking slum conditions associated with crime. Such work and job training programs as the Neighborhood Youth Corps, the Job Corps, the Youth Opportunity Centers, and Manpower Development and Training Act programs provide training, counseling, and work opportunities essential to break the pattern of unemployability that underlies so much of crime today. The Elementary and Secondary Education Act programs and the Head Start work with preschool children are aimed at readying disadvantaged children for school, improving the quality of slum education and preventing dropping out. Community action programs and the new Model Cities Program are concerned with strengthening the social and physical structure of inner cities, and thus ultimately with delinquency and crime prevention. As Chapter 1 of this report has pointed out, a community's most enduring protection against crime is to right the wrongs and to cure the illnesses that tempt men to harm their neighbors.

An Expanded Federal Effort

In the field of law enforcement and administration of justice the Federal contribution is still quite small, particularly in respect to the support it gives the States and cities, which bear most of the load of criminal administration. The present level of Federal support provides only a tiny portion of the resources the States and cities need to put into effect the changes this report recommends. The Commission has considered carefully whether or not the Federal Government should provide more support for such programs. It has concluded that the Federal Government should. In reaching this conclusion it has been persuaded, first, by the fact that crime is a national, as well as a state and local, phenomenon; it often does not respect geographical boundaries. The FBI has demonstrated the high mobility of many criminals. Failure of the criminal justice institutions in one State may endanger the citizens of others. The Federal Government has already taken much respon-

sibility in such fields as education and welfare, employment and job training, housing and mental health, which bear directly on crime and its
prevention. As President Johnson stated in his 1966 Crime Message to
Congress:

> *Crime does not observe neat, jurisdictional lines between city, State,*
> *and Federal Governments. . . . To improve in one field we must*
> *improve in all. To improve in one part of the country we must*
> *improve in all parts.*

Second, simply in terms of economy of effort and of feasibility, there are
important needs that individual jurisdictions cannot or should not meet
alone. Research is a most important instance. Careful experimentation with
and evaluation of police patrol methods, for example, or delinquency prevention programs, means assembling and organizing teams of specialists.
They can best be marshaled with the help of the Federal Government. It is
also important to make available the sorts of information that every jurisdiction in the Nation needs access to every day: wanted-person and stolen-
property lists, and fingerprint files, for example. Furthermore, the Federal
Government can do much to stimulate pooling of resources and services
among local jurisdictions.

Third, most local communities today are hard pressed just to improve
their agencies of justice and other facilities at a rate that will meet increases
in population and in crime. They cannot spare funds for experimental or
innovative programs or plan beyond the emergencies of the day. Federal
collaboration can give State and local agencies an opportunity to gain on
crime rather than barely stay abreast of it, by making funds, research, and
technical assistance available and thereby encouraging changes that in time
may make criminal administration more effective and more fair.

The Federal program the Commission visualizes is a large one. During
the past fiscal year the Federal Government spent a total of about $20
million on research into crime and delinquency, and another $7 million,
under the Law Enforcement Assistance Act, on research and demonstration
projects by local agencies of justice. The Commission is not in a position to
weigh [comparatively] . . . all the demands for funds that are made upon
the Federal Government. And so it cannot recommend the expenditure of a
specific number of dollars a year on the program it proposes. However, it
does see the program as one on which several hundred million dollars
annually could be profitably spent over the next decade. If this report has
not conveyed the message that sweeping and costly changes in criminal
administration must be made throughout the country in order to effect a
significant reduction in crime, then it has not expressed what the Commission strongly believes.

The Commission's final conclusion about a Federal anticrime program is
that the major responsibility for administering it should lie with the Department of Justice, and that the official who administers it for the Attorney

General should be a Presidential appointee, with all the status and prestige that inheres in such an office. In the Department of Justice alone among Federal agencies there is a large existing pool of practical knowledge about the police, the courts and the correctional system. The Federal Bureau of Prisons and the Federal Bureau of Investigation, each of which is already expanding its own support of State and local agencies, are parts of the Department of Justice. The Department of Justice has a Criminal Division, one of whose most important sections is concerned with organized crime and racketeering. It has the recently established Office of Criminal Justice, which has concentrated on criminal reform. Many of the research and demonstration portions of the Commission's program are already authorized under the Law Enforcement Assistance Act, which is administered by the Department of Justice. If it is given the money and the men it will need, the Department of Justice can take the lead in the Nation's efforts against crime.

In proposing a major Federal program against crime, the Commission is mindful of the special importance of avoiding any invasion of State and local responsibility for law enforcement and criminal justice, and its recommendation is based on its judgment that Federal support and collaboration of the sort outlined below are consistent with scrupulous respect for—and indeed strengthening of—that responsibility.

The Commission's Program

The program of Federal support that the Commission recommends would meet eight major needs:
(1) State and local planning
(2) Education and training of criminal justice personnel
(3) Surveys and advisory services concerning organization and operation of criminal justice agencies
(4) Development of coordinated national information systems
(5) Development of a limited number of demonstration programs in agencies of justice
(6) Scientific and technological research and development
(7) Institutes for research and training personnel
(8) Grants-in-aid for operational innovations.

State and Local Planning

The Commission believes that the process of State and local planning outlined in the preceding section of this chapter should be a prerequisite for the receipt of Federal support for action programs. It believes further that such planning should itself receive Federal support, and it recommends that planning grants be made available for this purpose. The Department of

Justice has already made grants of up to $25,000 to a number of State planning committees formed during the past year. It is clear that planning support in considerably larger amounts will be necessary if States and cities are to conduct a careful assessment of their needs and of ways to meet them.

Education and Training

This report has emphasized many times the critical importance of improved education and training in making the agencies of criminal justice fairer and more effective. The Federal Government is already involved to a limited degree in providing or supporting education and training for some criminal justice personnel. The FBI provides direct training of police officers at its academy in Washington and in the field. The Department of Justice's new Law Enforcement Assistance program has supported police curriculum development and training demonstration projects; the Department of Health, Education, and Welfare has done some research on education and training in the fields of juvenile corrections, mental health, and delinquency prevention; and the Department of Labor has recently initiated in a few large cities programs under the Manpower Development and Training Act to help prepare young men from slum areas for police work.

The Commission believes that Federal financial support to provide training and education for State and local criminal justice personnel should be substantially increased. Such support might take several forms. In the field of medicine forgivable loans have been used to help defray the costs of college education and to provide an incentive for further work in the field. Another plan would be to subsidize salary payments to personnel on leave for training or longer study programs, or to their interim replacements. Curriculum development programs like those conducted by the National Science Foundation are also much needed if those from different parts of the criminal justice system are to be jointly instructed in such subjects as, for example, the treatment of juveniles or the problems of parolees.

. . . . .

Surveys of Organization and Operations

Many criminal justice agencies willing to consider making changes are not sure what their needs are or how their practices compare to the best practice of the field. They need experienced advice about how to put changes into effect. State and local officials whom the Commission has consulted have pointed out that ineffectual administration can negate otherwise promising attempts to increase effectiveness against crime, and have urged that the Federal program help with this problem.

Management studies already have a long history in law enforcement.

Organizations like the IACP and the Public Administration Service have conducted them since the 1920's. The Children's Bureau has provided specialized assistance to many of the Nation's juvenile courts. In corrections, the Bureau of Prisons provides increasingly extensive consulting services to local authorities, having recently set up a special office to do so. The Justice Department's new Office of Criminal Justice has been able, with a relatively small amount of explanation and advice, to help stimulate local bail reform efforts. These valuable services have touched but a few of the thousands of agencies that could benefit by surveys and expert advice.

The Commission does not believe that the Federal Government itself should provide the staff to conduct studies or advise the very large number of local agencies that might wish such services. Federal assistance should be aimed instead at developing State or regional bodies with the skills to perform these services. In addition, the Federal Government could contract with private groups to conduct surveys and studies. Advice and studies by expert groups could become a valuable adjunct to the continuing work of State and local planning bodies. For example, they could assist police agencies that desire to reorganize their community relations programs, or correctional agencies seeking to establish halfway houses. In such cases, the studies might be a forerunner to more substantial grant-in-aid support.

Information Systems

Another way in which the Federal Government can collaborate with state and local criminal justice systems is by helping to improve the collection and transmission of information needed by the police, courts, and corrections agencies in their day-to-day work. The FBI already makes much important data available to local police agencies from its fingerprint files. The National Crime Information Center, now being developed by the FBI, will provide instantaneous response to computer inquiry by local agencies for information on stolen automobiles, wanted persons, certain identifiable types of stolen property, and the like.

In addition to this "hot" information, data on offenders needed by prosecutors, courts, and correctional authorities should be collected and made centrally available. . . . [T]he goal should be to develop an index drawn from the records of the criminal justice agencies across the country. With such an index a sentencing judge, for example, could learn where information might be found bearing on an offender's response to treatment in other jurisdictions. Disclosure of the information itself would remain, as at present, entirely within the discretion and control of the individual agency that held it. This would help avoid the dangers of developing national "dossiers" but would greatly speed collection of data for making decisions on disposition of cases—a major source of present delays and injustice.

At the State and local levels, enforcement activities against organized crime groups are for the most part nonexistent or primitive. . . . A principal need in this field is an effective system for receiving, analyzing, storing, and disseminating intelligence information. Many of organized crime's activities are national in scope, and even its small operations usually spill across city, county, and state lines. If investigators and prosecutors in separate jurisdictions are to make any headway at all against organized crime, they must work together; especially they must share information. There should be within the Department of Justice a computerized, central organized-crime intelligence system that handles information from all over the country. This system should be the center of a federally supported network of State and regional intelligence systems, such as those now being developed in New York and in the New England States.

In addition to information needed for operations, there should be available on a centralized basis statistical information on the criminal justice system itself. This is needed for assessing requirements and effectiveness. The FBI's Uniform Crime Reports service should be closely coordinated with this program, which also would include court, probation, prison, and parole statistics on such information as numbers and dispositions of cases, time intervals, and costs. Complementing such data would be special intensive surveys—of crime victims or insurance claims, for example—designed to ascertain more accurately the patterns of crime.

There are at present no centralized crime statistics apart from the UCR, although for many years it has been generally agreed in the field that the absence of information on all aspects of the criminal system has seriously impeded important research. Correlation of comprehensive statistics with surveys and other new methods for analyzing facts about crime is important not only to develop a national picture of crime's seriousness, but to provide a gauge by which police and other agencies can accurately determine the effect of their efforts on the amount of crime. The victimization survey undertaken by the Commission has shown the feasibility and usefulness of such surveys, in combination with UCR data, as the basis for statistical indices as comprehensive as those prepared by the Federal Government in the labor and agricultural fields.

Special Demonstration Projects

The Federal administering agency should be authorized to finance in a few places major demonstration projects designed to show all cities and States how much major changes can improve the system of criminal justice. For example, support could be provided to a police force that was prepared, on the basis of an organization study, to make fundamental personnel, management, and operational changes; or to a State or city wishing to plan for entirely new combinations of service between community-based correctional institutions and noncriminal agencies. The demonstration project authorization should also be broad enough to support cooperative programs under which various jurisdictions share needed services, such as police dispatching or short-term detention facilities, or even totally pooled police services.

In the earlier stages of the Federal program, these few major projects could serve as the primary laboratories for research and training, and the experience gained through them would provide a reference point for much of the work done by States and local communities under operational grants-in-aid. Thus, there should be special authorization for the systematic dissemination of the results of demonstration projects and for bringing State and local officials from other areas together to see model programs in operation.

Science and Technology

. . . [T]he skills and techniques of science and technology, which have so radically altered much of modern life, have been largely untapped by the criminal justice system. One extremely useful approach to innovation is the questioning, analytical, experimental approach of science. Systems analysis, which has contributed significantly to such large-scale government programs as national defense and mass transportation, can be used to study criminal justice operations and to help agency officials choose promising courses of action.

Modern technology can make many specific contributions to criminal administration. The most significant will come from the use of computers to collect and analyze the masses of data the system needs to understand the crime control process. Other important contributions may come, for example, from:

- ☐ Flexible radio networks and portable two-way radios for patrol officers.
- ☐ Computer assisted command-and-control systems for rapid and efficient dispatching of patrol forces.
- ☐ Advanced fingerprint recognition systems.
- ☐ Innovations for the police patrol car such as mobile teletypewriters, tape recorders for recording questioning, and automatic car position locators.
- ☐ Alarms and surveillance systems for homes, businesses and prisons.
- ☐ Criminalistics techniques such as voice prints, neutron activation analysis and other modern laboratory instrumentation.

The Federal Government must take the lead in the effort to focus the capabilities of science and technology on the criminal justice system.

It can sponsor and support a continuing research and development program on a scale greater than any individual agency could undertake alone. Such a program will benefit all agencies.

It should stimulate the industrial development, at reasonable prices, of the kinds of equipment all agencies need. A useful technique might be to guarantee the sale of first production runs.

It should provide funds that will enable criminal justice agencies to hire technically trained people and to establish internal operations research units.

It should support scientific research into criminal administration that uses the agencies as real-life laboratories.

Research

. . . There should be Federal support for specific research projects by individual scholars and by universities or research organizations. In many instances such projects should be carried out in conjunction with large police departments, correctional institutions, or other operating agencies. In addition to such project grants, the Commission believes the Federal Government should provide support for a number of institutes specifically dedicated to research into crime and criminal justice. Such institutes would bring together top scholars from the social and natural sciences, law, social work, business administration and psychiatry, and would be able to deal with the criminal justice system, from prevention to corrections, as a whole. Presumably most of these research institutes would be located at universities, although one or more might be independent.

These institutes would serve as the foundation for the other parts of the Federal program described here, both in the substance of the research they undertook and in the availability of their staff members as top-level consultants. They could provide training, through special seminars or degree courses, for senior administrators and specialist personnel. They could undertake studies of the effectiveness of various education and training programs. They could provide much of the data needed to conduct organization and operations studies and [could] seek and test new techniques for implementation. They could take major responsibility for analyzing data developed by the national information system, and they would propose and evaluate important new demonstration programs and provide consulting services.

Grant-in-Aid Support for New Programs

In addition to the forms of support described above, a major part of the Federal program should be grants-in-aid for a broad range of innovative State and local programs. The standards of this part of the program should preclude continuing support for such normal operational expenses as those for basic personnel compensation, routine equipment like police cars, or replacement of physical facilities like jails and courthouses. Support would instead be given to major innovations in operations, including especially the coordination of services among the parts of the system of criminal administration and among agencies in different jurisdictions.

The possibilities for such programs are as wide as the range of innovations State and local authorities propose to undertake. They might include:

- [ ] New police operations such as the storefront Community Service Officer program; sophisticated communications equipment; and regional laboratory facilities.
- [ ] Construction and operation of new corrections facilities to serve as a nucleus for community-based programs.
- [ ] Temporary salary support for new specialized personnel, such as computer experts, court management specialists, and classification or treatment experts for correctional facilities.

The Commission is confident that this eight-point program, if fully implemented, will do much to bring crime under control.

. . . . .

Conclusion

At its end, as at its beginning, this report on crime and criminal justice in America must insist that there are no easy answers. The complexity and the magnitude of the task of controlling crime and improving criminal justice is indicated by the more than 200 specific recommendations for action, and the many hundreds of suggestions for action, that this report contains. These recommendations and suggestions are addressed to cities, to States, to the Federal Government; to individual citizens and their organizations; to policemen, to prosecutors, to judges, to correctional authorities, and to the agencies for which these officials work. Taken together these recommendations and suggestions express the Commission's deep conviction that if America is to meet the challenge of crime it must do more, far more, than it is doing now. It must welcome new ideas and risk new actions. It must spend time and money. It must resist those who point to scapegoats, who use facile slogans about crime by habit or for selfish ends. It must recognize that the government of a free society is obliged to act not only effectively but fairly. It must seek knowledge and admit mistakes.

Controlling crime in America is an endeavor that will be slow and hard and costly. But America can control crime if it will.

> [*The President's Commission on Law Enforcement and Administration of Justice*, The Challenge of Crime in a Free Society (*Washington: U.S. Government Printing Office, 1967*), pp. 279–291.]